Russian-Ottoman Borderlands

Russian-Ottoman Borderlands

The Eastern Question Reconsidered

Edited by

Lucien J. Frary and Mara Kozelsky

The University of Wisconsin Press

The University of Wisconsin Press
1930 Monroe Street, 3rd Floor
Madison, Wisconsin 53711-2059
uwpress.wisc.edu

3 Henrietta Street, Covent Garden
London WC2E 8LU, United Kingdom
eurospanbookstore.com

Copyright © 2014
The Board of Regents of the University of Wisconsin System
All rights reserved. Except in the case of brief quotations embedded in critical articles and reviews, no part of this publication may be reproduced, stored in a retrieval system, transmitted in any format or by any means—digital, electronic, mechanical, photocopying, recording, or otherwise—or conveyed via the Internet or a website without written permission of the University of Wisconsin Press. Rights inquiries should be directed to rights@uwpress.wisc.edu.

Library of Congress Cataloging-in-Publication Data

Russian-Ottoman borderlands: the Eastern question reconsidered / edited by Lucien J. Frary and Mara Kozelsky.
    pages   cm
    Includes bibliographical references and index.
    ISBN 978-0-299-29804-3 (pbk.: alk. paper)
    ISBN 978-0-299-29803-6 (e-book)
    1. Eastern question.   2. Russia—Foreign relations—Turkey.
3. Turkey—Foreign relations—Russia.   4. Russia—History—1801–1917
5. Turkey—History—Ottoman Empire, 1288–1918.   I. Frary, Lucien J., editor of compilation.   II. Kozelsky, Mara, editor of compilation.
    D371.R87 2014
    949.6′03—dc23
    2013034802

For OUR PARENTS

Contents

Preface	ix
List of Abbreviations	xi
Introduction: The Eastern Question Reconsidered LUCIEN J. FRARY and MARA KOZELSKY	3
The Russian Protectorate in the Danubian Principalities: Legacies of the Eastern Question in Contemporary Russian-Romanian Relations VICTOR TAKI	35
"Dreadful Scenes of Carnage on Both Sides": The Strangford Files and the Eastern Crisis of 1821–1822 THEOPHILUS C. PROUSIS	73
Slaves of the Sultan: Russian Ransoming of Christian Captives during the Greek Revolution, 1821–1830 LUCIEN J. FRARY	101
Russia's Quest for the Holy Grail: Relics, Liturgics, and Great-Power Politics in the Ottoman Empire JACK FAIREY	131
The Crimean War and the Tatar Exodus MARA KOZELSKY	165
Russia, Mount Athos, and the Eastern Question, 1878–1914 LORA GERD	193

"Forty Years of Black Days"? The Russian Administration
   of Kars, Ardahan, and Batum, 1878–1918   221
   CANDAN BADEM

The Idea of an Eastern Federation: An Alternative
   to the Destruction of the Ottoman Empire   251
   JOHN A. MAZIS

Squabbling over the Spoils: Late Imperial Russia's Rivalry
   with France in the Near East   281
   RONALD P. BOBROFF

The Eastern Question in Turkish Republican Textbooks:
   Settling Old Scores with the European and
   the Ottoman "Other"   303
   NAZAN ÇIÇEK

Epilogue: Legacies of the Eastern Question   331
   LUCIEN J. FRARY and MARA KOZELSKY

Contributors   347
Index   351

Preface

The Eastern Question touched the lives of millions of people and dominated international relations between Europe, Russia, and the Ottoman Empire for more than a century. The legacy of the Eastern Question remains etched in the landscape from the Balkans to the Caucasus and continues to influence people living in these regions today. In recent decades, scholars have developed fresh insights into the religious, cultural, economic, and political aspects of the Eastern Question. Research in Russian and Ottoman archives has particularly challenged traditional interpretations, while new approaches have shifted attention from the governing elite to the subjects of empires and the peoples who lived in the borderlands. With this volume, we seek to highlight changes in the field and suggest new directions for the study of the Eastern Question.

The idea to form a collection of articles devoted to the Eastern Question originated in 2008 at a biannual meeting of the Association for the Study of Eastern Christian History and Culture, where we, the editors, began discussing the meaning and nature of what we consider the most important issue of international relations in the nineteenth century. Rigorous discussions, debates, and conversations with each contributor to this volume and with numerous scholars at two subsequent meetings of the Association for Slavic, East European, and Eurasian Studies sharpened our thinking and widened the perspective from which we view this historical phenomenon. In addition to the contributors, we wish to express our gratitude to the anonymous readers for their many excellent suggestions. We would also like to recognize Theofanis G. Stavrou, whose dedication to this field is a constant source of inspiration, and David Goldfrank, who has been a kind supporter of our project.

Harvard University and the Central Navy Museum in St. Petersburg granted permission to reproduce the map at the beginning of Victor Taki's chapter and the painting *Shipwreck off Mount Athos* by Ivan Aivazovsky for the cover, respectively. Sam Stutsman of the University of South Alabama created the map of the Ottoman Empire used at the beginning of the introduction. The chapter by Theophilus C. Prousis contains excerpts that have appeared earlier in his *Lord Strangford at the Sublime Porte (1822): The Eastern Crisis* (İstanbul: Isis Press, 2012). Finally, research grants, assistance from interlibrary loan, and other support from the University of South Alabama and Rider University have helped us toward the completion of this project.

List of Abbreviations

Archives

AVPRI	Arkhiv Vneshnei Politiki Rossiiskii Imperii, Moscow, Russia
AHMAE	Archives Historiques du Ministère des Affaires Etrangères, Paris, France
BOA	Başbakanlık Osmanlı Arşivi, İstanbul, Turkey
CDA	Centralen Dyrzhaven Arkhiv, Sofia, Bulgaria
GAARK	Gosudarsvtennyi Arkhiv Avtomna Respublika Krym, Simferopol, Crimea
GARF	Gosudarstvennyi Arkhiv Rossiiskoi Federatsii, Moscow, Russia
HAA	Hayastani Azgayin Arkhiv, Yerevan, Armenia
HHSA	Haus-, Hof- und Staatsarchiv, Vienna, Austria
OR RNB	Otdel rukopisei, Rossiiskaia Natsional'naia Biblioteka, St. Petersburg, Russia
RGADA	Rossiiskii Gosudarstvennyi Arkhiv Drevnikh Aktov, Moscow, Russia
RGIA	Rossiiskii Gosudarstvennyi Istoricheskii Arkhiv, St. Petersburg, Russia
RGVIA	Rossiiskii Gosudarstvennyi Voenno-Istoricheskii Arkhiv, Moscow, Russia
STsSA	Sakartvelos Tsentraluri Saistorio, Tbilisi, Georgia
TNA FO	The National Archives, Foreign Office, Kew, United Kingdom

Archival and Journal Notation

f.	*fond* (collection)
op.	*opis'* (inventory)
d.	*delo* (file)
kn.	*kniga* (book)
l., ll.	*list, listy* (leaf, leaves)

Russian-Ottoman Borderlands

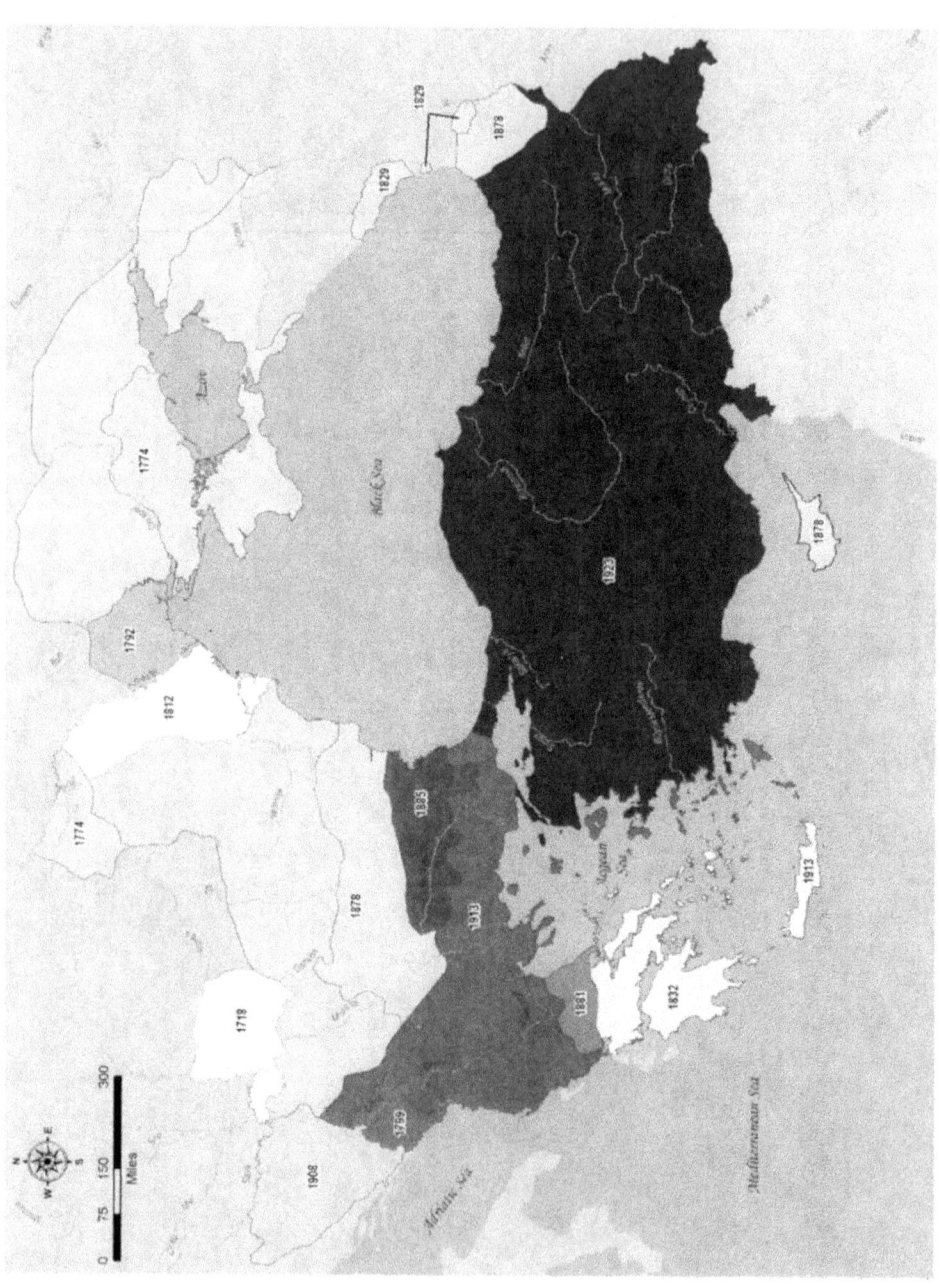

Introduction
The Eastern Question Reconsidered

LUCIEN J. FRARY and MARA KOZELSKY

As early as 1736, a treatise by Cardinal Alberoni of Spain, translated into English and published in London, proposed a joint effort among the European powers to conquer and divide the Ottoman Empire. The "perfidious and vast Empire of Turkey," he wrote, has been "in a languishing State for more than a Century." Alberoni attributed the decline of the Ottoman Empire to "a general Corruption and Venality, scarcely known in the World, since the time of the Romans." He urged "the Princes and States of *Christendom*" to unite in war against the armies of the sultan "to rescue Fellow Christians from the Tyranny and Bondage of the Infidels" and to reclaim the Holy Lands, thereby "perpetuating the Tranquility" of the world. Alberoni further characterized the Ottoman Empire as having a basis in "sacrilege . . . violence, treachery and oppression."[1] In a comprehensive design anticipating the Sykes-Picot Agreement of the twentieth century, Alberoni developed a recommendation for partitioning the Ottoman Empire among the small and large states of Europe.

Note: Map at left depicts the dissolution of the Ottoman Empire, Balkans to the Caucasus 18th to 20th c. (map created by Sam Stutsman at the University of South Alabama)

Although European approaches to the Ottoman Empire evolved over time, the notion that Europe had political and moral obligations to manage the Ottoman collapse persisted for centuries. Political leaders, memoirists, travelers, scholars, merchants, and critics generated thousands of works about the European response to perceived Ottoman decay and decline. Historians nearly matched that volume of output as they examined the resulting conflicts based on the language of nineteenth-century diplomats, who referred to the complex dynamics of European involvement in the Ottoman lands as the "Eastern Question." This Eastern Question involved a profound power struggle that precipitated numerous armed conflicts between the Ottoman Empire, Britain, Russia, and the other European powers and ignited the passions of native inhabitants. At its heart, the Eastern Question entailed the presumption of Western European states and Russia to manage the affairs of the Ottoman Empire.

Pinning down a concise definition of the Eastern Question has challenged historians in the past because contemporary interpretations changed according to its major episodes: the Greek Revolution (1821–30), the Crimean War (1853–56), the Eastern crisis of 1875–78, and the First World War. Intervening smaller-scale conflicts, such as the Russian-Persian War (1826–28), the ten-years' crisis (1831–41) evoked by the Egyptian Pasha Mehmed Ali, the Russian defeat of Shamil in the Caucasus (1859), the Young Turk Revolution (1908), the struggle for Macedonia, and the Balkan Wars (1912–13) also generated waves of contemporary speculation. Initially led by British and French publicists and politicians, Russian journalists began addressing the so-called Eastern Question in the 1830s, followed by Turkish critics later in the century. Subject populations of the Russian and Ottoman Empires likewise contributed their versions of the Eastern Question. In short, the Eastern Question varied tremendously according to the individual who posed it, from one historic moment and actor to the next.

J. A. R. Marriott's *The Eastern Question: An Historical Study of European Diplomacy* (1917) was the first major work to conceptualize the Eastern Question in its entirety. Until now, it remains the only detailed work of synthesis and theory. Conceived as Britain mobilized for war in 1914 and concluded while British troops were still in the trenches, Marriott's work interprets the history of the Eastern Question through the lens of the Great War. A subsequent effort by M. S. Anderson, *The Eastern Question: 1774–1923: A Study in International Relations* (1966), updated Marriott's approach in a sweeping synthesis for university students.

Although Marriott and Anderson incorporated some native and Russian voices, both works principally analyze the Eastern Question from a British diplomatic and political perspective. Their work rarely addresses the experiences of those living in the vast spaces along the Russian-Ottoman borderlands, from the Balkans to the Caucasus, where proposed solutions to the question made the greatest impression.

Since the publication of Anderson's survey, multiple waves of historical scholarship have enriched our view of the Eastern Question dramatically, allowing new perspectives to emerge. Scholars have shown, for example, that Russian rulers were not as desirous of absorbing Ottoman territories as nineteenth-century British diplomats feared. Researchers have investigated religious aspects of the Eastern Question, as well as the cultural and commercial networks involved. As new or revived nation states in the Balkans, the Black Sea region, and the Caucasus find their footing, regional scholars have begun exploring fresh perspectives and interdisciplinary approaches to construct their national pasts. Postcolonial studies, moreover, have shifted the historical focus from the decisions of the elites to the experiences of the subjects of empire. Scholars of Ottoman history have brought innovative analysis of Ottoman sources to the mainstream literature on the topic for the first time.

In recent decades, a more balanced view of the Eastern Question has materialized. A new, larger cast of players has entered the scene, and the geographic scope has broadened to encompass the states of the Black Sea and the Caucasus. Significantly, historians have challenged the very foundation of the Eastern Question, or the understanding that the Ottoman Empire was the "sick man of Europe."[2] The Ottoman Empire, as recent scholarship has shown, was no less stable than the other great empires that collapsed during the First World War. In contrast to the "decline narrative" often evoked by scholars, historians and social scientists have suggested that far from waning, the Ottoman Empire was centralizing and modernizing to reform and defend itself on its own terms.[3]

Our primary goal in this volume is to highlight the changes in the field by drawing together a sampling of current approaches. In contrast to the majority of traditional scholarship, which defines the Eastern Question through events or the immediate concerns of nineteenth-century diplomacy, strategic designs, and economic rivalry, this volume demonstrates that the Eastern Question was a much more complex phenomenon.[4] For the Ottoman Empire, the Eastern Question was a "Western Question," and from the perspective of those millions of peoples affected, it lacked many of the rational purposes that diplomats and historians have so painstakingly attributed to it. We define the Eastern Question as a historically evolving concept that originated in Europe's presumption to manage Ottoman affairs. We emphasize the human and grassroots aspects of the Eastern Question as well as its international framework in the Russian-Ottoman borderlands.

Essays in this collection explore the Eastern Question from the perspective of the Russian and Ottoman Empires and the borderlands in between. We aim to broaden the scope of the people, ideas, and events involved. We also hope to illuminate the reciprocal relationship between the great powers and the mass of populations affected by Eastern Question diplomacy. We emphasize that in addition to international relations, the Eastern Question involved the influences and consequences of foreign intervention. This includes sectarian violence and nationalist movements, economic rivalry and dislocation, migration and resettlement, colonial administration and regional identity. We wish to reveal the real and devastating consequences of Eastern Question political debates among the peoples living in the immense frontier zones of conflict and interaction. Our essays demonstrate that Eastern Question diplomacy and economic penetration were hardly isolated to the throne rooms and parliamentary halls, or even the battlefields. Rather, high-level diplomatic discourse on the Eastern Question affected the lives of millions of people in the lands between the Russian and Ottoman Empires. Not all this interaction was malignant, however. Although this volume tends to highlight negative aspects of the Eastern Question, we acknowledge that cross-cultural exchange and the expansion of knowledge had positive aspects as well.[5]

We further argue that the Eastern Question rivals the rise of Germany as the most prominent international problem shaping the course of modern European history prior to the First World War. The international tensions unleashed by the Eastern Question produced several cataclysmic wars from the end of the eighteenth century through the First World War that entangled all of Europe, consumed incalculable state resources, and cost millions of lives. The Eastern Question forced migrations of masses of peoples, produced ethnic cleansing and genocide, and remapped the European continent in its own image. No other international issue had the longevity or toll of the Eastern Question. The fundamental, transformative role of the Eastern Question in European history becomes apparent by looking beyond the great capitals of the West, London and Paris, and by incorporating into the mainstream narrative those cities, villages, nations, and empires on the eastern and southeastern periphery of the continent. When one views European history from the perspective of those peoples living in the Balkans, around the shores of the Black Sea, the Caucasus, and in present-day Russia and Turkey, the Eastern Question features paramount in shaping nineteenth-century international relations.

This collection of essays from multinational perspectives demonstrates that as the Eastern Question evolved in England, France, and Russia, it echoed differently in the Balkans, the Black Sea region, and the Caucasus. Each violent episode produced countless mass migrations, including the exodus of refugee Orthodox Christians from the Ottoman Empire to Russia, the flight of Ottoman Serbs to Habsburg lands, and the migration of millions of Muslims living in these regions to the domain of the sultan. The peoples who lived along Russian-Ottoman borders profoundly influenced the Eastern Question with their nationalist movements, cultures, and beliefs. Similarly, refugees displaced by the Eastern Question also shaped the internal political dynamic of their host nations.

This introduction outlines the history of Eastern Question scholarship in the nineteenth century as interpreted by Marriott, revised by Anderson, and as it evolves in new directions today. We emphasize the scholarship's Anglocentric origins and the prominent role of the Balkans in the international relations of the era. We highlight Russia's gradual entrance into contemporary scholarly speculation following the Crimean War, which by the nature of Russian colonial activity included special attention to present-day Ukraine, Crimea, and the Caucasus. Of central interest is the flourishing field of Ottoman history, which emerged as a major subject of inquiry with its own narratives and theoretical approaches after Anderson's survey appeared in the 1960s. Finally, while we retain the term "Eastern Question" in reflection of its prominence in centuries of international relations discourse, we underscore its formulation in Eurocentrism.

Evolution of the Eastern Question in European and Russian Thought

Although perceptions of Ottoman decline date to the early eighteenth century as evidenced by Alberoni's proposal, when exactly the "Eastern Question" first entered the lexicon of European diplomacy remains a mystery.[6] Scholars have suggested the term first gained wide currency sometime between the Congress of Vienna (1815) and the Congress of Verona (1822) to describe the military weakness and the apparent breakdown of financial and administrative controls in the Ottoman Empire.[7] For nearly a century afterward, contemporaries and historians have provided various definitions regarding the problem, its chronological origins, and its principal characteristics. Even the most cursory of historiographical surveys would suggest that scholars of the Eastern Question have reached no consensus on the nature of the problem and its scope.

With exceptions, the current convention in the literature is to date the "Eastern Question" to Russian expansion into Ottoman territory during the Russian-Ottoman wars of Catherine II. In particular, the 1768 war and the Treaty of Kuchuk Kainardji in 1774 served as a turning point in Russian relations with the Sublime Porte.[8] Historians might also date the origins of the Eastern Question to the Napoleonic Wars, when British studies, pamphlets, propaganda pieces, and Russophobic writings outlining the causes and course of Ottoman decline warned merchants about the possible threat of Russia's control of Mediterranean and Black Sea commerce. Although the term "Eastern Question" had not yet been coined, the specter of Ottoman decline provided a useful rallying point for those in the West who saw in Russia a potentially dangerous and hostile country. A range of new factors influenced subsequent Russian-British relations, including the status of the Ionian Islands and the Danubian principalities, the control of the Dardanelles, as well as Ottoman capitulations and commercial treaties.[9] Meanwhile, the Napoleonic invasion of Egypt in 1798 increased the imperialist threat to the Ottomans and displayed aspects of Eastern Question culture, such as attempts to translate revolutionary concepts from 1789 and afterward into a new political vocabulary for Muslim thinkers, as well as the scholarly and scientific investigations organized by the Institut d'Égypte.[10]

Significant groundwork for what soon would become known as the Eastern Question first appeared during the Greek Revolution, which detonated in 1821.[11] What began as a steady stream soon developed into a wave of works describing the Eastern crisis of 1831-41, which threatened the stability of the Ottoman Empire and envenomed the rivalries of European states for control of the so-called Near East and the balance of power on the continent.[12] At this time, the first books to contain the term in their titles, by Théodore Benazet and Charles Dupin, discussed the rise in prominence of Pasha Mehmed Ali of Egypt and the waning power of the Ottomans.[13] This genre, composed principally by British and French politicians, Orientalists and adventurers, demonstrates Western ambivalence about whom to support (Russia, the native peoples, or the Ottoman Empire) and the increasing stakes involved. Sectarian violence during the Greek rebellion, such as the massacre at Chios, in which Ottoman soldiers killed thousands of Greek Christians, left many Europeans leery of supporting the Ottoman Empire. Contemporary journalism and political debates reflected this lack of consensus, as the liberal public of Western Europe rallied behind the Greek cause. The lively public debate also reflected Western-centric and Christian-centric views by downplaying or ignoring Ottoman Greek atrocities against Ottoman Muslims. As the term became popular on the eve of the Crimean War, scholars and publicists began retroactively dating the beginning of the Eastern Question to the Ottoman conquest of Constantinople in 1453, the "Time of Cicero," or even as far back as the era of Homer.[14]

Much of the ambivalence about Europe's relationship to the Ottoman Empire had disappeared when the outbreak of the Crimean War in 1853 spawned a fresh phase of Eastern Question studies and pamphlet literature. During the Crimean War, Karl Marx composed a famous reflection on the Eastern Question in a series of letters submitted to the *New York Tribune*. Marx described the Eastern Question as diplomatic diversion from the forces of revolution at home and denounced the imperialist interests of the great powers. His work, which presented a materialist interpretation of the conflict and ascribed the religious impulses of the war to the manipulation of elites, inspired subsequent Western and Soviet studies for more than a century.[15] Simultaneously Marx identified Russia as the hostile power of the Crimean War. The continuing expansion of tsarist influence at the Sublime Porte sparked a surge of Russophobic literature, defined in part by the celebrated travel account of the Marquis de Custine and the prolific work of David Urquhart.[16] Much larger studies began to appear, including the two-volume collection of documents edited by A. Ubicini, titled *La questione d'Oriente innanzi l'Europa*, published in Milan in 1854, which focused on the holy places, then (as now) an area of intense international concern. Other books in this first flourish of serious scholarship surveyed society, religion, diplomacy, military strategy, and the economy.[17] The Crimean War also inspired a surge of irredentist and historical works among the Balkan peoples.[18] More broadly, Russia's ongoing struggle with Imam Shamil for the control of the northern Caucasus captured Western imaginations during the Crimean War and led to a smattering of books and articles.[19] A few Western European scholarly studies of "Tatary," Crimea, or the Caucasus also appeared at this time, with Western agents actively attempting to incite native rebellions among Muslim populations.[20]

Until the Crimean War, Russia often perceived its relationship with the Ottoman Empire as largely a local issue, an old dance between two rivals. Prior to the war, Russian scholars worked actively on the history of the Russian conquest of the steppe and other borderland regions with the Ottoman Empire such as the Crimea and the Caucasus, but without sustained reflection on the regions' significance for great-power politics. The appearance of English and French troops on Russian shores in 1854 came as a shock and inspired Russian scholars to join the Western debate.[21] The seminal work of Russian research on the Eastern Question was N. I. Danilevskii's *Rossiia i Evropa*, first published in article form in 1869.[22] The book reflected the intensified interest in the Balkans and Pan-Slavism among Russian readers, and Russia's role in the fate of the Orthodox world. Although shrouded in abstract terminology about a historical struggle between "cultural types," the book gained the interest of the Russian Foreign Ministry, which began to pursue a more active policy in the Balkans. The Eastern Question thus attracted serious attention from the Russian state, as well as the various circles in Russia's educated society. The keen interest of intellectuals in the role of Slavs in history and in the value of self-determination blended with important strategic and economic interests of the Russian Empire along its southern and western borders.[23] After Danilevskii's publication, a wave of work focusing on Russian foreign policy in the Balkans began to explore myths regarding Russia's historical mission to liberate Orthodox Christians.[24] Memoirs of Russian participants in Eastern Question conflicts also began to appear in print, including the multivolume *Russkie na Bosfore v 1833 godu* and *Dela Turtsii i Egipta v 1832 i 1833 godakh* by N. N. Murav'ev.[25] A valuable collection of treaties, edited and commented upon by T. Iuzefovich, reflected public interest in Balkan affairs.[26] Whereas many Russian works, including an essay by the philosopher and historian B. N. Chicherin, focused on the psychological and religious elements of Russia's Balkan entanglements, V. A. Ulianitskii's *Dardanelly, Bosfor i Chernoe more v XVIII veke* offered a pioneering study of the Russian-Tatar borderlands and the economic importance of the subject.[27]

Introduction

The outbreak of the Eastern crisis in 1875 and the resulting Russian-Ottoman War of 1877-78 inspired another major burst of historical and journalistic writing that marked a return to ambivalence about European states' relationship with the Ottoman Empire. Over the next decade, nearly five hundred titles touching on elements of this Eastern crisis appeared in the ten most popular monthly journals and magazines in Great Britain alone.[28] Perhaps the most famous works of this period are W. E. Gladstone's booklets titled *Bulgarian Horrors and the Question of the East* and *Lessons in Massacre*, and the articles in Fyodor Dostoevsky's *Dnevnik pisatelia*.[29] F. F. Martens, a legal expert attached to the Russian Foreign Ministry, mirrored Gladstone's work in semiofficial Russian publications.[30] Martens attempted to blend approaches by simultaneously supporting Russia's "historical role" as the leader of Orthodox Christians, while underscoring St. Petersburg's commitment to multilateral intervention. Paralleling this approach, the celebrated Russian historian S. M. Solov'ev's "Vostochnyi vopros" (written in 1876) considered the origins of the problem to lie "at the moment in history when European man realized the division between Europe and Asia, between the European and the Asian spirit."[31] Interspersing diplomatic narrative with commentary on geography, economy, and religion, Solov'ev supplied the groundwork for lengthier publications to follow, while supporting contemporary Russian policy in Poland and southeastern Europe.

Interpretations that highlighted fundamental contrasts between Christianity and Islam, divisions between East and West, and a religious calling to recover the Holy Land led scholars like Solov'ev to date the origins of the Eastern Question to the fourteenth century, when "Turks" first penetrated the Balkan Peninsula. Others looked to the Persian invasion of Greece in the sixth century BC. One of the most important Russian works, Sergei Zhigarev's two-volume *Russkaia politika v vostochnom voprose*, argued that the issue was "a difficult and complicated affair," involving the material interests of the East and the struggle of Orthodox Christians for freedom from Turkish rule.[32] Several years later, an innovative study by Max Choublier, titled *La question d'Orient avant la Traité de Berlin*, found the root of the problem in the eighteenth-century "decline" of the Ottoman Empire in the Black Sea. Choublier developed the concept further by showing how it enveloped many questions, including the Ottoman possessions in Europe, Asia Minor, Syria, and Egypt. He also warned of a possible resurgence of "Muslim fanaticism" in Asia and North Africa. Meanwhile, the development of Russian and European historiography of the Caucasus, Persia, and Afghanistan paralleled that of the Eastern Question in general.[33] Political events, such as Russia's penetration of the Caucasus, also helped inspire publication of the monumental, twelve-volume *Akty sobrannye Kavkazskoiu arkheograficheskoiu kommissiei*, among other Russian works on the region.[34]

Two great historians of the French Third Republic, Edouard Driault and Albert Sorel, devoted large portions of their scholarly careers to problems of the Ottoman Empire and the territories of what they described as the Near East.[35] Sorel's *La question d'Orient au XVIIIe siècle*, first published in 1889, pushed the origins of the question to the first partition of Poland. Driault's well-known study, *La question d'Orient*, published in 1898 and appearing in its ninth edition in 1938, reflected the popularity of the topic and the public desire for information.[36] Driault argued that the question emerged from the decline of Islam in Europe and Asia and focused foremost on the emergence of Christian Balkan states and the advance of Turkey's Christian neighbors.

By the beginning of the twentieth century, nearly all the early work done by Western Europeans and Russians reflected the values and interests of their social milieus. Even works by dissident Turkish intellectuals, who had just begun to enter the debates on the Eastern Question, reiterated Eurocentric perspectives.[37] Russian thought about the Eastern Question rarely entered Western studies. With few exceptions, the way in which the Eastern Question influenced Muslim populations remained largely unexamined. Largely due to conflict brewing in the Balkan Peninsula, scholars at the turn of the twentieth century perpetuated nineteenth-century essentialist thinking and stereotypes of Ottoman decline, while abandoning the emerging interest in the Eastern Question's relationship to the Caucasus and the region then known as Bessarabia.[38] With the onset of the First World War, Britain found itself on opposite sides of the conflict with the Ottoman Empire as the Eastern Question in public and scholarly discourse entered its final classic phase. In Britain, pundits and politicians assembled the most negative strains of Orientalist discourse about the Ottoman Empire to demonize it and draw attention to the persecution of subject populations. The work of Viscount James Bryce and Arnold J. Toynbee, both of whom were actively involved in publicizing the Armenian genocide of 1915, characterized this late trend. Neither man, moreover, saw the Armenian genocide as a new phenomenon or the inauguration of a new era of violence. Instead, these men understood the Armenian genocide as stemming from violent trends associated with the Eastern Question, particularly the Bulgarian massacres of 1875 and subsequent massacres of Armenians in 1895 and 1909.[39] Russian romanticizing of its historic role in liberating Ottoman Christians, meanwhile, dissolved in the collapse of its own empire. Soviet atheism, the revival of Marx's materialist interpretation of the Eastern Question, and Lenin's focus on nationalist movements in borderland territories emerged to take its place.[40]

The Eastern Question: The Search for New Definitions

The flood of journalistic literature that poured so freely throughout the nineteenth century virtually ceased with the collapse of the Ottoman Empire and the creation of the League of Nations mandate states in the 1920s. The Eastern Question gradually became an accepted component of nineteenth-century European history. As public attention waned, however, several scholarly studies that emphasized the Balkan states and the Black Sea in the context of the Eastern Question appeared, undoubtedly influenced by the war unfolding around them. The most significant general work of this era, Marriott's *The Eastern Question*, became the foundation for a general narrative on the subject until today. This 1917 publication (four later editions followed) became the first to harness all the various monographs on the subject into one continuous story.[41] Because Marriott's substantial tome established the model for most subsequent interpretations of the Eastern Question, it is worthy of scrutiny here.[42]

Marriott opens his book observing that despite the tremendous amount of energy dedicated to discussing the Eastern Question, no overarching study has been written. He comments that "monographs exist in plenty on special aspects of the problem, and many general Histories of Europe contain useful chapters on the subject," but analytical, comprehensive treatments are lacking.[43] He sets as his task the "sketching of the historical evolution of a problem which has baffled the ingenuity of European diplomatists in a general sense for more than 500 years, more specifically and more insistently, for about a century."[44]

Marriott's work synthesizes the vast literature and makes sense of the various articulations of the Eastern Question from its origins (as defined by him) to the present day. He traces the modern Eastern Question from the early rise of the Ottoman Empire in the fourteenth and fifteenth centuries through the First World War. He also provides the first theorization of the problem and attributes six major principles to it: the Ottomans in Europe; Balkan irredentism; Black Sea straits; Russian aspirations to the Mediterranean; the Habsburg interest in southeastern Europe; and finally, "the attitude of the European Powers in general, and England in particular" toward the subjects he identifies. To be sure, Marriott's work was groundbreaking. No other scholar had been brave enough to bring the disparate works on the Eastern Question together as a whole, and to theorize it. It became *the* uncontested authority on the subject, and continues to frame the field's understanding of the Eastern Question's major phases. Still, his work was very much a product of its era, imbued with the tensions of the Great War and the Eurocentric thinking of his age.

Foregrounding his work in essentialist thinking characteristic of his predecessors, Marriott argues that the Eastern Question existed "from time immemorial." He writes: "Europe has been confronted with an 'Eastern Question.' In its essence, the problem is unchanging. It has arisen from the clash in the lands of South Eastern Europe between the habits, the ideas, and preconceptions of the West and those of the East."[45] For Marriott, Ottoman Turks are "an alien substance . . . embedded in the living flesh of Europe."[46] It is not surprising, then, that Marriott with few exceptions expresses little interest in how the Eastern Question related to Muslim areas of Europe. Overlooking the problem for Crimea and the Caucasus, Marriott principally wove his narrative around Balkan affairs.[47]

Following Marriott's volume, several archival-based studies appeared in the 1930s, including those authored by Harold Temperley, R. W. Seton-Watson, and Vernon Puryear, prompting the need for a new synthesis.[48] A few decades later, M. S. Anderson, professor of history at the London School of Economics, published a comprehensive survey on the Eastern Question in 1966. With the exception of taking 1774 as his starting point, concluding his work with the First World War, and integrating data from recent studies, his framework deviated little from that of Marriott. Thus, the Balkan theater dominates the narrative at the expense of Muslim Europe, the chapter spread deviates little from Marriott's original conception, and the book retains a familiar focus on diplomacy. Anderson also uncritically shares Marriott's assumption that Ottoman "backwardness" led European powers to tangle in Ottoman affairs. While explicitly acknowledging that his work was "not original either in the information or the ideas provided," Anderson fulfilled a need for a new university textbook, as "no other book ha[d] been written in English at a moderate length" since Marriott.[49] Never conceived as a field shaper, Anderson's book has provided the general narrative and chronological scope of the Eastern Question for the last sixty years.[50]

Although several shifts in the literature have dated Anderson's useful survey, no comprehensive study of the Eastern Question has emerged to take its place. Thus, Nazan Çiçek, whose recent work analyzes the Turkish contribution to the Eastern Question, has noted, "even after Said's provocative work prompted a change of paradigm in Western scholars' approaches to the history of the East, the Eastern Question mainly remained a Western issue, which was analyzed according to its Western actors' thinking and policy-making patterns."[51] In *Orientalism*, Edward Said describes the Eastern Question as one of the most visible and enduring of the Orientalists' "flamboyant projects."[52] Without overstating Said's negative critique of Orientalists, it is worth noting that the history of the Eastern Question has often been told from a Western perspective. The better we understand the histories and motives of the Russian and Ottoman Empires, their relation to the other empires, and Russia's consistent reluctance to expand beyond the shores of the Black Sea, the more apparent it is that the Eastern Question was the product of perception rather than reality. Giving the full benefit of the doubt to the European diplomats of the time, we could attribute Eastern Question feuds and crises to consistent miscommunication and ignorant good intentions. In a more cynical view, harmful policies prompted by the Eastern Question have their roots in Western imperial ambitions, greed, and periodic hysteria.

In the last decades, significant advances have been made in Russian, Balkan, and Ottoman historiography. Work on the regional and national pasts of the Caucasus, Crimea, the Danubian principalities, and present-day Ukraine has increased as well. A growing number of scholarly articles and monographs touch on the intersection of the Russian-Ottoman Empires, forced and voluntary migrations, and the everyday experience of people living along the borderlands. Some of this work relates directly to the Eastern Question, but much research remains to be done before this historical phenomenon secures its rightful place in the general narrative of modern European history.[53]

Among the most important new trends influencing historical interpretation of the Eastern Question has been active research into Ottoman history by scholars using Ottoman sources. Kemal Karpat revitalized the study of Ottoman history for English language scholarship, freeing it equally from Eurocentric preoccupations with Ottoman decline and strictly controlled Turkish nationalist interpretations.[54] Characterizing the Eastern Question as a "moral and political justification for partitioning the Ottoman lands," Karpat has pointed to the delusory effects of European and Russian interference in Ottoman affairs.[55]

In recent years, numerous monographs have appeared revising standard narratives of Ottoman history.[56] As Nicholas Doumanis, Cem Emrence, Isa Blumi, and other specialists have recently emphasized, the cultural symbiosis and integrative policies of Ottoman rule helped sustain control over millions of peoples for hundreds of years. Religious tolerance, accommodation, and cultural syncretism—and not a policy of divide and rule—help explain Ottoman success among a heterogeneous mass.[57] Scholars have shown that the relatively tolerant nature of the Ottoman Empire enabled the elite at the Sublime Porte to share authority with local leaders, including spectacular figures, such as Ali Pasha of Tependenli and Mehmed Ali of Egypt, who have become integral to the Eastern Question narrative.[58] Elsewhere, scholarship on Ottoman history has reexamined the relationship between the Ottoman Empire and the West and the role of the Eastern Question in Ottoman affairs, including Nazan Çiçek's *Young Ottomans*, Candan Badem's *The Ottoman Crimean War*, and several essays in *War and Diplomacy* edited by M. Hakan Yavuz and Peter Sluglett.[59]

Work on Russia's involvement with the Eastern Question has grown at an even more rapid pace with substantial contributions made by Theofanis Stavrou, who has pioneered the study of Russia's Eastern Question among scholars working in the United States, and Charles and Barbara Jelavich.[60] Much of the recent literature on Russia's engagement in Eastern Question disputes has focused on the role of religion. Traditionally, scholars working from Anglocentric perspectives have attributed the Russian-Ottoman wars to Russian expansionist aims, despite the many examples of religion as a causal factor. Subsequently, a number of scholars, including Theophilus Prousis, Lora Gerd, Nikolai Lisovoi, and others, have taken Russia's commitment to protecting the rights of Ottoman Christians seriously. Collectively, they demonstrate that Orthodox belief and an Orthodox religious nationalism influenced Russia's political behavior vis-à-vis the Eastern Question.[61] Inflections of jihad with each major Russian-Ottoman war, as well as the pilgrimages of Russian Muslims in equal or greater numbers than Orthodox

Christian pilgrimages to the Ottoman Empire, suggest that Islam also had a role to play in the Eastern Question. This subject awaits sustained research.[62]

The renaissance of military and diplomatic history has brought new archival research to traditional accounts of Russian involvement in the Eastern Question.[63] For example, Alexander Bitis demonstrates the critical role played by the Russian military in prompting Russian involvement in the Greek Revolution, while John Daly's study of the navy during the same era reveals, among other things, the importance of the Caucasus to Russia's Eastern Question.[64] Vitalii Sheremet has written studies focusing on economic competition in Eastern Question conflicts in the first half of the nineteenth-century based on Russian and Turkish sources.[65] Focusing on the next major phase of the Eastern Question, David Goldfrank has argued that for Russia, the Crimean War involved both an Eastern and a Western Question, while, more recently, Goldfrank, Mara Kozelsky, L. V. Mel'nikova, Jack Fairey, and Orlando Figes have reinforced the importance of religion for all belligerent parties during the Crimean War.[66] Moving toward later periods, Ronald Bobroff, Michael Reynolds, and Sean McMeekin have emphasized that for Russia, conflict with the Ottoman Empire during World War I loomed as large as, or larger than, that with Germany.[67] Despite this rekindling of interest in war and the Eastern Question, its devastating results in the region from the Balkans to the Caucasus remains an understudied area of research.[68] Many volunteer legions took up arms against their imperial states during Eastern Question conflicts (Poles and Tatars against Russia; Greeks, Serbs, Bulgarians, and Armenians against the Ottoman Empire). These groups, which in many ways epitomize the depth of the displacement caused by the Eastern Question, have rarely been the subject of focused monographs.

As the preceding discussion suggests, we have much to learn about how the Eastern Question affected the borderland regions of and between empires. Several studies have demonstrated the importance of Greek, Romanian, and Polish lobbies in influencing international relations.[69] A. D. Panesh has contributed one of the few works on the Eastern Question in Circassia, showing how the tribes of the northern Caucasus maintained their independence in the face of British, French, Ottoman, and Russian efforts to embroil them in various conflicts.[70] These works suggest intriguing new directions for research.

Waves of Greek, Bulgarian, and Serbian refugees from the Ottoman Empire migrated to Russia with each convulsion of the Eastern

Question. Some thrived, but many perished upon arrival. With few exceptions, the experience of these groups remains relatively unknown.[71] As Balkan peoples migrated to Russia, millions of Muslims emigrated from Europe to the Ottoman Empire and present-day Turkey following the Treaty of Kuchuk Kainardji and on through the Treaty of Lausanne (1923).[72] All cases of mass migrations (in both directions) were accompanied by mass violence, whether connected to wars or massacres. These voluntary and forced migrations associated with the darker consequences of the Eastern Question constitute part of the same violent process that produced the Armenian genocide and the population exchange between the Greeks and the Turks at the end of the First World War and should be studied further.[73]

Finally, despite the many disastrous consequences of the Eastern Question, it did inspire well-meaning interest among many Europeans and Russians in the peoples and traditions of the Russian-Ottoman borderlands. Gary Bass and Davide Rodogno have shown, for example, that humanitarian intervention emerged in the Eastern Question.[74] Artwork and creative literature, business ventures and scientific enterprises produced in the interaction between natives and interlopers at the interstices of the Eastern Question similarly remain subjects worthy of further research.

Toward New Directions

The new research represented in this volume on the Russian and Ottoman Empires and the borderland regions in between calls for a rethinking of the Eastern Question, as the next wave of scholarship evolves. Each of the contributors to this volume has addressed some aspect of the Eastern Question in his or her research. The essays take both traditional and nontraditional approaches, reflecting our belief that the Eastern Question requires multiple modes of interpretation. Because the Eastern Question left an indelible mark on each of the nations and peoples it intersected, we have also urged our contributors to consider, when applicable, today's ongoing legacies.

Victor Taki opens the collection with a sweeping analysis of the development of Moldavian and Wallachian (modern Romanian) national consciousness. Analyzing discursive constructions of identity, Taki shows that the Eastern Question influenced how future Romanians viewed Turks, Russians, and themselves. His work also provides an excellent example of how borderland populations—in this case the

Moldavians and the Wallachians—influenced decisions of the great powers. John A. Mazis's chapter similarly explores how the Eastern Question prompted debate over statehood in Greece. In his essay, Mazis shows how a well-known Greek nationalist, Ion Dragoumis, rejected the Megali Idea (the Great Idea) in favor of an "Eastern Federation." Emerging out of the Greek War of Independence, the Megali Idea, or the Greek desire to recover Byzantine lands lost to the Ottoman Empire, simultaneously enabled the consolidation of Greek statehood and perpetuated violent conflict with the Ottoman Empire. In contrast to Greece's ambitious irredentist plan, some Greeks, like Dragoumis, actually encouraged a union with Turkey. Mazis explores the Eastern Federation concept and considers the implications should such a union have succeeded. Finally, Nazan Çiçek explores the Turkish nationalist response to the Eastern Question in "The Eastern Question in Turkish Republican Textbooks: Settling Old Scores with the European and the Ottoman 'Other.'" By studying representations of the Eastern Question in Turkish historical textbooks, Çiçek explains how Turkish nationalists of the twentieth century struggled to free Ottoman history from Western colonial presumptions.

In addition to a focus on nationalism, this volume underscores the central role of religion in the Eastern Question. Throughout the eighteenth and nineteenth centuries, Russia insisted upon the right to intervene on behalf of Orthodox Christians living in the Ottoman Empire, while conflict over the holy places helped bring the great powers to war on at least one occasion. Until recently, scholarship has dismissed religion, treating it as a smoke screen disguising other imperial motivations. Essays in this volume, however, begin with the premise that religious belief actually mattered. Jack Fairey offers one of the most cogent arguments for the importance of religion in the Eastern Question. Through an examination of three affairs involving Ottoman Christians, Fairey shows how Orthodox belief and culture framed international political behavior. With a similar interest in understanding the centrality of religion to the Eastern Question, Lora Gerd analyzes one of the most meaningful symbols of Russian interests in the Ottoman Empire: Mount Athos. A holy place second only, perhaps, to Christian sites in Palestine, Mount Athos attracted Russian pilgrims since medieval times and became one of the major Russian spiritual foundations in the Ottoman Empire, and hence a diplomatic flashpoint.

Several chapters in this volume deal with border crossings, in some variety or other, generated by the Eastern Question, whether depicting pilgrimages to Athos, the transfer of holy artifacts, or the movement of diplomats. Contributions by Lucien Frary, Mara Kozelsky, and Candan Badem deal more specifically with the dislocation and movement of peoples following each major war caused by the Eastern Question in the nineteenth century. A neglected aspect of Russian-Ottoman confrontations and the movements for independence in the Balkans is the enslavement of prisoners of war by Ottoman soldiers. Less onerous than the plantation form of slavery practiced in the Americas, Ottoman slavery existed well into the mid-nineteenth century and often served as punishment for rebellious religious and national groups. Frary shows how tales of Ottoman enslavement of Christians inspired humanitarian impulses in the Russian Empire and subsequent diplomatic debate during and after the Greek Revolution. Kozelsky analyzes the exodus of Crimean Tatars following the Crimean War as one of the many violent migrations associated with the Eastern Question. She explores Russian efforts to encourage migration and the ensuing crisis following the region's sudden population loss. In a subsequent chapter, Badem provides one of the first studies of Russian administration of Kars-Batum, a region Russia took from the Ottoman Empire in the war of 1878. Russian administrators, Badem argues, attempted to work with popular traditions, and when that failed, permitted mass migration. This region, as Badem shows, remains contested today by Armenian, Russian, Kurdish, and Turkish nationalists.

Diplomats began the Eastern Question, so diplomatic history plays an important role in this volume. Two chapters that tackle issues spread more than one hundred years apart explore the Eastern Question from various diplomats' point of view. Theophilus Prousis provides a sampling of the papers of the British diplomat Lord Strangford, who lived in İstanbul during the first phase of the Greek revolt, to provide a rare window into Ottoman affairs in the early 1820s. Here Prousis is less interested in the positions Strangford advocated for England. Instead, he is concerned with what Strangford witnessed: the turbulent beginning of the Greek rebellion and the fraught Ottoman response. These papers offer scholars and students uniquely valuable insight into the complexity of the Eastern Question, including sectarian conflict and the economic backdrop.

If Prousis sheds light on the opening of the Eastern Question, Ronald Bobroff brings us to its last phase in the context of European-Ottoman relations: the First World War. Through his analysis of French and Russian diplomatic exchange on the eve of war, Bobroff explores how rivalry over policy in the Ottoman Empire nearly dislodged the Franco-Russian alliance. He also examines the Russian contribution to the Sykes-Picot Agreement.

As the chapters in this volume suggest, echoes of the Eastern Question continue to resonate. No agreement regarding its final phase has emerged, and several scholars have suggested that the treaties settling the Ottoman collapse have marked a path toward new political problems in the Balkans and the Middle East.[75]

With this volume, we hope to open the debate on the Eastern Question in all its rich manifestations and thereby encourage a rethinking of this ever-pertinent historical phenomenon in the context of recent scholarship and different national experiences. The legacy of the Eastern Question remains evident today in debates over Turkey's entry into the European Union (EU), contemporary conflict over Cyprus, and the re-emergence of Turkey as a formidable power in the Middle East. As we argue in the epilogue to this book, the changing political alliances along the Black Sea, the enduring Russian concern over naval power and access to the straits, and the recurrent ethnic conflict and subsequent international crises in the Balkans and the Caucasus make revisiting the Eastern Question more relevant, and more imperative, than ever.

NOTES

1. *Cardinal Alberoni's Scheme for Reducing the Turkish Empire to the Obedience of the Christian Princes: And for a Partition of the Conquests. Together with a Scheme of a Perpetual Dyet for Establishing Publick Tranquility* (London: George Faulkner Bookseller, 1736), 1–7. Alberoni's scheme went through a number of reprints on the eve of the First World War, including a partial print in the *American Journal of International Law* 7, no. 1 (January 1913): 83–107. For Alberoni's acceptance into Eastern Question historiography, see J. A. R. Marriott, *The Eastern Question: An Historical Study in European Diplomacy* (Oxford: Oxford University Press, 1917), 5. Alberoni was an influential diplomat in the early eighteenth century as well as a cardinal. See Simon Harcourt Smith, *Cardinal of Spain: The Life and Strange Career of Alberoni* (New York: Knopf, 1944).

2. Tsar Nicholas I coined this phrase in his famous conversation with the British ambassador, Sir Hamilton Seymour, in 1853. H. W. V. Temperley, *England and the Near East: The Crimea* (London: Longmans, Green, 1936), 272, points out that the tsar referred not to "the sick man" but to the "dying bear."

"You may give him musk but even musk will not long keep him alive." See also R. W. Seton-Watson, *Britain in Europe, 1789-1914* (Cambridge: Cambridge University Press, 1937), 305.

3. See, for example, Carter Vaughn Findley, *Turkey, Islam, Nationalism, and Modernity: A History* (New Haven, CT: Yale University Press, 2010); Isa Blumi, *Reinstating the Ottomans: Alternative Balkan Modernities, 1800-1912* (New York: Palgrave Macmillan, 2011); idem, *Foundations of Modernity: Human Agency and the Imperial State* (New York: Routledge, 2012); M. Şükrü Hanioğlu, *A Brief History of the Late Ottoman Empire* (Princeton, NJ: Princeton University Press, 2008); Virginia Aksan, *Ottoman Wars, 1700-1870: An Empire Besieged* (Harlow, England: Pearson Longman, 2007); idem, "Finding the Way Back to the Ottoman Empire," *International History Review* 25, no. 1 (March 2003): 96-107.

4. For concise definitions of the Eastern Question that indicate the range and richness of the concept, see Theophilus C. Prousis, *Lord Strangford at the Sublime Porte (1822): The Eastern Crisis*, vol. 2 (İstanbul: Isis Press, 2012), 9, 12-13, 355-56; and idem, "Eastern Orthodoxy under Siege in the Ottoman Levant," *Modern Greek Studies Yearbook* 24/25 (2008/2009): 66.

5. For Russia, see David Schimmelpenninck van der Oye, *Russian Orientalism: Asia in the Russian Mind from Peter the Great to Emigration* (New Haven, CT: Yale University Press, 2011); for Western Europe, see Robert Irwin, *For Lust of Knowing: The Orientalists and Their Enemies* (London: Allen Lane, 2006).

6. A complete survey of the twists and turns of the Eastern Question in European thought, a subject worthy of a separate monograph, falls outside the confines of this introduction. The goal here, therefore, is to identify the major trends of historical writing about the Eastern Question in its most significant phases.

7. W. A. Phillips, "Eastern Question," in *Encyclopedia Britannica*, 11th ed. (New York: Encyclopedia Britannica, 1910-11), 8:112-18; A. S. Silun, "Vostochnyi vopros," in *Bol'shaia sovetskaia entsiklopediia*, 3rd ed. (Moscow: Sovetskaia Entsiklopediia, 1971), 5:408-9; I. S. Dostian, "Venskii kongress (1814-1815) i vostochnyi vopros," *Balkanskie issledovaniia* 18 (1997): 248-58; idem, "Balkanskii vopros v period venskogo kongressa (1814-1815)," *Études balkaniques* 1 (1971): 57-75; Tim Chapman, *The Congress of Vienna: Origins, Processes and Results* (London: Routledge, 1998), 71-73, 79-80; Harold Nicolson, *The Congress of Vienna: A Study in Allied Unity: 1812-1822* (New York: Harcourt, Brace, 1946), 243-44; Huseyin Yilmaz, "The Eastern Question and the Ottoman Empire: The Genesis of the Near East and the Middle East," in *Is There a Middle East? The Evolution of a Geopolitical Concept*, ed. Michael E. Bonine, Abbas Amanat, and Michael Ezekiel Gasper (Stanford, CA: Stanford University Press, 2012), 11-4. See also the thematic index in *Vneshniaia politika Rossii XIX i nachala XX v.: Dokumenty Rossiiskogo ministerstva inostrannykh del*, 16 vols. (Moscow: Nauka, 1960-94).

8. The text of the Kuchuk Kainardji agreement is published in T. Iuzefovich, *Dogovory Rossii s Vostokom politicheski i torgovye* (St. Petersburg: O. I. Baksta, 1869), 24-41. Important analyses include Roderic H. Davison, "'Russian Skill

and Turkish Imbecility': The Treaty of Kuchuk Kainardji Reconsidered," *Slavic Review* 35 (1976): 463-83; E. I. Druzhinina, *Kiuchuk-Kainardzhiiskii mir 1774 goda: Ego podgotovka i zakliuchenie* (Moscow: Nauka, 1955); and Virginia H. Aksan, *An Ottoman Statesman in War and Peace: Ahmed Resmi Efendi, 1700-1783* (Leiden: Brill, 1995), 163-69.

9. William Elton, *A Survey of the Turkish Empire* (London: T. Cadell and W. Davies, 1798); anonymous, *Observations on the Commerce of Great Britain with the Russian and Ottoman Empires: And on the Projects of Russia against the Ottoman and British Dominions* (London: J. Debrett, 1801); C. J. Liverpool, *A Vindication of the Convention Lately Concluded between Great Britain and Russia* (London: J. Wright, 1801); H. W. Williams, *Travels in Italy, Greece, and the Ionian Islands*, 2 vols. (Edinburgh: A. Constable, 1820). See also A. M. Stanislavskaia, *Rossiia i Gretsiia v kontse XVIII-nachale XIX v.: Politika Rossii v Ionicheskoi Respublike, 1798-1807 gg.* (Moscow: Nauka, 1976); and N. E. Saul, *Russia and the Mediterranean, 1797-1807* (Chicago: University of Chicago Press, 1970).

10. For reference to contemporary works on the French expedition to Egypt, see Darrell Dykstra, "The French Occupation of Egypt, 1798-1801," in *The Cambridge History of Egypt*, vol. 2, *Modern Egypt, from 1517 to the End of the Twentieth Century*, ed. M. W. Daly (Cambridge: Cambridge University Press, 1998), 113-38; Juan Cole, *Napoleon's Egypt: Invading the Middle East* (New York: Palgrave Macmillan, 2008); J. Christopher Herold, *Bonaparte in Egypt* (New York: Harper and Row, 1962). See also Salah al Din al-Boustany, ed., *The Journals of Bonaparte in Egypt*, 10 vols. (Cairo: Al-Arab Bookshop, 1971); 'Abd al-Rahman al-Jabarti, *Napoleon in Egypt: Al-Jabartī's Chronicle of the French Occupation, 1798*, trans. Shmuel Moreh (Princeton, NJ: Markus Wiener, 1993).

11. Among the more important works of this era, see William Wilkinson, *An Account of the Principalities of Wallachia and Moldavia* (London: Longman, Hurst, Rees, Orme, and Brown, 1820); J. M. Berton, *Les Turcs dans la Balance Politique de l'Europe au dix-neuvième siècle ou considérations sur l'usurpation et sur l'indépendance de la Grèce* (Paris: La Librairie Nationale et Etrangere, 1822); Edward Blaquiere, *The Greek Revolution: Its Origins and Progress* (London: G. and W. B. Whittaker, 1824); M. de Pradt, *L'Europe par rapport à la Grèce et à la réformation de la Turquie* (Paris: Béchet Ainé, 1826); R. L. Green, *Sketches of the Greek War of Independence* (London: Hurst, 1827); F. Pouqueville, *Histoire de la régénération de la Grèce*, 4 vols. (Paris: Firmin Didot, 1827); Thomas Gordon, *History of the Greek Revolution*, 2 vols. (Edinburgh: William Blackwood; London: T. Cadell, 1832); Konstantin Bazili, *Arkhipelag i Gretsiia v 1830 i 1831 godakh*, 2 vols. (St. Petersburg: Tip. N. Grecha, 1834).

12. See, for example, Alphonse Lamartine, *Vues, discours et articles sur la question d'Orient* (Paris: Charles Gosselin, 1840); A. F. Marmont, *The Present State of the Turkish Empire* (London: J. Ollivier, 1839); Nicolaòs Stephanopoli de Comnène, *Progrès social de l'Europe: Pensées d'un enfant de la Grèce sur les événemens d'Orient* (Paris: Debécourt, libraire-éditeur, 1841); George Gawler,

Tranquillization of Syria and the East (London: T. and W. Boone, 1845); K. M. Bazili, *Siriia i Palestina pod turetskim pravitel'stvom v istoricheskom i politicheskom otnosheniiakh* (Moscow: Tip. N. Grecha, 1862).

13. Théodore Benazet, *Question d'Orient* (Paris: C. Gosselin, 1836); Charles Dupin, *Discours sur la question de l'Orient* (Paris: Imprimerie Panckoucke, 1840).

14. M. N. Pokrovskii, "Vostochnyi vopros," *Bol'shaia sovetskaia entsiklopediia*, 1st ed. (Moscow: Sovetskaia Entsiklopediia, 1929), 13:310.

15. His daughter and son-in-law gathered the letters into the volume, Karl Marx, *The Eastern Question: A Reprint of Letters Written 1853–1856 Dealing with Events of the Crimean War*, ed. Eleanor Marx Aveling and Edward Aveling (London: S. Sonnenschein, 1897).

16. A. de Custine, *La Russie en 1839*, 2nd ed., 4 vols. (Paris: Librairie d'Amyot, 1843); D. Urquhart, *Portfolio, or, A Collection of State Papers*, 6 vols. (London: J. Maynard, 1836–37); idem, *The Spirit of the East*, 2 vols. (London: H. Colburn, 1838); idem, *Turkey and Its Resources: Its Municipal Organization and Free Trade* (London: Saunders and Otley, 1833); idem, *The Sultan Mahmoud and Mehemet Ali Pasha* (London: J. Ridgway, 1835); idem, *The Edinburgh Review and the Affghan War* (London: J. Maynard, 1843); G. de Lacy Evans, *On the Designs of Russia* (London: John Murray, 1828). See also G. H. Bolsover, "David Urquhart and the Eastern Question, 1833–37: A Study in Publicity and Diplomacy," *Journal of Modern History* 8 (1936): 444–67; J. H. Gleason, *The Genesis of Russophobia in Great Britain* (Cambridge, MA: Harvard University Press, 1950); Anta Dialla, *I Rosia apenanti sta Valkania: Ideologia kai politiki sto devtero miso tou 19ou aiona* (Athens: Ekdoseis Alexandreia, 2009), 73–89; Raymond T. McNally, "The Origins of Russophobia in France: 1812–1830," *American Slavic and East European Review* 17 (1958): 173–89; and Charles King, "Imagining Circassia: David Urquhart and the Making of North Caucasus Nationalism," *Russian Review* 66, no. 2 (2007): 238–55.

17. Emile de Girardin, *Solutions de la question d'Orient* (Paris: Librairie nouvelle, 1853); Edward H. Michelsen, *The Ottoman Empire and Its Resources*, 2nd ed. (London: W. Spooner, 1854); C. L. Graf von Ficquelmont, *Die religiöse Seite der orientalischen Frage* (Vienna: F. Manz, 1854); Christian Friedrich Wurm, *Diplomatische Geschichte der orientalischen Frage* (Leipzig: F. A. Brockhaus, 1858); C. H. Barault-Roullon, *Dangers pour l'Europe: Origine, progrès et état actuel de la puissance russe; Question d'Orient au point de vue politique, religieux et militaire* (Paris: J. Corréard, 1854); M. A. Melik, *L'Orient devant l'Occident* (Paris: A. Guyot et Scribe, 1856); A. A. Paton, *Researches on the Danube and the Adriatic; or Contributions to the Modern History of Hungary and Transylvania, Dalmatia and Croatia, Servia and Bulgaria*, 2 vols. (Leipzig: Brockhaus, 1861).

18. Ioannis Soutsos, *Apantisis Ellinos pros Anatolikon* (Athens: Typois Andr. Koromila, 1853); Alexandros Soutsos, *Alithis phasis tou anatolikou zitimatos* (Athens: D. Z. Gazi, 1854); K. N. Dosios, *Ellinismos i Rossismos* (Athens: S. K. Vlastou, 1854); G. D. Papanicolas, *Strike, but Hear! A New View of the Eastern*

Question (London: Edward Stanford, 1856); L. von Ranke, *Die serbische Revolution: Aus serbischen Papieren und Mittheilungen* (Berlin: Duncker und Humblot, 1844); idem, *The History of Servia, and the Servian Revolution*, trans. Mrs. Alexander Kerr (London: H. G. Bohn, 1847); Barthélemy-Sylvestre Cunibert, *Essai historique sur les révolutions et indépendance de la Serbie: Depuis 1804 jusqu'à 1850*, 2 vols. (Leipzig: F. A. Brockhaus, 1855); N. P. Popov, *Rossiia i Serbiia: Istoricheskii ocherk russkago pokrovitel'stva Serbii s 1806 po 1856 god*, 2 vols. (Moscow: Izd. K. Soldatenkova, 1869); Konstantinos Paparrigopoulos, *Istoria tou ellinikou ethnous*, 5 vols. (Athens: Eleftherodakis, 1860-74).

19. For a review of the contemporary literature on Shamil, see Thomas M. Barrett, "The Remaking of the Lion of Dagestan: Shamil in Captivity," *Russian Review* 53, no. 3 (1994): 353-66.

20. Frédéric Dubois de Montpéreux, *Voyage autour du Caucase, chez les Tcherkesses et les Abkhases, en Colchide en Géorgie, en Arménie et en Crimée; Avec un atlas géographique, pittoresque, archéologique, géologique*, etc., 6 vols. (Paris: Librairie de Gide, 1839-43); F. H. Müller, *Der ugrische Volksstamm; Oder Untersuchungen über die Ländergebiete am Ural und am Kaukasus, in historischer, geographischer und ethnographischer Beziehung*, 2 vols. (Berlin: Duncker und Humblot, 1837-39); F. P. Fonton, *La Russie dans l'Asie-Mineure* (Paris: Leneveu, 1840); Frédéric Bodenstedt, *Die Völker des Kaukasus und ihre Freiheitskämpfe gegen die Russen: Ein Beitrag zur neuesten Geschichte des Orients*, 2 vols. (Berlin: Decker, 1855).

21. On Tsar Nicholas I's imperviousness to the anti-Russian elements of the Eastern Question, see David Goldfrank, "Policy Traditions and the Menshikov Mission of 1853," in *Imperial Russian Foreign Policy*, ed. Hugh Ragsdale (Cambridge: Cambridge University Press, 1993), 119-58; and idem, "The Holy Sepulcher and the Origin of the Crimean War," in *The Military and Society in Russia, 1450-1917*, ed. Eric Lohr and Marshall Poe (Leiden: Brill, 2002), 491-506.

22. *Rossiia i Evropa: Vzgliad na kulturnye i politicheskie otnosheniia slavianskogo mira k germane-romanskomu* (St. Petersburg: Izdanie tovarishchestva obshchestvennaia pol'za, 1871). Danilevskii also published one of the first Russian studies of the Caucasus, *Kavkaz i ego gorskie zhiteli: V nynieshnem ikh polozhenii, s obiasneniem istorii, religii, iazyka, oblika, odezhdy, stroenii vospitanii, pravleniia, zakonov, korennykh obychaev, nravov, obraza zhizni, pishchi, obrazovaniia i torgovli khishchnykh gortsev Kavkaza* (Moscow: V. Gote, 1851).

23. Dialla, *I Rosia apenanti sta Valkania*; idem, "Russian Nationalism and the Eastern Question: The Case of Panslavism (1856-1878)," *Modern Greek Studies Yearbook* 24/25 (2008/2009): 73-91; Jelena Milojkovic-Djuric, *Panslavism and National Identity in Russia and in the Balkans 1830-1880: Images of the Self and Others* (Boulder, CO: East European Monographs, 1994).

24. Rostislav Fadeev, *Mnenie o Vostochnom Voprose: Po povodu poslednikh retsentsii na vooruzhenniia sily Rossii* (St. Petersburg: Tip. Departamenta Udelov, 1870); D. Bukharov, *Rossiia i Turtsiia: Ot vozniknoveniia politicheskikh mezhdu nimi otnoshenii do Londonskogo traktata 13/25 Marta 1871 g.* (St. Petersburg: Tip. F. S.

Sushchinskogo, 1878; originally published in French in 1877); A. V. Nekliudov, *Nachalo snoshenii Rossii s Turtsiei* (Moscow: Tip. Gattsuka, 1883); F. Uspenskii, *Kak voznik i razvivalsia na Rusi vostochnyi vopros* (St. Petersburg: Slaviansk. Blagotvoritel'noe O-vo, 1887).

25. N. N. Murav'ev, *Russkie na Bosfore v 1833 godu* (Moscow: Chertkov, 1869); idem, *Dela Turtsii i Egipta v 1832 i 1833 godakh: Diplomaticheskie snosheniia*, 4 vols. (Moscow: A. I. Mamontova, 1870); idem, *Voina za Kavkazom v 1855 godu*, 2 vols. (St. Petersburg: A. N. Demidova, 1877); see also, "Zapiski grafa A. I. Ribop'era," *Russkii arkhiv*, kn. 4 (1877): 460–506, kn. 5 (1877): 5–36.

26. T. Iuzefovich, *Dogovory Rossii s Vostokom*.

27. B. N. Chicherin, "Vostochnyi vopros s russkoi tochki zreniia 1855 goda," in S. P. Trubetskoi's *Zapiski kniazia S. P. Trubetskogo* (St. Petersburg: Sirius, 1906): 123–53 [originally published in *Blagonamerennyi*, no. 12 (1855), Leipzig, under the pseudonym Granovsky]; V. A. Ulianitskii, *Dardanelly, Bosfor i Chernoe more v XVIII veke* (Moscow: A. Gattsuka, 1883).

28. Nazan Çiçek, *The Young Ottomans: Turkish Critics of the Eastern Question in the Late Nineteenth Century* (London: I. B. Tauris, 2010), 1.

29. W. E. Gladstone, *Bulgarian Horrors and the Question of the East* (London: John Murray, Albemarle Street, 1876); idem, *Lessons in Massacre; or, The Conduct of the Turkish Government in and about Bulgaria since May, 1876* (London: J. Murray, 1877); Fyodor Dostoevsky, *A Writer's Diary*, trans. Kenneth Lantz, 2 vols. (Evanston, IL: Northwestern University Press); I. L. Volgin, "Nravstvennye osnovy publistsistiki Dostoevskogo: Vostochnyi vopros v *Dnevnike pisatelia*," *Izvestiia Akademii nauk SSSR (literatury i iazyk)* 30 (1972): 312–24. Two less emotional studies, by Edward Freeman, *The Ottoman Power in Europe; Its Nature, Its Growth, and Its Decline* (London: Macmillan, 1877); and Friedrich Gentz, *Zur Geschichte der orientalischen Frage* (Vienna: W. Braumüller, 1877), contrast with the voluminous pamphlet literature. The latter included such titles as *The Eastern Question: A Summary View of It for Busy Men, by One of Themselves* (Harrisburg, PA: C. H. Bergner, 1876); and E. T. Turnerelli's *The "Sacred Mission" of the Russian Wolf among the Christian Sheep of Turkey: Ought We to Oppose or Promote It?* (London: Haughton, 1876). See also R. W. Seton-Watson, *Disraeli, Gladstone and the Eastern Question: A Study in Diplomacy and Party Politics* (London: Macmillan, 1935); and Dwight E. Lee, *Great Britain and the Cyprus Convention of 1878* (Cambridge, MA: Harvard University Press, 1934).

30. F. F. Martens, "Étude historique sur la politique Russe dans la question d'orient," *Revue de droit international et de législation comparée* 9 (1877): 49–77; idem, *Die russische Politik in der orientalischen Frage* (St. Petersburg: H. Schmitz-dorff, 1877).

31. S. M. Solov'ev, "Vostochnyi vopros," in *Sobranie sochineniia S. M. Solov'eva* (St. Petersburg: Obshchestvennaia pol'za, 1882), 294.

32. S. Zhigarev, *Russkaia politika v vostochnom voprose*, 2 vols. (Moscow: Universitetskaia tipograiia, 1896), 1:49.

33. N. F. Dubrovin, *Istoriia voiny i vladychestva russkikh na Kavkaze*, 6 vols. (St. Petersburg: Tip. Departamenta udielov, 1871-88); V. A. Potto, *Kavkazkaia voina v otdel'nykh ocherkakh, episodakh, legendakh, i biografiiakh*, 4 vols. (Stavropol: Kavkazskii krai, 1994; first published in Tiflis, 1885-88); anonymous, *Contradictions of Lord Palmerston in Reference to Poland and Circassia, et caetera* (London: Hardwicke, 1863); G. D. C. Argyll, *The Eastern Question from the Treaty of Paris 1856 to the Treaty of Berlin 1878, and to the Second Afghan War*, 2 vols. (London: Strahan, 1879).

34. A. Berzhe, ed., *Akty sobrannye Kavkazskoiu arkheograficheskoiu kommissiei*, 12 vols. (Tiflis: Arkhiv Glavnago upravleniia namiestnika Kavkazskago, 1866-1904).

35. The "Near East" (*Proche-Orient, Blizhnii Vostok*) is a geographical term developed by European scholars and essayists in the nineteenth century. Many scholars retain its use to describe the western lands of the Ottoman Empire. For a discussion of this term, see Yilmaz, "The Eastern Question and the Ottoman Empire," 11-35; Nikki R. Keddie, "Is There a Middle East?," *International Journal of Middle Eastern Studies* 4, no. 3 (1973): 255-71; and Roderic Davison, "Where Is the Middle East?," *Foreign Affairs* 38 (July 1960): 665-75.

36. Edouard Driault, *La question d'Orient, 1918-1937: La paix de la Méditerranée* (Paris: F. Alcan, 1938); Albert Sorel, *La question d'Orient au XVIIIe siècle: Le partage de la Pologne et le traité de Kaïnardji* (Paris: E. Plon, Nourrit et Cie, 1889).

37. See Çiçek, *Young Ottomans*.

38. On Bessarabia, see Andrei Kushko and Viktor Taki, with the assistance of Oleg Groma, *Bessarabiia v sostave rossiiskoi imperii, 1812-1917* (Moscow: Novoe Literaturnoe Obozrenie, 2012).

39. See Bryce's "Preface" to Toynbee's *The Murderous Tyranny of the Turks* (New York: George H. Doran, 1917); and Arnold J. Toynbee, *The Armenian Atrocities: The Murder of a Nation* (London: Hodder and Stoughton, 1915).

40. See, for example, V. I. Lenin, "National and Colonial Questions, for the Second Congress of the Communist International," http://marxists.anu.edu.au/archive/lenin/works/1920/jun/05.htm; and "Events in the Balkans and in Persia," http://www.marxists.org/archive/lenin/works/1908/oct/16.htm. Quoting Marx, Pokrovskii, "Vostochnyi vopros," 13:309, 321-22, emphasizes the Ottoman "feudal yoke," Western imperialism, and the hostile nature of tsarist foreign policy.

41. Among the most enduring specialized studies written around this time are the publications of R. W. Seton-Watson, *The Southern Slav Question and the Hapsburg Monarchy* (London: Constable, 1911); idem, *The Balkans, Italy, and the Adriatic* (London: Nisbet, 1916); idem, *The Rise of Nationality in the Balkans* (London: Constable, 1917); see also George Abbott, *Turkey, Greece, and the Great Powers: A Study in Friendship and Hate* (New York: M. Mcbride, 1917). Naturally, not all works published during the war dealt exclusively with the Balkans. Interest in Germany and the Eastern Question had arisen as well. See, for

example, Heinrich von Treitschke, *Germany, France, Russia and Islam* (London: Jarrold and Sons, 1915).

42. Marriott states in his *Memories of Four Score Years: The Autobiography of the Late Sir John Marriott* (London: Blackie & Son, 1946), 154, "Few of my books have evoked more cordial encomiums from those qualified to bestow them than *The Eastern Question*; quite recently it was described by an expert as a 'classical work,' and I think I may, without immodesty, claim that it is now accepted as the standard work on the subject with which it deals."

43. Marriott, *Eastern Question*, 2. The fourth and last edition was reprinted as late as 1963.

44. Ibid., 203.

45. Ibid., iii.

46. Ibid., 3.

47. Written in the wake of the Armenian massacres and the disastrous Greek invasion of Anatolia in 1919-23, Arnold Toynbee's *The Western Question in Greece and Turkey: A Study in the Contact of Civilizations* (Boston: Houghton Mifflin, 1922) provided the sole antidote to pro-Western, Balkan-centric accounts akin to Marriott. The fierce public controversy sparked by Toynbee's volume marked a turning point in his career and led to his resignation from the Koraes Chair of Modern Greek and Byzantine History at King's College, London. See Richard Clogg, *Politics and the Academy: Arnold Toynbee and the Koraes Chair* (London: Frank Cass, 1986); and idem, *Anglo-Greek Attitudes: Studies in History* (New York: Palgrave Macmillan, 2000), 36-59.

48. Temperley, *England and the Near East*; Vernon Puryear, *England, Russia, and the Straits Question, 1844-1856* (Berkeley: University of California Press, 1931); idem, *International Economics and Diplomacy in the Near East: A Study of British Commercial Policy in the Levant, 1834-1853* (Stanford, CA: Stanford University Press, 1935); R. W. Seton-Watson, *Disraeli, Gladstone and the Eastern Question*. See also Philip Mosley, *Russian Diplomacy and the Opening of the Eastern Question in 1838 and 1839* (Cambridge, MA: Harvard University Press, 1934); and the work of Puryear's student Mose Lofley Harvey, "The Development of Russian Commerce on the Black Sea and Its Significance" (PhD diss., University of California, Berkeley, 1938).

49. M. S. Anderson, *The Eastern Question, 1774-1923: A Study in International Relations* (London: Macmillan, 1966), ix. Anderson published a companion volume of documents, *The Great Powers and the Near East, 1774-1923* (London: Edward Arnold, 1970).

50. Since Anderson's work, A. L. Macfie, *The Eastern Question, 1774-1923* (London: Longman, 1989; rev. ed. 1996) is the only other mainstream survey in English. Also meant for college students and one-quarter of the length of Anderson's work, Macfie's volume is supplemented by a selection of primary documents.

51. Çiçek, *Young Ottomans*, 6.

52. Edward Said, *Orientalism* (New York: Vintage, 1979), 73-76.

53. A number of important works have also appeared about the Eastern Question from Western European perspectives since the publication of Anderson's survey, including Karl A. Roider, *Austria's Eastern Question, 1700-1790* (Princeton, NJ: Princeton University Press, 1982); Allan Cunningham, *Anglo-Ottoman Encounters in the Age of Revolution: Collected Essays* (London: F. Cass, 1992); idem, *Eastern Questions in the Nineteenth Century: Collected Essays* (London: F. Cass, 1993); Matthew Gibson, *Dracula and the Eastern Question: British and French Vampire Narratives of the Nineteenth-Century Near East* (New York: Palgrave McMillan, 2006); and Miloš Ković, *Disraeli and the Eastern Question* (Oxford: Oxford University Press, 2011).

54. Both the Ottoman and the early Turkish Republican state tightly controlled the publication of historical narratives around state interests, and only recently has the state opened up history for a much wider public interpretation. For a good discussion about the relationship between the Turkish state and its control over the past, see Wendy Shaw, "The Rise of the Hittite Sun," in *Selective Remembrances: Archaeology in the Construction, Commemoration, and Consecration of National Pasts*, ed. Phillip Kohl, Mara Kozelsky, and Nachman Ben-Yahuda (Chicago: University of Chicago Press, 2008), 163-88. See also Candan Badem, *The Ottoman Crimean War (1853-1856)* (Leiden: Brill, 2010), 1-39.

55. Kemal Karpat, *The Politicization of Islam: Reconstructing Identity, State, Faith and Community in the Late Ottoman State* (Oxford: Oxford University Press, 2001), 14-15; idem, "The Transformation of the Ottoman State, 1789-1908," *International Journal of Middle East Studies* 3, no. 3 (1972): 258; idem, *Social Change and Politics in Turkey: A Structural-Historical Analysis* (Leiden: Brill, 1973); idem, *An Inquiry into the Social Foundations of Nationalism in the Ottoman State: From Social Estates to Classes, from Millets to Nations* (Princeton, NJ: Princeton University Press, 1973); and idem, *Ottoman Population 1830-1914. Demographic and Social Characteristics* (Madison: University of Wisconsin Press, 1985). For a longer discussion of Karpat's foundational contribution to Ottoman historiography, see Aksan, "Finding the Way Back to the Ottoman Empire."

56. Recent revisionist work in Ottoman history includes Suraiya N. Faroqhi, *Pilgrims and Sultans: The Hajj under the Ottomans, 1517—1683* (London: I. B. Tauris, 1994); idem, *Approaches to Ottoman History: An Introduction to the Sources* (Cambridge: Cambridge University Press, 1999); idem, *Subjects of the Sultan: Culture and Daily Life in the Ottoman Empire* (London: I. B. Tauris, 2000); *The Cambridge History of Turkey*, vol. 3, *The Later Ottoman Empire, 1603-1839*, ed. Suraiya N. Faroqhi (Cambridge: Cambridge University Press, 2006); Selim Deringil, *Conversion and Apostasy in the Late Ottoman Empire* (New York: Cambridge University Press, 2012). For a good summary of trends in the field, see Jun Akiba, "Preliminaries to a Comparative History of the Russian and Ottoman

Empires: Perspectives from Ottoman Studies," in *Imperiology: From Empirical Knowledge to Discussing the Russian Empire*, ed. Kimitaka Matsuzato (Sapporo: Hokkaido University Press, 2007), 33-49.

57. Nicholas Doumanis, *Before the Nation: Muslim-Christian Coexistence and Its Destruction in Late Ottoman Anatolia* (Oxford: Oxford University Press, 2013); Cem Emrence, *Remapping the Ottoman Middle East: Modernity, Imperial Bureaucracy, and the Islamic State* (London: I. B. Tauris, 2012); Blumi, *Foundations of Modernity*; idem, *Reinstating the Ottomans*; Evangelia Balta and Mehmet Ölmez, eds., *Between Religion and Language: Turkish-Speaking Christians, Jews and Greek-Speaking Muslims and Catholics in the Ottoman Empire* (İstanbul: EREN, 2011).

58. Katherine Fleming, *The Muslim Bonaparte: Diplomacy and Orientalism in Ali Pasha's Greece* (Princeton, NJ: Princeton University Press, 1999); Khaled Fahmy, *All the Pasha's Men: Mehmed Ali, His Army, and the Making of Modern Egypt* (Cambridge: Cambridge University Press, 1997). See also Eugene Rogan, *Frontiers of the State in the Late Ottoman Empire: Transjordan, 1850-1921* (Cambridge: Cambridge University Press, 1999); Frederick Anscombe, *The Ottoman Gulf: The Creation of Kuwait, Saudi Arabia, and Qatar* (New York: Columbia University Press, 1997); Dina Rizk Khoury, "The Ottoman Centre versus Provincial Power-Holders: An Analysis of the Historiography," in *The Cambridge History of Turkey*, vol. 3, *The Later Ottoman Empire, 1603-1839*, ed. Suraiya N. Faroqhi (Cambridge: Cambridge University Press, 2006), 135-56.

59. See Badem, *Ottoman Crimean War*; Çiçek, *Young Ottomans*; Caesar E. Farah, *Politics of Interventionism in Lebanon; 1830-1861* (London: I. B. Tauris, 2000); M. Hakan Yavuz and Peter Sluglett, eds., *War and Diplomacy: The Russo-Turkish War of 1877-1878 and the Treaty of Berlin* (Salt Lake City: University of Utah Press, 2011).

60. Theofanis G. Stavrou, *Russian Interests in Palestine: A Study of Religious and Educational Enterprise* (Thessaloniki: IMXA, 1963); Theofanis G. Stavrou and Peter Weisensel, *Russian Travelers to the Christian East from the Twelfth to the Twentieth Century* (Columbus, OH: Slavica, 1986), as well as the journal edited by Stavrou, *The Modern Greek Studies Yearbook* (1985-present); Barbara Jelavich, *Russia's Balkan Entanglements, 1906-1914* (New York: Cambridge University Press, 1991); Barbara and Charles Jelavich, *Establishment of the Balkan Nation States, 1804-1920* (Seattle: University of Washington Press, 1977); Barbara Jelavich, *History of the Balkans*, 2 vols. (Cambridge: Cambridge University Press, 1983).

61. Theophilus C. Prousis, *Russian Society and the Greek Revolution* (DeKalb: Northern Illinois University Press, 1994); Lora Gerd, *Konstantinopol'skii Patriarkhat i Rossiia 1901/1914* (Moscow: Indrik, 2012); idem, *Konstantinopol i Peterburg: Tserkovnaia politika Rossii na pravoslavnom Vostoke, 1878-1898* (Moscow: Indrik 2006); N. N. Lisovoi, *Russkoe dukhovnoe i politicheskoe prisutstvie v Sviatoi Zemle i na Blizhnem Vostoke v XIX-nachale XX v.* (Moscow: Indrik, 2006); idem, ed., *Rossiia v Sviatoi Zemle: Dokumenty i materialy*, 2 vols. (Moscow:

Mezhdunarodnye otnosheniia, 2000); Stephen K. Batalden, *Catherine II's Greek Prelate: Eugenios Voulgaris in Russia 1771-1806* (Boulder, CO: East European Monographs, 1982); Gregory Lynn Bruess, *Religion, Identity and Empire: A Greek Archbishop in the Age of Catherine the Great* (Boulder, CO: East European Monographs, 1997); Derek Hopwood, *The Russian Presence in Syria and Palestine, 1843-1914: Church and Politics in the Near East* (Oxford: Clarendon Press, 1969).

62. On Russian hajj, see Eileen Kane, "Odessa as a Hajj Hub, 1880s-1910s," in *Russia in Motion: Essays on the Politics, Society, and Culture of Human Mobility, 1850-Present*, ed. John Randolph and Eugene Avrutin (Chicago: University of Illinois Press, 2012), 107-25.

63. V. N. Vinogradov, *Dvuglavnyi rossiiskii orel na Balkanakh, 1683-1914* (Moscow: Indrik, 2010); idem, ed., *Vek Ekateriny II: Dela balkanskie* (Moscow: Nauka, 2000); E. P. Kudriavtseva, *Rossiia i stanovlenie serbskoi gosudarstvennosti, 1812-1856* (Moscow: Kvadriga, 2009); G. A. Georgiev et al., *Vostochnyi vopros vo vneshnei politike Rossii: Konets XVIII-nachalo XX veka* (Moscow: Nauka, 1978); I. S. Dostian, *Rossiia i Balkanskii vopros* (Moscow: Nauka, 1972).

64. Alexander Bitis, *Russia and the Eastern Question, 1815-1833* (Oxford: Oxford University Press, 2006); John Daly, *Russian Seapower and "The Eastern Question," 1827-1841* (Annapolis, MD: Naval Institute Press, 1991).

65. V. Sheremet, *Voina i biznes: Vlast', den'gi i oruzhie; Evropa i Blizhnii Vostok v novoe vremiia* (Moscow: Tekhnologicheskaia shkola biznesa, 1996); idem, *Osmanskaia imperiia i Zapadnaia Evropa vtoraia tret' XIX v.* (Moscow: Nauka, 1986).

66. David Goldfrank, *The Origins of the Crimean War* (London: Longman, 1994); idem, "The Holy Sepulcher and the Origin of the Crimean War," in *The Military and Society in Russia: 1450-1917*, ed. Eric Lohr and Marshall Poe (Leiden, The Netherlands: Brill, 2002), 491-506; L. V. Mel'nikova, *Russkaia Pravoslavnaia Tserkov i Krymskaia Voina, 1853-1856 gg.* (Moscow: Kuchkovo pole, 2012); Orlando Figes, *The Crimean War: A History* (New York: Metropolitan Books, 2011). While not from the Russian perspective, Winfried Baumgart, *The Crimean War* (London: Oxford University Press, 2008) has probably provided the most substantial revision of the conflict since the publication of Anderson's survey.

67. Ronald Bobroff, *Roads to Glory: Late Imperial Russia and the Turkish Straits* (London: I. B. Tauris, 2006); Michael Reynolds, *Shattering Empires: The Clash and Crash of Ottoman and Russian Empires, 1908-1918* (Cambridge: Cambridge University Press, 2011); Sean McMeekin, *The Russian Origins of the First World War* (Cambridge, MA: Harvard University Press, 2011). See also Andrew Rossos, *Russia and the Balkans: Inter-Balkan Rivalries and Russian Foreign Policy, 1908-1914* (Toronto: University of Toronto Press, 1981).

68. The only book devoted to the civilian experience of the Crimean War, for example, dates to 1904: Arsenii Markevich, *Tavricheskaia guberniia vo vremia Krymskoi Voiny* (1904; repr., Simferopol: Binez, Inform, 1994).

69. Radu Florescu, *The Struggle against Russia in the Romanian Principalities* (Iasi: Center for Romanian Studies, 1997); Robert A. Berry, "Czartoryski's Hôtel

Lambert and the Great Powers in the Balkans, 1832-1848," *International History Review* 7, no. 1 (1985): 45-67; and more recently, Radosław Żurawski vel Grajewski, *Wielka Brytania w "dyplomacji" księcia Adama Jerzego Czartoryskiego wobec kryzysu wschodniego (1832-1841)* (Warsaw: Wydawn. Nauk. Semper, 1999); Jelena Milojković-Djurić, *The Eastern Question and the Voices of Reason: Austria-Hungary, Russia, and the Balkan States, 1875-1908* (Boulder, CO: East European Monographs, 2002). For an interesting discussion of the origins of the Eastern Question in Balkan affairs, see Zdenko Zlatar, *Between the Double Eagle and the Crescent: The Republic of Dubrovnik and the Origins of the Eastern Question* (Boulder, CO: Eastern European Monographs, 1992).

70. A. D. Panesh, *Zapadnaia Cherkesiia v sisteme vzaimodeistviia rossii s turtsiei, angliei, i imamatom shamiilia v XIXv (do 1864)* (Maikop: Adygeiskii respublikanskii institut gumanitarnykh issledovanii im. T. M. Kerasheva, 2007).

71. For demographic analyses of Greek movements during Russian-Ottoman wars, see the foundational works of G. L. Arsh, including "Grecheskoe emigratsiia v Rossiiu v kontse XVIII-nachale XIX v.," *Sovetskaia etnografiia*, no. 3 (1969): 85-95; and *Eteristskoe dvizhenie v Rossii: Osvoboditel'naia bor'ba grecheskogo naroda v nachale XIX v. i russko-grecheskie sviazi* (Moscow: Nauka, 1970). See also Shteliian Shterionov, *Gertsite po Bulgarskite zemi pres XVIII-XIX vek (do 1878 g.)* (Sofia: Faber, 2008); idem, *Migratsiiata na Gretskoto naselenia, obitavashto Bulgarskite zemi pres XVIII-XIX vek (do 1878 g.)* (Sofia: Faber, 2009); John Mazis, *The Greeks of Odessa: Diaspora Leadership in Late Imperial Russia* (Boulder, CO: East European Monographs, 2004); M. A. Aradzhioni, *Greki Kryma i priazov'ia izucheniia i istoriografiia etnicheskoi istorii i kult'tury (80-e gg XVIII v. 90-e gg XX v.)* (Simferopol: Simferopol'skii gos. universitet, 1999); A. Mikaelian, *Na krymskoi zemle: Istoriia armianskikh poselenii v Krymu* (Erevan: Izd-vo Aiastan, 1974); Nina Noskova, *Krymskie bolgary v XIV-nachale XX v.: Istoria i kul'tura* (Simferopol: SONAT, 2002).

72. Justin McCarthy, *Death and Exile: The Ethnic Cleansing of Ottoman Muslims, 1821-1922* (Princeton, NJ: Darwin Press, 1996); Alan W. Fisher, "Emigration of Muslims from the Russian Empire in the Years after the Crimean War," *Jahrbücher für Geschichte Osteuropas* 35 (1987): 356-71; idem, *The Russian Annexation of Crimea, 1772-1783* (Cambridge: Cambridge University Press, 1970); Bryan Glyn Williams, "The Hijra and Forced Migration from Nineteenth-Century Russia to the Ottoman Empire: A Critical Analysis of the Great Crimean Tatar Emigration, 1860-1861," *Cahiers du monde russe* 41, no. 1 (2000): 79-108; Mark Pinson, "Demographic Warfare—an Aspect of Ottoman and Russian Policy, 1854-1866" (PhD diss., Harvard University, 1970).

73. As the Armenian genocide unfolded, contemporary observers like Marriott and Toynbee saw this human disaster as developing from the Eastern Question and directly connected to the long history of sectarian violence in the Ottoman Empire. Thus, for example, Toynbee connected the Armenian genocide to the policies of Sultan Abdülhamid II, whose "Balkan experience had

taught him the policy of keeping the races of his empire in hand by setting them to massacre one another." Post–World War II scholarship has associated the Armenian genocide with later atrocities of the twentieth century. For Toynbee on the Armenians, see Toynbee, *Armenian Atrocities,* 21. For the argument that the population exchange and the Armenian genocide were products of twentieth-century violence, see Norman Naimark, *Fires of Hatred: Ethnic Cleansing in the Twentieth Century* (Cambridge, MA: Harvard University Press, 2001).

74. Gary Bass, *Freedom's Battle: The Origins of Humanitarian Intervention* (New York: Knopf, 2008); and Davide Rodogno, *Against Massacre: Humanitarian Intervention in the Ottoman Empire, 1815–1914* (Princeton, NJ: Princeton University Press, 2011).

75. Edward Knox, *The Making of a New Eastern Question: British Palestine Policy and the Origins of Israel, 1917–1925* (Washington, DC: Catholic University Press, 1981); Carl L. Brown, *International Politics and the Middle East: Old Rules, Dangerous Game* (Princeton, NJ: Princeton University Press, 1984); Harry J. Psomiades, *The Eastern Question: The Last Phase; A Study in Greek-Turkish Diplomacy* (Thessaloniki: IMXA, 1968).

Map of Moldavia and Wallachia, 1782. (reprinted with permission from the Pusey Map Collection at Harvard University)

The Russian Protectorate in the Danubian Principalities
Legacies of the Eastern Question in Contemporary Russian-Romanian Relations

Victor Taki

In 1890, the soon-to-be leader of the Romanian Liberal Party, Dimitrie Alexandru Sturdza, published a booklet titled *Europa, Rusia și România*, in which he presented his country as the avant-garde force of European civilization in the upcoming struggle with the mass of Slavic peoples mobilizing against Europe under the Russian scepter.[1] Citing different statistical sources, the brochure calculated the comparative strength of the two opposing forces and attempted to anticipate the outcomes of the future confrontation between East and West. The maps charting the geography of this confrontation constitute perhaps the most interesting aspect of this small book. The Kingdom of Romania together with the predominantly ethnically Romanian lands of the Russian and the Austro-Hungarian Empires constituted an "advance bastion" protruding well into the mass of Slavic peoples and connected to Sturdza's "fortress Europe" by the Hungarian and Austrian isthmus. To the north, separated by the mass of western Slavs, lay a flank rampart in the shape of Eastern

Prussia, the Baltic provinces of the Russian Empire, and Finland. Another bulwark located to the south consisted, rather unexpectedly, of Greece and Turkey, which Sturdza did not hesitate to place together despite the dramatic confrontations that the two had undergone in the nineteenth century, and the even more traumatic ones that were still to come. Sturdza's imagined geography thus split the European continent along a much more entangled line than the one Winston Churchill drew between Stettin and Trieste half a century later.

Had Sturdza the possibility to travel 120 years into the future, he would undoubtedly be happy to see his optimistic expectation of "Europe's" victory in its confrontation with Russia confirmed. The "frontier of civilization" has been pushed well eastward, while the western and southern Slavic peoples who previously nearly encircled the "Romanian bastion" have been largely incorporated into "the fortress." Sturdza's only possible cause for concern would be the unstable state of the erstwhile southern flank, where Turkey currently engages in economic cooperation with Russia. In the late nineteenth century, the prospect of a Russian-Ottoman cooperation indeed seemed unnatural and unrealistic, but this was (and still is!) even more true of Sturdza's proposed idea that Turkey and Greece together could form a "rampart" against some external assailant. The fact that Sturdza was capable of identifying such a force indicates his tendency to conceive of the Eastern Question as subordinate to the issue of Slavic unity and ultimately of Russia's relation to Europe. Sturdza shared this tendency with the Russian Pan-Slavist writers Rostislav Andreevich Fadeev and Nikolai Iakovleich Danilevskii, whose works he cited and whose visions in some respects constituted a mirror image of his own ideas.[2] The fact that the Russian writers and the Romanian author reinterpreted the Eastern Question as the problem of relations between Russia and Europe is all the more striking if one takes into account how differently the two sides conceived the relations between each other.

In order to explain this conjunction of similarities and differences between the authors, whose mode of thinking still has some influence in contemporary Russia and Romania, this chapter traces the historical evolution of Russian-Romanian relations and of the ways in which the two nations perceived each other in the context of the Eastern Question. The chapter demonstrates that the mutual perceptions of Russians and Romanians correlated with their evolving conceptualizations of the Eastern Question and the role of their respective countries in it. Initially defined by common Orthodox faith, relations between Russia and the

Romanian principalities of Moldavia and Wallachia became considerably secularized by the turn of the nineteenth century. With the emergence of modern nationalism, both Romanians and Russians became increasingly sensitive about their ethnic differences. In parallel, earlier projects placing the principalities under the Russian protectorate gave way to concerns about the place of Romanians in the prospective union of the Slavic peoples. Increasingly negative mutual perceptions constitute one of the most significant legacies of the Eastern Question in contemporary Russian-Romanian relations. An emphasis on collective perceptions helps transcend the traditional historiographical treatment of the Eastern Question as the story of diplomacy and war. It reveals an enduring relevance of the Eastern Question for understanding present-day international relations on the eastern borders of the EU.[3]

This chapter also argues for a greater importance of the Romanian principalities in the Russian-Ottoman encounter and the international relations of the eighteenth and nineteenth century more broadly. Contacts between Russian rulers and the elites of these two Ottoman tributary polities were the most important manifestations of Russia's influence in the European Turkey that generated the Eastern Question as we know it. In an effort to secure the historical privileges of the principalities, the Moldavian and Wallachian boyars suggested to Russian foreign-policy makers their basic strategy of interference in the relations between the sultan and his Christian subjects. Later, the discourse of the Ottoman "capitulations" to Moldavia and Wallachia served the Romanian leaders in playing Turkey off against Russia in order to widen their political autonomy. The activities of Romanian leaders revealed the limits of Russia's influence in the Balkans, even if they were not the immediate cause of the Crimean War and the subsequent abolition of the Russian protectorate over the principalities. The history of the Russian protectorate over Moldavia and Wallachia thus reveals that the standard accounts of the Eastern Question have not given to the borderland elites the attention that they merit.

The Danubian Principalities and Russia

"The light comes to us from Moscow," wrote the metropolitan of Moldavia Dosifei in the late seventeenth century. A major religious writer, Dosifei occupies pride of place in the history of the Moldavian Church due to the Romanian translations of the Old Church Slavonic liturgical books. Printed on a press that he received from the Muscovite tsar

Feodor Alexeevich in 1681, these translations made it possible to conduct the religious services in Romanian.[4] Dosifei headed the Moldavian Church for fourteen years, during which on two occasions (in 1674 and 1684) he participated in negotiations with Moscow with the goal of bringing Moldavia under Muscovite suzerainty.[5] This did not strengthen Dosifei's credentials in the eyes of Moldavia's Ottoman overlords, and eventually he had to leave for Poland in the train of Jan Sobieski's army retreating from Moldavia in 1686. On several occasions during his stay in Polish exile, Dosifei, like many other high Orthodox clergymen from the Ottoman Empire, sent for and received financial help from Moscow.[6] Although some accounts indicate that Dosifei died in Zolkiev (Poland) in 1696, according to others he came to Russia that year, was favorably received by Peter the Great, and died in Moscow in 1701, shortly after being named the metropolitan of Azov.[7]

Dosifei's activities illustrate both the initial attitudes of the Moldavian and Wallachian elites toward Muscovite Russia and the mediatory role of the high Orthodox clergy in the early relations between the principalities and the sole sovereign Orthodox power. They demonstrate that the Christian leaders of southeastern Europe quickly recognized the opportunities resulting from the emergence of Russia and the beginning of the Ottoman retreat from Europe. Thus, some fifty years earlier in 1649, the patriarch of Jerusalem, Paisios, sent a message to Tsar Aleksei Mikhailovich with an invitation to join the Moldavian and Wallachian princes on a campaign to take İstanbul, "for now the strength of the Turk [was] exhausted."[8] The Moldavian metropolitan Gedeon brought the same message from the *hospodars* Vasilie Lupu (1634-53) and Gheorghe Ștefan (1653-58), who proposed, respectively, an anti-Ottoman alliance and the acceptance of Moscow's sovereignty over the principality.[9] The Greek clergy propagated the idea of an anti-Ottoman struggle later in the century. Thus, in 1688, the archimandrite Isaiah of St. Paul's Monastery on Mount Athos brought messages to Moscow from a former patriarch of Constantinople, Dionysios, the Wallachian prince Șerban Cantacuzino, the Moldavian prince Constantine Cantemir, and the Serbian patriarch Arsenije III.[10] On their behalf, Isaiah summoned the young Russian tsars Ivan and Peter to a holy war for the liberation of the Orthodox Church and declared, "At present the whole Turkish state has received a harsh punishment from God and the great Muslimhood [*busurmanstvo*] is coming to utter ruin."[11]

Remarkably, such pleas reveal that the Greek Orthodox subjects of the sultan came to perceive the Muscovite tsars as their intercessors before the latter were ready and willing to adopt such a posture themselves. Thus, despite agreeing to accept Moldavia under his suzerainty in 1656, Alexei Mikhailovich ultimately refused to dispatch to Iași the embassy that was supposed to administer the principality's oath of loyalty to the tsar.[12] Five years later, Alexis ordered the governor of Kiev to declare to the representative of the Moldavian *hospodar* Constantin Șerban that "there [was] an old friendship" between the sultan and the tsar and thus the latter could not accept the former's subject "under his high hand."[13] Alexei Mikhailovich was clearly unwilling to antagonize the Ottomans, much like his father Mikhail Feodorovich, who in 1641 returned to them the Azov fortress captured by the Don Cossacks several years previously. As a result, almost two decades elapsed between Patriarch Paisios's message to Alexis and the outbreak of the first Russian-Ottoman War of 1677–81.

In the course of the Russian-Ottoman wars of the late seventeenth and the eighteenth century, appeals for protection and declarations of loyalty to the tsars became routine in the addresses of the *hospodars*, boyars, and high clergymen. Peter the Great received requests for a protectorate or an alliance from one Wallachian and three Moldavian princes before concluding the Lutsk treaty of April 1711 with Moldavian *hospodar* Dimitrie Cantemir, on the eve of the ill-fortuned Pruth campaign.[14] Defeated by the tsar at Poltava in 1709, the Swedish king Charles XII fled to the Ottoman fortress Bender on the Dniester, where, with the help of the Crimean khan and French diplomacy, he managed to provoke another war between Russia and the Ottoman Empire.[15] A brief overview of conditions of the Russian-Moldavian treaties concluded up to that historical turning point demonstrates that from the beginning the Moldavian and Wallachian princes and boyars were ready to submit under the "high sovereign hand" of the tsar on certain conditions. The latter usually included internal autonomy and the preservation of their traditional rights and laws of the country. Thus, the treaty of 1656 between Gheorghe Ștefan and Aleksei Mikhailovich stipulated that the Moldavian *hospodar* always be elected from the natives of Moldavia, retain his traditional prerogatives, and reestablish his authority over cities alienated into Ottoman-controlled *reaya* districts.[16] Similarly, the conditions on which the Moldavian boyars were ready to swear loyalty to Tsar Alexis in 1674 referred to the "customs of our land" and the "old rights" and stipulated the right to elect the *hospodar* as well as the secular and ecclesiastical officials. The boyars also asked to restore the territorial integrity of the principality, which, under the influence of Polish political notions, they called a commonwealth (Rech Pospolitaia).[17] Finally, the diploma issued by Peter the Great to Cantemir secured the latter's hereditary rule over Moldavia and asserted the plenitude of the *hospodar*'s authority over the boyars, the cities, and the Ottoman *reayas* "in accordance with the ancient Moldavian custom."[18]

For almost a century after the Pruth debacle, no Moldavian or Wallachian prince wanted or dared to conclude the treaties of alliance with or become a subject of the Russian tsar.[19] Phanariote Greeks, who, after 1711, maintained the thrones of Moldavia and Wallachia, were too closely controlled by the Ottomans. As cultural foreigners, they did not enjoy substantial support among the largely autochthonous boyar class.[20] Phanariotes were aristocratic natives of the Phanar district in Constantinople who provided important diplomatic services to the Ottomans in the post-Karlowitz period. Rooted in the political tradition of the Byzantine Empire, whose reincarnation they sometimes secretly envisioned, Phanariote Greeks were generally inimical to protonationalist manifestations of other Orthodox subject peoples of the sultan that were incompatible with this Megali Idea. The period of their rule in the principalities (1711/1716-1821) is characterized by latent intra-elite tensions within the boyar class between the autochthonous elements and the Greeks who came to the principalities in the suites of the Phanariote princes. For this reason, the Russian-Ottoman wars of 1735-39 and 1768-74 occasioned the formation of pro-Russian boyar factions that perceived Russian rule as a means to consolidate their hold on the principalities.[21] In 1736-37, the Wallachian envoy to Anna Ioannovna, P. Drăgunescu, reported that the boyars of the principality "slavishly request[ed] not to leave [them] among other enslaved people, but to deliver [them] and make [them] subjects of [His] Orthodox Majesty."[22] In September 1739, their Moldavian counterparts "accepted with a great and ineffable tearful joy" the authority of the empress and signed with the commander of the Russian army, Burkhard Christoph von Münnich, a convention according to which Moldavia relinquished its right to conduct an independent foreign policy and undertook to maintain a twenty-thousand-strong Russian army in return for internal autonomy.[23] In 1769, the delegations of the Wallachian and Moldavian boyars arrived at the court of Catherine II with the offer to bring the principalities under the Russian scepter. The offer was received favorably but did not lead to the conclusion of a formal treaty because of the unwillingness of the empress to provoke the Habsburg monarchy or other European powers.[24]

These attempts to enact a vision of Russia as the protector of the Orthodox principalities cost the Moldavian and Wallachian elite dearly, while bringing nothing or very little in return. For various reasons, the treaties of alliance and suzerainty signed in 1656, 1711, and 1739 remained a dead letter. The *hospodars*, boyars, and clergymen who signed these treaties eventually had to emigrate or face severe punishment from the Ottomans. A similar fate awaited those who collaborated with the Russians in the last two wars of the century. Negotiations with the Orthodox power had their price, as the Moldavian metropolitan Dosifei had demonstrated.[25] More generally, the pro-Russian boyars could not fail to become more cautious, in view of the fact that Russian troops abandoned the principalities as many times as they occupied them.[26]

The leaders of the pro-Russian faction started considering political alternatives after the elusive response of Catherine II to the Moldavian and Wallachian deputations in 1770 made it clear that the empress would neither have the principalities "joined to the most happy provinces of Russia" nor insist on their independence (as she did with respect to Crimea).[27] In particular, they must have suggested that, in their negotiations with the Porte, the Russian diplomats demand the recognition of those "rights and privileges that the principalities enjoyed at the beginning of the Ottoman overlordship."[28] In a striking instance of the "invention of the legal tradition," the leader of the pro-Russian Wallachians, Mihai Cantacuzino, produced the texts of the Ottoman "capitulations" granted to the fifteenth-century Wallachian princes Mircea the Old and Laiota Basarab.[29] These "capitulations" stipulated the full autonomy of the principality, preservation of its faith, the nonaccession of the Muslims in its territory, the appointment of the elected natives as *hospodars*, the inviolability and nontaxation of the Wallachians on business in the Ottoman Empire, and their right to emigrate from the principality.[30] In parallel, the Moldavian boyars formulated the theory of "capitulations" in their memorandum addressed to Austrian and Prussian representatives at the Congress of Focșani in 1772.[31]

The final text of the Kuchuk Kainardji treaty of 1774 contained a somewhat different version concerning the status of Moldavia and Wallachia within the Ottoman Empire. Even though the restoration of the traditional privileges of the principalities was announced, the text mentioned only the preservation of faith and the right of the inhabitants to immigrate to other countries. Other aspects of the "capitulations," most importantly the election of native *hospodars*, were omitted.[32] Other stipulations of Article 16 (amnesty for the participants of war on

Russia's side and Russia's right to make "representations" on behalf of Moldavia and Wallachia) constituted the new prerogatives of the Romanov empire, rather than the ancient "privileges" of the principalities. Each of the subsequent Russian-Ottoman treaties (Jassy, 1792; Bucharest, 1812; the Convention of Akkerman, 1826) would confirm the clauses of Kuchuk Kainardji, while a special *hatt-i sheriff* issued by Selim III in 1802 under Russian pressure fixed the seven-year term of appointment for the *hospodars* and made their deposition conditional upon Russia's consent.[33]

After 1774, Russian diplomacy used the "capitulations" as a means of applying extra pressure on the Ottomans during negotiations as well as an instrument of continued interference in the relations between the sultan and the principalities.[34] Nevertheless, in the long run, the main beneficiaries of the discourse of "rights and privileges" were the elites of Moldavia and Wallachia. By the second or third decade of the nineteenth century, the latter were disillusioned by the tendency of St. Petersburg to view the principalities as bargaining chips in negotiations with the Ottomans. The Russian annexation of Bessarabia in 1812 demonstrated that the tsar was no more committed to the territorial integrity of the principalities than were the sultans, when they alienated substantial portions of Moldavian and Wallachian lands into *reayas*, or the Habsburg emperors, when they annexed Little Wallachia and Bucovina in 1718 and 1774 respectively.[35] Nevertheless, many of the boyars still expected political benefits from cooperation with Russia. Their attitude is perhaps best expressed by the author of the anonymous memorandum on the principalities written in the wake of the Bucharest treaty: "There is a received opinion that the principalities of Moldavia and Wallachia are pro-Russian. This opinion needs to be qualified. It is true if one understand this inclination as a necessity, a request for protection. However, this opinion is no longer founded if one understands it as a demand to pass under Russian dominance."[36]

The political language employed by the boyars in their relations with the Russian emperor in the early nineteenth century indicates that the latter was for them no longer a champion of Orthodoxy, whose subjects they were "slavishly requesting" to become, but rather the guarantor of secular rights and privileges that had been granted by the sultans centuries earlier. Thus, in their address to Nicholas I following the outbreak of the war of 1828-29, the Wallachian boyars expressed conviction that the emperor would secure their "stable and legal existence, guarantee the laws and customs of [their] ancestors, their property" and religion.³⁷ Russian vice-chancellor K. V. Nesselrode replied that "their destinies [were] protected from any design of conquest" and that the tsar's goal was "legal order," "the benefits of regular and stable administration," and the "inviolability of the privileges" that they possessed.³⁸ Accordingly, the Treaty of Adrianople of 1829 mentioned "special capitulations on the basis of which the principalities Moldavia and Walachia subordinated themselves to the supreme authority of the Sublime Porte" and confirmed "the rights, privileges and advantages" granted thereby.³⁹

The period between the Treaty of Kuchuk Kainardji and that of Adrianople therefore constituted a new stage in Russian-Moldavian-Wallachian relations.⁴⁰ As always, the boyars sought to build ties with the Russian rulers on a contractual basis. However, if earlier the "rights and privileges" conditioned Russian-Moldavian and Russian-Wallachian negotiations and treaties (as in 1656, 1711, and 1739), from the early 1770s onward they also affected the trilateral relations between Russia, the Ottoman Empire, and the principalities. The autochthonous elites of Moldavia and Wallachia now expected Russia to be the guarantor of the "capitulations" granted by the Ottomans. Once the Russian-Ottoman treaties recognized the "capitulations" as authentic, the boyars acquired a legal basis for the defense of their autonomy. Russian protection was seen as legitimate so long as Russia performed the functions of the guarantor of the "capitulations" granted to the principalities by the third party. Russia's ability to instrumentalize the issue of "rights and privileges" would therefore be limited as soon as the Ottoman Empire (or some other great power) decided to treat the "capitulations" as seriously as did the Moldavian and Wallachian elites.⁴¹

This became obvious already in 1822, when in the wake of the Greek uprising in the principalities, the Porte decided to appoint the new *hospodars* from the ranks of autochthonous boyars, thereby ending a century of Phanariote rule. Although St. Petersburg insisted for several years on a status quo ante 1821, it eventually had to enforce the switch to the autochthonous princes in the Convention of Akkerman of 1826. Together with the ambiguous position of Russian authorities with respect to the Etaireia conspiracy that organized the rebellion, this intransigence produced a lasting impression that Russia supported "the Greeks," that is, the Phanariotes.⁴² In the meantime, the Ottomans took credit for restoring the main clause of the "capitulations," namely, the rule of autochthonous princes, without any Russian pressure, in fact despite it. Predictably, a considerable number of boyars in both principalities became pro-Ottoman.⁴³ As was the case of the some Bulgarian leaders later in the century, the Turkophiles within the Moldavian and Wallachian elites proved to be quite capable of combining professions of loyalty to the Ottomans with an attempt to attract the attention of the European powers to the status of the principalities.[44]

However, the implications of the new trilateral Russian-Ottoman-Romanian relations informed by "capitulations" were not immediately obvious to the Russians. This is clear from their rather cavalier treatment of the clauses of the Akkerman convention and the Adrianople treaty. Thus, in 1828 the Russian occupation authorities discontinued the work on the Organic Statutes that was started under the autochthonous *hospodars* in accordance with the convention. The Russian Ministry of Foreign Affairs recognized that a legal definition of relations between the princes and the boyar elites was necessary in order to overcome the political crisis in the principalities triggered by the uprisings of 1821. Yet the fruits of boyar efforts to elaborate these Organic Statutes in 1827-28 did not satisfy the Russian ministry. Different boyar committees, whose members were handpicked from the great boyars on the indications of the Russian consul, started work anew in June 1829.[45] Second- and third-rank boyars criticized the committees as too narrow and oligarchic and evoked the ancient laws and customs, such as the passage of the legal codes by the Assembly of the Land (Adunarea Obștească).[46] The same applied to the "Extraordinary Assemblies of Revision" convoked in 1831 to endorse the Organic Statutes.[47] Another perceived violation of the spirit and letter of "capitulations" came with the appointment of the new *hospodars* by the Porte on Russia's suggestion, even though the Organic Statues presupposed their election by the Extraordinary Assemblies (Adunări Obștești Extraordinare).

The greatest tensions, however, came after the evacuation of Russian troops in 1834, when the Wallachian assembly was forced, upon the initiative of the Russian consul, to vote the notorious "additional article" that prohibited the assemblies from changing the statutes without permission of the sovereign and the protecting powers.[48] All three princes who ruled between 1834 and 1848 proved capable of frustrating the assemblies, either on their own, as was the case of the Moldavian *hospodar* Michael Sturdza, or under Russian pressure, as was the case of the Wallachian princes Alexandru Ghica and Gheorghe Bibescu.[49] Whatever the circumstances, the frustrated opposition was likely to interpret such incidents as Russian intrigues. As a result, in 1848 the Wallachian and Moldavian revolutionaries saw their task as the abolition of the Organic Statutes and Russian hegemony.

The story of the emergence of modern Romanian nationalism in the proclamations and programs of "the generation of 1848" usually focuses on the "discovery" of the Latin origin of the Romanians and the attendant French republican influences.[50] However, one should not exaggerate the immediate impact of these developments on the relations of the "young Romanians" with their neighbors on the east or south. The first implication of the "return to the origins" was an internal political one. Together with the critique of the lord-and-peasant relations, fixation on the language and Romanic revalorization of history were aspects of imagining a modern national community over deep social and cultural divisions that characterized Moldavian and Wallachian society. These three facets of nation building according to Miroslav Hroch find their best embodiment in the figure of Mihai Kogălniceanu, who advocated the abolition of corvées, championed the Romanian language, and pioneered the publication of historical sources, including the texts of the "capitulations."[51]

At the same time, their self-identification as people of Latin origin did not immediately place the leaders of the "forty-eighters" in antagonistic relations with the surrounding Slavic peoples. During the 1830s and 1840s, Polish revolutionaries found refuge in the principalities, while Wallachian oppositionists, both in the principality and in Paris, were in touch with the leader of the Polish political emigration, Adam Czartoryski.[52] The idea of a Balkan federation, which Czartoryski first articulated as a foreign minister of Alexander I in 1804-6, framed the cooperation between the "young Romanians" and the southern Slavic leaders. The consciousness of Latin roots did not prevent some of the Romanians from participating in the abortive Bulgarian conspiracies in the early 1840s or maintaining the contacts with Miloš Obrenović and the Serbian "constitutionalist" party, both of which were alienated by the Russian hegemony in Belgrade.[53] Thus, fear of the "Slavic encirclement" that gripped D. A. Sturdza half a century later was not yet a significant component of the anti-Russian sentiment that characterized the younger generation of the boyars on the eve of the revolution of 1848.

Nor should one overestimate the role of the pro-French orientation in the concrete actions of the "forty-eighters." The role of progressive French writers and educators in shaping their outlook was admittedly paramount as was the role of the February revolution in triggering the events in Iași and Bucharest. However, the failure of the Second Republic to provide more than moral support confined the "young Romanians" to the traditional maneuvering between the tsar and the sultan, which made the Wallachian Revolution of 1848 an issue of Russian-Ottoman relations par excellence.[54] These relations not only made possible both the actual outbreak and the crushing of the revolution but also determined the strategy of the revolutionaries themselves.

This strategy consisted in portraying themselves as loyal Turkish subjects who sought to restore Ottoman legality, order, and ultimately sovereignty over the principalities threatened by the Russian intrigues.[55] To Suleiman Pasha, the Ottoman representative dispatched to Wallachia in spring 1848, the revolutionaries suggested that the sultan abrogate the Organic Statute in favor of the old "capitulations," which the statute had supposedly violated. In response to the circular of Nicholas I on 19 July 1848, threatening to exercise his right of protectorate, the Wallachian regency (one of the incarnations of the revolutionary government) responded with a lengthy memorandum affirming the right of the nation to regulate its political existence on the basis of the Ottoman "capitulations." The rhetoric of the revolutionary members of the regency also revealed the characteristic tendency of Moldavian and Wallachian elites to interpret Russia's self-assumed function of protector and guarantor of the "capitulations." In view of multiple violations of the "capitulations" by the Russian government in the post-1829 period, the Wallachian revolutionaries could easily argue that Russia had forfeited its status as legitimate guarantor.[56]

This strategy of appeal to the Ottoman "capitulations" as the basis of Romanian self-determinations continued in the early 1850s.[57] Indicative in this respect is the case of Ion Ghica, the representative of the Wallachian revolutionary government in İstanbul and future prime minister of Romania. Addressing the Romanian political emigrants as well as the progressive European public at the beginning of the Crimean War, Ghica dismissed as unrealistic several alternative solutions to the Romanian question: a confederation of national republics in the spirit of Giuseppe Mazzini, Alexandre-August Ledru-Rollin, and Louis Blanc failed to take into consideration multiple conflicts between the subject peoples of Austria and Turkey; a big Romanian nation-state between the Dniester and the Tisza would not be allowed by Austria and Russia, who had annexed territories with the predominantly ethnic Romanian population; a smaller Romanian duchy under a German prince created with Russia's help would not receive an international guarantee of its existence, in the absence of which it was likely to become the prey of Russia's Pan-Slavic designs. Instead, Ghica sought to remind the Romanians that they "were existentially related" to Turkey and that the latter, in its turn, had no chance to survive without the Romanians. As a "diehard nationality," the Romanians could constitute the "political frontier" of Turkey that Russia would not be able to leap over. All it took to make them such a frontier was to "render to the principalities the full extent of their rights on the basis of capitulations."[58]

In 1853–56, Romanian revolutionary leaders couched their support of the Ottomans in broader generalizations about Russia as an "Asiatic despotism," which were particularly widespread among the European liberals and radicals in this period.[59] Thus, in 1853 Ghica remarked on a transformation without precedent in history, whereby after a centuries-long struggle, "Christian Europe" was ready to ally itself with Turkey, whose government "took the initiative of reforms and progress." In a statement that undoubtedly reflected the attitude of many of his revolutionary associates, Ghica claimed that "the Danube and the banks of the Bosphorus were to become the site of the quarrel between autocratic absolutism and European civilization."[60]

Drawing on voluminous nineteenth-century literature on "the Russian menace," the interpretation of Russian-European relations formulated by the Romanian revolutionary exiles in the period between 1848 and the end of the Crimean War proved to have a lasting influence on the Romanian perception of Russia.[61] The case of Dimitrie Alexandru Sturdza, considered at the beginning of our discussion, demonstrates that the Romanian elites later in the century tended to view contemporary European politics from the perspective of the early 1850s, when, without precedent in its previous or subsequent history, imperial Russia indeed confronted a European coalition. Educated Romanians could not fail to be deeply impressed by two things: that the Crimean War was triggered by Russia's occupation of Moldavia and Wallachia in July 1853, and that Russia's defeat led to the abolition of its protectorate over the principalities.

Three basic stages in the evolution of Moldavian and Wallachian perceptions of the Russian protectorate emerge from the evidence presented thus far. During the early period, from the mid-seventeenth century to the Treaty of Kuchuk Kainardji of 1774, the Russian protectorate was seen within the broader framework of common Orthodox faith. From the earliest attempts to transfer the principalities under Russia's suzerainty, the princes and the boyars conditioned their entrance on the preservation of the ancient laws, rights, and privileges of the two countries. By the early 1770s, the Moldavian and Wallachian elites adopted a subtler strategy to secure their autonomous status as their homelands repeatedly served as the main battleground for Russian-Ottoman wars. With the formulation of the theory of Ottoman "capitulations," Russia became perceived as the guarantor of the "rights and privileges" granted by the Ottoman rulers of the fifteenth and sixteenth centuries but violated by their successors. Finally, in the context of the Greek crisis of the 1820s, and certainly after the Treaty of Adrianople, the erstwhile anti-Ottoman implications of the discourse of "capitulations" gave way to the anti-Russian ones. By the 1840s, the younger generation of Romanian elites viewed the Russian protectorate over the principalities as a much greater danger to their nation-building project than the increasingly formal Ottoman suzerainty. In this situation, the Romanian leaders found it profitable to speak of the Ottoman capitulations as the foundations of their national independence and defend them from Russian encroachments. An analysis of the discourse of capitulations offered in this section illustrates both the role of the Moldavian and Wallachian elites in the Eastern Question and the importance of the latter to the emergence of modern Romania.

The Wallachian revolutionaries of 1848 used the "capitulations" to legitimize their nation-building program and encourage the Ottoman government to resist Russian hegemony in the principalities. Russia's defeat in the Crimea, which ended its protectorate over the principalities and eventually made possible their unification, also contributed to the persistent tendency of the modern Romanian elites to conceptualize their relations with Russia within the framework of the latter's "civilizational" conflict with "Europe." The remainder of this chapter traces a parallel evolution of Russian perceptions of Romanians. It concludes with an examination of the legacies of the Russian protectorate in present-day relations between Russia, Romania, and Turkey.

The Discovery of Romanians in Nineteenth-Century Russia

As he reflected on the geographical position of the Romanians in 1828, Russian diplomat Felix Petrovich Fonton could not conceal his regret about "these eight million people foreign to the Slavs [who] had settled here on the beautiful slopes of the Carpathians, drawing a wedge between the Slavic tribes and preventing their unification." If instead of these Romanians, reasoned Fonton, there had been Serbs or Bulgarians, "how easy it would have been to solve the Eastern, or better to say, the Slavic question."[62] Once he entered the subjunctive mood, the young

Russian found it difficult to stop: "If instead of the traitor Brâncoveanu and an indifferent people used to oppression, Peter the Great in his campaign had encountered here the stout and honest Bulgarians or valiant Serbs, the result would have been different. Then the point of gravity of Russian policy would move to the south and then perhaps not the eccentric, cold, and granite St. Petersburg, but splendid Kiev would have become the second capital of our state!"[63]

This passage was part of the "Humorous, Political, and Military Letters" that Fonton addressed to a friend from the headquarters of the Russian army fighting against the Ottomans on the Danube in 1828-29. The light and jocular tone of these letters written by a youthful diplomat suggests that the author did not take all too seriously his observations about the fatal role that the Romanians played in Russian history. Nevertheless, they indicate a disturbance that the presence of the Romanians created on the smooth surface of the Russian imperial vision. Despite the tendency of Russian authors to speak of the Balkan population in essentialist terms based on a shared language and religion, educated Russians were increasingly aware of the perceived and real differences between particular Orthodox subject peoples of the sultan and increasingly better disposed toward some of them than to others. This sensitivity was the result of a secularization of the mental outlook of the Russian elites since the late seventeenth century that led to the separation of religion and ethnicity in the perception of self and others. With time, the appreciation of differences of historical origin, language, and above all the putative collective character led to the "discovery" of particular nations within broader premodern religious communities.

The main sources of information on the Christian population of the Ottoman Empire in the sixteenth and seventeenth centuries were the Greek Orthodox prelates who periodically came to Muscovy in the hope of obtaining material support for the Eastern churches. Under their influence, the tsars gradually assumed the posture of the champions of Orthodoxy. This conditioned the Russian perception of the population of southeastern Europe well into the eighteenth century. The rhetoric that sought to win the support of the Orthodox peoples during the eighteenth-century wars predictably focused on what the peoples of the region had in common, rather than on their peculiarities. Thus, during the Pruth Campaign of 1711, Peter the Great issued a manifesto that addressed the population of Moldavia and Wallachia "as well as Greeks, Serbs, Bulgarians, Slavs, Albanians and other Christian peoples" and announced the war for the "liberation of the suffering Christians from the barbarian yoke."[64] The parallel manifesto addressed by Peter the Great to the prince-bishop of Montenegro likewise spoke about the suffering of the "Christian church" and "Christian flock" under the rule of the Ottoman "barbarians."[65] At the beginning of the Russian-Ottoman War of 1768-74, Catherine the Great appealed to the "Slavic peoples of the Orthodox faith," but the text of her manifesto applied this category indiscriminately to the "Christian population of Moldavia, Wallachia, Muntenia [sic], Bulgaria, Bosnia, Herzogovina, Macedonia and Albania."[66] The ethnic categories were thus still subsumed under common religious identity, even though the anti-Muslim rhetoric of Catherine's manifesto was somewhat toned down in comparison with Peter's address.

The situation changed in the course of the Russian-Ottoman War of 1768-74, which brought the Russians into more direct contact with the population of the European Turkey. The war, mainly fought in Moldavia and Wallachia, led the Russians to "discover" the Greeks rather than the Slavs or the Romanians. The emergence of the "Greek myth" in Russian culture can be explained by the Westernization of the Russian upper classes and the appropriation of the legacy of the classical antiquity.[67] Within the framework of this myth, Russian-Ottoman rivalry was sometimes represented as a reincarnation of the Persian Wars, and, as a result, the Greeks were singled out from the mass of Ottoman Christians. The "Greek project" of Catherine the Great turned traditional championship of Orthodoxy into the objective of restoration of the Greek Empire, which often made Russian Philhellenes ignore the tensions between the Greeks and the non-Greeks of the Balkans.

The political developments of the French Revolution and the Napoleonic era compromised the ability of Philhellenism to serve as an ideological and cultural binder between the autocracy and the Westernized Russian elites.[68] In the context of the Europe-wide confrontation between the absolutist regimes and revolutionary France, the republican connotations of Greek antiquity appeared increasingly problematic to Russian rulers. These connotations were even more at odds with the mystical Christian ideology of the Holy Alliance proposed by Alexander I after the defeat of Napoleon as a way of consolidating the antirevolutionary unity of the European monarchs. When Alexander Ypsilanti, the leader of the Philiki Etaireia uprising in Moldavia and Wallachia in February 1821, asked Alexander I, whose former aide-de-camp he was, to help the Greeks in their struggle against the Ottomans, the emperor's legitimist convictions superseded his Hellenic sympathies. Official repudiation of the uprising followed. Despite the persistence of Philhellenism among educated Russians, the failure of the Etaireia uprising made many doubt that modern Greeks possessed the valor of their Athenian and Spartan ancestors. In the meantime, Russians were adopting increasingly critical views of the Phanariotes and their oppression of the Orthodox population of European Turkey in general and of the principalities of Moldavia and Wallachia in particular. The early Russian descriptions of the principalities portrayed the local population as the victim of predatory Phanariote princes and the boyars corrupted by the latter's influence.[69]

The crisis of the Greek myth in Russian culture was accompanied by the growth of Pan-Slavism. The first Serbian uprising of 1804-13 made Russians increasingly aware of the existence of southern Slavs. This awareness manifested itself early on in various political visions, namely, the project of the Balkan federation proposed to Alexander I by his minister for foreign affairs, Adam Czartoryski, in 1804-6.[70] The Russian press of the second and third decades of the nineteenth century portrayed the Serbian leader George Petrovitch as a romantic freedom fighter, whose bravery and courage the leaders of the Etaireia failed to match. By the 1820s, the southern Slavs were well on the way to replacing the Greeks in the Russian discourse of the Balkans. In the course of the war of 1828-29, the Russian army went as far as Adrianople, which for the first time brought the Bulgarians to the attention of the young Russian officers (like the future Slavophile Aleksei Stepanovich Khomiakov), or of the young diplomats, like Fonton. At this time, Pan-Slavic attitudes were still rather vague but nevertheless widespread enough to make the head of the Russian provisional administration in Moldavia and Wallachia (1829-34), General Pavel Dmitrievich Kiselev, pursue the goal of "the unity of the great Slavic family."[71]

Pan-Slavic ideas marked Russia's policy regarding the Eastern Question at an early stage, as evidenced by the project for the general peace written by the Russian consul in Iaşi, Vasilii Feodorovich Malinovskii, and by Adam Czartoryski's plan for a Balkan federation.[72] However, in such projects traditional Russian intervention on behalf of the Orthodox coreligionists was still poorly differentiated from championship of the Slavic cause. Even more importantly, this Pan-Slavism was not conditioned by the awareness of the existing tensions in the relations between southern Slavs and their non-Slavic neighbors, including the Greeks and the Romanians. Finally, while these Pan-Slavic schemes were potentially incompatible with the existence of the Ottoman, Austrian, or

Napoleonic Empires, they still did not have the anti-Westernism characteristic of later Russian Pan-Slavism. Indeed, it is difficult to find a more European thinker and politician than Czartoryski.

The emergence of the Slavs from the shadows of the Greeks was paralleled by a period of uncertainty about the population of Moldavia and Wallachia. Initially, the Russians saw both Romanians and southern Slavs as victims of Ottoman (and Greek) dominance. Characteristic in this respect was an overview of the Slavic population of European Turkey published in 1825 by A. M. Spiridov, a secretary at the Russian consulate in Bucharest at the time of the Etaireia uprising in the principalities. Spiridov attributed the failure of Alexander Ypsilanti to secure broad support on both sides of the Danube to "a general and unchangeable prejudice [*predubezhdenie*] of all the Slavic peoples of the Ottoman Empire toward the Greeks."[73] According to Spiridov, these Greeks were no longer "sons of glory . . . who would be ready to die for the motherland. Their places were taken by treacherous courtiers, of debauched morals, avid for money grabbing." After the Ottoman conquest of Constantinople, the Greeks of the capital used treachery and intrigue to subjugate valiant Slavs.[74] Interestingly enough, Spiridov viewed the Romanians as members of the greater Slavic family, the existence of which was in his opinion testified by "the similarity of tongues, mores, customs, names of persons, towns, villages, rivers, lakes, settlements, and finally, by their faith."[75] This passage reveals a basic characteristic of Pan-Slavic discourse that consisted in understating the differences between different members of the "Slavic family."

Spiridov was not the only one to believe in the Slavic origin of the Romanians. Similar ideas were articulated in the late 1820s by Iurii Ivanovich Venelin, a Transcarpathian Rusyn, and a self-identified Bulgarian intellectual known for his association with the Pan-Slavist historian Mikhail Mikhailovich Pogodin, the Slavophile A. S. Khomiakov, and the Aksakov brothers, Konstantin Sergeevich and Ivan Sergeevich. Venelin's main goal was to affirm the centrality of Bulgarians within the emergent Pan-Slavic historical narrative.[76] In order to link the historical narratives of southern and eastern Slavs, Venelin was prepared to redescribe the entire history of Moldavia and Wallachia as the history of the Bulgarians. The predominance of the Slavonic element (*Slovene*) in Moldavia and Wallachia, according to Venelin, could be demonstrated by the prevalence of Slavonic toponyms in the principalities as well as the usage of the Slavonic language by the upper classes and in government correspondence. In his opinion, the linguistic and cultural peculiarity of the Romanians was the result of the Ottoman conquest. In order to break the natural connection that existed between Russia and Moldavia and Wallachia, the Turks established Phanariote rule, replaced Slavonic with the Wallachian language in churches, and assimilated the Bulgarian nobility of the principalities through their intermarriage with the Greeks.[77]

The great uncertainty about the early history of Moldavia and Wallachia explains why theories that appear eccentric in retrospect possessed a minimum plausibility to contemporaries. However, in the long run, Romanian linguistic and cultural distinctiveness proved impossible to ignore. By the mid-nineteenth century, broad generalization about the origins of Moldavians and Wallachians gave way to the academic study of the language and literature of the principalities. This helped to dispel the earlier superficial impression of similarity between Slavs, on the one hand, and Moldavians and Wallachians, on the other. Thus, in 1840, the recently appointed first chair of Romanian at St. Petersburg University, Iakov Danilovich Ginkulov, in his authoritative *Nachertanie pravil moldovlakhiiskoi grammatiki* found it possible to speak of a single Romanian language and classified it as a branch of Latin in terms of the predominant vocabulary.[78]

Political and cultural changes in Moldavia and Wallachia in the second quarter of the nineteenth century likewise alerted the educated Russians to the distinctiveness of Romanians. As they confronted these changes, some Russian observers of the principalities reacted with exasperation. This was the case of the famous traveler Egor Petrovich Kovalevskii, who passed through the principalities in the early 1840s on his way to Montenegro. Professing Pan-Slavic views, Kovalevskii could not help wondering how "this relatively small people surrounded by Slavic tribes and sharing their faith, performing its divine service and conducting its correspondence in the same language, and entering into frequent and close relationships with them, [was] presently so different from them in its spirit and its moral direction."[79] The fundamental irony of the situation consisted in the fact that such an outcome was to a large extent the product of Russia's own policies in the principalities.

The end of the Phanariote regime in Moldavia and Wallachia and a series of political reforms sponsored by Russian occupation authorities in the wake of the Russian-Ottoman War of 1828-29 stimulated the cultural Westernization of the Romanian upper classes and the development of modern Romanian nationalism.[80] The transformation of cultural practices involved gradual replacement of the Oriental vestments by

Occidental fashions and the growing currency of French in place of Greek as the language of politics and high culture.[81] Anatole Demidoff's *Voyage dans la Russie méridionale et la Crimee par la Hongrie, la Valachie et la Moldavie* of 1837 contains the following description of the Bucharest beau monde on the promenade set up during the Russian occupation of Wallachia several years previously: "In the same carriage you would see women imitating Viennese fashions and coquetry, young men dressed in European black suits together with an old boyar with a venerable and noble countenance, a long, absolutely white beard, and monumental headwear introduced here by Phanariotes."[82]

The same mixture of Oriental traits and westward inclinations characterized, in the opinion of Russian commentators, the mentality and political orientation of Moldavian and Wallachian elites.[83] According to Ivan Petrovich Liprandi, an amateur Orientalist and veteran of the Russian-Ottoman War of 1828–29, "the influence of the Phanar made [them] completely different from the nobility of all other European countries" and as a result, their nature "contain[ed] a singular inclination for plots and intrigues."[84] On the other hand, Liprandi deplored the "pernicious" or "bizarre" ideas of the Western-educated boyars of the younger generation who believed "that the Wallachians were the true descendants of the ancient Romans, shared a common origin with Western Europeans, and therefore should try to imitate them in everything from the language to the way of thinking, mores, government, and even religion." Liprandi noted with regret that the new Wallachian writers were trying to seduce away the simple people instinctively drawn to Russia by gradually replacing numerous Slavic words with Italian, French, or Latin ones as well as by Latinizing the Cyrillic script.[85]

The new political attitudes of the Romanian elites and the generational change that produced them did not escape the most perceptive Russian observers of Moldavia and Wallachia. Thus, at the beginning of the Crimean War in 1853, Petr Vladimirovich Alabin, an officer in the Russian army occupying the principalities, noted, "The venerable boyars, who witnessed our deeds for their fatherland, those who remember acutely how we with our own hands broke the yoke, which weighted upon them, how we extracted them from the abyss of ignorance and semisavagery—these venerable elders have either left the political life or have passed away altogether." This, according to Alabin, left Russians without local support. "The majority of the Moldavian and Wallachian intelligentsia are hostile toward us, for it belongs to the new generation, whose liberal ideas were frustrated in 1848 because of us." As a result, "there is no one to raise a voice for us. Whatever good we have done for Moldavia and Wallachia is forgotten, although it cost us a lot of blood. Now they remember only that we did not allow the principalities to adopt the forms upon which, in their opinion, depends the happiness of a country." Alabin was also aware of the broader political philosophy that underlay the new attitude toward Russia. "The revolutionary party of Moldavians and Wallachians," he observed, "consider us to be the enemies of civilization, who are not only willing to suppress the democratic elements, upon which they are going to build a new and, in their opinion, a great structure, but also deprive them of their fatherland by annexing the Danubian principalities." Unlike some of his comrades-in-arms in the Russian occupation army, Alabin remained unconvinced by the outward expressions of sympathy, loyalty, and love demonstrated by Romanians in 1853, noting, "If we happen to lose this war, they will no longer be constrained by anything and will try to pay us back for 1848."[86]

Whereas a direct observer like Alabin could sense acutely the state of mind of the emergent Romanian society, the Russian Pan-Slavic visionaries in the second half of the nineteenth century tended to underplay the importance of the attitude of the Romanian elites towards the prospect of Pan-Slavic union. Mikhail Pogodin overlooked it completely when he stated in 1854 that "Moldavia, Wallachia and Transylvania [would] have to join [the projected] union."[87] Others treated the opinions of the Romanian elites rather dismissively as a shortcoming of the Romanian national character that their unification with the Slavs would be able to cure. Thus Nikolai Danilevskii in his famous *Rossiia i Evropa* (1869) argued, "[Only] with the support of Slavdom, to which they are closely related, will the Romanians be able to overcome the Gallomania that consumes them as well as the imitativeness of their pitiful intelligentsia."[88] Those for whom the distinctiveness of Romanians was a potential problem for Slavic unity viewed it as a result of their Oriental character (Kovalevskii), or their infatuation with everything French (Danilevskii) or both (Liprandi).

For Russian writers of the second half of the nineteenth century, the boyar origin of the Romanian political class represented perhaps the most important marker of difference between the Romanians and the Slavs south of the Danube, who lacked aristocracy in the conventional sense of the terms. While the Pan-Slavic writers disliked this feature of Romanian society, the main conservative critic of Pan-Slavism, Konstantin

Nikolaevich Leont'ev, found that the existence of a native aristocracy (i.e., the boyars) positively distinguished the Romanians from southern Slavs. According to Leont'ev, it enabled Romania to withstand the pernicious influence of European democracy better than Serbia or Bulgaria, where the lack of nobility only aggravated the populist tendencies implicit in any national liberation movement.[89] In Leont'ev's scheme, the boyar class in Romanian principalities played the same role that Danilevskii attributed to Islam for the "Christian East" as a whole: both served to protect the Orthodox population from the corrupting influence of Western Christianity, Romano-Germanic civilization, and modern European democracy.[90]

Both the Russian Pan-Slavist writers and their critics during the 1860s, 1870s, and 1880s shared the assumption that Russia's conflict with the Ottoman Empire over the issue of the Orthodox coreligionists was ultimately secondary to the confrontation between Russia and the European powers in the question of Slavic unity. In the framework of this vision, relations with Romanians were no longer an aspect of Russian-Ottoman relations for the Russian writers (as they had been for tsarist diplomacy) but a function of Russia's relations with "Europe." Among the major Russian Pan-Slavists, Rostislav Fadeev was the one who expressed this idea with the greatest clarity. Fadeev envisioned Slavic unity as the "entire group of peoples connected to Russia by the historical destiny of coreligionists and compatriots."[91] He thus included in it the Greeks and the Romanians, "especially the former, who [had] grown together with Slavdom particularly strongly and [would] have to share its lot." According to Fadeev, the Romanians were incapable of "assembling the disparate branches of their tribe trampled just as the Slavs by foreign oppression." Like other Danubian peoples, the Romanians, in Fadeev's opinion, faced the historical choice: to align themselves with Russia or to become Austrian provinces with the subsequent demotion of the Romanians to the status of an inferior race. He pointed to the Habsburg drive toward the Balkans and the lower Danube, which became only stronger after Prussia defeated Austria in 1866 in the struggle for Germany and started encouraging the Austrian-Hungarian expansion in the southeast. The French commitment to the Romanian cause was disproved, according to Fadeev, by the French offer of Serbia and Romania to the Habsburgs in return for their secession of Galicia to support the second Polish uprising in 1863. With so many false friends around, the Romanians were bound to succumb to Magyarization and Germanization unless they allied themselves with

Russia. Finally, in a statement that demonstrates the indebtedness of the Pan-Slavic discourse to the rhetoric of tsarist manifestos, Fadeev claimed that Russians were "the only people interested in Romanian independence [*samostoiatel'nost'*] and the only one that created and supported this independence."[92]

The Russian discovery of Romanians in the nineteenth century was a complex process that involved growing awareness of the ethnic diversity and ethnic conflicts existing beneath the common religious identity of the Orthodox population of the Ottoman Empire. This process was conditioned by the gradual secularization of the outlook of the Russian elites, manifested, among other things, in the "Greek myth" of the late eighteenth century and the later Pan-Slavism. At the same time, the Russian discovery of Romanians was the product of the transformations in European Turkey and in particular of the political crisis of the 1820s, which revealed with clarity the tensions between the Greeks, on the one hand, and southern Slavs and Romanians, on the other. Post-1821 political and cultural changes in Moldavia and Wallachia limited the tendency of early Russian Pan-Slavists to dissolve Romanians in the Slavic ocean. As a result, the distinctiveness of Romanians became increasingly visible against the background of Slavic unity constructed by Russian writers.

As the Pan-Slavist writings demonstrate, some educated Russians of the second half of the nineteenth century were as likely as their Romanian counterparts to perceive Russian-Romanian relations as an aspect of Russia's relations with Europe. Obviously, the Russian and the Romanian ways of viewing these relations were very different. Asserting, as did some Romanian nationalists, the irreconcilable character of Russia's conflict with Europe, the Russian Pan-Slavists of the 1860s and the 1870s still viewed Romania as an ally and member of the prospective Slavic union, despite the "unhealthy" Gallomania of the Romanian elites. Broad theories overlooked or underestimated the strength of anti-Russian sentiment in a small country that lay on the way to the Balkans. In this respect, one can say that the discovery of the Romanians in nineteenth-century Russia remained incomplete.

The Nineteenth-Century Legacies in Current Russian-Romanian Relations

It would be erroneous to argue that Fadeev's and Sturdza's visions of Russian relations with Europe determined Russian-Romanian relations in the late nineteenth to early twentieth century. At the same time,

Russian Pan-Slavism and the Romanian perceptions of Russia certainly presented obstacles and constraints that the nineteenth-century diplomats of the two countries found difficult to overcome. The troubled history of Russian-Romanian cooperation in 1877-78 amply demonstrates that on both sides pragmatic considerations were at the mercy of assumptions about imperial honor, inviolability of the nation, and historically divergent understandings of Russia's "protection" of the principalities. It proved very difficult to make the Romanian side sign a military convention regulating the passage of Russian troops through Romanian territory. Although sympathetic to the idea, the government of Ion C. Brătianu was apprehensive lest Russia reestablish the protectorate and feared for the territorial integrity of the country.[93] The foreign minister Mihai Kogălniceanu, himself an advocate of the convention, faced strong objections in the Senate on the part of Sturdza, who defended a Turkophile position and advocated neutrality.[94]

After the war, the allies clashed on the issue of southern Bessarabia, a territory that Russia had ceded to Moldavia in 1856 and demanded back in 1878 in exchange for Dobrogea.[95] In a desperate defense of their country's territorial integrity at the Berlin Congress, Ion C. Brătianu and Mihai Kogălniceanu once again evoked the Ottoman "capitulations" and Russia's own treaties with Turkey.[96] For their part, the Russian ministers A. M. Gorchakov and P. A. Shuvalov presented the exchange of southern Bessarabia for the territorially larger Dobrogea as yet another manifestation of traditional Russian benevolence to the principalities. They also described Romanian "ingratitude" for the "Russian blood" shed for the liberation of this country, an argument that would find much greater resonance with Russian public opinion than with European diplomats.[97] Resolved in Russia's favor, this conflict confirmed the apprehensions of the Romanian elites about their imperial neighbor, and strengthened the anti-Russian sentiments that characterized modern Romanian nationalism. As for the Russians, they found one more pretext to regret, as did Felix Fonton in 1828, that God decided to place Romanians on Russia's way toward the southern Slavs.

With time, the constraining influences of national perceptions were bound to increase, if only because of the liberalization of politics and the concomitant rise of the power of public opinion. The period between the outbreak of the First World War and Romania's entry into the war on the side of the Entente (and therefore of Russia) witnessed intense polemics between the partisans of the Entente and Germanophiles, in the course of which the latter used the entire arsenal of anti-Russian arguments.[98] Now, at a time of increasingly populist politics in both Russia and Romania, perceptions inherited from the past are as capable as ever of influencing the relations between the two countries. The ideas that the nationalist intellectuals formulated a century and a half ago in quite different circumstances demonstrate remarkable tenaciousness in both countries at present.

The dramatic events of the twentieth century shaped the mutual perceptions of Russians and Romanians in a more evident, if not necessarily deeper, way. The background of contemporary Russian-Romanian relations would be incomplete without the "unification" of Bessarabia with Romania in the wake of the Bolshevik takeover, the Molotov-Ribbentrop Pact, Romania's participation in World War II, its subsequent transformation into a Soviet satellite, the reemergence of nationalist discourse under Nicolae Ceaușescu, and finally the reopening of the prospect of reunification of the Republic of Moldova with Romania and the emergence of the Transnistria in the late 1980s and early 1990s. Nevertheless, the basic ways in which present-day Russian and Romanian elites perceive the relationship between the two countries had arguably crystallized by the end of the nineteenth century and in fact by the mid-1800s.

Like the Romanian revolutionary émigrés in the early 1850s, present-day Romanian politicians and foreign-policy makers perceive their country's relation with the Russian Federation under the species of the latter's relations with the West. Similar to their nineteenth-century predecessors, they do not see Russia as part of "European civilization" and assume that tensions between Russia and the West are irreconcilable. In fact, much of Bucharest's post-1989 foreign strategy relied on such irreconcilability and used its implications to facilitate Romania's entry into Western political organizations. Although the special political relationship between Romania and Turkey ceased to exist 130 years ago, there are manifestations of the Turkophile attitudes of nineteenth-century Romanian elites today just as there is evidence of continuous apprehension and hostility towards Russia. Like Ion Ghica at the outbreak of the Crimean War, Teodor Baconschi, the Romanian foreign minister from 2009 to 2012, assumed Turkey to be part of the West and found it less difficult to imagine Turkey in Europe than do many Western European politicians.[99] Having acquired both NATO and EU membership during the first decade of the twenty-first century, Romanian foreign-policy makers proved much more receptive to the idea of Turkish accession to the EU than they were to the prospect of a special partnership between Europe and Russia.

For their part, Moscow's officials and political commentators likewise subsume Russian-Romanian relations under Russia's relations with the West. On multiple occasions, domestic uses of anti-NATO rhetoric were deemed more important than the annoyance that such rhetoric could cause in Bucharest. On the other hand, the growing popularity of Eurasianism and other anti-Western ideologies among the broader Russian society resulted in the resurrection of the Pan-Slavic approaches to Romania. Under their influence, the radical nationalist writers have either made strong anti-Romanian jibes or assumed, even more implausibly than Fadeev and Danilevskii, that Romania can be Russia's ally in the confrontation with the West. Thus, the notorious Alexander Gelievich Dugin essentially reproduced Danilevskii's argument when he pressed for Moldova's unification with Romania and the latter's joining the anti-Atlantic coalition led by Russia.[100] However extravagant its source, the idea was rearticulated in June 2004 by a liberal political observer Stanislav Aleksandrovich Belkovkii as a way of solving the Transnistrian conflict, whereupon it received some resonance with the political commentators in Romania and Moldavia.[101]

Although the historical perceptions discussed in this essay stand in the way of greater pragmatism in Russian-Romanian relations for both sides concerned, there are important differences in the way these perceptions relate to the policies that the two countries pursue toward each other. Whereas Russia is Romania's main "other," the reverse is not true. As a result, the role of nineteenth-century Russian stereotypes about the Romanians in the populist foreign-policy rhetoric of Vladimir Putin is necessarily much smaller than the place of traditional nineteenth-century clichés about the "Russian danger" in the foreign political discourse of the similarly populist President Traian Băsescu. Therefore, ideological legacies that the Russians inherited from the time of the Eastern Question at least potentially represent less of an obstacle for a pragmatic Russian policy toward Romania than do similar legacies for a pragmatic Romanian policy toward Russia.

In their pursuit of a more active role in the Black Sea region, Romania's foreign-policy makers will most likely continue their attempts to isolate Russia through participation in energy projects like Nabucco, special partnerships with Georgia and Azerbaijan, and a favorable attitude toward Turkey's aspirations to EU accession.[102] However, the prospects of this policy are unclear in view of Romania's territorial disputes with Ukraine as well as the apparent strength of the Russian-Turkish partnership, which is more than an outcome of Turkey's frustration on the European front. On the other hand, in view of Russia's apparent readiness to pursue its energy projects with any of the Black Sea states, including Romania, one can question the wisdom of formulating the Black Sea problem as that of "too much Russian presence." Until Romania became a NATO and EU member in 2002 and 2007 respectively, the strategy of inflating Russia's influence helped Romanian foreign-policy makers facilitate their country's entry into these international organizations. By the time of the resolution of Romania's security and "civilizational" dilemmas, the struggle between Europe and Russia as portrayed by Dimitrie Alexandru Sturdza in 1890, if indeed there was such a struggle, had been resolved manifestly in favor of the former. From that moment onward, continued commitment to the past vision, which has fulfilled its historical function, can only lead Romanian policy makers to squander important opportunities in the present and the future.

NOTES

1. Dimitrie Alexandru Sturdza, *Europa, Rusia și România* (Bucharest: Stabilimenul Grafic I. V. Socecu, 1890). For a discussion of Sturdza's ideas in the context of Russian and Romanian geopolitical thought of the late nineteenth to early twentieth century, see Andrei Cusco, "Frontiers, Geography, and the Spatial Limits of Modernity through the Lens of Russian and Romanian Intellectuals (Late 19th and Early 20th Century)," in *New Europe College: Petre Țuțea Program Yearbook*, ed. Irina Vainovski Mihai (Bucharest: New Europe College, 2009), 79–120.

2. R. A. Fadeev, *Mnenie o vostochnom voprose* (St. Petersburg: Tipografia Departamenta Udelov, 1870); N. Ia. Danilevskii, *Rossiia i Evropa* (1869; Moscow: Blagoslavlenie. Institut Russkoi Tsivilizatsii, 2011).

3. The groundbreaking study of the role of the discourses of otherness in international relations is Iver B. Neumann, *Uses of the Other: "The East" in European Identity Formation* (Minneapolis: University of Minnesota Press, 1999); and idem, *Russia and the Idea of Europe: A Study of Identity in International Relations* (London: Routledge, 1996).

4. See Dosifei's request for a printing press addressed to the patriarch of Moscow Ioakim, 15 August 1679, *Istoricheskie sviazi narodov SSSR i Rumynii v XV–nachale XVIII v.: Dokumenty i materialy*, ed. Ia. S. Grosul, 3 vols. (Moscow: Nauka, 1965–70), 3:58.

5. For the addresses of Moldavian *hospodars* and the tsar's responses in 1674 and 1684, see *Polnoe Sobranie Zakonov Rossiiskoi Imperii* (hereafter *PSZ*), ser. 1, vol. 2, 965-71 and 957-59 respectively.

6. See Dosifei's request to that effect addressed to Ivan V and Peter I, 23 November 1688, *Istoricheskie sviazi narodov SSSR i Rumynii*, 3:99-100.

7. On Dosifei, see S. N. Cheban, *Dosifei, mitropolit Sochavskii i ego knizhnaia deitelnost'* (Kiev: M. T. Meinander, 1915); I. D. Grekul, *Dosoftei, svet prikhodit iz Moskvy* (Kishinev: Kartia Moldoveneaska,1960); Arsenii Stadnitskii, *Issledovania po istorii moldavskoi tserkvi* (St. Petersburg: Tipografia Vaisberga i Gershunina, 1904), 52-56.

8. N. F. Kapterev, *Kharakter otnoshenii Rossii k Pravoslavnomu Vostoku v XVI i v XVII stoletiiakh* (Moscow: Tip. L. F. Snegireva, 1885), 262-63. The founder of the Bogoiavlenskii monastery, Arsenii Sukhanov, who traveled across the Ottoman Empire in 1649-53 and again in 1654, added, "All Christians are envisioning Aleksei Mikhailovich taking Constantinople." Cited in B. M. Dantsig, *Blizhnii Vostok v russkoi nauke i literature* (Moscow: Glavnaia redaktsia vostochnoi literatury, 1973), 32.

9. Dimitrie G. Ionescu, "Tratatul lui Gheorghe Stefan cu Ruşii," *Revista istorica romina*, no. 3 (1933): 241-46; D. M. Dragnev, ed., *Ocherki vneshnepoliticheskoi istorii moldavskogo kniazhestva (posledniia tret' IV-nachalo XIX v.)* (Kishinev: Shtiintsa, 1987), 218-19. See also Silviu Dragomir, *Contribuţii privitoare la relaţiile biserici româneşti cu Rusia în veacul XVII* (Bucharest: Şosec C. Sfetea. Librărie Naţională, 1912).

10. Dragnev, *Ocherki vneshnepoliticheskoi istorii*, 234. The corulers Ivan V and Peter I as well as Tsarevna Sofiia responded favorably to Cantacuzino's desire to be "under the high hand of their tsarist majesties" and suggested coordinating the military activities. For Moscow's response to Cantacuzino's request, see *PSZ*, ser. 1, vol. 2, 959-62. However, the failure of the Crimean campaign of 1689 made this alliance inconsequential.

11. Kapterev, *Kharakter*, 271; see also A. A. Kochiubinskii, *Snoshenia Rossii pri Petre Pervom s iuzhnymi slavianami i rumynami* (Moscow: Universitetskaia tip., 1872), 6-7.

12. Dragnev, *Ocherki vneshnepoliticheskoi istorii*, 219-20.

13. See the corresponding rescript in *PSZ*, ser. 1, vol. 2, 964-65.

14. The *hospodars* who approached the tsar were Constantin Brâncoveanu (1690, 1698) in Wallachia and Antioh Cantemir (1699), Constantin Duca (1701), and Mihai Racoviţă (1704) in Moldova. See *Istoricheskie sviazi narodov SSSR i Rumynii*, 3:114-18, 132-35, 166, and 204-6. On Peter's relations with the *hospodars* prior to 1711, see *Ocherki vneshnepoliticheskoi istorii Moldavii*, 240-42; and G. S. Ardeleanu, "Ştiri din correspondenţa lui Petru I," *Studii şi cercetări de istorie medie*, no. 1 (1950): 192-208. On the Lutsk treaty, see Ion Focşeneanu, "Tratatul de la Luţk şi Campania Ţarului Petru I în Moldova (1711)," in *Studii privind relaţiile romîno-ruse* (Bucharest: Academia Republicii Populare Romîne, 1963),

1-55; Ion Eremia, "Consideratii privid tratatul moldo-rus de la 1711," in *Frontierile Spațiului Românesc în Contextul European*, ed. Sorin Șipoș, Mircea Brie, Florin Șprengeu, and Ion Gumenâi (Chișinau: Editura Cartdidact, 2008), 102-20.

15. H. B. Sumner, *Peter the Great and the Ottoman Empire* (Oxford: B. Blackwell, 1949), 37-38; Brian L. Davis, *Empire and Military Revolution in Eastern Europe: Russia's Turkish Wars of the Eighteenth Century* (London: Continuum, 2011), 159-63.

16. See the "articles" submitted by the Moldavian metropolitan Gedeon and logothete Necul on 12 May 1656, which stipulated that the Moldavian *hospodar* "remain in the same rank" as his predecessors prior to the Ottoman vassalage and that his "honor and rank do not get ruined ... as it was not ruined by the godless ones." The articles were confirmed by the tsar on 20 May 1656, after which the Moldavian representatives swore the oath of loyalty to the tsar. See *PSZ*, ser. 1, vol. 2, 385-90. The term *reaya* originally designated the nonmilitary population of the Ottoman Empire. With time, it was applied to the territories exempt from the jurisdiction of the Moldavian and Wallachian princes and subordinate to the governors of the Ottoman fortresses of Turnu, Giurgiu, Brăila, Reni, and Ismail on the Danube and Bender and Hotin on the Dniester. The population of these territories had to sustain the Ottoman garrisons.

17. See "Stat'i prislannyie iz Varshavy k tsariu Alexeiu Mikhalovichu ot volokhskikh boyar Radula i Petrashki na kakikh usloviakh zhelaiut oni byt' v rossiiskom poddanstve," *PSZ*, ser. 1, vol. 2, 971-72.

18. "Diplom, dannyi vakakhskomu kniaziu Dmitriiu Kantemiru," *PSZ*, ser. 1, vol. 4, 659-61.

19. With the exception of the prince of Moldavia Alexandru Mavrocordat Firaris (the Fugitive), who in 1787 defected to the Russians, the only *hospodar* to accept Russian suzerainty in the post-1711 period was the Wallachian prince Constantine Ypsilanti. Ypsilanti did so at the outbreak of the Russian-Ottoman War of 1806-12 in the expectation of establishing the dynastic rule of the Ypsilanti over both principalities. See George F. Jewsbury, *Russian Annexation of Bessarabia, 1774-1828: A Study of Imperial Expansion* (Boulder, CO: East European Monographs, 1975), 37-43. Vladimir Mischevca and Periklis Zavitsanos, *Principele Constantin Ypsilanti* (Chișinău: Civitas, 1999).

20. Phanariote rule in Moldavia and Wallachia constitutes a controversial subject in Romanian historiography. In the nineteenth century, critical evaluations by Mihai Kogălniceanu, *L'Istoire de la Dacie, des Valaques Trasdanubiennes et de la Valachie* (Berlin: Librairie B. Behr, 1854), 372; and A. D. Xenopol, *Epoca Fanarioților pâna la 1812* (Iași: Editura librăriei școalelor Frații Saraga, 1896) gave way to more positive appraisals by Nicolae Iorga, *Byzance après Byzance* (Bucharest: L'Institut d'Etudes Byzantines, 1935); and Florin Constantiniu and Șerban Papacostea, "Les réformes des premiers princes Phanariotees en Moldavie et en Valachie: Essai d'interpretation," *Balkan Studies* 13, no. 1 (1972): 89-118.

For a recent discussion of the role of the Phanariotes in the Ottoman governance, see Christine M. Philliou, *Biography of an Empire: Governing the Ottomans in an Age of Revolution* (Berkeley: University of California Press, 2011), 5-37.

21. E. B. Shul'man, "Prorusskaia partia v Valakhii i ee sviazi s Rossiei, 1736-1737," in *Russko-rumynskie i rumynsko-russkie otnoshenia* (Kishinau: Shtiintsa, 1969), 7-41. At the time of the Pruth campaign, there was likewise a pro-Russian party in Wallachia led by Toma Cantacuzino, whose personal rivalry with the *hospodar* Constantin Brankovianu was one of the factors behind the latter's "betrayal" of Peter the Great. See Victor Țvircun, "Viața și activitatea contelui Toma Cantacuzino în Rusia (I)," *Revista Istorică* 21, nos. 5-6 (2010): 501-16.

22. Cited in L. E. Semenova, *Kniazhestva Moldaviia i Valakhiia, konets XIV-nachalo XIX vv.: Ocherki vneshnepoliticheskoi istorii* (Moscow: Indrik, 2006), 316. On Drăgunescu's mission, see E. B. Shul'man, "Missia valashskogo vornika P. Drăgunescu v Rossiiu (1736-1737 gg.)," in *Vekovaia druzhba* (Kishinev: Shtiintsa, 1963), 211-39; Dragnev, *Ocherki vneshnepoliticheskoi istorii*, 262.

23. See D. F. Maslovskii, *Stavuchanskii pokhod: Dokumenty 1739 g*. (St. Petersburg: Voenno-uchebnyi komitet Glavnogo Shtaba, 1892), 187-88; Dragnev, *Ocherki vneshnepoliticheskoi istorii Moldavii*, 271-73.

24. Dragnev, *Ocherki vneshnepoliticheskoi istorii Moldavii*, 298-99; Semenova, *Kniazhestva Moldaviia i Valakhiia*, 320-21.

25. Although all Russian-Ottoman treaties beginning with Belgrade (1739) contained a clause about the nonpunishment of "the subjects of both empires which in the course of war defected to the opposite side," there was little or no practical possibility to enforce this clause, as the considerable Romanian immigration to Russia during the eighteenth century demonstrates. See A. Vianu, "Cîteva date privitoare la emigrarea romînilor în sudul Rusiei în secolul al XVIII-lea," in *Studii privind relațiile romîno-ruse* (Bucharest: Academia Republicii Populare Romîne, 1963), 57-65.

26. It is noteworthy that during the war of 1787-92 there were hardly any appeals on the part of the boyars to make Moldavia and Wallachia Russian provinces. Instead, Wallachian boyars addressed to both Russia and Austria two memoranda in which they effectively demanded the end of the Phanariote regime and the restoration of the historical autonomy of the two principalities under the rule of autochthonous princes. By historical autonomy, the boyars implied a restoration of the national militia and the abolition of the Ottoman monopoly on foreign trade. See Vlad Georgescu, ed., *Mémoires et projets de réforme dans les principautés roumaines, 1769-1830: Répertoire et textes inédits* (Bucharest: Association internationale d'études du Sud-Est Européen, 1970), 10.

27. Cited in Semenova, *Kniazhestva Moldaviia i Valakhiia*, 36.

28. Ibid., 38.

29. The Moldavian counterparts of these Wallachian forgeries were the treaties between Selim I and Bogdan III (1511) and Suleiman II and Petru Rareș (1545). There were multiple editions of the capitulations during the nineteenth

century. See, for example, M. Mitilineu, ed., *Colecțiune de tratatele și convențiunile ale României cu puterile straine* (Bucharest: Noua tipografia ale laboratorilor români, 1874), 6, 18, 35, 51. For the French translation of the first two treaties, see Felix Colson, *De l'État présent et de l'avenir de principautés de Moldavie et de Valachie* (Paris: A. Pougin, 1839), 323-25. Most specialists on the subject of capitulations indicate that these texts were presented by Mihai Cantacuzino to Count Grigorii Orlov during the Congress of Foșcani in August 1772. See "Memoire addressé au Comte Orlov," 6 August 1772, in *Genealogia Cantacuzinilor*, ed. Nicolae Iorga (Bucharest: Institut de Arte grafice și Editură Minerva, 1902), 492-508. For a dissenting opinion, see Semenova, *Kniazhestva Moldaviia i Valakhiia*, 31-65.

30. The issue of the Ottoman capitulations to the principalities generated a voluminous literature and an unending historiographical debate. The Romanian historians of the twentieth century demonstrated that the texts of capitulations published by their nineteenth-century predecessors were in fact late eighteenth-century forgeries (the earliest extant copy is dated 1804). The predominant opinion of present-day Romanian historiography is that, although forgeries, the "capitulations" were predated by the actual Ottoman *ahd-names* and *hatti-i sheriffs* issued by the sultans to the *hospodars* in the fifteenth and the early sixteenth century, the copies of which were later lost. However, the texts of these original *hatt-i sheriffs* and *ahd-names* still remain to be discovered in the Ottoman archives. For an overview of the historiography of "capitulations," see Semenova, *Kniazhestva Moldaviia i Valakhiia*, 21-31. On the "uses" of capitulations by the nineteenth-century Romanian nation-builders, see the discussion later in this chapter.

31. Constantin Giurescu, *Capitulațiile Moldovei cu Poarta Ottomană* (Bucharest: Institut de Arte Grafice Carol Göbl, 1908), 6-11.

32. T. P. Iuzefovich, *Dogovory Rossii s Vostokom* (St. Petersburg: Tip. O. I. Baksta, 1869), 32-34.

33. On the latter, see G. S. Grosul, *Dunaiskie kniazhestva v politike Rossii, 1774-1806* (Chișinău: Shtiintsa, 1975), 154-65.

34. Apart from the treaties that Russia concluded with the Ottoman Empire after 1774, the manifestos of the Russian rulers and their generals to the population of the principalities during the Russian-Ottoman wars also referred to local laws and privileges. Thus, Peter the Great's manifesto of 8 May 1711 addressed to Moldavians and Wallachians, as well as other Christians of the Ottoman Empire, promised to "leave each country under its old laws" and to "confirm their old rights and privileges." See *Istoricheskie sviazi narodov SSSR i Rumynii*, 3:333. P. A. Rumiantsev's manifesto to the population of Moldavia of 22 September 1788 announced the preservation of "local laws" and confirmed the rights of inhabitants. See RGVIA, f. VUA, d. 2391, part 2, ll. 383.

35. The name of Bessarabia initially applied only to the lands between the Black Sea littoral and lower courses of the Pruth, the Danube, and the Dniester.

Although by the end of the fourteenth century Moldavian princes extended their sovereignty over these territories, their hold remained tenuous. In the first half of the fifteenth century, these lands temporarily passed under the control of the Wallachian princely family of the Bassarabs, which explains the origin of the toponym. Following a protracted resistance to the Ottoman advance, the most notable Moldavian ruler, Stephen the Great (1457–1504), eventually had to accept the status of a sultan's vassal and cede the fortresses of Kilia and Akkerman with the surrounding districts to Bajezed II in 1484. Some fifty years later, Suleiman the Magnificent consolidated Ottoman control over Moldavia, by constructing the fortress of Bender on the Dniester and alienating into *reaya* a still larger chunk of the territory between the Dniester and the Pruth. In the meantime, the steppe land between the fortresses (whose number was augmented by the construction of Ismail and Reni in the early 1600s) became the abode of the seminomadic Nogai subjects of the Crimean khans, themselves vassals of the Porte. The alienation of the Khotin district into *reaya* in 1713 further limited the territories that were under direct jurisdiction of the Moldavian princes east of the Pruth. Following the extension of the Russian borders to the Pruth and the Danube in 1812, the name of Bessarabia, hitherto applied only to the southern part of the Pruth-Dniester mesopotamia, came to designate the entire territory between the Dniester, the Pruth, the Danube, and the Black Sea. On the Ottoman *reayas* along the Danube and the Dniester, see Laurențiu Râdvan, *At Europe's Borders: Medieval Towns in the Romanian Principalities* (Leiden: Brill, 2010), 248–55, 495–97, 516–14, 543–44; on the temporary Austrian annexation of Oltenia (Little Wallachia), see Șerban Papacostea, *Oltenia sub stapânirea austriaca, 1718–1739* (Bucharest: Editura Enciclopedica, 1998). On the Russian annexation of Bessarabia, see Jewsbury, *Russian Annexation of Bessarabia*; and Andrei Cusco and Victor Taki, with participation of Oleg Grom, *Bessarabiia v sostave Rossiiskoi imperii, 1812–1917* (Moscow: Novoie Literaturnoie obozrenie, 2012).

36. "Mémoire concernant le statut international des Principautés, le caractère des relations de la Moldavie avec la Turquie et la Russie, ainsi que l'influence de ces relations sur les rapports sociaux internes," in *Mémoires et projets de réforme*, 98.

37. "Adresse du Divan de Valachie à l'empereur de Russie," 4 May 1828, Bucharest, in *Annuaire historique universel* (Paris: Fantin, 1829), 89.

38. Ibid.

39. Article 5 in Iuzefovich, *Dogovory Rossii s Vostokom*, 74.

40. For this period, see Grosul, *Dunaiskie kniazhestva v politike Rossii*; and Jewsbury, *Russian Annexation of Bessarabia*, 7–55.

41. Apart from the Moldavian memorandum on capitulations addressed to the Prussian and Austrian representatives in 1772, the Moldavian and Wallachian boyars submitted three additional memoranda on the same subject to the Ottoman government in August and September 1774. See *Mémoires et projets de réforme*, 8. In 1790, the Wallachian divan addressed to the Russian and

Austrian governments a memorandum on the international statute of the principalities and the principles on which their relations with the Ottoman Empire should be based. See N. Iorga, "Viaţa unui mitropolit de altădată," *Convorbiri literare*, no. 11 (1901): 1126-31.

42. See, George F. Jewsbury, "The Greek Question: The View from Odessa, 1815-1822," *Cahiers du monde russe* 40, no. 4 (1999): 751-62.

43. I. C. Filitti, *Framântarile politice si sociale în Principatele Române de la 1821 la 1828* (Bucharest: Cartea Românească, 1932) remains one of the best accounts of this period. See also Anastasie Iordache, *Principatele Romnâne în epocă modernă*, vol. 1, *Domniile pământene şi ocupaţia rusească* (Bucharest: Albatros, 1996).

44. See the memorandum addressed to the British Ambassador in Constantinople Lord Stratford Canning by Ionica Tautul, the leader of the middle and lower rank Moldavian boyars during the 1820s, in *Mémoires et projets de réformes*, 170-72.

45. V. Ia. Grosul, *Reformy v dunaiskikh kniazhestvakh i Rossiia* (Moscow: Nauka, 1966), 145-47; Iuliu C. Ciubotaru, "Lucrări şi proecte in vederea elaborării regulamentului obştesc al Moldovei din anul 1827," in *Regulamentul Organic al Moldovei*, ed. Dumitru Vitcu and Gabriel Bădărău (Iaşi: Junimea, 2004), 77-78.

46. "Requêtes des mécontents moldaves," AVPRI, f. 331, op. 716/1, d. 10, ll. 4-19; "Projet d'adresse (en traduction littérale) saisi dans les papiers du spathar Sion," ibid., ll. 53-57.

47. See reports of the Russian provisional authorities on the adoption of the project of the statutes by the assemblies of revision: Kiselev to Nesselrode, 30 April 1831, Iaşi, RGIA, f. 958, op. 1, d. 625, "Donesenia Russkikh konsulov iz Bucharesta i Iass vitse-kantsleru K. V. Nesselrode ob ustroistve kniazhestv Vlakhii i Moldavii," ibid., ll. 90-93, 258-58.

48. Radu Florescu, *The Struggle against Russia in the Danubian Principalities, 1821-1854: A Problem of Anglo-Turkish Diplomacy* (1962; Iaşi: Center for Romanian Studies, 1997).

49. On Sturdza's relations with the opposition, see Gheorghe Platon, *Moldova si începuturile revolutiei de la 1848* (Chisinau: Universitas, 1993), 110, 122-25. In 1844, Bibescu prorogued the assembly after it refused to approve the mining concessions to the Russian engineer Trandafilov. See Barbara Jelavich, *Russia and the Formation of the Romanian National State, 1821-1878* (Cambridge: Cambridge University Press, 1984), 38; Florescu, *Struggle against Russia*, 144.

50. See, for instance, Nicolae Iorga, *Histoire des relations entre la France et les Roumains* (Paris: Payot, 1918); John C. Campbell, *French Influence and the Rise of Romanian Nationalism: The Generation of 1848 (1830-1857)* (New York: Arno Press, 1971); Mihai Dimitrie Sturdza, *Românii între frica de Rusia şi dragostea de Franţa* (Bucharest: Roza Vânturilor, 2006).

51. Miroslav Hroch, "From National Movement to the Fully-Formed Nation: The Nation-Building Process in Europe," in *Mapping the Nation*, ed. Gopal Balakrishnan (New York: Verso, 1996), 78-97, esp. 79.

52. Campbell, *French Influence*, 52, 54-55, 115, 117.

53. Ibid., 69-74. On the Russian influence in Serbia and the reactions of Miloš Obrenović and the "constitutionalists" to it, see Stevan K. Pavlowitch, *Anglo-Russian Rivalry in Serbia 1837-1839: The Mission of Colonel Hodges* (Paris: Mouton, 1961); E. P. Kudriavtseva, *Rossiia i Serbia v 30-kh-40-kh gg. XIX veka* (Moscow: Institut Rossiiskoi Istorii RAN, 2002), 52-81, 99-112.

54. The best essay-length discussion of the revolution is Dan Berendei, *1848 în Țările Române* (Bucharest: Editura Stiintifica si enciclopedica, 1984); the most complete treatment is Cornelia Bodea, *1848 la Români*, 2 vols. (Bucharest: Editura Enciclopedica, 1998); see also Gheorghe Platon, *Geneza revolutiei române de la 1848: Introducere în istoria moderna a României* (Bucharest: Junimea, 1980); and Keith Hitchins, *The Romanians, 1774-1866* (Oxford: Clarendon Press, 1996), 231-73.

55. It is noteworthy that Constantinople was the first capital to which the Wallachian revolutionaries dispatched their first foreign representative, Ion Ghica, in late May 1848, before the outbreak of the revolution.

56. "Răspunsul locotinenței domnești la circularea rusească din 19 iulie, 1848," in *Anul 1848 în Principatele Române*, ed. Ioan C. Brătianu, vol. 4 (Bucharest: Carl Göbl, 1903), 157-67. Even more explicitly, this tendency to present Wallachian revolution as a return to the spirit and letter of the Ottoman "capitulations" can be found in the accounts of 1848 events written by one of the leaders of the revolutionary government and the spiritual father of the "1848 generation," Ion Heliade Rădulescu. See J. R., *Le Protectorat du Czar* (Paris: Comon, 1850); J. Eliade Radulesco, *Mémoires sur l'histoire de la régénération Roumaine, ou sur l'évènements de 1848 accomplis en Valachie* (Paris: Librairie de la Propagande démocratique et sociale Européenne, 1851).

57. Shortly before the revolution was crushed, one of its leaders, Alexandru Golescu, addressed a memorandum to the democratic public in Western Europe that referenced the ancient treaties of the principalities with the Ottoman Empire that had been violated by Russia. See "Istoricul ultimelor evenimente petrecute in Principale, memoriu de Al. G. Golescu," in *Anul 1848 în Principatele Române*, vol. 4 (Bucharest: Institut de Arte Grafice Carol Göbl, 1903), 634-70.

58. G. Chanoi [Ion Ghica], *Dernière occupation des principautés par la Russie* (Paris: J. Dumaine, 1853), 18-20.

59. An element of the *longue durée* of European intellectual history, the perception of Russia as despotic was particularly strong during the 1830s, 1840s, and early 1850s. See Martin Malia, *Russia under Western Eyes: From Bronze Horseman to Lenin's Mausoleum* (Cambridge, MA: Harvard University Press, 1999); Ezequiel Adamovsky, *Euro-Orientalism: Liberal Ideology and the Image of Russia in France, 1740s-1880s* (Bern: Peter Lang, 2006); Iver B. Neumann, *Russia and the Idea of Europe: A Study of Identity in International Relations* (London: Routledge, 1996); and Marshall Poe, *A People Born to Slavery: Russia in Early Modern European Ethnography, 1476-1748* (Ithaca, NY: Cornell University Press, 2000).

60. Chanoi, *Dernière occupation des principautés*, 12.

61. On the role of the political exile in the Romanian national movement, see Angela Jianu, *A Circle of Friends: Romanian Revolutionaries and Political Exile, 1840-1859*, Balkan Library Studies 3 (Leiden: Brill, 2011).

62. F. P. Fonton, *Vospominania*, vol. 1 (Leipzig: F. Wagner, 1862), 37.

63. Ibid., 38. Constantin Brâncoveanu (1688-1716) was a *hospodar* of Wallachia, who in the course of the Pruth campaign failed to support Peter the Great despite a secret agreement to this effect. Brâncoveanu decided to ally with the Ottomans due to his rivalry with Peter's Moldavian ally Dimitrie Cantemir, the slowness of Russian progress, and the quicker than expected mobilization of the Ottoman troops.

64. Published in *Istoricheskie sviazi narodov SSSR i Rumynii*, 3:331.

65. A. L. Narochnitskii and N. Petrovich, eds., *Politicheskie i kul'turnye otnosheniia Rossii s iugoslavianskimi zemliami v XVIII v. Dokumenty* (Moscow: Nauka, 1984), 29-30.

66. See A. N. Petrov, *Voina Rossii s Turtsiei i s pol'skimi konfederatami, 1769-1774*, vol. 1 (St. Petersburg: Eduard Veimar, 1866), 103-6.

67. A. L. Zorin, *Kormia dvuglavnogo orla: Literatura i gosudarstvennaia ideologiia v Rossii v poslednei treti XVIII-pervoi treti XIX veka* (Moscow: Novoie Literaturnoie Obozrenie, 2004), 31-61; V. I. Proskurina, *Mify imperii: Literatura i vlast' v epokhu Ekateriny II* (Moscow: Novoie Literaturnoie Obozrenie, 2006), 149-94.

68. Theophilus Prousis, *Russian Society and the Greek Revolution* (DeKalb: Northern Illinois University Press, 1994), 26-53.

69. [Johann Christian von Struve], *Travels in the Crimea: A History of the Embassy from St. Petersburg to Constantinople in 1793* (London: S. Hamilton, 1802), 90, 257; A. F. Langeron, "Journal des campagnes faites en service de Russie," in *Documente privitoare la istoria Românilor*, supp. 1, vol. 3 (Bucharest: Socec, 1889), 73.

70. George Vernadsky, "Alexandre Ier et le problème slave pendant la première moitié de son règne," *Revue des Études Slaves* 7, nos. 1-2 (1927): 94-111.

71. Kiselev to Butenev, 19 June 1833, Bucharest, AVPRI, f. 133, op. 469, d. 141, l. 207.

72. On Malinovskii's project, see I. S. Dostian, "Evropeiskaia utopia V. F. Malinovskogo," *Voprosy istorii*, no. 6 (1979): 32-46; On Czartoryski's plans in 1804-6, see Vernadsky, "Alexandre Ier," 94-111; Patricia Grimsted, *The Foreign Ministers of Alexander I: Political Attitudes and the Conduct of Russian Diplomacy, 1801-1825* (Berkeley: University of California Press, 1969); and W. H. Zawadzki, *A Man of Honour: Adam Czartoryski as a Statesman of Russia and Poland, 1795-1831* (Oxford: Oxford University Press, 1993).

73. A. M. Spiridov, "Kratkoie obozrenie narodov Slavianskogo plemeni obitaiushchikh v Evropeiskoi chasti Turetskoi Imperii," *Severnyi Arkhiv*, no. 14 (1825): 86.

74. Ibid., 87-90.

75. Ibid., 93.

76. Iu. I. Venelin, *Drevnie i nyneshnie Bolgare v politicheskom, narodopisnom, istoricheskom i religioznom ikh otnoshenii k Rossiainam*, vol. 1 (Moscow: Universiteskaia tip., 1829).

77. Iu. I. Venelin, "Zamechania na sochinenie gospodina Iakovenko o Moldavii i Valakhii i proch. (pervoie pis'mo k izdateliu Moskovskogo Vestnika)," *Moskovskii Vestnik*, no. 15 (1828): 269–71.

78. Ia. D. Ginkulov, *Nachertanie pravil moldovlakhiiskoi grammatiki* (St. Petersburg: Imperial Academy of Sciences, 1840), i–iii. Other useful works by Ghinkulov include *Sobranie sochinenii i perevodov, v proze i stikhakh, dlia upazhnenia v valakho-moldavskom iazyke, s prisovokupleniem slovaria i sobrania slavianskikh pervoobraznykh slov, upotrebliaemykh v iazyke valakho-moldavskom* (St. Petersburg: Imperial Academy of Sciences, 1841); idem, *Vyvody iz vlakho-moldavskoi grammatiki* (St. Peterburg: Imperial Academy of Sciences, 1847); idem, *Karmannaia knizhka russkikh voinov v pokhodakh po kniazhestvam Moldavii i Valakhii*, pts. 1–2 (St. Petersburg: Imperial Academy of Sciences, 1854).

79. E. P. Kovalevskii, "Vospominania o beregakh nizhnego Dunaia," *Biblioteka dlia chtenia* 65 (July 1844): 1; summary in *Zhurnal Ministerstva Narodnogo Presviashchenia* 44, nos. 10–12 (1844): 178–79.

80. On the reforms of the early 1830s, see I. C. Filitti, *Principatele Române de la 1828 la 1834: Ocupaţa rusească şi Regulamentul organic* (Bucharest: Institut de Arte Grafice "Bucovina," 1934); Grosul, *Reformy v dunaiskikh kniazhestvakh*; Alexander Bitis, *Russia and The Eastern Question: Army, Government, and Society, 1815–1833* (Oxford: Oxford University Press for the British Academy, 2006), 426–64; and Victor Taki, "Between *Polizeistaat* and *Cordon Sanitaire*: Epidemics and Police Reform during Russian Occupation of Moldavia and Wallachia, 1828–1834," *Ab Imperio*, no. 4 (2008): 75–112.

81. See Neagu Djuvara, *Între Orient şi Occident: Ţările române le începutul epocii moderne* (Bucharest: Humanitas, 1995); Pompiliu Eliade, *Influenta franceza asupra spiritului public în România: Originile; Studiu asupra starii societatii românesti în vremea domniilor fanariote*, trans. Aurelia Dumitrascu (1898; Bucharest: Humanitas, 2000); idem, *La Roumanie au XIX-e siecle*, vol. 2, *Les trois presidents plenipotentiaires (1828–1834)* (Paris: Hachette, 1914).

82. Anatole Demidov, *Voyage dans la Russie méridionale et la Crimée par la Hongrie, la Valachie et la Moldavie* (Paris: Ernest Bourdin, 1840), 108. For a more detailed treatment of the Russian perception of Moldavia and Wallachia as frontiers of civilization, see Victor Taki, "Moldavia and Wallachia in the Eyes of Russian Observers," *East-Central Europe/L'Europe du Centre-Est* 32, nos. 1–2 (2005): 199–224.

83. Some of the more Western-minded Russian observers noted with approval that, solemn and immobile, the bearded Moldavian and Wallachian patriarchs looked not unlike the pre-Petrine Muscovite boyars. See Filip Vigel, "Zamechania na nyneshnee sostoianie Bessarabskoi oblasti," *Russkii Arkhiv* 80, no. 1 (1893): 1–34.

84. I. P. Liprandi, *Dunaiskie kniazhestva* (Moscow: Izdanie Imperatorskogo Obshchestva Istorii i Drevnostei Rossiskikh, 1877), 5.

85. Ibid., 6-8.

86. P. V. Alabin, *Chetyre voiny: Pokhodnye zapiski v 1849, 1853, 1854-56, 1877-78 gg.*, vol. 2 (Samara: I. P. Novikov, 1888), 43.

87. M. M. Pogodin, *Istoriko-politicheskie pis'ma i zapiski v prodolzhenie Krymskoi voiny* (Moscow: Tip. Moskovskogo Universiteta, 1874), 120.

88. Danilevskii, *Rossiia i Evropa*, 486.

89. K. N. Leont'ev, "Plody natsional'nykh dvizhenii na pravoslavnom vostoke," in his *Sobranie sochinenii*, 9 vols. (Moscow: Izd. V. M. Sablina, 1912-13), 6:233.

90. Danilevskii, *Rossiia i Evropa*, 380-81.

91. Fadeev, *Mnenie o vostochnom voprose*, 52.

92. Ibid., 52-53.

93. On the complex negotiations that preceded the conclusion of the convention, see Jelavich, *Russia and the Formation of the Romanian National State*, 241-56.

94. "Discursul lui Mihai Kogălniceanu asupra politicei externe a Românei în condiţii crizei orientale (Şedinţa Senatului României din 17 [29] Aprilie 1877)," in *Discursuri şi dezbateri parlamentare (1864-2004)*, ed. G. Buzatu (Bucharest: Editura Mica Valahia, 2004), 83-98.

95. Jelavich, *Russia and the Emergence of the Romanian Nation-State*, 277-86; Cusco and Taki, *Bessarabiia v sostave Rossiiskoi imperii*, 234-60.

96. *Les Protocoles du Congrès du Berlin* (St. Petersburg: Trenke et Fusnot, 1878), 49-50.

97. Ibid., 47-48.

98. Vladlen Vinogradov, *Rumynia v gody Pervoi Mirovoi Voiny* (Moscow: Nauka, 1969), 52-71.

99. "Teodor Baconschi: Turcia are vocaţia istorică şi politică de a face parte din UE," http://tinyurl.com/ks986mr (accessed 13 January 2013).

100. Alexandr Dugin, *Osnovy geopolitiki* (Moscow: Arctogeia-tsentr, 2000), 220. Danilevskii described the unification of Romania with part of Transylvania, Bucovine, and part of Bessarabia "with the consent and cooperation of Russia, under whose impartial and pacifying influence the Romanians would be able to successfully withstand Magyarization." See Danilevskii, *Rossiia i Evropa*, 486.

101. Belkovsky reiterated his plan more recently; see http://www.moldovanova.md/ru/publications/show/280 (accessed 9 November 2011). For the Romanian responses to what came to be termed as the "Belkovsky Plan," see http://www.revista22.ro/proiectul-belkovski-transnistria-contra-basarabia-977.html (accessed 9 November 2011).

102. On Romania's cooperation with Georgia and Azerbaijan, see Sabina Fati, "Moscova şi Ankara nu văd cu ochi buni extinderea influenţei militare şi energetice pregătită la Bucureşti. De ce se tem Rusia şi Turcia de România,"

April 18, 2011. Available at http://www.romanialibera.ro/actualitate/mapa
mond/de-ce-se-tem-rusia-si-turcia-de-romania-222755.html (accessed 11
September 2011). On Romania's attitude towards Turkey's EU accession, see
http://www.euractiv.ro/uniunea-europeana/articles%7CdisplayArticle
/articleID_12711/.html.

"Dreadful Scenes of Carnage on Both Sides"
The Strangford Files and the Eastern Crisis of 1821–1822

Theophilus C. Prousis

Lord Strangford, an experienced diplomatic official with previous postings to Portugal, Brazil, and Sweden, served as Britain's ambassador to the Sublime Porte from 1821 to 1824, an especially turbulent time in Ottoman-European encounters. As the Ottoman Empire coped with a series of challenges, Strangford sent hundreds of reports to the London Foreign Office. His correspondence detailed the state of the sultan's realm at a tense but pivotal moment in the Eastern Question, that precarious web of European power, rivalry, and intrigue in the remarkably resilient Ottoman Empire, which still possessed strategic lands and vital waterways in the Levant, or eastern Mediterranean. Rebellion broke out in the Danubian principalities, the Peloponnese, and other Greek-inhabited regions of the Ottoman Empire. War between Russia and Turkey loomed, largely over Ottoman actions that abrogated Russian-Ottoman treaties. Ottoman restrictions disrupted European trade. Politics clashed with religion. Sectarian abuse and violence deepened the

Portrait of Percy Clinton Sidney Smythe, 6th Viscount Strangford, 1820-24. (reprinted with permission from the Trustees of the British Museum)

Greek-Ottoman divide. Administrative disorder heightened public uncertainty, government factions contested the sultan's rule, and border disputes sparked hostility between Turkey and Persia.

The virtually untapped Strangford treasure trove, located in the National Archives, Kew, UK, provides an invaluable resource on Ottoman domestic and foreign affairs, European interests in the Near East, and Greek stirrings for national independence. The Strangford files, much like the Dashkov papers in Russian archives, hold potential riches for scholars working in Ottoman, Mediterranean, borderlands, and especially Eastern Question history.[1] Against the backdrop of an intensifying crisis in the Near East, Strangford chronicled a volatile situation from Constantinople, the epicenter of the upheaval. The messy realities at the core of this unfolding cataclysm featured the escalating cycle of Greek-Ottoman fighting and reprisal; the Ottoman massacre of Greek residents on Chios; the discord among Greek rebels; the debates among Ottoman officials about military and administrative reform; and the dogged efforts of European envoys like Strangford to pacify the Greek uprising and reduce Russian-Ottoman tension.[2] Britain's ambassador probed all these ramifications, along with the predictable matter of British trade in the troubled Levant. His communiqués also recounted his persistent attempts to persuade the Porte to evacuate Ottoman troops from the Danubian principalities, to appoint new *hospodars* or governors, and to remove Ottoman impediments against Black Sea and Mediterranean shipping.

Strangford's description of these topics sharpens our view of the complex nature of the Eastern Question in the early nineteenth century, when the Ottoman Empire faced internal and external pressures spawned by war, revolt, administrative breakdown, and European intervention. Archives and manuscripts like the Strangford collection widen our approach to the Eastern Question, from a purely great-power military, naval, and diplomatic rivalry to a more varied and dynamic contest. European strategic, commercial, religious, and other objectives entwined with the unpredictable circumstances of the Ottoman Empire. By relating specific episodes of janissary unrest, Greek sedition, economic dislocation, and public insecurity, the writings of Strangford elucidate not just the overlapping problems at the crux of the Eastern Question but also the human element at the grassroots, institutional, and policy-making levels of Ottoman society. Rich in texture and detail, these snapshots depict commercial disruption, sectarian strife, administrative disorder, and foreign meddling in the embattled Ottoman East.

The Greek revolution, which erupted in the Danubian principalities and spread to the Morea, Attica, Thessaly, Macedonia, and the Aegean Archipelago, triggered an Eastern emergency with European-wide repercussions. The established order of legitimacy confronted the principles of liberty and nationality, and the unrest morphed into the prolonged Greek conflict.[3] This struggle drained Ottoman resources and revenues; stoked dissension among factionalized Greeks; provoked outside intervention that resulted in an independent Greek kingdom;

and inspired incendiary outbursts in Europe, Russia, and the Balkans. The Greek uprising also eventually led the Porte to accelerate its program of centralizing reforms for the purpose of modernizing the empire.[4] Already in the opening months of the disturbance, European envoys and consuls had to cope with the seemingly intractable realities of the Eastern quandary: the flare-up of sectarian strife, the dislocation of trade, the upsurge in piracy, and the risk of war between Russia and Turkey, especially after the Russian legation severed official ties with the Porte and left Constantinople in the summer of 1821.

In taking measures to crush the Greek mutiny, the Porte infringed on specific articles in Russian-Ottoman treaties and thus antagonized official relations between the two empires. Reprisals against the Greeks, most notably the execution of Ecumenical Patriarch Grigorios V in April 1821, breached the Porte's promise in the Treaty of Kuchuk Kainardji (1774) to shelter the faith and churches of Ottoman Orthodox Christians.[5] Trade obstacles seemingly contravened Russia's right of unimpeded merchant navigation in the straits, guaranteed by Kuchuk Kainardji and the Treaty of Commerce (1783). The Porte's dismissal of the *hospodars* of Moldavia and Wallachia, accusing them of abetting the agitation, undermined the sultan's imperial decree of 1802, and subsequent stipulations in the Treaty of Bucharest (1812), sanctioning Russian consent in the appointment and deposition of *hospodars*. Facing strong public clamor for intervention on behalf of persecuted Greeks, and despite urgent calls by high-ranking officials for military action to rectify broken treaties, Alexander I upheld the order of legitimacy. The tsar deplored the rebellion as a menace to Europe's peace and security and to the principles of monarchical solidarity and political stability; he also advocated the Porte's swift suppression of the disorders before they engulfed other regions. At the same time, the tsarist regime requested the strict observance of treaties, intent on using them as instruments for exerting pressure on Turkey.

The Foreign Ministry's dual approach of censuring the revolt but insisting on complete compliance with treaty accords became the basis for Russian policy in 1821. Russia's ambassador in Constantinople, Grigorii Aleksandrovich Stroganov, rebuked the insurrection but remonstrated for Orthodox brethren, protested violations of trade clauses, and counseled moderation and restraint in Ottoman treatment of non-insurgent Greek Christians.[6] For a host of reasons, however, the Porte strongly suspected Russian complicity in the turmoil: Russia's past wars against Turkey; its self-proclaimed guardianship of Orthodox

Christians under Ottoman rule; its generous support of Greek migration to southern Russia, in particular the distribution of land grants and tax exemptions to Greek settlements in recently annexed Ottoman territories; and its extensive network of Greek protégés in Black Sea and Aegean commerce. Furthermore, Greek merchants in Odessa participated in the national ferment that produced the Philiki Etaireia (Society of Friends), the secret society that launched the insurgence of 1821. Founded in Odessa (1814) and headquartered in Kishinev, this conspiratorial organization recruited members and monies from Greek centers in Russia and came under the leadership of Alexander Ypsilanti, a Greek general in the Russian army and an aide-de-camp of the tsar. Also, Russia refused to extradite rebels who fled to Bessarabia, in particular the *hospodar* of Moldavia, Michael Soutso, who joined the Philiki Etaireia and took part in the Ypsilanti upheaval.[7] Treaty provisos crumbled not just because of the Porte's plausible, but mistaken, accusations of the Russian government's entanglement in the subversion but also because of the outbreak of sectarian rage in Constantinople, Smyrna, and elsewhere. Ironically, treaties that sought to maintain cordial ties between Russia and Turkey and safeguard Russian activities in the Near East did neither.

In an ultimatum delivered to the Porte on 6/18 July 1821, Russia demanded the evacuation of Ottoman troops from the Danubian principalities, the restoration of damaged churches and religious properties, the protection of Orthodox Christians, and the guarantee of commercial rights. If the sultan did not accept these terms, Russia would have to offer asylum and assistance to all Christians subjected to "blind fanaticism."[8] The expiration of the Russian note's prescribed eight-day deadline without the Porte's full compliance, followed by Ambassador Stroganov's departure from the Ottoman capital, severed official relations between Russia and Turkey, the two realms most profoundly affected by the uproar of 1821. Thus began a strange twilight period of no war yet no peace. Alexander I proved reluctant to act unilaterally without the sanction of the Concert of Europe and dreaded the prospect of a Russian-Turkish clash that would disrupt the status quo, incite revolts elsewhere, and jeopardize the balance of power in Europe. Firmly committed to the Concert of Europe, the tsar suspected that a Jacobin directing committee in Paris had instigated trouble in the Balkans. Yet the Eastern quagmire thickened, Greek-Ottoman fighting intensified, Russian-Ottoman affairs festered, and treaty vows shattered amid war and revolution in the Levant.

Britain remained neutral in the Greek-Ottoman feud of 1821 yet pursued its own strategic, political, and commercial ends. Above all, Foreign Secretary Castlereagh resolved to avert war between Russia and Turkey, to maintain the Ottoman Empire as a bulwark against the perceived peril of Russian expansion, to extend British trade in the Levant, and to safeguard Britain's protectorate over the Ionian Islands.[9] All these objectives framed Lord Strangford's responses to the Eastern predicament. Despite his considerable skill, finesse, and energy in striving to calm Russian-Ottoman antagonism and to mollify the Greek havoc, he remains a controversial figure. As the chief representative of British policy in the Near East, he chided Stroganov for his harsh tone toward the Porte and falsely implicated several tsarist officials, including Russia's ambassador, in the subversive Philiki Etaireia. Yet Strangford worked tirelessly with his European and Ottoman counterparts to neutralize a dangerous situation, to shield Orthodox Christians, and to reestablish tranquility in Moldavia and Wallachia. He became convinced that the Porte's timely restoration of order, most notably the safekeeping of sacred shrines and the evacuation of troops from the Danubian principalities, would forestall Russian-Ottoman hostilities. Through steadfast negotiation, Strangford and his colleagues sought to prevent a great-power war and to defuse the Greek insurgency.[10]

Along with his foreboding of a Russian-Ottoman confrontation, Strangford registered concern over the impending danger of anti-Greek reprisals—what he termed "atrocious and sanguinary proceedings" and "a spirit of relentless fanaticism." Attacks against Greek Christian property and churches became all too palpable to the British envoy, who bemoaned "the prolongation of that system of sanguinary persecution."[11] Violent incidents heightened the mood of disquiet and trepidation in Constantinople, especially at European embassies, obviously caught off guard when the sultan ordered the execution of Constantine Mourousi, an Ottoman Greek who served as grand dragoman (interpreter or translator) of the Porte. The death of the ecumenical patriarch and other church hierarchs amplified the perceived sectarian character of the Greek-Ottoman collision.[12] Strangford's dispatches portrayed an escalating Eastern flashpoint, fueled largely by the danger of partisan slaughter in the capital and other embattled areas. With indelible images and scenes, his writing evoked the religious wrath and nationalistic ferocity that prolonged, as well as exemplified, the Greek-Ottoman fight. Random and deliberate violence, retribution and excess, by both Greeks and Turks, took place in Moldavia, Constantinople, Smyrna,

Aivali, and Tripolitsa. A progression of retaliation and vengeance exacerbated the Eastern emergency, magnified the human cost of the conflict, and made diplomatic mediation all the more difficult and imperative.

Perhaps the most infamous of these outrages occurred on the island of Chios. The Chios catastrophe epitomized both the folly and the fury of the Greek revolution, eliciting horrific reminders of fire and sword memorialized in Eugène Delacroix's edgy *Massacre at Chios* (1824), the expressive painting that inspired European sympathy and support for the Greek cause. Located only five miles from the Turkish mainland, Ottoman Chios enjoyed relative autonomy, prospered economically, and blossomed into a commercial hub, perhaps the richest island in the Aegean, perfectly situated along the main shipping routes in the Levant. Renowned for its physical beauty, mild climate, fertile soil, and resourceful population, and supposedly the birthplace of Homer, Chios featured merchant-funded schools and hospitals and a printing press that produced new editions of the ancient Greek classics. When a band of misguided adventurers from nearby Samos landed in March 1822 and raised the flag of liberation, most Chiotes remained skeptical; they understandably feared that Samiote foolhardiness and bravado might jeopardize their coveted autonomy and prosperity. Cautious Chiotes questioned the prospect of successful rebellion, given their island's proximity to Turkey and its distance from the main Greek naval base at Hydra. Fears became reality when the Ottoman navy approached in April 1822. The Samiote "liberators" fled to the mountains or to their awaiting boats, leaving Chios to a bitter fate of plunder, savagery, and slavery. Ottoman regular and irregular forces exacted a terribly high price in retribution, looting and burning the island, slaughtering unarmed residents, and enslaving thousands. Massacre, captivity, and flight greatly diminished the island's Greek population, from nearly 120,000 to some 20,000.[13]

Throughout these mounting pressures during the opening two years of the crisis, Strangford counseled restraint and caution. He rebuffed Ottoman complaints that the tsarist regime stood behind the Ypsilanti expedition. He advised the Porte to put its trust in the tsar's revulsion of revolution. He protested the execution of the patriarch. And he repeatedly tried to assuage the anger and resentment that incited further atrocities by the belligerents. Far from disloyal to Stroganov, he echoed his Russian colleague on several crucial issues yet criticized his provocative demeanor and language, such as Stroganov's sweeping assertion that Russia had the right not just to protect the sultan's Christian subjects but to denounce the Ottoman Empire's existence as "incompatible with the stability and security of the Christian faith."[14] Although Strangford did not succeed in thwarting a rupture in Russian-Ottoman relations, he exhorted the Porte to observe the strict letter of existing treaties—by withdrawing Ottoman troops from the Danubian principalities, by repairing damaged churches, and by protecting Greek Orthodox subjects.

The narratives of Strangford reflect the advantages and limitations of primary sources written by Europeans in the Ottoman Islamic world in the early nineteenth century. Their commentaries conveyed conventional Western views of the Ottoman Empire, perceptions that stigmatized the Ottoman other with occasional distortion, bias, and exaggeration. Envoys and consuls—and not just British representatives—depicted Ottoman officialdom in a mostly negative light, accenting episodes of oppression and abuse by pashas, janissaries, and customs officers. Many of these authorities, portrayed as rapacious, corrupt, and arbitrary, interfered in the administration of European diplomatic and commercial concessions—the capitulations—and thus complicated European-Ottoman interactions. Through their anecdotes and choice of words, Western records alluded to commonly accepted European images of the Ottoman Empire, fast approaching what became known as "the sick man of Europe" in Western political discourse and popular opinion.[15]

Yet the dispatches excerpted here elucidate some of the essential benefits of Western firsthand testimony on the Eastern Question. Strangford relied on a circle of sources, gathering intelligence from merchants, travelers, protégés, consuls, and dragomans; from high-ranking as well as regional Ottoman officials; and from other European envoys. Sifting through these different accounts, the ambassador chronicled what he deemed the most critical realities in Constantinople, the geopolitical heart of the Ottoman Empire, and addressed a range of topics beyond the political and diplomatic facets of the Eastern crisis. Moreover, given Strangford's access to highly placed authorities in the central government and their protracted deliberations, his correspondence sheds light on how Ottoman officialdom perceived and reacted to the Greek sedition. The very specificity and urgency of his reports deepen our understanding of the multiple issues, such as sectarian friction and religiously tinged Russian-Ottoman tension, which marked an age of upheaval in the Ottoman Levant.

Documents

These passages introduce readers to the various concerns that not only preoccupied Strangford but characterized Eastern Question diplomacy during the Eastern crisis. Document 1 suggests the intrigue and duplicity that accompanied European dealings with Ottoman court favorites and influential advisers of the sultan. Selections 2 and 3 highlight the crux of Strangford's overarching task: to defuse Russian-Ottoman tension and avoid war between Russia and Turkey. Documents 4, 7, 8, and 10 demonstrate the prominence of commerce in Eastern Question negotiations during this troubled period, especially in view of the disruption of trade caused by the Greek revolt. Selections 5 and 9 deal with the Chios massacre, while document 6 focuses on the festering problem of orderly governance in the Danubian principalities. All these sources are located in the Foreign Office holdings of the National Archives, Kew (TNA FO).[16] When the manuscript has a word or phrase underlined for emphasis, I have retained the original format. In most matters of wording, grammar, punctuation, and citation of numbers, I have retained Strangford's format, including his archaisms and inconsistent spellings. All explanatory material in brackets is mine.

1. TNA FO 78/106, FF. 14–16, 10 JANUARY 1822 (No. 3) (Secret)

[Strangford to Castlereagh re: the possibility of influencing Halet Efendi, the main adviser and close confidante of Sultan Mahmud II, by a bribe.][17]

Among the means which have occurred to my colleagues and to me, as likely to influence the Turkish policy in the present crisis, the employment of a sum of money has more than once been under consideration.

That Halet Efendi, the sultan's sole favourite and principal adviser, is accessible to corruption, is as certain as that his power over his imperial master is unbounded. A negotiation of this nature (supposing it to be previously authorized by Your Lordship) would of course require the utmost delicacy and circumspection. But it does not appear to be impracticable, or unlikely to be successful.

The fear of the janissaries is (confidentially) admitted by the Turkish government as a chief reason for their delay in completely evacuating the Principalities and in nominating the *hospodars*.

On <u>this</u> ground, the offer of money might be made to Halet Efendi. He might be told, that immediately on orders being given for the removal of the troops, and on the publication of a decree appointing the *hospodars*, a sum would be secretly placed in his hands, to be applied, at his sole discretion, to the purpose of quieting any opposition or discontent which those measures might excite among the janissaries.

Halet Efendi is too wealthy to be tempted by an inconsiderable offer. Perhaps one thousand purses, or between twelve and thirteen thousand pounds sterling, though in itself, a large sum, would not be considered by the allied cabinets as bearing any proportion to the expenditure of treasure which a war between Russia and Turkey might hereafter impose upon the governments of Europe.

2. TNA FO78/106, FF. 204–12A, 25 FEBRUARY 1822 (NO. 27)

[Strangford to Castlereagh re: the British ambassador's conference with Ottoman ministers on the demands submitted to the Porte by the tsarist regime.]

My conference with the Turkish ministers took place at the house of the *reis efendi* [Ottoman foreign minister] on Saturday the 16th instant.

It was originally intended by the Porte that this meeting should be of a private and confidential character; but in consideration of the important interests which it involved, I requested the Turkish ministers to consent that it should be conducted in the most formal and official way. . . .

Your Lordship will perceive that in the absence of any late instructions from His Majesty's government, I regulated my language according to the more recent intelligence which my colleagues had received from their respective courts, founded upon their knowledge of the intentions of Russia in case the Porte should not accede to her demands with regard to the Principalities.

The intelligence thus received, left no room to doubt that a further resistance to the Russian demands would be followed by war; and that the month of March would be the term of the emperor's forbearance.

On this point my conference principally turned—<u>peace</u>, and the active good offices of the allies for the future, in case the Divan should accede to the Russian propositions—<u>war</u>, and the cessation of all friendly intervention on the part of the allies if it should refuse, or delay to admit them.

In placing this alternative before the Turkish ministers, with all possible frankness, though at the same time, with all the conciliatory forms of friendship, I could hardly avoid making use of language which I fully expected would have been ill-received by Ottoman pride.

But I was completely mistaken. Everything which I uttered was placed to its true account; the friendly part which England was acting, seemed to be thoroughly and gratefully felt; and on no previous occasion did I ever experience such marked attention—such perfect amenity—and such invincible, I might say, such provoking good humour. It was difficult to avoid entertaining a suspicion that they had already made up their mind to grant what I demanded—that they were resolved to keep this determination a secret—and that they were amusing themselves with the anxiety and agitation under which they saw me evidently labouring.

There were none of those offensive allusions, upon this occasion, with which the language of the Turkish ministers formerly abounded—and no insolent reference was made to the union of the Koran and the sabre, or to the irresistible might of an Empire armed in defence of its religion.

The result of the conference may be summed in a very few words. The Russian demands were admitted in the most unequivocal manner, and a solemn promise to execute them with the least possible delay, was given, together with a declaration that the Divan was seriously occupied in actually carrying them into effect. But no positive term for the accomplishment of this engagement was appointed.

Were we to judge merely from the text of those assurances, it would certainly seem that little real progress had been made in the negotiation. But I cannot avoid thinking that I have gained much more than appears on the face of the protocol. To say nothing of the tone and manner of the Ottoman ministers, and of the various favourable indications which they presented, it is quite impossible for me to suppose that such language as that which was held to them, in the name of the king of England, can be altogether without effect. The confidence which this government places in His Majesty, and in the friendship of Great Britain, is certainly greater than that which it is disposed to shew towards any other of the allies; and I have every reason to hope that such full credit is given to us for the <u>disinterestedness</u> of our advice, as will ensure its being finally and speedily accepted.

But I have other grounds on which to found these hopes. Private assurances have been repeatedly sent to me, since the day of my conference, by some of the ministers with whom I am in more confidential relations (particularly by the *kapudan pasha* [grand admiral of the Ottoman navy]), that all matters would be settled to my satisfaction—but that I must allow the government to do things in its own way.

3. TNA FO 78/106, ff. 252–55, 25 February 1822 (No. 29)

[Strangford to Castlereagh re: the issue of direct negotiations between Russia and the Ottoman Empire.]

Your Lordship will perceive from the report of my last conference, that there is no immediate hope of inducing the Porte to accede to the very desirable proposition of opening a direct negotiation with Russia. The unconquerable feeling of Turkish pride will stand in the way of such an arrangement, and the pretence, that, as they were not the <u>first</u> to break the ordinary relations between the two governments, they are not called upon to be the <u>first</u> to renew them, will, I apprehend, be obstinately adhered to. At all times, the reluctance of the Turks to engage in negotiation at a distance from the seat of their own government, has been notorious, and I do not imagine that there is anything in the present question, which will induce them to relinquish that system of habitual distrust which characterizes them.

If the virtual admission of most of the demands of Russia (which we may consider as having already taken place), and the fair and honest execution of those which yet remain to be fulfilled, should be considered by the emperor of Russia as sufficiently re-establishing the state of things which existed previously to the departure of his minister, it is only to His Imperial Majesty's magnanimity that we can look for the renewal of the direct official intercourse between the two governments. I should deceive Your Lordship were I to indicate the slightest hope that the <u>first</u> step towards it, would be taken by the Porte. But I think that in still further satisfaction of His Imperial Majesty's dignity, it would not be found impossible to procure from the Porte, if not a positive request, at all events, the expression of a strong wish that a Russian minister should be sent to Constantinople. The principal difficulty in the way of a negotiation to obtain such a declaration from the Porte, would be the individual exception with which they would most probably seek to accompany it, and which would (perhaps with reason) be considered as offensive to the emperor's dignity.

This government has certainly manifested of late, a wish to have it generally understood that it was on the point of renewing its official relations with Russia, and the language now held upon this subject is very different from that which prevailed some time ago. There is a very wealthy and respectable corporation of Turkish merchants ... who trade with the Black Sea. These persons presented a memorial to the Porte on the 21st instant, respecting a valuable ship belonging to them, which the crew, composed of Greeks, had carried into Odessa, and sold to a Russian merchant there, at the beginning of the rebellion. The *kiahya bey* [Ottoman minister of the interior] told them, in reply, to have a little patience, and that as soon as matters were settled with Russia, their ship would undoubtedly be restored to them. This assurance not appearing to satisfy the merchants, Gianib Efendi, who was present (and who of all the Turkish ministers is the least likely to make any declaration of a pacific tendency), added—"Matters are now almost finally adjusted. I pledge myself that in one month, or in six weeks at furthest, a Russian minister will be here, and the two governments will be better friends than ever."—The satisfaction with which this intelligence was received by the public, among whom it was speedily circulated, must have proved to the Ottoman ministers (if indeed they could have had any doubt on the subject) the unpopularity of a Russian war, and the desire of all the wealthy and respectable classes for the preservation of peace with their mighty neighbour.

4. TNA FO 78/107, ff. 142–44a, 10 April 1822 (No. 47)

[Strangford to Castlereagh re: the steps taken by the Porte to repress the abuses of foreign-flagged vessels.][18]

The Turkish government continues to employ very strict measures to repress those abuses of foreign flags which have so long prevailed here, to the great disgrace of such missions as have converted them into a source of pecuniary profit.

Although the right of the Porte to investigate the nationality of the ships which enter and depart from this harbour cannot be disputed, its ignorance of European forms and usages, often leads it into wrong modes of applying a principle, otherwise perfectly justifiable in itself. Frequent disputes arise in consequence between the government and certain of the foreign ministers—and it is to be lamented that some of the latter should occasionally forget that they are called upon at this moment to watch over higher and more important interests, and should exhaust their time and their temper in paltry squabbles, and in seeking to defend cases which could not be justified according to any navigation code in Europe.

The missions to which we are indebted for the trouble and vexations now imposed upon our trade, are those of Naples, Denmark, and Holland. The chargés d'affaires of these courts have long made a public traffic of their national flags, which became at length so notorious as to rouse the attention of the Porte, and to induce her to establish a system of scrutiny, of which the inconveniences are general in their operation upon all the missions at this residence, even upon those against which no accusation has ever been urged.

Nor is it only with reference to our commerce and navigation that we have to complain of the prejudices which the respectable part of the *corps diplomatique* now suffer in consequence of the improper behaviour of the three chargés d'affaires already mentioned. The Porte seeks to retrench many of the immunities which we have enjoyed from time immemorial, on account of the flagrant abuse of them committed by some of the individuals whom we are unfortunately compelled to consider as our colleagues. I allude particularly to the right of importing wine for the use of our families. This privilege is now a daily subject of contention with the Porte, owing to the dishonourable conduct of M. Navoni, the Neapolitan agent, who has made prodigious sums of money by lending his name to the publicans of Pera, whom he has thus for several years supplied with liquors, on a fixed and most profitable percentage. The whole conduct of this man is a perpetual scandal — and I speak the sentiments of every mission here, which has the slightest regard for its own honour, when I say that it is a disgrace to the court of Naples that such a person should be charged with the conduct of its affairs, and should be permitted to prostitute the name of a public minister, in such a shameful manner as we have lately witnessed.

5. TNA FO 78/107, FF. 227–30, 25 APRIL 1822 (NO. 55)

[Strangford to Castlereagh re: the Ottoman attack on Chios and the recapture of that island by the *kapudan pasha*'s fleet.][19]

The Turkish expedition against Chios has been successful.

We are yet without complete details of this transaction, but from all that can be collected, it seems to have been productive of dreadful scenes of carnage on both sides.

On the first appearance of the *kapudan pasha*'s formidable fleet, the Greeks who were stationed between Chesme, on the mainland, and Chios (to prevent the troops assembled at the former place from crossing over), cut their cables, and effected their escape, leaving Chios to its fate.

This circumstance enabled six thousand of the Chesme troops to join the *kapudan pasha*, who, on the 11th instant proceeded to summon the insurgents to surrender, offering pardon to all who should lay down their arms, and giving them eight hours to consider . . . his proposals.

The insurgents rejected this offer—and instantly attempted to carry the castle by escalade, thinking that they could effect that object, and secure themselves in the fortress before the *kapudan pasha* could have time to disembark his troops. In this they were mistaken—they were vigorously repulsed by the garrison, and in the meanwhile, the *kapudan pasha* landing about nine thousand men, and the former making a sortie, they were enclosed between two fires; lost all their artillery, amounting to twenty pieces, which was speedily turned against them, and after a short and most bloody resistance, took to flight, and were pursued in all directions. It is said that the loss on both sides amounts to fifteen thousand men. No quarter was given after the action. Every person taken with arms in his hands was instantly put to death. The women and children have been thrown into slavery. Previously to the action, and on the first appearance of the fleet, the Catholic inhabitants had shut themselves up in their convent. They have been protected by the *kapudan pasha*, who has stationed a guard for their security, and who has received numbers of them on board of his fleet, where they are treated with the utmost kindness. The Catholic Greeks have, as Your Lordship is aware, never taken any part in the insurrection, and, as well at Chios, as in all the other islands, have constantly maintained their allegiance to the sultan.

The *kapudan pasha* has left a considerable body of troops on the island, who will, I fear, pursue the work of destruction to the very utmost. The Samiote Greeks, whose unfortunate expedition to Chios has been the cause of the calamity which has overwhelmed that once happy and flourishing island, took no part in the combat, and basely fled to Psara, hastily embarking on the side opposite to that where the Turkish troops landed.

The *kapudan pasha* is said to have proceeded to the Morea, with the intention of attacking some of the insurgent islands in his way.

I have the honour to enclose a translation of the placard which accompanied the exhibition of heads, standards, and other trophies, sent to the Porte by Vahid Pasha, the governor of Chios.

6. TNA FO 78/108, FF. 50-59, 10 May 1822 (No. 70)

[Strangford to Castlereagh re: the nomination of the new *hospodars* and the proposed changes in the administration of the Danubian principalities.][20]

At the council held on Monday, . . . [the] question of nominating the new princes [*hospodars*], and of choosing them from among the native boyars, was proposed to the *ustaas* [officers] of the janissaries who were present, and unanimously approved. The slight offered to the Greek nation by this selection, has more than any other cause, induced the janissaries to approve of the nomination of princes being carried into effect. Had the choice of the government fallen upon Greeks, I am convinced that the janissaries would have resisted to the very utmost.

In truth, the policy of the Porte seems now to be decided; and its resolution to reduce the Greek nation to a state of absolute nullity, may be considered as irrevocably fixed. That *imperium in imperio* [empire within an empire, or state within a state] which had made such silent but rapid progress during the last thirty years, will exist no longer. The great source of Greek influence, and with it, of that hitherto exercised by Russia, will now be cut off, by the employment of Turkish subjects as the future dragomans of the Porte, and by the selection of natives to govern the two Principalities. Some observations which were lately made to me on this subject by one of the most intelligent Turks I have hitherto known, are perhaps not unworthy of Your Lordship's attention.

"What has Russia gained," he asked, "by precipitating the Greek affair? For that it originated in the hopes held out by her ministers at St. Petersburg, and her agents in Turkey, no man who has his eyes and ears, can for a moment doubt. However, praise be to God, that she acted as she did. But for the conduct of her consuls in the Archipelago, and the intemperance of her minister here, in hurrying matters to an extremity, we should have gone on in a false and fatal security. The

Greeks would have, slowly perhaps, but surely, appropriated to themselves, the entire government of this Empire. In commerce and in affairs of state, they were already all powerful, and nobody among us had begun to suspect the gradual encrease of their influence. Had this state of things gone on for thirty years more, we should have been lost. Russia has done us a great service without intending it. She held a lever in her hands, with which she could at any time, have shaken this Empire to the foundation. It is now broken. She has (also without meaning it) rendered us another service. The powers of Europe have taught her, that she cannot make war upon us under flimsy pretences. I was in the ministry when the Holy Alliance was proclaimed; and when all my colleagues were frightened by it, I said, that if the sovereigns of Europe acted up to their word, the Holy Alliance would, one day, be our barrier against Russia. If I am not now in the ministry, it is owing to what I <u>then</u> said, and to the indignation with which it was received. But I was in the right. Had it not been for that alliance, which has now proved to Russia that she is but <u>one</u>, and the other states of Europe are <u>many</u>, we should have ere now been fighting against Russia for the possession of Constantinople. This result was not foreseen by Stroganoff [Stroganov] when he sought to excite his government against us. The Russian influence here is no more. She will again seek to exert it, under pretence of settling the affairs of the Principalities, and of restoring to them the blessings of peace and good order. But we mean to deprive her of this pretence. We shall anticipate her, by our new arrangements for the relief of Wallachia and Moldavia; and when her minister returns here, he will find that everything is done, and that he has no excuse for meddling in our affairs."

Your Lordship may depend upon the fidelity with which the above observations are reported.

7. TNA FO 78/108, ff. 167–69A, 10 June 1822 (No. 85)

[Strangford to Castlereagh re: the British embassy's successful resistance against the Porte's endeavor to search British ships in the harbor of Constantinople.]

Your Lordship is aware that many of the most essential of our commercial privileges here, do not depend upon the positive letter of our treaties with the Porte, but are derived from the stipulations of those subsisting between Turkey and Russia, inasmuch as the arrangement concluded in 1802, placed us upon the footing of the most favoured nation.

Whatever advantages therefore are accorded to Russia by treaty, we have a right to claim, even though they should not be specifically provided for in our own capitulations.[21]

Among the new arrangements established by the Porte for the purpose of preventing the abuses in foreign navigation which have been detected here, is the practice of causing ships to be visited at the moment of their departure, by the officers of the Porte, in order to ascertain whether the cargoes correspond with the manifests.

This new regulation has hitherto been exercised with great severity, and has been the subject of loud and violent complaints on the part of the foreign merchants.

By the 55th Article of our capitulations, the right of the Porte to make this visit or search on board of our ships is clearly admitted. But on the other hand, in her treaty with Russia, this right is as positively abrogated, as far as the navigation of that power is concerned.

Conceiving that we are entitled, in virtue of the arrangement of 1802 to every advantage possessed by Russia, I have strenuously resisted the claim set up by the Porte, to examine our ships, demanding for them, the same exemption which is accorded to those of Russia.

This attempt on my part was attended with considerable difficulty, as all the other missions here had yielded to the pretensions of the Porte, and had admitted her right of searching the ships of their respective nations.

I will not trouble Your Lordship with the details of a negotiation, which has occupied me almost incessantly for the last three weeks, and I confine myself to a communication of its successful result, as announced in the accompanying official report from my first dragoman [Francis Chabert].

The British navigation in this port is now placed upon a footing quite distinct as far as relates to the right of search, from that of any other nation. I am very unwilling that we should be exposed to the jealousy likely to arise from this circumstance, but as one of my first duties here is to assist our commerce, I cannot think that I ought to reject any exemption from inconvenience which I may be able to procure for it, from a principle of delicacy, because other missions may not have succeeded in obtaining it for their respective countries. If it were [a] question of any positive and <u>exclusive favour</u> to our commerce, I certainly should not think it worth being purchased at the price of the discontent of my colleagues, but as the present arrangement relates merely to relief from a great and serious inconvenience, I conceive that I am bound to do all that I can in behalf of my countrymen, without any tenderness for the jealous feelings of merchants belonging to other nations.

8. TNA FO 78/108, FF. 261–64, 25 JUNE 1822 (NO. 97)

[Strangford to Castlereagh re: the *reis efendi*'s confidential proposal on commercial matters.]

I have the honour to transmit a copy of an unexpected communication which has been made to me by the *reis efendi*.

After stating that the restrictive measures which have lately been adopted by this government with regard to foreign commerce, are aimed prospectively at Russia, and destined to prevent the navigation of the Greeks from being carried on almost exclusively under the flag of that country—and after renewing his promise that the British trade should continue to be exempted from the effects of the new regulations, the *reis efendi* expresses the wish of this government that the commerce of its *reaya* [tax-paying Orthodox Christian] subjects, hitherto conducted under Russian protection, should be transferred to Great Britain. He adds to this (sufficiently obscure) proposal, a request that I would concert with him as to the means of carrying the dispositions of the Porte into effect, in such a way as to be reciprocally beneficial to England and to Turkey.

Even were this overture likely to be advantageous to our commerce and navigation (which it certainly is not), I am persuaded that Your Lordship would not conceive the present to be a proper moment for accepting from the Porte any invidious distinction in our favour.

But while I act in conformity to what I presume will be Your Lordship's opinion, by declining to avail myself of the *reis efendi*'s proposition, I feel persuaded that I am not sacrificing any real advantage to the commercial interests of His Majesty's subjects. Their navigation does not require any new stipulations to support it, for the political circumstances of this Empire have, of themselves, been sufficient to place it in a more flourishing condition, and to give it a greater extension [than] it ever before possessed. The Greek carrying trade is extinct, or more properly, the greater part of it is now lodged in our hands or in those of the Ionians. It seems therefore better to leave matters as they are, and to suffer our commerce to profit by the natural course of events, without seeking to foster it by new arrangements between the two governments.

In this opinion, I have desired M. Chabert to thank the *reis efendi* for his communication; adding, however, that it was only valuable to me as a mark of His Excellency's confidence and of his good-will towards the nation with whose interests I am charged—but that I did not see how the proposal which he had made to me, could be turned to the advantage of either country. I observed, moreover, that discovering in this overture a sincere proof of his desire to favour our commerce, it would encourage me, when a proper opportunity occurred, not to make new demands in behalf of it, but to invite him to define and settle certain rights (with reference in particular to our Black Sea trade) to which we had an undoubted claim, but which had either lapsed into oblivion, or had never hitherto been recognized with sufficient precision by the Ottoman government.

9. TNA FO 78/108, FF. 303–07, 26 JUNE 1822 (NO. 101)

[Strangford to Castlereagh re: naval clashes off Chios between Greek and Ottoman ships.]

The [Austrian] internuncio [Rudolf von Lützow] having delayed the departure of the post until this day, I am enabled to have the honour of reporting to Your Lordship that most unwelcome and disastrous intelligence has arrived from the Turkish fleet before Chios.

On the night of Wednesday last, the Greeks attacked the *kapudan pasha*'s vessel (a three-decker) and two other ships of the line, with their fire ships. The crews of the two smaller vessels of the line succeeded in extinguishing the flames, but the admiral's ship was blown up, and the *kapudan pasha* perished, together with all his officers and crew. The body of the *kapudan pasha* was picked up, floating on the sea, and was interred at Chios on the following day.

I sent M. Chabert to the Porte early this morning, to ascertain from the *reis efendi* the truth of this intelligence, a rumour of which had reached me last night, but in such a vague manner that I did not report it in my dispatches to Your Lordship. The *reis efendi* fully confirmed the particulars which I have related as above; and though deeply affected with the disgrace thus brought upon the Ottoman arms, endeavoured to assume an appearance of the utmost indifference.

The loss of the finest and largest vessel in the Turkish fleet, and of the only commander of any skill in naval matters whom this government possessed, must undoubtedly be a cause of the greatest mortification to the Porte—while it will proportionally augment the audacity of the Greeks. I dread the exasperating effect which this affair may have on the public mind at Constantinople and Smyrna, and still more those measures of barbarous policy to which this government will too probably have recourse for the sake of calming it. Nor can I look without apprehension to the unfavourable influence which this disaster may have on the progress of the negotiation, which I had flattered myself was so near to a successful termination.

10. TNA FO 78/110, ff. 18–25, 3 September 1822 (No. 145)

[Strangford to Castlereagh re: Russia's demand for the retraction of Ottoman regulations on navigation in the Black Sea.]

It appears that the Russian government has invited the British and Austrian missions at St. Petersburg to propose to the internuncio and to me, the employment of our joint efforts for the purpose of procuring from the Porte the abrogation of the system on which she is now acting with respect to foreign navigation.

The Russian government, while it admits that these regulations are justified by the enormous abuses which have been committed here, and that they contain nothing contrary to treaty, discovers in them, notwithstanding, a clear indication of an unfriendly if not a decidedly hostile disposition towards Russia, on the part of the Turkish government.

The regulations of the Porte respect those nations which have not acquired by treaty the right to navigate in the Black Sea. The Turkish ministers say that this privilege was granted to those nations who enjoy it, either in consequence of a war, at the end of which the Porte yielded it, or of some amicable negotiation at which an equivalent for it was granted by the other contracting party—that the Porte is ready to concede the navigation of the Black Sea to those powers who are willing to negotiate, and to grant a fair compensation for it in some shape or other, but that she will not suffer those powers to defraud the interests of the Porte, by surreptitiously availing themselves of an advantage for which other states have been content to pay.

This is the principle on which the Porte is now acting. Its attention to the question of foreign navigation, has been provoked by the multiplied and scandalous abuses of foreign flags which have prevailed in the chanceries of the Dutch, Danish, and Neapolitan missions—abuses, which I am obliged to say, have been equally injurious to the interests of the Porte and disgraceful to the legations which have practised them.

That Russia in particular has no just ground of complaint against these regulations, may be inferred both from the fact that since the departure of her minister, the navigation of bona fide Russian vessels has been constantly respected, and has never been interrupted, but also from the indulgence which the Porte, in the very face of those regulations, has extended to vessels which have no right to be considered as <u>Russian</u>. In August last, a number of Genoese and Sardinian vessels arrived here under the Russian flag, with the intention of proceeding to the Black Sea. Their owners being apprehensive of a Russian war, changed their flag for that of France, which M. de Viella, the French chargé d'affaires, accorded to them. Under that flag they accordingly proceeded to the Black Sea; on their return from which, every one of them, on their arrival at Constantinople, was permitted by this government to resume the Russian flag, under which they had originally sailed, and to which they were in point of <u>strict right</u>, as little entitled as to that of France, or of any other country except their own.

I do not therefore perceive on what ground Russia is (at least for the present) justified in complaining against the new regulations of the Porte; nor how I can charge myself with the office of supporting these complaints.

But there is, moreover, another consideration of which, as long as it shall be my <u>first</u> duty to watch over British interests, I must not permit myself to lose sight. The restrictions of the Porte with respect to the navigation of other countries, have produced such a sudden and extensive effect in favour of that of Great Britain, and the British shipping interests in the Levant have been so greatly benefitted by their operation, and by the exclusion of, what may be termed <u>interlopers</u>, from the trade of the Black Sea, that I can hardly venture to do anything which may disturb the progress of these advantages, without Your Lordship's express commands.

NOTES

1. I am compiling four volumes of Strangford's dispatches from his ambassadorship at the Porte (1821-24). Volumes 1 and 2 have already appeared: Theophilus C. Prousis, *Lord Strangford at the Sublime Porte (1821): The Eastern Crisis* (İstanbul: Isis Press, 2010); idem, *Lord Strangford at the Sublime Porte (1822): The Eastern Crisis* (İstanbul: Isis Press, 2012). Excerpts from these works can be found in Theophilus C. Prousis, "Eastern Orthodoxy under Siege in the Ottoman Levant: A View from Constantinople in 1821," *Modern Greek Studies Yearbook* 24/25 (2008/2009): 39-72; idem, "British Embassy Reports on the Greek Uprising in 1821-1822: War of Independence or War of Religion?," *Archivum Ottomanicum* 28 (2011): 171-222. For biographical information on Strangford (1780-1855), see Prousis, *Lord Strangford at the Sublime Porte (1821)*, 326. On the Dashkov collection in the Russian State Historical Archive, St. Petersburg, and its importance for studying imperial Russian activities in the Near East, see Theophilus C. Prousis, *Russian-Ottoman Relations in the Levant: The Dashkov Archive*, Minnesota Mediterranean and East European Monographs, no. 10 (Minneapolis: Modern Greek Studies Program, University of Minnesota, 2002). Dmitrii V. Dashkov (1784-1839), an adviser at the tsarist embassy in Constantinople from 1817 to 1823, inspected Russian consulates in the Levant, visited sacred sites on Mount Athos and in Palestine, and recorded his observations on Greek and Ottoman affairs in a variety of proposals, memoranda, and dispatches.

2. The Eastern crisis of the 1820s forms part of the larger canvas of internal and external challenges that destabilized and thus restructured the Ottoman Empire in the late eighteenth and early nineteenth centuries. See Virginia H. Aksan, *Ottoman Wars, 1700-1870: An Empire Besieged* (Harlow, England: Pearson Longman, 2007), 180-342; Caroline Finkel, *Osman's Dream: The Story of the Ottoman Empire, 1300-1923* (New York: Basic Books, 2005), 289-446; Suraiya Faroqhi, ed., *The Cambridge History of Turkey*, vol. 3, *The Later Ottoman Empire, 1603-1839* (New York: Cambridge University Press, 2006); Frederick F. Anscombe, ed., *The Ottoman Balkans, 1750-1830* (Princeton, NJ: Markus Wiener, 2006); Fikret Adanir and Suraiya Faroqhi, eds., *The Ottomans and the Balkans: A Discussion of Historiography* (Leiden: Brill, 2002). European consuls often described the state of the Ottoman Empire during these unsettled times. See Theophilus C. Prousis, *British Consular Reports from the Ottoman Levant in an Age of Upheaval, 1815-1830* (İstanbul: Isis Press, 2008); G. L. Arsh, *Eteristskoe dvizhenie v Rossii: Osvoboditel'naia bor'ba grecheskogo naroda v nachale XIX v. i russko-grecheskie sviazi* (Moscow: Nauka, 1970); 29-76; Eleutherios Prevelakis and Kallia Kalliataki Mertikopoulou, eds., *Epirus, Ali Pasha, and the Greek Revolution: Consular Reports of William Meyer from Preveza*, 2 vols., Monuments of Greek History, no. 12 (Athens: Academy of Athens, 1996).

3. On the Greek revolution, see Aksan, *Ottoman Wars*, 285-305; David Brewer, *The Greek War of Independence: The Struggle for Freedom from Ottoman*

Oppression and the Birth of the Modern Greek Nation (Woodstock, NY: Overlook Press, 2003); Petros Pizanias, ed., *The Greek Revolution of 1821: A European Event* (İstanbul: Isis Press, 2011); Douglas Dakin, *The Greek Struggle for Independence, 1821-1833* (London: Batsford, 1973). For a recent Russian perspective on the Greek awakening, based largely on Russian and Greek sources, see Olga E. Petrunina, *Grecheskaia natsiia i gosudarstvo v XVIII-XX vv.: Ocherki politicheskogo razvitiia* (Moscow: KDY, 2010), 100-222. The Greek revolt exerted a profound impact on great-power politics and diplomacy in the Near East. For this European, including Russian, perspective on the Eastern quagmire of the 1820s, see M. S. Anderson, *The Eastern Question, 1774-1923* (London: Macmillan, 1966), 1-77; Paul Schroeder, *The Transformation of European Politics, 1763-1848* (Oxford: Clarendon Press, 1994), 614-21, 637-64; idem, *Metternich's Diplomacy at Its Zenith, 1820-1823* (Austin: University of Texas Press, 1962), 164-94, 223-25; A. V. Fadeev, *Rossiia i vostochnyi krizis 20-kh godov XIX veka* (Moscow: Nauka, 1958); G. L. Arsh and V. N. Vinogradov, *Mezhdunarodnye otnosheniia na Balkanakh 1815-1830 gg.* (Moscow: Nauka, 1983), 127-295.

4. With the benefit of Ottoman archives, several scholars have examined the effect of the Greek uprising on Ottoman reforms of administrative and military institutions and on the ruling hierarchy's exposure to such secular concepts as nation, citizen, liberty, and national independence. See the studies by Hakan Erdem: "'Do Not Think of the Greeks as Agricultural Labourers': Ottoman Responses to the Greek War of Independence," in *Citizenship and the Nation-State in Greece and Turkey*, ed. Faruk Birtek and Thalia Dragonas (New York: Routledge, 2005), 67-84; idem, "The Greek Revolt and the End of the Old Ottoman Order," in Pizanias, *Greek Revolution of 1821*, 257-64. Also see Nikos Theotokas and Nikos Kotaridis, "Ottoman Perceptions of the Greek Revolution," in Pizanias, *Greek Revolution of 1821*, 265-73; Vitalii Sheremet, "The Greek Revolution of 1821: A New Look at Old Problems," *Modern Greek Studies Yearbook* 8 (1992): 45-55.

5. The landmark Treaty of Kuchuk Kainardji (1774) ended Ottoman hegemony over the Black Sea region and marked imperial Russia's emergence as a Near Eastern power. In addition to the commercial, consular, and territorial concessions granted to Russia, the treaty stipulated that the sultan would protect Orthodox Christians in the Aegean Archipelago, the Danubian principalities, and western Georgia. The tsarist government subsequently, and speciously, declared that this pledge gave Russia leverage to interfere in Ottoman affairs on behalf of all Orthodox Christians. On this significant but controversial treaty, see Prousis, *Russian-Ottoman Relations in the Levant*, 5-7, 142; Aksan, *Ottoman Wars*, 157-60; Jacob C. Hurewitz, ed., *The Middle East and North Africa in World Politics: A Documentary Record*, 2nd rev. ed., 2 vols. (New Haven, CT: Yale University Press, 1975), 1:92-101; Roderic H. Davison, *Essays in Ottoman and Turkish History, 1774-1923: The Impact of the West* (Austin: University of Texas Press, 1990), 29-59. On the treaty's impact on the Greek national awakening,

see the essay by G. L. Arsh, "Gretsiia posle Kiuchuk-Kainardzhiiskogo mira," in *Istoriia Balkan: Vek vosemnadtsatyi*, ed. V. N. Vinogradov (Moscow: Nauka, 2004), 445-66.

6. On Russia's official policy toward the Greek uprising of 1821, in particular the tsar's delicate balancing act between upholding legitimacy and intervening on behalf of Greek coreligionists, see Theophilus C. Prousis, *Russian Society and the Greek Revolution* (DeKalb: Northern Illinois University Press, 1994), 26-30, 185-87; idem, *Russian-Ottoman Relations in the Levant*, 25-27; Barbara Jelavich, *Russia's Balkan Entanglements, 1806-1914* (New York: Cambridge University Press, 1991), 49-75; I. S. Dostian, *Rossiia i balkanskii vopros* (Moscow: Nauka, 1972), 196-238; Fadeev, *Rossiia i vostochnyi vopros*, 36-91; V. I. Sheremet, *Voina i biznes: Vlast', den'gi, i oruzhie; Evropa i Blizhnii Vostok v novoe vremia* (Moscow: Tekhnologicheskaia shkola biznesa, 1996), 218-86; Alexander Bitis, *Russia and the Eastern Question: Army, Government, and Society, 1815-1833* (Oxford: Oxford University Press, 2006), 104-21, 161-67.

7. On these various connections between Russia and the Greeks, see Prousis, *Russian Society and the Greek Revolution*, 3-24; Arsh, *Eteristskoe dvizhenie v Rossii*, 129-76, 200-222, 245-96; G. L. Arsh, *Grecheskaia kul'tura v Rossii XVII-XX vv.: Sbornik statei* (Moscow: Institut slavianovedeniia RAN, 1999); Iu. D. Priakhin, *Greki v istorii Rossii XVIII-XIX vekov: Istoricheskie ocherki* (St. Petersburg: Aleteiia, 2008); I. Nikolopulos, *Greki i Rossiia XVII-XX vv.: Sbornik statei* (St. Petersburg: Aleteiia, 2007). Precisely because of these deep-seated Russian-Greek ties, the Ottoman government suspected Russia's direct involvement in the Greek agitation.

8. The tsarist ultimatum of 6/18 July 1821 appears in print in Ministerstvo inostrannykh del SSSR, *Vneshniaia politika Rossii XIX i nachala XX v.: Dokumenty Rossiiskogo ministerstva inostrannykh del*, 17 vols. (Moscow: Nauka, 1960-2005), 12 (1980):203-10. The old-style Julian calendar, used in Russia until 1918, lagged twelve days behind the new-style Gregorian calendar in the nineteenth century.

9. On British policy under Foreign Secretary Castlereagh toward the Greek insurgence and the larger Eastern crisis in 1821-22, see Charles Webster, *The Foreign Policy of Castlereagh, 1815-1822: Britain and the European Alliance*, 2nd ed. (London: G. Bell, 1934), 349-86; Charles W. Crawley, *The Question of Greek Independence: A Study of British Policy in the Near East, 1821-1833* (Cambridge: Cambridge University Press, 1930; repr., New York: H. Fertig, 1973), 17-42; V. N. Vinogradov, *Velikobritaniia i Balkany: Ot Venskogo kongressa do Krymskoi voiny* (Moscow: Nauka, 1985), 31-55, for a Russian view of Castlereagh's policy.

10. On Strangford's efforts at the Porte, see the essay by Allan Cunningham ("Lord Strangford and the Greek Revolt") in Allan Cunningham, *Anglo-Ottoman Encounters in the Age of Revolution: Collected Essays*, ed. Edward Ingram (London: Frank Cass, 1993), 188-232; Radu R. Florescu, *The Struggle against Russia in the Romanian Principalities: A Problem in Anglo-Turkish Diplomacy, 1821-1854* (Iaşi: Center for Romanian Studies, 1997), 109-12, 123-47; idem, "Lord Strangford

and the Problem of the Danubian Principalities, 1821-24," *Slavonic and East European Review* 39, no. 93 (1963): 472-88; Crawley, *Question of Greek Independence*, 17-22; W. David Wrigley, *The Diplomatic Significance of Ionian Neutrality, 1821-1831* (New York: Peter Lang, 1988), 156-62, 166-69, 177-86; Irby C. Nichols Jr., "Hellas Scorned: The Affair of the Ambassadorial Address to the Greeks, 1821," *East European Quarterly* 9, no. 3 (1975): 279-92. For a more nuanced and complete picture of Strangford's observations and negotiations, see the first two volumes of my Strangford compendium, cited above in note 1.

11. Prousis, *Lord Strangford at the Sublime Porte (1821)*, 68-69, 77-78.

12. On the executions and other excesses in Constantinople, see Brewer, *Greek War of Independence*, 103-11; Christine M. Philliou, *Biography of an Empire: Governing Ottomans in an Age of Revolution* (Berkeley: University of California Press, 2011), 71-73, 85-86, 91, 210-13; Robert Walsh, *A Residence at Constantinople*, 2 vols. (London: F. Westley and A. H. Davis, 1836), 1:308-20.

13. On the Chios disaster, see Brewer, *Greek War of Independence*, 154-67, largely based on the contemporary diplomatic accounts, including some of Strangford's writings, published in Philip P. Argenti, ed., *The Massacres of Chios Described in Contemporary Diplomatic Reports* (London: John Lane, 1932). Also see William St. Clair, *That Greece Might Still Be Free: The Philhellenes in the War of Independence*, 2nd rev. ed. (Cambridge: Open Book, 2008), 78-81, 227; Helen Long, *Greek Fire: The Massacres of Chios* (Bristol, England: Abson Books, 1992), 9-113; Davide Rodogno, *Against Massacre: Humanitarian Interventions in the Ottoman Empire, 1815-1914; The Emergence of a European Concept and International Practice* (Princeton, NJ: Princeton University Press, 2012), 66-72; Gary J. Bass, *Freedom's Battle: The Origins of Humanitarian Intervention* (New York: Knopf, 2008), 67-75. Philip Mansel, in *Levant: Splendour and Catastrophe on the Mediterranean* (London: John Murray, 2010), 50, writes: "Chios was the first Levantine paradise to be destroyed. The Greek island which least wanted independence suffered most because of it."

14. Prousis, *Lord Strangford at the Sublime Porte (1821)*, 137-41.

15. On the views of European travelers, consuls, and other visitors who recorded their observations of the Ottoman Levant in the eighteenth and nineteenth centuries, see Allan Cunningham, *Eastern Questions in the Nineteenth Century: Collected Essays*, ed. Edward Ingram (London: Frank Cass, 1993), 72-107; Prousis, *Lord Strangford at the Sublime Porte (1821)*, 43-44, 335. On British literary and travelogue descriptions of the Ottoman Empire in particular, see Gerald Maclean, *The Rise of Oriental Travel: English Visitors to the Ottoman Empire, 1580-1720* (New York: Palgrave Macmillan, 2004); idem, *Looking East: English Writing and the Ottoman Empire before 1800* (New York: Palgrave Macmillan, 2007); Filiz Turhan, *The Other Empire: British Romantic Writings about the Ottoman Empire* (New York: Routledge, 2003); Christine Laidlaw, *The British in the Levant: Trade and Perceptions of the Ottoman Empire in the Eighteenth Century* (New York: Tauris, 2010). Tsar Nicholas I coined the term "sick man" when

contemplating the Ottoman Empire's imminent demise. See Orlando Figes, *The Crimean War: A History* (New York: Metropolitan Books, 2011), 105; Trevor Royle, *Crimea: The Great Crimean War, 1854-1856* (New York: Palgrave Macmillan, 2004), 10, 26.

16. See Prousis, *Lord Strangford at the Sublime Porte (1822)*, 27-28, 62-67, 92-93, 105-6, 126-29, 149-50, 166-67, 174-75, 231-33.

17. Strangford's correspondence in 1821-22 (see the many references in the first two volumes of my Strangford project) made frequent reference to this prominent Ottoman official. As a close adviser to Mahmud II, Halet Efendi (Mehmed Said) supported the sultan's political drive to restore centralized absolute rule and to curb the powers of *ayans*, or provincial notables, in Anatolia and the Balkans. In organizing some of the military expeditions against regional chieftains, Halet sought to strengthen his own antireform base among the janissaries and their allies and to eliminate contenders for power in the provinces. While he ardently backed the suppression of Ali Pasha's revolt, he worked against the sultan's proposed military reforms. A target of growing criticism because of Ottoman military setbacks in the Peloponnese in 1821, Halet Efendi eventually fell from favor in the sultan's inner circle. Exiled from the capital, Halet Efendi was executed on the sultan's orders in late 1822. See Finkel, *Osman's Dream*, 430-31; Aksan, *Ottoman Wars*, 285-89, 314; Philliou, *Biography of an Empire*, 43-44, 54-59, 75-77, 96-99, 103; Brewer, *Greek War of Independence*, 103, 109, 166.

18. The topic of abuses committed by European-flagged merchant vessels in the Ottoman East belongs to the larger story of the capitulations—the capitulatory agreements between the Porte and European powers, including the numerous irregularities and misuses that became part of the capitulatory system in Ottoman-European relations. For an overview, with the relevant bibliography, see Maurits H. van den Boogert, *The Capitulations and the Ottoman Legal System: Qadis, Consuls, and Beratlis in the 18th Century* (Leiden: Brill, 2005); Prousis, *British Consular Reports from the Ottoman Levant*, 15-22, 103-5, 127-28, 167-68, 229-32.

19. This report appears in Argenti, *Massacres of Chios*, 11-12.

20. Strangford made abundant reference to the status of the Danubian principalities during the Eastern turmoil, focusing in particular on the evacuation of Ottoman troops and the appointment of new *hospodars*. The disturbances of 1821 prompted the sultan to replace Greek Phanariote governors with *hospodars* drawn from native boyars in Moldavia and Wallachia. See Philliou, *Biography of an Empire*, 65-104; Florescu, *Struggle against Russia in the Romanian Principalities*, 124-42.

21. On British capitulations in the Ottoman Empire, see Hurewitz, *Middle East and North Africa*, 1:34-41, 189-91.

The Aurut Bazaar, or Slave Market. (lithograph from Thomas Allom, *Constantinople and the Scenery of the Seven Churches of Asia Minor, Illustrated. In a Series of Drawings from Nature by Thomas Allom. With an Historical Account of Constantinople, and Descriptions of the Plates, by the Rev. Robert Walsh* [London: Fisher, Son, 1838], vol. 1)

Slaves of the Sultan
Russian Ransoming of Christian Captives during the Greek Revolution, 1821–1830

LUCIEN J. FRARY

The people of Russian lands were involved in the Crimean Tatar and Ottoman slave trade from at least the second half of the fifteenth century.[1] By the sixteenth century, Crimean Tatars, Nogais, Kalmyks, and Kazakhs raided Russian territories annually, with the goal of enslaving as many Russians as they could take away. Disputes over ransom prices, conflicts regarding fugitives, hazardous exchanges of plunder and military captives, bandit raids, and territorial rivalries were common realities in the shared Russian-Ottoman frontier.[2] Commercial connections and cultural interactions, infused at times by religious antagonism, guaranteed close, if discordant, contacts between the people living along the margins of empires. Despite fresh interest in borderland studies and the relatively large literature devoted to the Russian-Ottoman wars, the fates of the men and women captured and enslaved in the borderland conflicts of the eighteenth and nineteenth century remain an unexplored avenue of scholarship.[3] Indeed, the study of war captives in general is a neglected field, not only in the context of the Eastern Question but also in the history of the modern world before the twentieth century. Detailed studies of the operational, strategic, and diplomatic aspects of the Russian-Ottoman wars exist, but few European scholars and Russian specialists have attempted to determine the fate of war captives, even though archival sources are perhaps more accessible to researchers in Europe and Russia than to their Turkish colleagues.[4] This chapter attempts to uncover a small portion of this experience, by focusing on the Christians enslaved by Ottomans during the Greek Revolution and the Russian Empire's attempt to redeem them.[5] The Russian response to the sectarian violence that accompanied the taking of slaves is an important subtheme of this chapter. The violence was so severe that many Russian officials described the Ottoman response to the Greek Revolution as a "war of extermination."

In the early months of 1821, when the Sublime Porte received news of the Greek revolt, the Islamic authorities called on all faithful Muslims to avenge the actions of the Christian insurgents. Subsequently, Ottoman soldiers stormed the settlements of Orthodox Christians throughout the Aegean Islands, the Peloponnese, and the Greek-speaking mainland, capturing, pillaging, and enslaving entire populations. Thousands of the *reaya* (Ottoman tax-paying subjects) ended up as slaves in Muslim households and farms, where they began new lives as servants, laborers, and, in some cases, companions of their Muslim masters. Of course, the enslavement of prisoners was in no respect the monopoly of the Ottomans. This practice was typical and, at times, officially sanctioned by European powers, at least until the eighteenth century.[6] Although historians have often underscored the harsh repression of the Ottoman government and Muslim civilian population against the Christian Orthodox, part of the violence can be explained by the actions of the Greek insurgents in the opening phase of the conflict. As the insurrection spread, Greek rebels rounded up, enslaved, sold, and slaughtered Muslims and Ottoman civil servants (especially tax officials) in Arcadia, Monemvasia, Navarino, Kalamata, Tripolitza, and elsewhere. The spotlight here is on one side of this phenomenon: individuals who began their lives as free Ottoman Christians, but who became subject to slavery once the revolt against the sultan permitted their capture according to Islamic law (sharia).

Research for this chapter draws principally from Russian consular archives.[7] By the early nineteenth century, Russia maintained permanent consular posts at the most significant centers of trade and strategic influence in the "Christian East" (i.e., the jurisdiction of the Ecumenical Patriarchate, from the Balkans to Egypt).[8] The duties of Russian consular agents in the major towns and cities of the Ottoman Empire ranged widely. Consuls were expected to keep detailed records of the economic conditions within their sphere of jurisdiction, which made them well acquainted with commercial routes and cargos. Agents were required to gather information on military affairs and naval exercises and compose summary reports on politics and society for their superiors in Constantinople and St. Petersburg. On the eve of the outbreak of the Greek Revolution, Russia had posts (often staffed by non-Russians, especially Greeks) at İstanbul, the Dardanelles, Alexandria, Smyrna, Athens, Patras, Santorini, Cyprus, and other regions in the eastern Mediterranean and the Balkans. Largely untapped sources from embassy and consular posts, such as İstanbul (Grigorii Stroganov, Matvei Minchaki), Smyrna (Spyridon Destunis), the Aegean archipelago (Ioannis Vlassopoulos), the Dardanelles and Thessaloniki (Angelos Mustoksidi), and northern Greece (Ioannis Paparrigopoulos) present abundant firsthand testimony on the Greek revolt, the sectarian violence committed on both sides of the conflict, and the rivalries among European powers in the Near East.

Russian foreign ministry archives also contain scores of petitions for tsarist help from distressed relatives of captives. Family members and friends of the Christian prisoners of war made immediate efforts to redeem them. Individuals, as well as entire families, were relocated to places as distant as eastern Anatolia, the Rhodope mountains, and Egypt. Hundreds of people faced tragic dilemmas and searched for the means and methods to locate relatives. As Orthodox Christians (often with connections in diaspora centers in southern Russia), many injured parties naturally sought the protection of the Russian Empire. Greek supplicants of Constantinople were perhaps the most vociferous. Grievances, private letters, even poems and songs found in files at the Archive of the Foreign Policy of Imperial Russia contain fascinating stories of scores of slaves.[9] Written or transcribed in amazingly diverse orthography in Russian, Italian, Greek, French, and Turkish by rich and poor, literate and illiterate individuals, these untapped sources provide a rare glimpse into life during uncertain times. Furthermore, Russian archival materials shed fresh light on the Ottoman judicial procedure, ethnic customs, Muslim and Christian gender roles, and the functioning of slavery as an institution. Finally, Russian consular reports reveal one of the first state-driven humanitarian interventions of the nineteenth century and probe the roots of humanitarian movements and government responses in the nineteenth-century Ottoman Empire.[10]

Ottoman Responses to the Outbreak of the Greek Revolution

The Greek Revolution began in February 1821 when Alexander Ypsilantis, a dashing lieutenant general in the Russian army, led an army of a few thousand volunteers across the Pruth into Moldavia and announced a Balkan-wide uprising against the sultan. Issuing a proclamation summoning Greeks to participate in "the fight for faith and motherland," Ypsilantis sent written appeals to the tsar for aid.[11] Although Ypsilantis's forces in the Danubian principalities (Moldavia and Wallachia) failed to achieve success, a series of unrelated rebellions broke out in the Peloponnese and on the Greek mainland in the following weeks. Meanwhile, the Greek merchant marine began attacking Ottoman vessels in the Aegean, while smaller revolts against contingents of Ottoman soldiers erupted in Attica, Thessaly, and Epirus. A decade of warfare ensued that laid waste to vast territories and destroyed countless lives. The Greeks, disorganized, prone to infighting, and typically low on funds, often stood near complete defeat. Atrocities occurred on both sides, as religious and social antagonisms exacerbated ethnic tensions.[12]

From the beginning, the Greek-Ottoman confrontation was fought with incredible brutality.[13] Perhaps based more on religious than nationalist distinctions, recent scholarship has pointed to the wider array of motivations behind the pattern of excesses and atrocities, including calculated political strategy, family feuds, territorial disputes, and economic discrimination. In the terrible opening months of the revolution, scores of thousands of Turks and Greeks died, while only a small portion of them lost their lives to actual combat. In Kalavryta and Kalamata, Greek irregulars massacred the Muslim population, despite promises of sparing them. In innumerable villages, the Christians slaughtered entire Muslim populations, including at least fifteen thousand (of a population of forty thousand) in the Peloponnese alone.[14] Perhaps the most infamous Greek massacre of Muslims occurred at Tripolitza in October 1821, when the capitulation of the besieged Ottoman garrison turned into a chaotic assault as notorious as the worst atrocities of the twentieth century.[15] Muslim male and female inhabitants of all ages were annihilated, their stone buildings destroyed, their farmhouses burned. In Missolonghi, in western Greece, entire families were exterminated, and women were enslaved by wealthy Greek families.[16] In Patras, the relatively well-organized Greek inhabitants rallied behind the banner of their archbishop, Germanos, who informed the Russian consul Ioannis Vlassopoulos of their "firm resolution to die before submitting to the yoke."[17] In late March, some five thousand armed Greeks stormed the town's citadel, laying waste to Muslim dwellings. In response, Vlassopoulos lamented, "the intimidated Turkish government" was readying a large group of troops from Rumelia to put down the insurgents in Patras without mercy. "The Turks, unsettled by their belief of an impending emancipation," were no longer in a state to listen to reason. "Despairing of my inability to efface this vulgar spirit, and the impressions motivated by deception, perversity, and prejudice," Vlassopoulos warned, "the disruption of order in this country appears all too imminent."[18] On Palm Sunday, 3 April, in retaliation for Greek excesses, an Ottoman force under Iussuf Pasha attacked the city, surprising the rebels and forcing them to take flight.

In the wake of the Ottoman military victory at Patras, Ottoman soldiers took revenge on the Greeks for their earlier brutality by setting their houses on fire. The troops went berserk, beheading forty Greeks, desecrating their corpses, and turning the once-bustling commercial port into a wasteland. Reverend Robert Walsh, the chaplain of the British embassy, reported a rumor circulating in İstanbul that "certain sacks filled with two thousand five hundred pair of ears cut off from the slain [were] sent as a present to the sultan by the pasha, as vouchers for his victory." Exhibited before the gate of the Seraglio in piles, "the ears were generally perforated, and hanging on strings. The noses had one lip and a part of the forehead attached to them, the chins had the other, with generally a long beard; sometimes the face was cut off whole, and all the features remained together."[19]

Vlassopoulos was forced to depart after his home was set on fire by a Muslim mob.[20] He attributed the insurrection to the Greek's desire to "escape from the yoke of slavery" and "deliver themselves from the evils of despotism." Much to his dismay, Vlassopoulos learned that the Russian consular agent in Navarino had been killed.[21] The Russian vice consul on Zante, Antoine F. Sandrini, estimated total losses of the Christian community at Patras, at 180 million piastres.[22]

Particularly violent confrontations between Christians and Muslims took place in Constantinople, Smyrna, and Samos.[23] Perhaps the most conspicuous example of blatant violence against the innocent occurred when, on Easter Sunday, an urban mob in İstanbul executed the eighty-year-old ecumenical patriarch, Grigorios V, and other prominent members of the clergy. The Ottomans displayed his corpse, with those of five bishops, on a gate in the Greek quarter with a *fetva* (religious ruling) accusing him, pinned to his body. Reverend Walsh recorded that the rabble of the city reveled in defiling the patriarch's body and cast it into the harbor.²⁴

The execution and defilement of the patriarch created one of the most intense confrontations in the diplomatic history of the Eastern Question. Claiming that the violence against Orthodox churches and clergy violated the Treaty of Kuchuk Kainardji (1774), the Russian government attempted to intervene, putting forward humanitarian motives. The Russian ambassador to the Sublime Porte, Grigorii Stroganov, sought a collective statement on behalf of the European powers, condemning the execution of the patriarch and the massacres of innocent Christians. Stroganov argued that a "specter of religious war" was threatening the Near East, warning of the "religious fanaticism of the Turks" against the Christians.²⁵ He complained bitterly: "The blood of our brothers flows all around, and the innocent are exterminated in the street to avenge a few of the guilty," and claimed that "if the Turks continued exterminating the Greek nation [*les Turcs continuent, s'ils ne tendent qu'à exterminer la nation grecque*]," Russia would have to intervene.²⁶ After months of negotiations, the Ottoman divan refused to accept a Russian ultimatum regarding the security of Orthodox Christians and their churches. In late July, Stroganov formally broke relations and departed from the Ottoman capital, barely escaping imprisonment by Ottoman authorities himself.²⁷

The public execution of the ecumenical patriarch, together with the atrocities against numerous bishops and clergy, set the tone for future Russian-Ottoman relations. News reports regarding the massacres of Christians and the enslavement of women and children sparked an intense reaction from the Russian public. The defilement of the corpse of the patriarch symbolized the Ottoman attitude toward Eastern Orthodox Christians in general and turned the Greek rebellion into a sacred national crusade. The religious dimension of the conflict fueled what Russian officials increasingly perceived as a war of extermination (*guerre d'extermination*) against infidels, an unwelcome prototype of the "ethnic cleansing" of the following century.²⁸ By 1826, Russian foreign minister Karl V. Nesselrode warned of "the extermination of the Greeks of the Morea and their replacement with Egyptians" and called for a "mediation to interpose in favor of the Greeks before the Egyptian Pasha [would] conquer the region and exterminate the inhabitants." Ominously, Nesselrode conjured the image of "an existing plan, or some sort of convention between the Pasha of Egypt and the Porte that [had] as its goal the extermination of the Greeks [*qui auroit pour but l'extermination des grecques*]."[29] European observers responded with outrage; hundreds of volunteers flooded into Greece with their romantic fantasies and heady dreams of freedom and independence, in what historians have later described as the Philhellenic movement.[30] Meanwhile, European cabinets and the Russian Foreign Ministry struggled to maintain the status quo and prevent the Greek rebellion from igniting a general conflagration of the Eastern Question.[31]

The Greek insurgency created a terrifying threat to European peace. Whereas the actions in İstanbul were committed in plain sight and in front of European observers, other atrocities were committed in a less public venue, far from journalistic eyes. In June 1821, the Muslim authorities and civilians of the prosperous commercial port of Smyrna plundered the Greek quarter of the city and murdered hundreds of Christians. Unruly janissaries together with random violence between Christians and Muslims caused sectarian friction, social chaos, and a complete breakdown of trade. Writing from Smyrna in July, Russian consul Spyridon Destunis recorded the following impressions in his diary: "Throngs of armed janissaries roamed about the city in the morning and committed various outrages. They killed Greeks, both men and women, whomever they happened to come across. It was a terrifying, unforgettable day! They resembled hunters pursuing people as their prey! To see defenseless, unarmed Christians falling like sheep from the bullets and sword blows of these hard-hearted criminals!"[32] Of Greek extraction, Destunis sympathized with the Christians involved. The severance of Russian-Ottoman relations forced him to abandon his post.[33] Out of humanitarian concern for the Christian population, the Russian Foreign Ministry prepared plans for military intervention. Unilateral intervention, however, was not an option, as Tsar Alexander set international collaboration above humanitarian motives.

Of all the major trading centers of the Aegean, the island of Chios became the focal point of particularly vicious Ottoman vengeance. In the years preceding the Greek Revolution, no area of the empire was more blessed by good fortune. Western influences were strong due to centuries of intermittent occupation by Italian city-states. The islanders had enriched themselves through commerce and the production of cotton, silk, and citrus fruit. Besides a few hundred soldiers in the garrison of the harbor of Chora, the island's central town, the Muslim-Turkish presence was minimal. A light tax burden and a high degree of local autonomy brought prosperity to the Chiotes. The British army officer Thomas Gordon described the Chiotes before the Greek insurrection as "mild, gay, lively, acute, industrious, and proverbially timid, they succeeded alike in commerce and literature; the females were noted for their charms and grace, and the whole people, busy and contented, neither sought nor wished for a change in their political condition."[34] Unfortunately for the islanders, their Greek-speaking relatives held visions of independence that were more ambitious.

When news of the uprising reached Chios, the native leadership professed their loyalty to the sultan and promised to abstain from action. The arrival of rebel messengers from Hydra, led by Lykourgos Logothetis, and approximately fifteen hundred refugees from Samos ended the island's tranquility. This Greek horde looted Muslim warehouses, defamed mosques, and filled their vessels with treasure. In April 1822, the Ottoman garrison exchanged cannon fire with a contingent of Greeks. The clash resulted in the dispatching of a powerful Ottoman fleet under the *kapudan pasha* Kara Ali with more than four thousand Muslim infantry. When they arrived, these troops inflicted horrendous reprisals on the Christian inhabitants.[35] According to Gordon, "Mercy [among the Ottomans] was out of the question, the victors butchering indiscriminately all who came in their way; shrieks rent the air, and the streets were strewed with the dead bodies of old men, women, and children; even the inmates of the hospital, the madhouse, and the deaf and dumb institution, were inhumanely slaughtered."[36] European observers concur that thousands of persons of every age and sex were massacred at the storming of the island.[37] Thousands were enslaved and more than twenty thousand hanged, starved, or tortured to death.

As refugees and asylum seekers clustered together for safety in numbers, the Ottoman soldiers turned from massacre to the more profitable business of enslavement. Gordon estimated that by the end of May 1822, forty-five thousand Chiotes had been dragged into slavery.[38] Although the Ottoman *kapudan pasha* Kara Ali attempted to ban the export of slaves, he thought otherwise upon learning that the soldiers were executing their prisoners instead.[39] Ships laden with captives soon appeared in the slave marts of Constantinople, Egypt, and the Barbary Coast. The slave market at Smyrna attracted Muslim buyers from all parts of Asia Minor. The flood of fresh captives brought prices down, and captives from Chios were being sold for as little as fifty Turkish *kuruş* (i.e., two bits).[40]

Reverend Walsh had difficulty conveying the scope of atrocities when he visited Chios a few months after its destruction. According to his estimate, the original population of seventy thousand had been reduced to less than half. Towns had been attacked, houses destroyed, and lives wasted. "If you think the ruins of Chios like any other effects of modern war, you are entirely deceived," he wrote. "We met nothing that had life, in the country no more than in the city; the very birds seemed to have been scared away by the carnage."[41] He went on to describe terrified young girls in the slave market who had lost all chance of redemption. In Europe and Russia, the events on Smyrna and Chios swayed public opinion overwhelmingly in favor of the Greeks.

In the wake of the Chios massacre, European and Russian newspapers began reporting the details of the atrocities, particularly the taking of slaves. Accounts of atrocities committed by Muslims against Christians clearly outranked the memory of the massacres of Muslims in Philhellene and Western press accounts.[42] In France, Eugène Delacroix painted his gigantic oil *Les Scènes des Massacres de Scio*, which created an immense impression on the public when it was unveiled. In the center of the work stands a naked Greek woman in the ropes of slavery, as well as a woman being raped by a Turk in a fez. Another Delacroix painting, *La Grèce sur les ruines de Missolonghi*, is an allegory of vanquished Greece imploring European assistance.[43] These works of art fueled public debate already kindled by the Philhellenic movement and various philanthropic organizations. Rescuing the Greeks from slavery and destruction became a common theme of European and Russian art and journalism as the movement for abolition of slavery gained momentum.

The dramatization of the Greek-Ottoman cataclysm by Delacroix and other contemporaries has dominated the historical narrative obscuring a more accurate view. As the Philhellenes continued to engage in "freedom fighting," the Ottoman army remained firmly committed to putting down the revolt. Furthermore, the sultan's policy toward enslaved war captives was not always malicious.[44] For example, in Bursa in August 1822, some Ottoman soldiers and officials wanted to sell some of the boys and girls that had been enslaved on Chios, but the authorities intervened and ordered the return of these slaves to their homes because they were members of pardoned villages. A *fetva* was issued indicating that it was contrary to the sharia to enslave pardoned *reaya*. The Ottoman government dealt carefully in certain cases of unlawful enslavement of Christians and investigated scenarios that appeared contrary to the religious law.[45]

Despite the public furor, the European powers remained reluctant to intervene. In the years following the outbreak of the revolution, thousands of Christians in the Greek provinces were rounded up by Ottoman troops and retailed to Muslims who had the means to acquire them. Ottoman slave traders regularly sold individuals in public slave markets to the highest bidder. European observers, rather hypocritically, were appalled by the phenomenon. Russia, as the traditional protector of Orthodox Christians, responded by launching a nationwide relief campaign to redeem the Christian captives.

Ottoman Enslavement of Christian Captives: The Russian Response

As the only independent Orthodox nation in the world, the Russian state and society reacted with determination against Ottoman anti-Christian reprisals. Leading officials in the Russian Ministry of Foreign Affairs, the Holy Synod, the War Ministry, and other echelons of the state apparatus launched a nationwide relief effort. This remarkable act of philanthropy led to the collection of hundreds of thousands of rubles from the Russian people and the imperial family. The process began in November 1822, when the Russian Holy Synod issued an *ukaz* calling for donations. "The generosity of the Russian church consists, as always, as an energetic paradigm of the exploits of love for Christianity." The stated goal was the ransoming and resettling of "Greeks taken into captivity as slaves by Ottoman soldiers in Sidon, Kassandra, and on the island of Chios."[46] In the following months, Russian consuls and their agents extended their search to encompass the whole Near East.

Although a thorough survey of the Ottoman system of slavery lies outside the confines of this chapter, some comments may help clarify the conditions and process of enslavement that the Greek captives endured. Distinct from the form of slavery imposed by Europeans on plantation field workers in the New World, the Ottoman system of slavery was not based on the *need* for human labor, nor was the Ottoman system arguably as onerous as the serfdom imposed on the peasantry of Eastern Europe during the same period. Generalizations of this sort are a chancy business, but the "comparatively mild character" of Ottoman bondage was due, in part, to the fact that owners did not esteem their slaves primarily for their economic usefulness. Although enslaved people in Ottoman domains typically did not want to remain in a condition of bondage, the Ottoman system of enslavement tended to exhibit a sense of "attachment" or "mode of belonging" to a social unit or group, such as a family or a household and brought certain economic and psychological advantages.[47] Although scholars in the past two decades have begun to challenge perceptions regarding the "good treatment" of Ottoman slaves, the combination of Ottoman laws and social guidelines that affected the lives of slaves deserves our attention, if not approbation.[48]

In all premodern Islamic societies, private individuals could own slaves. Islam sanctioned slavery as long as the captive individuals were not already Muslim and had not submitted to a Muslim ruler through the traditional capitation tax. Whereas many societies developed forms of slavery, few exhibited such a diverse and stratified system of human bondage as did the Ottoman society. There were many types of Ottoman slaves, including elite military-administrative slaves and female consorts or wives, nonelite agricultural and industrial slaves, and menial bondsmen and bondswomen.[49] The backbone of the Ottoman military machine (the janissary corps) was founded on the *devshirme* ("gathering" or "handpicking")—a type of enslavement. Under the *devshirme*, Ottoman officials took male Christian children, usually ranging in age from seven to eighteen, from Christian families (primarily in the Balkans) at an interval of several years and trained them in the military and administration.[50] Many captives from conquered lands also performed domestic tasks in Ottoman households. Slaves were used to satisfy the desires of Ottoman notables for prestige; conspicuous consumption played a part in elite households. Furthermore, Ottoman magnates often employed large and well-armed slave households for the purposes of personal safety and political power. Precaution and pragmatism impelled Ottoman dignitaries to regard their slaves with at least a modicum of respect, if not kindness, especially since they could be well armed, disciplined, and trained.

When the Ottomans were in a position of military supremacy, most of the enslaved people of the empire were prisoners of war, acquired through conquest in Europe, the Black Sea, and the Mediterranean. By the eighteenth century, most people became slaves through commerce rather than warfare. This was mainly due to the slowing pace of military conquest as well as the shifting nature of the global slave trade. After the great period of Ottoman expansion, the original sources of slaves, based on military success, shifted to a system of networking in human bondage. Crimean Tatar merchants provided the bulk of supply for the Black Sea trade until the mid-eighteenth century; numerous towns and cities of North Africa served as markets for the demand of Mediterranean, Indian Ocean, and Persian Gulf consumers. İstanbul and Cairo, the two largest cities of the empire, constituted the principle destination points for markets dealing in slaves. Estimates regarding the quantity of slaves indicate that approximately sixteen thousand to eighteen thousand men and women were transported into the Ottoman Empire from Africa per year during most of the nineteenth century.[51]

It is impossible to know how many Christians the Ottomans took into slavery during the Greek Revolution or from where. Russian archives contain petitions from locations such as Trebizond, Smyrna, Crete, and Missolonghi, which represented additional targets of Christian enslavement. Remote areas such as Monemvasia, Samothrace, and the island of Psara figure large in the tally of Greek Christian slaves.[52] Overall, most captives appear to have been women and children. If entire families were captured, often the reports say nothing more than, for example: "Stephanos the Greek merchant's family was taken captive on the island." That the Ottoman market was still flooded with slaves five years after hostilities ceased serves as one indicator of the volume of human trafficking. For example, while in the bazaar in Constantinople in 1834, Konstantin Bazili, a well-known Russian diplomat, traveler, and author, observed that "attractive female slaves were valued from 15 to 25,000 piastres (5 to 5,000 rubles); but if she [was] really beautiful and of a good height, the value could rise to 40,000 or 50,000 piastres."[53]

The highest echelons of Russian officialdom could not resist the temptation to intervene. The enslavement of Greek-Christians generated a serious, sustained effort to ransom the captives, on behalf of the Russian state and society, involving nobles as well as peasants, even serfs(!).[54] Thousands of unnamed Russians, in addition to members of the imperial family, donated substantial sums. A special commission was formed in Constantinople to locate the captives. This risky business involved a handful of the tsar's most loyal Greeks.

Although the paper trail extended from obscure Aegean islands, Black Sea ports, St. Petersburg, and beyond, the main undertaking of slave manumission resided with Russian consuls and their agents in Ottoman territories. Russian consuls served as the principle mediators in ransoming Christian captives. The governor of Novorossiia and Bessarabia, Mikhail S. Vorontsov, who proposed that the Russian state become more involved, triggered concrete action. He had need for concern, for Odessa, the wealthiest Greek center in Russia, was being flooded by thousands of refugees. Greek communities also set an example by contributing pledges to assist those fleeing hostilities as soon as the revolution broke out. Impressive personal offerings came from prominent merchant-philanthropist families.[55]

In June 1824, Vorontsov ordered Matvei Minchaki (Minciaky), the chargé d'affaires of the Russian embassy in the Ottoman capital, to employ the significant resources now at his disposal (one hundred thousand Ottoman piastres) to locate and ransom Christian slaves.[56] Vorontsov wrote, "Since the disasters at Chios in 1822, a subscription has been opened in Russia for the ransoming of the unfortunate Greeks who have fallen into slavery. This subscription has produced considerable funds. A committee composed of the principle refugee bishops of Bessarabia has been in charge of collection." Acknowledging the difficulties embedded in the task, Vorontsov advised him "to acquire information about numerous individuals [they knew had] been enslaved."[57] He also instructed Minchaki to form a commission of people of integrity who would assist him. Ottoman regulations on the slave trade were to be followed punctiliously. Vorontsov included a special short list of about a dozen Greeks who had fallen into slavery: Aspasia Silvia (the niece of a Russian naval officer); two daughters of Artietu Ataliotissa (a Greek merchant), now residing in Bursa and İstanbul; Zanni, son of Antonio Evmorfopoulos (a Greek merchant in İstanbul); Michael and Coco Parembli, from Smyrna; Stamatis and Nikorisi, sons of Andreas Jalussi of İstanbul; and several others.[58]

Not long after receiving his instructions, Minchaki discovered that the two Ataliotissa daughters were going to be sold in the public marketplace in Constantinople. Since time was of the essence, he employed a Greek from Smyrna named Psaki to verify the girls' identity. Upon confirmation, he gave the mother 4,500 piastres (2,565 rubles) to ransom her daughters.[59] Although beginning in rather piecemeal fashion, this sort of endeavor provided Minchaki and his agents with the experience to continue on a larger scale.

By January 1825, Minchaki had succeeded in forming a special commission dedicated to ransoming Christian slaves. Vorontsov's instructions regarding how he was to employ the one hundred thousand piastres were clear: first, the commission was not to dissolve until the slaves mentioned were liberated; second, agents involved were to ensure the credibility of the transactions and obtain receipts; third, they were to collect as much information as possible about other slaves; and fourth, a certain Mr. Pezer, a merchant from Smyrna and Constantinopolitan, was to act as the primary negotiator. No money was to be exchanged until the name, owner, location, and price was established. An appendix to the instructions contains a list of more than two hundred families from Smyrna and Anatolia as well as the names of captives taken on Chios.[60] The list highlights the range of individuals, including slave number 52: a certain Marie, wife of Hadji Nikolas Chaviara with two of his daughters, two sons, and another young woman with two infants. Taken from the village of Thera near Smyrna, the family had become separated: the two boys were being held in Scala Nuova; the two girls were in a village near Odemissi, "but nothing [was] known about the others." Slave number 92 on the list: "Theodoroula, wife of Batty of Odessa," was being held in Pergamum with fourteen members of her family, "of whom [they had] heard nothing." According to Vorontsov's list, nearly sixty slaves were being held in Pergamum alone.[61]

The leading members of Minchaki's special commission included the honorary counselor Baron Konstantin Hubsch; the Swiss national and Russian agent Jacques Dantz (also a merchant of the first guild in Odessa); Zakharia Zakharov, a Greek merchant of the third class in Taganrog; and Konstantin Valsamaky, a Greek merchant of Odessa, third class (the latter's signature is particularly prominent on the sales' receipts).[62] These individuals forwarded their reports to the Russian embassy in Constantinople, which passed them on to St. Petersburg. Vorontsov praised Minchaki for the "very agreeable list of representatives" that he nominated for the ransoming of slaves. "The zeal that the commission has not ceased to demonstrate since it has been activated," Vorontsov added, "will be well recompensed." Indeed, Vorontsov noted that he would send a special report on the matter directly to the tsar.[63]

By the summer of 1825, Russian efforts came to fruition, and the commission discovered that many individuals had already been ransomed for between 500 and 3,000 piastres. In August and September, Minchaki reported that seventy-three slaves had been purchased for 51,546 piastres. Detailed sales receipts including the names of the captives, the owners, the interpreters and notaries involved, as well as the price and place were forwarded to Russian authorities in Odessa and St. Petersburg. Meanwhile, St. Petersburg began to pursue more-concrete methods to pacify the region, including negotiations with Great Britain (which culminated in the St. Petersburg Protocol) and dispatching a large naval force to the Aegean. In November, Vorontsov had to caution Minchaki not to exhibit *excès de zèle* in his operations but to confine his agents to ransoming the captives designated on the lists. He also warned against making these lists known to the public, for that would appear tactless and offensive and might raise the asking price.[64]

The Russian state reacted swiftly when the lives and faiths of Christians were threatened, since individuals, who in their tender years became members of Muslim households, oftentimes assimilated to their local environment and converted to Islam. At times the members of the commission encountered instances of apostasy. For example, after locating two children from the family of Alexander Loukou, Baron Hubsch was informed by local merchants (Alessandro Skanavi and Etienne Koumela) that both Nikolas and Frangouli Loukou had "gone Turk" and therefore did not warrant further consideration.[65] Many more examples of the abandonment of individuals who had apostatized exist in Russian Foreign Ministry archives. Often formerly Christian slaves rose to positions of prominence in Ottoman affairs. For example, one of the children (renamed Ibrahim Edhem) taken from the Greek island of Chios in 1822 became grand vizier in 1877–78.[66] Another youth enslaved during the Greek revolt, Georgios Stavrolakis, eventually became prime minister of Tunis more or less continuously from 1837 to 1873.[67]

As the traditional protector of the Orthodox world, the Russian state expended great energy to prevent young people from "going Turk" or abandoning their Christian faith. Reports of apparent Islamization from local authorities meant an end to Russian relief aid, although at times not before judicial inquiry. Legal cases were often needed to clearly establish a person's confessional status. For example, in 1826 the father of a girl ransomed with Russian aid was arrested by Turkish authorities and forcibly detained, because his daughter had reportedly converted to Islam. After a Russian agent intervened, a tribunal led by the local imam and four Turks testified that the girl had not embraced Islam. She was allowed to return with her father to Chios, although the transaction cost the Russian government extra.[68] Sometimes certain family members converted, while others resisted; the reasons why are strong subjects for comparative analysis. In recent years, Ottomanists have convincingly demonstrated that forced Islamization was rare; most converts did so voluntarily.[69] Yet according to Russian reports from the 1820s, the maxim "There is no compulsion in religion" (Sura II, the Quran) was not always revered.

The search for slaves continued in March 1826, and Vorontsov forwarded the commission another 65,000 piastres, followed by yet another 60,000 in October.[70] In August 1826, Minchaki reported that 231 slaves had been ransomed for 170,721 piastres and asked the Russian government for an additional 100,000 piastres.[71] Indeed, just as Russia formed a coalition with Great Britain and France to pacify the region, the efforts to ransom slaves began to succeed. The commission members were rewarded for their efforts: Honorary Counselor Hubsch received the Cross of St. Vladimir, the Swiss national Dantz was promoted to counselor of commerce, and Zakharia Zakharov and Konstantin Valsamaky were given gold medals.[72] The awards were accompanied with 10,000 rubles that the emperor designated for the victims of Missolonghi.

In the documentation of the period, one finds many individual cases that illustrate the plight of the enslaved. For instance, Ioannis Vlassopulos, now the Russian consul on the island of Poros, forwarded a petition to the embassy in Constantinople from a certain Jean Argiri, native of the island of Poros, who sought to redeem his daughter, Marie, who had been abducted in 1827. The girl, fourteen years old, was sold into Ottoman slavery, and the father did all he could to obtain her release. Evidently a well-off individual, Argiri wrote a letter (in Italian) in 1829 in which he claimed, "Since the destruction of Psara by the Turkish army I have been fatally disgraced by the loss of my only daughter named Marie."[73] After months of searching, he had at last found her with a Turkish family in Constantinople. "Since relations between Russia and the Porte have become stable," Argiri wrote, "articulated by the glorious peace of Adrianople [ending the Russian-Ottoman War of 1828–29], I thought that in the glorious name of the monarch of Russia, the loving father and magnanimous benefactor of the Greek nation, you would end my bitter calamity by sending a mission to Constantinople to liberate my only daughter." Action was immediately necessary, insisted Argiri, lest the poor girl abandon her religion and become Muslim (*e perdens nella maomettana*). Unfortunately, it proved impossible to determine the name of the girl's master, and Vlassopulos was unable to recover Argiri's daughter.[74]

Hundreds of what we may call emancipation sales receipts found their way into Russian archives. These quittances are particularly interesting sources. An excerpt from one reads as follows: "The undersigned Katerigno, daughter of Giorgos Arkonty, Sciote, finding myself a slave in possession of the Tartar Mahmud Aga, declare to have received from Mr. Zakharia Zakharov of this village the sum of 1,500 piastres, which serves for my ransom from the aforementioned Mahmud Aga, in faith of which I have been released." Another sales receipt states: "The undersigned Antonin, son of George Triknoeti, aged eight years and a native of Psara, slave under the ownership of Mehmet Hoza who lives in Ginzirli *han* [suburb of Constantinople], declares to have received from the Russian agent Zakharia Zakharov two thousand piastres for the purpose of my repurchase from the hands of the above said Mehmet, in faith of which I will attest." The young Antonin signed with an "X," and several eyewitnesses certified the document in Italian and Greek.[75] The names of the people involved (most were illiterate) in these quittances underscore ethnic and linguistic diversity: Sofoula Boulazenna, Nicolo Zolota, Michel Baraki, Basil Schina, Theodoros Benaki, and Maria Ladakia.

In another example, a slave trader named Halif Kadine from the Sultan Mehmed district of Constantinople sold four slaves to the Russian special commission. According to the consular report, Miltiades, aged four from Missolonghi; Marie, the wife of Constandi Christodoulos of the Peloponnese with her son Themistokles; and a girl named Despina cost the Russian commission three thousand Turkish piastres.[76] Although ransomed, Despina was tormented by the memory of her abduction; she reportedly had lost "her sense of strength of mind."[77]

As the Greek Revolution reached its final phase, Russian foreign minister Nesselrode had reason to be pleased. He singled out Count F. P. Pahlen (the temporary acting governor of Novorossiia and Bessarabia) for his ardor in ransoming Greek slaves. He congratulated Minchaki and spurred on the other Russian agents as well.[78] By the summer of 1827, the Russian relief aid had led to the emancipation of 360 individuals for 290,000 piastres.[79] Although the number of individuals liberated did not reflect the total of those enslaved, the process indicates the care with which the Russian state employed its funds and the respect it showed toward Ottoman laws and customs, even during times of war.

In 1826, the Russian Foreign Ministry sent Alexander I. Ribop'er (Ribeaupierre) as the primary plenipotentiary (he soon became ambassador) to the Sublime Porte. Ribop'er wrote copious memoranda on the Greek revolt based on intelligence from agents throughout the Aegean, the Morea, and the Ionian Islands. Minchaki stepped down as chargé d'affaires. The outbreak of war between the Ottomans and the Russians a few months later, however, ended the ransoming efforts. Minchaki must have had mixed feelings when reflecting upon the many individuals still in captivity as well as those who had apostatized. The embassy took over the few thousand piastres remaining from the relief drive.[80]

Nevertheless, the Russian-sponsored effort to ransom Christian slaves did not end immediately. In 1830, the government of the newly formed independent Greek state in Nafplion (the first Greek capital) acquired sufficient stability and recognition to plea for foreign intercession. The appeal, written by Iakovos Rizos-Neroulos, a talented literary scholar and Greece's first foreign minister, was signed by President Ioannis Kapodistrias, the well-known diplomat and former Russian foreign minister. It reached Viktor N. Panin, the Russian representative in Nafplion in January. Accompanying the official letter for intervention were the lists of more than five hundred families taken captive and held at Smyrna, Galata, Alexandria, Bursa, Magnesia, and elsewhere. The Greek government stated that it was prepared to issue new passports and certificates of travel if Russia would persuade the Sublime Porte to release the victims and compensate their owners.[81] Panin forwarded the messages to Ambassador Ribop'er and complained of formidable obstacles due to Muslim property rights. "Yet I don't doubt Your Excellence will try, in the interests of humanity and religion to release the unfortunate captives."[82] He tried to assure Kapodistrias of Russia's zealous intensions and encouraged the Greek government to release Turkish prisoners of war.[83]

Ribop'er in turn began to pressure the grand vizier to end the enslavement of war captives in general. Citing Islamic law, the Porte replied that the slaves were private property and the just fruits of war. Ribop'er observed, "The Turks always considered the Greeks their slaves and their property, by the right of war."[84] The most frequently cited text was Quran 47:4: "When you meet the unbelievers, smite their necks; then, when you have made wide slaughter among them, tie fast the bonds. Then set them free, either by grace or ransom, till the war lays down its load."[85] Thus with moral and material backing, Ottoman soldiers, often underpaid and overexposed to danger, took matters into their own hands by either killing or enslaving the "infidels" they encountered. Nevertheless, Ribop'er did not cease to track down enslaved Christians. For example, pressuring the Porte to respond to repeated complaints from the families of enslaved individuals who felt compelled to adopt Islam, but claimed to have done so for pragmatic reasons, led to an official proclamation from the Ottoman government. The Ottoman notice addressed "to the *kadis*, *voivodes*, and others, resident in the regions comprising the three divisions of Asia and the three divisions of Europe," proclaimed that the captives who have embraced Islam "but never ceased to desire their homeland . . . and [had] constantly tried to escape . . . [were] no longer of utility to their proprietors or patrons." These individuals "should be sent back to their countries."

The statement praised the patron-masters for their compassion, assuring them of future benedictions.[86]

Ribop'er was not alone in his efforts to redeem Christian slaves on behalf of the Russian Empire. The Russian vice consul in Thessaloniki, Angelos Mustoksidi, was one of the most energetic exponents of the cause of Greek Christians enslaved during the War for Independence.[87] His strong relations with Ottoman authorities and tireless efforts on behalf of Christian captives led to the emancipation of hundreds of individuals. When he arrived at his post in Thessaloniki soon after the end of hostilities, Mustoksidi was appalled at the large number of Christian slaves in Epirus, Thessaly, and Macedonia. He noted, "The Turks don't wish to be deprived of their slaves, particularly those who are young and good looking, but they are willing to sell them for a profit." Mustoksidi complained of forced conversions, the debauchery of young women, and terrible acts of injustice.[88] In response to letters of protest from Greek families, Mustoksidi petitioned the Ottoman government. His negotiations with the governor of the region, Mehmed Reşid, permitted several hundred families to settle in the Greek kingdom.[89] Mustoksidi provided his personal funds to assist the families in uniting with their compatriots.[90]

Well over a year after the Greek-Ottoman war ended, while on a special mission in 1831 in Albania and Epirus (lands still under Ottoman control), the Russian consul in northern Greece, Ioannis Paparrigopoulos, repeatedly complained of the wretched plight of Christian slaves in Turkish custody. Their families still sought Russian intercession, and Paparrigopoulos was eager to oblige. In a letter (coauthored by the British consul in Preveza, William Meyer) Paparrigopoulos beseeched Mehmed Reşid, now the grand vizier, to deliver a *boujouli* (official rescript) to all the pashas and muftis in the area to emancipate all the captives and allow them to return to their homes. The involvement led to official orders from the Sublime Porte to grant the safe passage of all captives and all individuals who once were slaves and had since been set free. Paparrigopoulos was impressed that "even after years of misery they [had] refused to give up the religion of the fathers."[91]

Nevertheless, some evidence suggests that not all the people taken captive were unhappy with their new lot in life. For example, when Ottoman-Egyptian forces began evacuating the Morea in 1828, many Greek female hostages wished to board vessels bound for Egypt. A French observer was puzzled by their resolution to openly renounce the land (*patrie*), religion, and regions of their birth, especially when bound for a country where sickness, fear, and death would promptly greet them.[92] Such images add nuance and complexity to the Ottoman system of slaves, European interventions, and the life and times of people in the eastern Mediterranean during the tumultuous opening decades of the nineteenth century.

When Greece at last became independent in 1830, the new government under President Kapodistrias petitioned Russian agents to investigate slavery and exert further pressure on the Porte to free Christian captives. Greek agents compiled extensive detailed lists of slaves' names, location upon capture, and status inside Turkish- and Arabic-speaking lands. Individuals and families remained far from their homelands. Unfortunately for the families of the enslaved, the Ottoman government considered the individuals involved to be the private property of their owners and concluded that forcible emancipation was illegal.[93] According to Gianib Efendi, the Ottoman *chiaus bashi* (head of the sultan's palace police), the captives "were condemned to slavery by Mussulman laws and religion—which not only permitted, but enjoined such a disposal of the wives and children of their enemies. . . . Why do not the Christian sovereigns interfere to prevent the emperor of Russia from sending his subjects to Siberia?"[94] It should be noted that many captives became integrated into Ottoman society and may not have experienced terribly oppressive lives as slaves of the sultan.

Ottomans gave up the practice of enslaving prisoners after the 1828–29 war with Russia. The launching of the Tanzimat (Restructuring), by Sultan Abdülmecid I (1839–61), spelled the beginning of the end of the Ottoman slave system, although the process was gradual and no distinct abolition decree was issued (as in the case of the United States and the West Indies).[95] Soldiers were obliged to return "kidnapped" Christians to the Russians during the next major war in the Crimea.[96] Although the penal code of 1858 imposed punishments for kidnapping and enslaving people, complete abolition did not occur until the early twentieth century and the founding of the Turkish Republic.

More research into the system of Ottoman slavery needs to be conducted before we can fully understand its place in the Eastern Question. Preliminary conclusions based on research presented here suggest that, at the very least, Russian efforts succeeded in reuniting hundreds of families. Russian intervention also raised awareness about Ottoman slavery in diplomatic circles and perhaps even prompted some reflection on Russia's own system of coerced labor. Moreover, it is clear that the system of slavery occupied a central concern of Russian diplomacy with the Porte, which continued through the Crimean War. Russia, as demonstrated by the efforts to free slaves, *did* have real, pressing concerns about Ottoman treatment of Christian populations, while refugees in the Russian Empire, such as the Greeks living in Odessa, compelled Russian officials to take stands on sensitive political issues.

NOTES

1. The major studies of Russian slavery are Richard Hellie, *Slavery in Russia, 1425-1725* (Chicago: University of Chicago Press, 1982); idem, "Russian Slavery and Serfdom, 1450-1804," in *The Cambridge World History of Slavery*, vol. 3, *AD 1420-AD 1804*, ed. by David Eltis and Stanley L. Engerman (Cambridge: Cambridge University Press, 2011), 275-95; idem, "Slavery among the Early Modern Peoples on the Territory of the USSR," *Canadian American Slavic Studies* 17 (1983): 454-65; and idem, "Migration in Early Modern Russia, 1480-1780s," in *Coerced and Free Migrations: Global Perspectives*, ed. David Eltis (Stanford, CA: Stanford University Press, 2002), 292-323. Ottoman specialists in Russia have yet to examine the system of Ottoman slavery based on Russian or Ottoman archival sources. For a survey of Russian historiography on slavery, see Richard Hellie, "Recent Soviet Historiography on Medieval and Early Modern Russian Slavery," *Russian Review* 35, no. 1 (January 1976): 1-32; and idem, "Muscovite Slavery in Comparative Perspective," *Russian History* 6, no. 2 (1979): 133-209. See also, Liubov Kurtynova-D'Herlugnan, *The Tsar's Abolitionists: The Slave Trade in the Caucasus and Its Suppression* (Leiden: Brill, 2010).

2. Michael Khodarkovsy, *Where Two Worlds Meet: The Russian State and the Kalmyk Nomads, 1600-1771* (Ithaca, NY: Cornell University Press, 1992); idem, *Russia's Steppe Frontier: The Making of a Colonial Empire, 1500-1800* (Bloomington: Indiana University Press, 2002); Daniel Brower and Edward Lazzerini, *Russia's Orient: Imperial Borderlands and Peoples, 1700-1917* (Bloomington: Indiana University Press, 1997); Willard Sunderland, *Taming the Wild Field: Colonization and Empire on the Russian Steppe* (Ithaca, NY: Cornell University Press, 2002).

3. On the Russian-Ottoman wars, see V. N. Vinogradov, *Dvuglavnyi rossiiskii orel na Balkanakh, 1683-1914* (Moscow: Indrik, 2010); Alexander Bitis, *Russia and the Eastern Question: Army, Government, and Society, 1815-1833* (Oxford: Oxford University Press, 2006); and Virginia Aksan, *Ottoman Wars, 1700-1870: An Empire Besieged* (Harlow, England: Longman/Pearson, 2011). On the Russian and Ottoman military, see J. L. H. Keep, *Soldiers of the Tsar: Army and Society in Russia, 1462-1874* (Oxford: Clarendon Press, 1985); and Rhoads Murphy, *Ottoman Warfare, 1500-1700* (London: UCL press, 1999).

4. For an introduction to the subject of prisoners of war in the Ottoman Empire, see Suraiya Faroqhi, *The Ottoman Empire and the World around It* (New York: I. B. Tauris, 2007), 119-36. On the Habsburg Empire, see Karl A. Roider,

Austria's Eastern Question, 1700-1790 (Princeton, NJ: Princeton University Press, 1982), 16; and the published documents about freeing slaves, in Karl Jahn, *Türkische Freilassungserklärungen des 18. Jahrhunderts (1702-1776)* (Naples: Istituto Universitario Orientale di Napoli, 1963).

5. Of vital importance, academic and public interest in the study of enslavement in the Ottoman and other Islamic societies has exhibited an impressive surge in the past two decades or so. See the relevant chapters in *The Cambridge World History of Slavery*, vol. 3. For detailed accounts of the Ottoman slave system, see Ehud Toledano, *As If Silent and Absent: Bonds of Enslavement in the Islamic Middle East* (New Haven, CT: Yale University Press, 2007); idem, *Slavery and Abolition in the Ottoman Middle East* (Seattle: University of Washington Press, 1997); idem, *The Ottoman Slave Trade and Its Suppression* (Princeton, NJ: Princeton University Press, 1982); Y. Hakan Erdem, *Slavery in the Ottoman Empire and Its Demise, 1800-1909* (New York: St. Martin's Press, 1996); Suraiya Faroqhi, *Studies of Ottoman Men and Women: Establishing Status, Establishing Control* (İstanbul Eren, 2002); Halil Inalcik, "Servile Labor in the Ottoman Empire," in *Studies in Ottoman Social and Economic History* (London: Variorum, 1985), vii; Yaron Ben-Naeh, "Blond, Tall with Honey-Colored Eyes: Jewish Ownership of Slaves in the Ottoman Empire," *Jewish History* 20, no. 3/4 (2006): 315-32. See also Geza David and Pal Fodor, eds., *Ransom Slavery along the Ottoman Borders: Early Fifteenth-Early Eighteenth Centuries* (Boston: Brill, 2007); Daniel Pipes, *Slave Soldiers and Islam* (New Haven, CT: Yale University Press, 1981); Shaun E. Marmon, ed., *Slavery in the Islamic Middle East* (Princeton, NJ: Princeton University Press, 1999); Alan Fisher, *A Precarious Balance: Conflict, Trade, and Diplomacy on the Russian-Ottoman Frontier* (İstanbul: Isis Press, 1999), 27-46, 77-138; Bernard Lewis, *Race and Slavery in the Middle East* (Oxford: Oxford University Press, 1990); and William G. Clarence-Smith, *Islam and the Abolition of Slavery* (Oxford: Oxford University Press, 2006).

6. Evidence exists for Ottoman prisoners being used as slaves in southern Italy and France in the early 1800s. See Salvatore Bono, *Schiavi musulmani nell'Italia moderna: Galeotti, vu' cumpra', domestici* (Naples: Edisioni Scientifiche Italiane, 1999).

7. The documents in this essay come from the AVPRI, specifically *fondy* 133 (Kantseliariia MID), 159 (Formuliarnye spiski), 165/2 (Afiny-missiia), 180 (Posol'stvo v Konstantinopole); and RGADA. The document's place of composition and date (the Julian calendar used by Russia followed twelve days behind the Gregorian calendar in the nineteenth century) is followed by the archival reference. Selected Russian archival reports during these years are published in Ministerstvo Inostrannykh Del Rossiiskoi Federatsii, *Vneshniaia politika Rossii XIX i nachala XX v.: Dokumenty Rossiiskogo ministerstva inostrannykh del*, 16 vols. (Moscow: Nauka, 1960-94), hereafter *VPR*.

8. The first durable diplomatic stations were founded in the eighteenth century. On the Russian consular system during this era, see Lucien J. Frary,

"Russian Consuls and the Greek War of Independence (1821-31)," *Mediterranean Historical Review* 28, no. 1 (June 2013), 46-65. For the broader background, see G. L. Arsh, *Albaniia i Epir v kontse XVIII-nachale XIXv* (Moscow: Akademii Nauk, 1963); I. S. Dostian, *Russkaia obshchestvennaia mysl' i balkanskie narody: Ot Radishcheva do dekabristov* (Moscow: Nauka, 1980); Constantin Papoulidis, "À propos de l'œuvre des employés grecs du Ministère des Affaires Étrangères de la Russie impériale aux XVIIIème, XIXème et XXème siècles," *Balkan Studies* 35 (1994): 5-14; idem, "K voprosu o deiatel'nosti grekov, sluzhivshikh v MID Rossiiskoi Imperii v XVIII-XX vv.," in *Grecheskaia kul'tura v Rossii, XVII-XX vv.*, ed. G. L. Arsh (Moscow: Nauka, 1999), 44-50; Ioannis Nikolopulos, "Ioannis Paparigopulos—eterist, rossiiskii konsul, grecheskii zemlevladelets," in *Greki i Rossiia XVII-XX vv.* (St. Petersburg: Aleteiia, 2007), 120-48; and Theophilus Prousis, *Russian-Ottoman Relations in the Levant: The Dashkov Archive*, Minnesota Mediterranean and East European Monographs, no. 10 (Minneapolis: University of Minnesota, 2002).

9. An elaborate message to the tsar composed by more than a dozen Greek notables is contained in AVPRI, f. 133, op. 468, d. 8192.

10. Two recent studies emphasize the Eastern Question as the crucial factor leading to modern theories and techniques of humanitarian intervention: Gary J. Bass, *Freedom's Battle: The Origins of Humanitarian Intervention* (New York: Alfred A. Knopf, 2008); and Davide Rodogno, *Against Massacre: Humanitarian Interventions in the Ottoman Empire* (Princeton, NJ: Princeton University Press, 2012).

11. A contemporary Russian translation of Ypsilantis's proclamation appears in *Russkii arkhiv* (1868): 294-97. Russian official policy and the ensuing War of Independence is covered in Theophilus Prousis, *Russian Society and the Greek Revolution* (DeKalb: Northern Illinois University Press, 1994), 26-83; Alexander Bitis, *Russia and the Eastern Question: Army, Government, and Society, 1815-1833* (Oxford: The British Academy, 2006), 98-121; Barbara Jelavich, *Russia's Balkan Entanglements (1806-1914)* (Cambridge: Cambridge University Press, 1991), 49-75; and Olga E. Petrunina, *Grecheskaia natsiia i gosudarstvo v XVIII-XX vv.: Ocherki politicheskogo rasvitiia* (Moscow: KDU, 2010), 147-93. The relevant documents from the Russian Foreign Ministry for the period 1821-30 are published in *VPR*, vols. 12-16. The much neglected Ottoman perspective is provided by H. Şükrü Ilicak, "The Revolt of Alexandros Ipsilantis and the Fate of the Fanariots in Ottoman Documents," in *The Greek Revolution of 1821: A European Event*, ed. Petros Pizanias (İstanbul: Isis Press, 2011), 225-39.

12. Three excellent studies of the War of Independence exist in English: David Brewer, *The Greek War of Independence* (Woodstock, NY: Overlook Press, 2001); Douglas Dakin, *The Greek Struggle for Independence, 1821-1833* (Berkeley: University of California Press, 1973); George Finlay, *History of the Greek Revolution*, 2 vols. (London: William Blackwood and Sons, 1861); see also the historiographical survey in N. P. Diamandouros, ed., *Hellenism and the Greek War of Liberation (1821-1830)* (Thessaloniki: IMXA, 1976), 193-230. On atrocities

against the Muslim community, see Justin McCarthy, *Death and Exile: The Ethnic Cleansing of Ottoman Muslims, 1821–1922* (Princeton, NJ: Darwin Press, 1995), 1–22.

13. Maria Efthymiou, "Continuities and Ruptures in a Revolution: Practices, Morals, Ideologies and Violence in the Greek Revolution of 1821," in *La société grecque sous la domination ottoman: Économie, identité, structure sociale et conflits*, ed. Maria Efthymiou (Athens: Hêrodotos, 2010), 259-324.

14. Dakin, *Greek Struggle*, 59; Finlay, *History of the Greek Revolution*, 1:172, 179, 181–82, 184–88, 199–203; Thomas Gordon, *History of the Greek Revolution*, 2 vols. (London: William Blackwood and T. Cadell, 1832), 1:149, 168–69.

15. Dakin, *Greek Struggle*, 66–67; idem, *British and American Philhellenes during the War of Greek Independence, 1821–1833* (Thessaloniki: IMXA, 1955); 28–30; Edward Blaquiere, *Report on the Present State of the Greek Confederation, and on Its Claims to the Support of the Christian World* (Athens: Istoriki kai Ethnologike Etairia tis Ellado, 1974), 11; idem, *The Greek Revolution: Its Origins and Progress* (London: G. and W. B. Whittaker, 1824), 153; W. Alison Phillips, *The War of Greek Independence, 1821–1833* (New York: Smith Elder, 1897), 60–61; Gary J. Bass, *Freedom's Battle*, 64–66.

16. Rodogno, *Against Massacre*, 65; McCarthy, *Death and Exile*, 11-2.

17. Archbishop Germanos of Patras, Bishop Procopius of Kalavyta, Andreas Zaimis, Andreas Londos, and Venezelos Ruffos to Vlassopoulos, 26 March 1821, AVPRI, f. 180, op. 517, d. 1221 (1821), ll. 45–47.

18. Vlassopoulos to Stroganov, Patras, 13 March 1821, AVPRI, f. 180, op. 517, d. 1221 (1821), ll. 45–47.

19. Robert Walsh, *A Residence at Constantinople*, 2 vols. (London: Frederick Westley and A. H. Davis, 1836), 1:335-37. On the frenzy of fighting in Patras, see Brewer, *Greek War of Independence*, 70–78; Gordon, *History of the Greek Revolution*, 1:145-49, 154-57, 233, 297-301; Finlay, *History of the Greek Revolution*, 1:186-87; Theophilus C. Prousis, *Lord Strangford at the Sublime Porte (1821): The Eastern Question* (İstanbul: Isis Press, 2010), 27-28.

20. Stroganov supported his "totally merited" departure and commended Vlassopoulos for "following instructions with prudence and loyalty." Stroganov to Vlassopoulos, Pera, 3 May 1821, AVPRI, f. 180, op. 517, d. 1221 (1821), ll. 71–72.

21. Vlassopoulos to Stroganov, Patras, 4 March 1821; Vlassopoulos to Stroganov, Patras Bay, 27 March 1821; Vlassopoulos to Stroganov, Ithaca, 20 April 1821, *VPR*, 12:47–48, 86–88, 126–27; Vlassopoulos to Kapodistrias, Ithaca, 29 April 1821; Vlassopoulos to Pouqueville, Ithaca, 26 April 1821, RGADA, f. 15, op. 1, d. 326, ll. 204-8, 215; Stroganov to Vlassopoulos, Pera, 9 May 1821, AVPRI, f. 180, op. 517, d. 1221 (1821), l. 68.

22. Sandrini to Nesselrode, Zante, 18 April 1821, *VPR*, 12:123.

23. Eyewitness accounts include Walsh, *Residence at Constantinople*; and Theophilus Prousis, "Smyrna 1821: A Russian View," *Modern Greek Studies Yearbook* 7 (1991): 145–68.

24. Walsh, *Residence at Constantinople*, 1:311-20; Charles Frazee, *The Orthodox Church and Independent Greece, 1821-1852* (Cambridge: Cambridge University Press, 1969), 22-35; Prousis, *Russian Society and the Greek Revolution*, 28, 55-56.

25. Stroganov to Nesselrode, Constantinople, 10 April 1821, *VPR*, 12:113-16.

26. Stroganov to Nesselrode, Constantinople, 28 May 1821, *VPR*, 12:162-65; C. W. Crawley, *The Question of Greek Independence: A Study of British Policy in the Near East, 1821-33* (Cambridge: Cambridge University Press, 1931), 18; Rodogno, *Against Massacre*, 68.

27. *VPR*, 13:113-19, 132-33, 154-59, 162-68, 176-78, 203-10, 224-27, 637-48; Prousis, *Russian Society and the Greek Revolution*, 37-38; idem, *Russian-Ottoman Relations in the Levant*, 27; idem, *Lord Strangford at the Sublime Porte (1821)*, 97-102, 109-111, 120-21, 124, 145, 161-62, 169.

28. The phrase "guerre d'extermination" appears in the dispatches and draft position papers of the Russian ambassador to Great Britain, Christopher Lieven, as early as 1824. On the Russian negotiations with the British cabinet (more than six thousand manuscript pages), see "Pacification de la Grèce," AVPRI, f. 133, op. 468, d. 12960-67; see also V. N. Vinogradov, "Les discussions sur la Grèce à Londres," in *Les relations gréco-russes pendant la domination turque et la guerre d'indépendance grecque* (Thessaloniki: IMXA, 1983), 133-60; and C. A. Vacalopoulos, "L'attitude de la Russie face à la question de l'indépendance grecque considérée par l'Ambassadeur russe Lieven (mai 1829)," in *Les relations gréco-russes pendant la domination turque et la guerre d'indépendance grecque* (Thessaloniki: IMXA, 1983), 160-69.

29. Nesselrode to Minchaki, St. Petersburg, 3 March 1826; Nesselrode to Lieven, St. Petersburg, 10 June 1826; Nesselrode to Lieven, Moscow, 17 September 1826, AVPRI, f. 133, op. 468, d. 12960, ll. 174, 332, 374.

30. On the Philhellenic movement, see Roderick Beaton, *Byron's War: Romantic Rebellion, Greek Revolution* (Cambridge: Cambridge University Press, 2013); William St. Clair, *That Greece Might Still Be Free: The Philhellenes in the War of Independence*, 2nd ed. (Cambridge: Open Book, 2008); Denys Barau, *La cause des Grecs: Une histoire du mouvement philhellene (1821-1829)* (Paris: Éditions Champion, 2009); Dakin, *British and American Philhellenes*; and C. M. Woodhouse, *The Philhellenes* (London: Hodder and Stoughton, 1969).

31. The hawks in the Russian Foreign Ministry attempted to convince Tsar Alexander I to intervene. Torn between his desire to maintain the European coalition and his commitment to protect Christians under threat, Tsar Alexander failed to develop a clear-cut policy in relation to the Greek rebellion. Alexander's contradictory stance enabled the Greek struggle to remain a mostly internal Ottoman affair in the early 1820s. See Prousis, *Russian Society and the Greek Revolution*, 26-83.

32. Prousis, "Smyrna 1821," 156.

33. For the British perspective, see Richard Clogg, "Smyrna in 1821: Documents from the Levant Company Archives in the Public Record Office," *Mikrasiatika Chronika* (1972), 15:313-71; for the French view, see Henri Mathieu,

La Turquie et ses different peuples (Paris: E. Dentu, 1857), 311. See also Rodogno, *Against Massacre*, 66–68; Bass, *Freedom's Battle*, 56, 57.

34. Gordon, *History of the Greek Revolution*, 1:351.

35. The massacre on Chios has been the subject of several recent studies: H. Long, *Greek Fire: The Massacre of Chios* (Bristol: Abson, 1992); Rodogno, *Against Massacre*, 68–70; Bass, *Freedom's Battle*, 67–75; Brewer, *Greek War of Independence*, 154–67. For additional detail, see S. G. Vios, ed., *I sphagi tis Hiou eis to stoma tou Hiakou laou* (Chios: Omereio Pnevmatiko Kentro Dimou Hiou, 2006); Apostolos Vakalopoulos, *Istoria tou neou ellinismou*, 6 vols. (Thessaloniki: n.p., 1973–82), 6:65–124; Philip Argenti, ed., *The Massacres of Chios Described in Contemporary Diplomatic Reports* (London: John Lane, 1932); idem, *Bibliography of Chios from Classical Times to 1936* (Oxford: Oxford University Press, 1940), 415–34. The dispatches of the British ambassador to the Porte, Lord Strangford, constitute an invaluable record of the incident. See Theophilus C. Prousis, *Lord Strangford at the Sublime Porte (1822): The Eastern Question* (İstanbul: Isis Press, 2012), 81–258, 334–71.

36. Gordon, *History of the Greek Revolution*, 1:358.

37. See the reports in Prousis, *Lord Strangford at the Sublime Porte (1822)*; and Argenti, *Massacres of Chios*.

38. Gordon, *History of the Greek Revolution*, 1:361.

39. Brewer, *Greek War of Independence*, 162. According to Lord Strangford, the *kapudan pasha* "redeemed with his own money a vast number of the wretched women and children whom the Turkish trips had sold as slaves." See Prousis, *Lord Strangford at the Sublime Porte (1822)*, 123.

40. Erdem, *Slavery in the Ottoman Empire*, 26.

41. Walsh, *Residence at Constantinople*, 1:398–409, 2: 6–10. The periodical *Vestnik Evropii*, no. 9/10: 152–54, no. 13/14: 156–59 reported on the massacre. See also Prousis, *Russian Society and the Greek Revolution*, 61–62.

42. Jean Dimakis, *La guerre d'indépendance Grecque vue par la presse française (période de 1821 à 1824)* (Thessaloniki: IMXA, 1968); R. L. Green, *Sketches of the War in Greece* (London: Hurst, 1827); F. Pouqueville, *Histoire de la regeneration de la Grèce*, 4 vols. (Paris: Firmin Didot, 1827); Rodogno, *Against Massacre*, 69–70; Bass, *Freedom's Battle*, 67–75.

43. Nina Athanassoglou-Kallmyer, *French Images from the Greek War of Independence, 1821–1830: Art and Politics under the Restoration* (New Haven, CT: Yale University Press, 1989), 30–31.

44. Rodogno, *Against Massacre*, 72–78; Bass, *Freedom's Battle*, 47–151. For the Ottoman view of the war, based primarily on Ottoman archives, see Erdem, "'Do Not Think of the Greeks as Agricultural Laborers': Ottoman Responses to the Greek War of Independence," in *Citizenship and the Nation-State in Greece and Turkey*, ed. Faruk Birtek and Thalia Dragonas (New York: Routledge, 2005), 67–84; idem, "The Greek Revolt and the End of the Old Ottoman Order," in *The Greek Revolution of 1821: A European Event*, 260–63; Christine Philliou, *Biography*

of an Empire: Governing Ottomans in an Age of Revolution (Berkeley: University of California Press, 2011), 65-81.

45. Erdem, *Slavery in the Ottoman Empire*, 20-26.

46. Ukaz of the Holy Synod, 29 November 1822, *VPR*, 12:605-6. For an assortment of supplications from the families of the victims and the Russian response, see AVPRI, f. 180, op. 517/1, d. 2614 (1824-27). Compilations of statistics and yearly *otchety* are available in *VPR*, 12:605-6, 14:18, 217-18, 333, 711-12, 718-22, 741-43, 774-76.

47. On families and households in the Ottoman Empire, see Alan Duben and Cem Behar, *Istanbul Households: Marriage, Family, and Fertility, 1880-1940* (Cambridge: Cambridge University Press, 1991); Suraiya Faroqhi, *Stories of Men and Women: Establishing Status, Establishing Control* (İstanbul: Eren, 2002); Madeline C. Zilfi, "Servants, Slaves, and the Domestic Order in the Ottoman Middle East," *Hawwa* 2, no. 1 (2004): 1-33. See also Toledano, "Enslavement in the Ottoman Empire," 34-38.

48. See the general discussion in Toledano, "Enslavement in the Ottoman Empire," 31-34. See Zilfi, "Servants, Slaves, and the Domestic Order," on how manumitted slaves, especially women, became a form of cheap labor.

49. See Metin Kunt, *All the Sultan's Servants: The Transformation of Ottoman Provincial Government, 1550-1650* (New York: Columbia University Press, 1983); Suraiya Faroqhi, "The Ruling Elite between Politics and 'the Economy,'" in *An Economic and Social History of the Ottoman Empire, 1300-1914*, ed. Halil Inlcik and Donald Quataert (Cambridge: Cambridge University Press), 564-636; H. Sahillioğlu, "Slaves in the Social and Economic Life of Bursa in the Late 15th and Early 16th Centuries," *Turcica* 17 (1985): 43-112; Erdem, *Slavery in the Ottoman Empire*, 11-17.

50. The principle works on the *devshirme* include V. Demetriades, "Some Thoughts on the Origins of the Devşirme," in *The Ottoman Emirate (1300-1389)*, ed. Elizabeth A. Zachariadou (Rethymnon: University of Crete, 1993), 67-76; V. L. Ménage, "Sidelights on the Devshirme from Idris to Sa'duddin," *Bulletin of the School of Oriental and African Studies* 18 (1956): 181-83; idem, "Some Notes of the Devshirme," *Bulletin of the School of Oriental and African Studies* 18 (1964): 64-78; J. A. B. Palmer, "The Origin of the Janissaries," *Bulletin of the John Rylands Library* 35 (1952-53): 448-81; Basilike Paoulis, *Ursprung und Wesen der Knabenlese im osmanischen Reich* (Munich: R. Oldenbourg, 1963); R. C. Repp, "A Further Note on the Devshirme," *Bulletin of the School of Oriental and African Studies* 31 (1968): 137-39; S. Vryonis, "Isidore Glabas and the Turkish Devshirme," *Speculum* 31 (1956): 433-43; idem, "Seljuk Gulams and Ottoman Devshirme," *Der Islam* 41 (1965): 224-52; Elizabeth A. Zachariadou, "Les 'janissaires' de l'empereur byzantine," in *Studia Turcologica memoriae Alexii Bombaci dicata* (Naples: Herder, 1982), 591-97. For accessible syntheses, see Colin Imber, *The Ottoman Empire, 1300-1650* (New York: Palgrave, 2002), 128-43; and Bruce Masters, "devşirme," in *Encyclopedia of Ottoman History* (New York: Facts on File, 2009), 183-85.

51. Toledano, "Enslavement in the Ottoman Empire," 26; Ralph Austen, "The 19th Century Islamic Slave Trade from East Africa (Swahili and Rea Sea Coasts): A Tentative Census," *Slavery and Abolition* 9 (1988): 21-44; idem, "The Mediterranean Islamic Slave Trade out of Africa: A Tentative Census," *Slavery and Abolition* 13 (1992): 214-48; see also Paul E. Lovejoy, *Transformations in Slavery: A History of Slavery in Africa*, 2nd ed. (Cambridge: Cambridge University Press), 135-59. Specialists have yet to provide estimates regarding the total volume of coerced migration from the Black Sea shores and the Caucasus, a precise calculation of which is most likely impossible. In borderland regions like the Crimea, reasonable estimates suggest that a substantial portion of the population consisted of slaves of former slaves. On numbers of slaves in the early modern period, see Hellie, *Slavery in Russia*, 679-89. On the Crimean Tatar traffic, see Fisher, *Precarious Balance*.

52. Much of the population of Psara was enslaved or massacred. According to George Finlay, about seven thousand people lived on the island before the revolution. See Finlay, *History of the Greek Revolution*, 2:152.

53. K. M. Bazili, *Ocherki Konstantinopolia*, 2 pts. (St. Petersburg: N. Grech, 1835), pt. 2, 158. The term "piastre" or "piaster" comes from the Italian *piastra*, or "thin metal plate." Piastre was another name for *kuruş*, the standard unit of currency in the Ottoman Empire until 1844. It was subdivided into forty *para*, each of three *akçe*. For details on the exchange rate, see Şevket Pamuk, "Money in the Ottoman Empire, 1326-1914," in Inlcik and Quataert, *Economic and Social History of the Ottoman Empire*, 945-80.

54. For the context of Greek relief aid, see Prousis, *Russian Society and the Greek Revolution*, 55-83.

55. Ibid., 69.

56. Selected material from the writings of Minchaki are published in *VPR*, vols. 13-16. Russian agents reported to him from Zakynthos (Anton Sandrini), Corfu (S. P. Popandopoulo), Mytilini and Syros (S. L. Svilarch), Santorini (B. Marchesini), Naxos (K. Raftopoulos), Samos (G. Svoronos), Mykonos (Pietro Kordia), Tinos (Ivan Dzhani), Cyprus (Mario Santi), and elsewhere. See, "Delo ob uchrezhdenii konsul'stv," AVPRI, f. 165/2, op. 507, d. 78 (1829); AVPRI, f. 165/2, op. 507, d. 163 (1831).

57. Vorontsov to Minchaki, Odessa, 2 June 1824, AVPRI, f. 180, op. 517/1, d. 2614, ll. 1-2.

58. Ibid., 2.

59. Minchaki to Vorontsov, Constantinople, 27 August 1826, AVPRI, f. 180, op. 517/1, d. 2614, ll. 79-80.

60. "Liste d'esclaves à racheter à Smirne et aux environs, ainsi que dans les autres parties de la Anatolie," "Liste d'esclaves à racheter dans l'île de Chio," January 1825, AVPRI, f. 180, op. 517/1, d. 2614, ll. 8-18.

61. Ibid., ll. 11, 13.

62. Vorontsov to Minchaki, Odessa, 20 October 1826; Minchaki to Vorontsov,

Buyukdere, 25 September 1826, AVPRI, f. 180, op. 517/1, d. 2614, ll. 55-56, 134-35.

63. Vorontsov to Minchaki, Odessa, 20 October 1826, AVPRI, f. 180, op. 517/1, d. 2614, l. 55.

64. Minchaki to Vorontsov, Buyukdere, 4 October 1825; Vorontsov to Minchaki, Odessa, 14 August 1825; Vorontsov to Minchaki, Odessa, 21 November 1825, AVPRI, f. 180, op. 517/1, d. 2614, ll. 102, 19-39, 45.

65. Hubsch to Minchaki, Pera, 2 August 1825, f. 180, op. 517/1, d. 2614, ll. 166-68.

66. Erdem, *Slavery*, 26.

67. Magali Morsy, *North Africa, 1800-1900: A Survey from the Nile Valley to the Atlantic* (London: Longman, 1984), 185.

68. Hubsch to Minchaki, Pera, 4 August 1826, AVPRI, f. 180, op. 517/1, d. 2614, ll. 194-200.

69. Antonina Zhelyazkova, "Islamization in the Balkans as a Historiographical Problem: The Southeastern-European Perspective," in *The Ottomans and the Balkans: A Discussion of Historiography*, ed. Fikret Adanir and Suraiya Faroqhi (Leiden: Brill, 2002), 223-66; Selim Deringil, "'There Is No Compulsion in Religion': On Conversion and Apostasy in the Late Ottoman Empire, 1839-1856," *Comparative Studies in Society and History* 42, no. 3 (2000): 547-75; Colin Heywood, "Bosnia under Ottoman Rule, 1463-1800," in *The Muslims of Bosnia-Herzegovina: Their Historic Development from the Middle Ages to the Dissolution of Yugoslavia*, ed. Mark Pinson (Cambridge, MA: Harvard University Press, 1994), 22-53.

70. Vorontsov to Minchaki, Odessa, 12 March 1826; Vorontsov to Minchaki, Odessa, 4 October 1826, AVPRI, f. 180, op. 517/1, d. 2614, ll. 48, 54.

71. Minchaki to Vorontsov, Buyukdere, 4 August 1826, AVPRI, f. 180, op. 517/1, d. 2614, ll. 127.

72. Vorontsov to Minchaki, Odessa, 20 October 1826, AVPRI, f. 180, op. 517/1, d. 2614, ll. 55-56.

73. Jean Argiri to Vlassopulo, Poros, 3 January 1830, AVPRI, f. 180, op. 517/1, d. 1228 (1830), l. 4.

74. Vlassopulo to Ribop'er, Poros, 4 January 1830, AVPRI, f. 180, op. 517/1, d. 1228 (1830), l. 3.

75. Constantinople, 17 September 1826, AVPRI, f. 180, op. 517/1, d. 2611 (1825-26), l. 126.

76. Constantinople, 12 November 1826, AVPRI, f. 180, op 517/1, d, 2611 (1825-26), l. 211.

77. Ibid.

78. Nesselrode to Pahlen, St. Petersburg, 22 March 1827, AVPRI, f. 180, op. 517/1, d. 2614, l. 67.

79. Minchaki to Pahlen, Buyukdere, 10 May 1827, AVPRI, f. 180, op. 517/1, d. 2614, ll. 155-56.

80. Ribop'er to Hubsch, Pera, 16 November 1827, AVPRI, f. 180, op. 517/1, d. 2614, l. 252.

81. Kapodistrias and Rizos-Neroulos to Panin, Nafplion, January 1830; Rizos-Neroulos to Panin, Nafplion, 2 May 1830, AVPRI, f. 180, op. 517/1, d. 1796 (1830), ll. 40–52, 261.

82. Panin to Ribop'er, Naples de Romani, 3 February 1830, AVPRI, f. 180, op. 517/1, d. 1796 (1830), l. 39.

83. Panin to Kapodistrias, Nafplion, 5 February 1830, AVPRI, f. 180, op. 517/1, d. 1796 (1830), l. 62.

84. Ribop'er to Panin, Buyukdere, 24 February/8 March 1830, AVPRI, f. 180, op. 517/1, d. 1796 (1830), ll. 343–44.

85. Cited in Clarence-Smith, *Islam and the Abolition of Slavery*, 25. On details regarding the Ottoman emancipation of slaves, see Erdem, *Slavery in the Ottoman Empire*, 152–84.

86. Ribop'er to Panin, Buyukdere, 16 July 1830, AVPRI, 165/2, op. 507, d. 40 (1828), ll. 246–48.

87. On Mustoksidi, see Lucien J. Frary, "Russian Interests in Nineteenth Century Thessaloniki," *Mediterranean Historical Review* 23, no. 1 (June 2008): 15–33.

88. Mustoksidi to Rikman, Thessaloniki, 15 December 1830, AVPRI, f. 180, op. 517/1, d. 1294 (1830), ll. 108–11.

89. Mustoksidi to Panin, Thessaloniki, 12 February 1831, AVPRI, f. 165/2, op. 507, d. 154 (1831), ll. 140–42; for a petition from Greek captains addressed to Mustoksidi, see, ll. 143–44.

90. The Russian government reimbursed him twenty-five thousand piastres to save Greek slaves. See "Mustoksitsi, Anzhelo Arsen'evich," AVPRI, f. 159, op. 464, d. 2343.

91. Paparrigopoulos and Meyer to Mehmet Reshid Pasha, Ochrid, 27 July 1831, AVPRI, f. 165/2, op. 507, d. 163 (1831), l. 56. A full summary of the negotiations with the grand vizier is contained in Paparrigopoulos to Rikman, Nafplion, 25 August 1831, AVPRI, f. 165/2, op. 507, d. 163 (1831), ll. 38–45.

92. J. Mangeart, *Souvenirs de la Morée* (Paris: Igonette, 1830), 41.

93. Ribop'er to Panin, Buyukdere, 24 February 1830, AVPRI, f. 180, op. 517/1, d. 1796 (1830), ll. 343–46.

94. Prousis, *Lord Strangford at the Sublime Porte (1822)*, 133–34.

95. During this period, enslaved people used the government decrees as tools to achieve their freedom. See Toledano, *Ottoman Slave Trade*; idem, "Ottoman Conceptions of Slavery in the Period of Reform, 1830s–1880s," in *Breaking the Chains: Slavery, Bondage and Emancipation in Modern Africa and Asia*, ed. Martin A. Klein (Madison: University of Wisconsin Press, 1993), 37–63; Erdem, *Slavery in the Ottoman empire*; Clarence-Smith, *Islam and the Abolition of Slavery*, 104–18; Lewis, *Race and Slavery in the Middle East*, 78–81, 160–61.

96. Toledano, *Ottoman Slave Trade*, 24–26; Erdem, *Slavery in the Ottoman Empire*, 29–33, 44–45, 196.

Russia's Quest for the Holy Grail

Relics, Liturgics, and Great-Power Politics in the Ottoman Empire

JACK FAIREY

A development common to all the social sciences since the end of the Cold War has been a renewed appreciation for the social and political power of religion.[1] In keeping with this trend, a growing number of historians have self-consciously sought (in the words of Philip Gorski) "to bring religion back in" to the writing of modern political and social history. In European history, the resulting "religious turn" has yielded valuable insights on a range of topics from the origins of Westphalian sovereignty to the rise of nationalism, the public sphere, and the modern state.[2] Historians of the Ottoman Empire, similarly, have paid increasing attention to the political history of religion and religious institutions, especially as these affected the internal cohesion of the empire and the formation of those modern states and nations that would eventually replace it.[3]

The impact of Ottoman religious affairs on modern international relations, however, has been less studied. One striking example of this

View of Constantinople by Evening Light by Ivan Aivazovsky. (reprinted with permission from the Peterhof Museum, Russia)

neglect is the history of the Crimean War between Russia and the Ottoman Empire, Britain, and France in 1853-56. The Crimean War is not normally treated as "a religious conflict," yet its origins were inextricably bound up with religious actors and issues. The dispute was, for example, the last major European war in which a combatant cited explicitly religious factors as a casus belli. In 1853, the Russian government based its entire case for war on its claim that the Ottoman government was carrying out a deliberate campaign of interference in Orthodox religious affairs. The purpose of this campaign, St. Petersburg declared, was to undermine the political and social position of the Orthodox Church in the Near East and thereby to strike at Russian influence throughout the region.[4] In June 1853, Tsar Nicholas I announced that all his efforts to bring the sultan to reason on the issue had failed; the sole alternative that remained was a resort to force. Holy Russia had no choice but to "march to the defense of the Orthodox Faith."[5]

Chancellor Karl Vasil'evich Nesselrode enlarged upon his sovereign's accusations regarding the religious causes of the conflict in a memorandum, dated 2 March 1854. This memorandum, though ostensibly for internal use, was clearly aimed at a wider audience. "For a long time now," the chancellor complained, "all the acts of the Turkish Government toward us, as toward the Eastern Church in Turkey, have born an evident stamp of hostility." As evidence, Nesselrode cited a long list of offenses committed by the Sublime Porte against the Orthodox Church, including:

> direct interference in internal [ecclesiastical] affairs ... constant irregularities in the election of the patriarchs; ... obstacles of every sort placed in the way of the development of the Bulgarian and Bosnian Churches, of the instruction of the indigenous clergy, and of the religious education of the population ... ; prohibition or partial laceration of sacred texts ordered by the Greek-Slavic clergy from Russia for their own use, ... ; a thousand things, in other words, which, taken separately have only a relative importance, but which, taken all together, have proven to us for some years past the well-developed intentions of the Turkish government to contribute to the increase of other sects, in order to diminish, along with our authority, the number of those whom it envisages to be adherents of Russia.[6]

The tsar and his ministers were convinced, moreover, that the Porte had not arrived at these policies independently: the British, French, and Austrian embassies had incited the Ottomans to adopt an interventionist course. Russian statesmen concluded that the future of Orthodoxy itself was under threat in the Near East, and that a binding engagement from the Ottoman sultan was necessary to preserve the religious status quo from such a hostile constellation of forces. In order to secure a comprehensive guarantee of Orthodox rights in the Near East, Nicholas I was prepared—though reluctant—to set the entire region ablaze.

The Ottoman, British, and French governments each vigorously denied these allegations. The Ottoman declaration of war in October 1853, for example, categorically refuted the tsar's complaints: there had been no campaign of interference in Orthodox affairs, and the Ottoman government had no intention of compromising the rights and privileges of the Orthodox Church in any way. The tsar's demands for a formal guarantee were therefore unnecessary and little more than "a pretext for war."[7] The British Foreign Secretary, Lord Clarendon, similarly claimed to be mystified by Nesselrode's references to a concerted political campaign against Orthodoxy in the East. The Porte, he conceded, had mismanaged the dispute between Catholics and Orthodox over the holy places in Palestine, but this was an isolated problem and it had, in any case, been resolved in the spring of 1853 to the satisfaction of all sides. "Where then," Clarendon demanded rhetorically, "are the causes which Count Nesselrode, appealing to impartial Europe, assumes will justify the position now taken by Russia?"[8]

Rejection of the Russian government's casus belli left European and Ottoman statesmen with only two alternatives: either the tsar was acting from misplaced zeal, or he had aggressive designs against the Ottoman Empire. Most contemporaries favored the latter conclusion. Lord Palmerston, for one, insisted in parliament that what Russia demanded from the sultan was an injurious pretention to "stand between the Sultan and his subjects—that if those subjects should feel aggrieved they should go to St. Petersburg instead of to Constantinople for redress, and that they should apply for the protection of the Czar instead of appealing to the justice of the Sultan."[9] Russia, in other words, was making false charges of religious persecution in order to legitimize its claim to a protectorate over Ottoman Christians."[10] The ultimate purpose of that protectorate, in turn, was to reduce Sultan Abdülmecid to "a mere vassal of the [Russian] Emperor."[11]

Historians since have tended to perpetuate this false dichotomy by leaving the Russian government's central charges unexamined. Studies on the origins of the Crimean War have instead focused either on the "big picture" of inter-European imperial rivalries, personal ambitions, and economic competition or on the details of how diplomacy failed to prevent the catastrophe.[12] In either case, without a reevaluation of Russia's claims, its government and autocrat must come off poorly, as their intransigence seems otherwise the product of incompetence, madness, or overweening ambition.

In the nineteenth century and for the first half of the twentieth, the abundance and accessibility of English diplomatic sources and memoirs encouraged historians to place the burden of guilt for the conflict on Russia. As Brison Gooch concluded in his 1956 survey of the historiography of the Crimean War, the most common understanding of the conflict at its first centenary was that it had been "fought in defense of the Ottoman Empire . . . for the status quo and against Russian encroachment."[13] Historians of Russia undermined these assumptions over the last several decades by presenting evidence that the tsar harbored no secret designs on the Ottoman Empire and that Russian concern over mistreatment of the Orthodox Church was genuine.[14] This evidence, however, has not led to a reexamination of Nesselrode's central accusation regarding the existence of a long-standing and systematic campaign of interference in Ottoman Orthodox affairs.[15] Instead, most modern writers have merely upgraded Russian motives from aggression to incompetence, on the continuing assumption that complaints about the affairs of the Orthodox community were exaggerated or, if true, inconsequential.

This chapter takes a contrary view and provides three concrete examples of precisely the sort of "direct interference" in Orthodox affairs during the decade leading up to 1853 that Nesselrode complained of and that other governments denied existed. The first example is an attempt by Ottoman and British statesmen in 1852 to interfere in the custodianship of an Orthodox relic known as the Ayion Potirion (Holy Grail) of Vlatades monastery. The second example is a sporadic campaign waged by the British embassy over three decades to have the Ottoman government censor Orthodox liturgical prayers. The final example consists of a series of attempts by Ottoman and Western diplomats during the 1840s and 1850s to secure the appointment or dismissal of high-ranking Orthodox clergymen.

It is noteworthy that in each of these cases the Ottoman, British, and French foreign ministries—no less than the Russian—treated disparate and apparently trivial incidents as symptoms of a larger international contest over Ottoman Christian affairs. Diplomats on all sides agreed, moreover, that this contest was unprecedented, that it touched upon vital political and economic interests, and that it showed a worrying, upward trajectory. For at least a decade leading up to the Crimean War, in other words, diplomats had commented on the increasing involvement of European states in Ottoman Christian affairs and the likelihood that these intrigues would lead to serious international complications.

The cases described here thus both substantiate Russian complaints and illustrate the many strategic functions of religion in the history of the Eastern Question. Religion was much more, for example, than just a motivating and organizing principle for competition that pitted Orthodox Russians and "Greeks" [*Rum*] against Catholic Frenchmen, Muslim Turks, and Protestant Englishmen. Religious institutions in themselves provided an important venue for political competition, as states attempted to project "soft power" not only along confessional lines but *across* them. The fear that so exercised Russian statesmen in 1853 was precisely that other states were learning to poach supporters from pro-Russian religious constituencies like the Orthodox Church more effectively. Hitherto the principle way of attracting the political sympathies of Eastern Christians had been to convert them to a different religion; by the 1850s it seemed possible to achieve many of the same goals by recasting Orthodoxy itself as something that could be "pro-Ottoman," "pro-British," "pro-French," and so on. The resulting efforts of the powers to invest religious sites, objects, and institutions with their own distinctive political stamp meant that disputes over obscure details of religious life quickly became bound up with wider struggles for ascendancy in the Near East. In response, all the great powers felt a new compulsion to monitor the internal affairs of Ottoman Christians and to take positive steps to counteract the baleful influences that they supposed their rivals were exercising in manifold, subtle ways under the auspices of religion. The following three cases illustrate the intensity of this surveillance and its unfortunate effects.

The Ayion Potirion of Vlatades

On 8 October 1850, Charles Blunt, British consul in Thessaloniki and a long-time resident of the Ottoman Empire, sent an agitated dispatch marked "Confidential" to his superior in İstanbul, Lord Stratford Canning de Redcliffe. He was concerned, he explained to the ambassador, about events then occurring at the Orthodox monastery of Vlatades [Çavuş Manastir], a Byzantine-era establishment situated high on the heights of the acropolis overlooking the port of Thessaloniki. Among the many relics preserved at the monastery, Blunt noted, "there exists deposited part of a drinking cup made out of the skin of a dried gourd, such as may be seen used, at the present day by the peasants in Turkey. This cup, or rather remains of one, is said to be (although there are no traditionary [sic] documents in support of the assertion) the same used by Our Saviour at the 'Last Supper!'"[16]

The origins of the relic known in Greek as the Ayion Potirion or Ayiakoupa were conveniently lost in the mists of time. A visiting Russian pilgrim, Andrei Nikolaevich Murav'ev, speculated in 1849 that it had been the emperors of Constantinople who first encased the relic in silver and that they had later given it to the Bagratid kings of medieval Georgia as part of some marriage-alliance.[17] The Bagratids, in turn, were supposed to have brought the cup to the Georgian monastery of Iviron on Mount Athos at some point during the Middle Ages. During Byzantium's declining centuries, Iviron lost control of the cup and it somehow passed into the hands of the monks of Vlatades. In the late eighteenth century, the cup lost its original form when mutinous janissaries pillaged Vlatades and broke the relic into pieces to facilitate the process of stripping away the silver chasing.[18] The monks decided to remake the reliquary as three separate silver cups that could be either nested one within the other or used separately. The Ayiakoupa enjoyed considerable renown in the Balkans for its miraculous powers, and the monks of Vlatades often took it on circuits of the countryside to bless the populace.

In the late 1840s, the relic came to the attention of a member of the Russian imperial elite, General Ivan Savvich Gorgoli, a senator of Greek origins although both he and his parents had been born and raised in Russia.[19] Gorgoli became intrigued and he sent a message to the Russian vice-consul in Thessaloniki, an Ionian Greek by the name of Angelos Mustoksidi, requesting the latter's assistance in securing a private purchase of the relic. As this request came from a privy councilor to the tsar, Mustoksidi gave the request his full attention. The vice-consul seems also to have privately considered the acquisition a worthy goal, so he was not deterred when the monastery rejected his first request for one of the three cups. Mustoksidi knew that the exarch of Vlatades, Bishop Veniamin Karypoglou of Servia and Kozani, approved of his proposal. The vice-consul therefore continued to nurture "the hope of one day procuring for Russia a portion of this precious relic."[20]

In the spring of 1850, Mustoksidi convinced Bishop Veniamin to raise the issue again with the monks and the committee of local lay notables who assisted with the management of the monastery's affairs. This time, the guardians of the Potirion proved more amenable. Their change in attitude does not seem to have been rooted in financial considerations, as Mustoksidi noted that the monastery had no pressing debts or needs at the time.[21] Instead, the brethren had realized that Mustoksidi's request might open up much wider vistas for the monastery than a simple, one-time purchase by a Russian nobleman. The monastery, they announced, was still not interested in selling the Ayion Potirion to Senator Gorgoli, but it *was* willing to make a voluntary gift of the largest of the three silver vessels to the empress of Russia, Alexandra Fedorovna. This gift would be contingent, however, on the Russian and Ottoman governments granting the monastery permission to send its own delegation to St. Petersburg to present the relic in person to the tsarina.[22]

This counteroffer was a deft move on the part of the monastery that entirely transformed the nature of the transaction. Whereas originally, Mustoksidi had offered to broker a private purchase that would have linked the monastery to Russia tangentially, the monks were proposing to initiate a public and politically charged relationship with the Russian imperial family. In a sense, they would be putting the tsarina in their debt. It was not unknown for hierarchs to show their appreciation for

Russian support by sending small relic fragments as gifts, but few ordinary monasteries had ever made such a significant donation to the imperial family.[23] So different was the nature of the new arrangement that at first Mustoksidi balked and told the monks that their proposal went beyond his instructions. Mustoksidi sent a letter on 5 June to his superiors requesting instructions and enclosing a formal letter from the monastery offering the tsarina the relic.

Bishop Veniamin, in the meantime, urged Mustoksidi to take custody of the relic until a clear decision was made. Mustoksidi agreed, and the Potirion was conducted through the city from Vlatades to the Russian consulate with great fanfare. The monastery, confident that its gift would be accepted, proceeded with the selection of an emissary to convey the Potirion to St. Petersburg. Veniamin's archdeacon, also named Veniamin, was chosen for this purpose. The community decided to enhance the gravitas of their envoy by elevating Archdeacon Veniamin to the rank of archimandrite in a ceremony at the Orthodox cathedral of St. Dimitrios.[24]

The public celebrations that attended the appointment and elevation of the new Archimandrite Veniamin attracted negative attention to the monastery's plans. In particular, the celebrations aroused the suspicions of the British consul, Charles Blunt, who wanted to know what all the commotion was about. Blunt's investigations led him to a different understanding of events than we find in the letters of Mustoksidi. Blunt reported that the monastery had never altered its initial refusal to sell the Potirion. He claimed that the Russian consul had tricked the monks into giving up control of the relic by asking them to bless the Russian consulate with holy water sprinkled from the chalice. Once the relic was within the walls of the consulate, Mustoksidi was supposed to have requested that it be installed temporarily in the consular chapel so that he and his staff might enjoy its continued blessings. In Blunt's words: "The Cup was brought . . . the Consulate purified, but the relic never left."[25] With this achieved, Mustoksidi had then supposedly "induced" the local Orthodox community "to present this Relic to the Emperor of Russia" by promises of imperial largesse. The differences between Blunt's characterization of events and Mustoksidi's are obvious and fundamental. Whereas Mustoksidi ascribes the initiative to local Christians, Blunt depicts the latter as dupes manipulated by a Russian agent acting on orders from St. Petersburg.

At first glance, Blunt's preoccupation with the incident seems odd. Certainly, the event was curious, but one would hardly have thought that it required serious diplomatic attention either from the British consulate or from his superiors. Blunt saw things in a very different light. "I take the liberty of reporting the details to Your Excellency," Blunt prefaced his report, "under the impression that they may be interesting; the more so, I venture to add ... as the whole affair leads me to think, that Russian Policy, in this instance, aims at some hold upon the fanatical feelings of the Christians of the Greek Church, in these districts, as the depositary of Sacred Relics of the Oriental Church."[26] Russia, in other words, was stealing a march on the other European powers in the race for the hearts and minds of Christians in the Near East. Not only was this new addition to "Holy Russia's" stockpile of relics likely to give it heightened prestige and an added aura of sanctity in the Orthodox world, but the exchange would open a new relationship between the Russian government and one of the most important monasteries in the region. "It may be easy to suppose," he complained, what sort of impression the upcoming visit to the glittering court of St. Petersburg would make on the mind of whichever "ignorant deacon, from the wilds of Macedonia" was tasked with conveying the relic to Russia, "and what would be that individual's report upon his return, respecting not only the magnanimous clemency of the [tsar], but also of [the Russian emperor's] attachment to his co-religious brethren in Turkey!"[27]

Not all was lost, however, since Blunt had good reason to hope that the deal could still be scuttled. Rumors that the local *reaya* were about to send their own special emissary (i.e., Archimandrite Veniamin) to the imperial court in St. Petersburg had raised hackles not only at the British consulate but also among the Muslim community of Thessaloniki. One prominent notable, Ahmed Kasım Efendi, had complained vigorously to the governor of Thessaloniki, Yakub Paşa Karamanoğlu, that the donation should not be permitted.[28] Yakub Paşa was reluctant to get involved, but Ahmed Efendi threatened that he would complain to the Porte if the governor failed to keep the pretentions of local Christians in check. As a result, when the Russian legation in İstanbul finally approved the donation and Archimandrite Veniamin applied to the governor's office in early September 1850 for the necessary travel papers [*yol teskere*], his request was denied. Yakub Paşa justified the decision by noting that the Potirion was a valuable antiquity. Under the terms of recent decrees prohibiting the export of archaeological treasures, it could not be removed without the express approval of the Ottoman foreign ministry.[29] Mustoksidi made the necessary application and waited for a response.

From September 1850, the accounts of Blunt and Mustoksidi separate irreconcilably. According to Blunt, the Russian consul first tried bullying the governor and then resorted to deception:

> The Russian Consul ... called upon Yacoub Pasha, and used every effort to convince his Excellency, that he was injuring the interests of the Monastery, *for the Emperor of Russia would richly endow it, when in possession of this Sacred Relic.* Yacoub Pasha was proof against all the efforts of the Russian Consul, telling him that this Relic, he considered as property of the Sultan and that he could not allow its extraction without a special order from the Porte—The Russian Consul however, did not return the Relic to the Monastery but sent it off to Constantinople by the last Steamer! His Excellency Yacoub Pasha is highly indignant at this double dealing of Mr. de Mustoxidi, and sent for the Arch Bishop of Salonica demanding ... a full detail of all the proceedings of this affair. ... The Pasha has already reported this case to the Porte, but there is a meeting of the Council today especially called to draw up a Basmata [*sic*] of all the facts relating to this singular case.[30]

Blunt was sure the Russian consulate would use all its wiles to get around this ban. The outcome of the affair would therefore depend on whether the central government in İstanbul supported the governor in his attempts to frustrate Russian designs. Blunt clearly expected that Ambassador Canning would use his influence to stiffen the Porte's resolve and ensure that the Grail—all of it—remained in Thessaloniki.

The correspondence of Mustoksidi shows no trace of the deliberate deception Blunt alleges. On the contrary, what is most striking about the numerous letters between Mustoksidi and the Russian legation in İstanbul during the fall of 1850 is their naive optimism.[31] Mustoksidi was mystified by Ottoman objections to the donation, and he appears entirely unaware of the role being played behind the scenes by the British consulate. He found the officious interference of the Ottoman authorities all the more strange, in that "the Turks" traditionally stayed out of such matters. Mustoksidi explained away these anomalies by placing the blame squarely on two notorious "troublemakers" on the municipal council, Gavril Zakadi and Ahmed Kasim, who had forced the governor's hand. He confidently predicted that the whole thing would soon blow over and that the Porte would soon grant Archimandrite Veniamin his travel permit.

As it became clear, however, that the objections of the Ottoman government were *not* going away, the vice-consul became increasingly indignant. The Ottoman government, he fumed, had no business involving itself in such affairs. The object in question was, after all, not some antiquarian objet d'art but a religious relic. It was the legal property of

Vlatades, and the monastery was within its rights to donate it to whomever it wished. He further noted that amateur archaeologists had been looting the East of antiquities for years with or without formal permission. It therefore seemed all the more arbitrary for the governor to invoke the law on antiquities in this particular instance. Beyond these considerations, Mustoksidi worried that the Ottoman government was establishing an unsettling precedent for ignoring the liberties and privileges not just of Vlatades but of the Orthodox Church generally. In his opinion, the Russian government should not permit the Porte thus to "encroach on the rights of the church."[32] Mustoksidi therefore insisted on retaining the relic, even after the Russian embassy warned him in December 1850 that it did not look as if the necessary approval would ever be forthcoming.[33]

The outcome of the story is uncertain. According to the memory preserved at Vlatades itself, Mustoksidi's persistence won out, and the Ottoman government finally permitted the monastery to send one of the relics to Russia in December 1856.[34] The specific destination of the relic in Russia, however, was not recorded, and the precious vessel seems to have immediately disappeared from view. The fact that the Russian government donated a large silver crucifix and a gilded *evangelion* to the monastery soon thereafter supports this version of events, as does the tsar's decision in 1852 to present Mustoksidi with the Cross of St. Anne for his part in the affair.[35] Mustoksidi thus seems to have sent *something* to Russia, but it is difficult to see how this could have been one of the original chalices. A catalog of the relics held at Vlatades dating from 1821 records three cups, Mustoksidi in his reports states clearly that there were only three, and the number held today at Vlatades is exactly three.[36] Where did the monastery suddenly find a fourth Grail? It is also difficult to credit that such a rare and venerable relic could have arrived at St. Petersburg without fanfare or that the Russian Church could somehow have lost track of it subsequently. It is tempting to hypothesize instead that either the monks or Mustoksidi decided to circumvent the objections of the Porte by sending a replica. It is certainly suggestive that in 1850 Mustoksidi reported sending Senator Gorgoli "exact models of the three cups and the pieces contained in each."[37] It may well be that is all Mustoksidi ever sent.

Prayer Books and Liturgical Commemorations

British efforts to disrupt religious ties between Russia and Ottoman Christians were not limited to the control of relics like the Potirion.

British diplomats also showed a surprisingly keen interest in the contents of Slavonic, Greek, and Armenian liturgical books, many of which were printed in Russia but destined for use in the Ottoman Empire. In particular, the British embassy suspected Russia of using liturgical prayers to sow political disloyalty among Ottoman Christians.

British agents noted with disapproval, for instance, that Orthodox clergymen generally did not mention either Sultan Abdülmecid or the Ottoman dynasty by name in the intercessory prayers of the liturgy known as litanies [*ektenia/synapti*]. Whereas service books published in Russia and Serbia contained specific references to the reigning sovereign, Ottoman service books referred only vaguely to "our kings" [*vasileis*] without specifying whether this meant all monarchs or only Orthodox Christian rulers.[38] Ottoman texts of the liturgy of St. John Chrysostom thus commemorated "our most pious and God-protected kings and all those in palace and camp."[39] Other intercessory prayers were more specific, however, invoking divine assistance for "the mighty and holy Orthodox emperor [*Orthodoxou Aftokratoros*]"—a formulation that after the fall of Byzantium could refer only to the tsar of Russia.[40]

Tacit liturgical references to the Romanovs became more explicit in the early nineteenth century as Russian influence in the Ottoman Empire grew. By the 1840s, for example, churches under the Patriarchate of Jerusalem were reading the following prayers in the part of the Great Ektenia formerly reserved for "our most pious kings":

[Officiant] For our most pious, most autocratic Great Lord Nicholas Pavlovich, emperor of all Russia, and for his spouse the most pious Lady and great Empress Alexandra Fedorovna let us pray to the Lord.
[Congregation] Lord, have mercy.
[Officiant] For the Crown Prince, pious Lord Tsarevich and Grand Duke Alexander Nikolaevich and his spouse the pious Lady Tsarevna and Grand Duchess Maria Alexandrovna let us pray to the Lord.
[Congregation] Lord, have mercy
[*followed by intercessions for the various grand dukes and duchesses of the Romanov dynasty*][41]

To British ears, such prayers smacked of treason.

Orthodox clergymen could at least excuse themselves on the grounds that their liturgy had always commemorated "our most pious and Christ-loving emperors"—whatever that phrase was taken to mean; in the case of the Armenian Apostolic (Gregorian) Church, on the other hand, liturgical links to Russia were all the more problematic for being quite recent.⁴² Prior to the 1800s, Russia had meant little to Ottoman Armenians, who regarded the Muscovites—when at all—as a remote country peopled by heretics. This disinterest changed over the first decades of the nineteenth century as Russia expanded rapidly into the Caucasus, acquiring Armenian lands from Persia by the Treaty of Turkmenchai (1828) that included Echmiadzin, the seat of the supreme patriarch and catholicos of all Armenians. The Russian government was keen to expand its influence further in the Near East, and as Paul Werth has shown, it immediately perceived the potential of the Catholicosate as a means "to project imperial Russian power across the southern frontier and to maximize its leverage in manipulating neighbouring states."⁴³ Already in March 1829, Nicholas I was ordering his ministers to investigate how Russia might use the relics held at Echmiadzin of St. Gregory the Illuminator to attract the sympathies of Ottoman Armenians.⁴⁴ In order to convert the Armenian Church into a more serviceable and reliable institution, Nicholas issued a statute [*polozhenie*] in 1836 reorganizing the Catholicosate. The statute specified, for example, that the tsar would henceforward appoint all catholicoi at his pleasure. "All liturgical services conducted in Armenian churches" were to commemorate "His Imperial Majesty and His August Dynasty"—and to do so *before* the prayers for the catholicos and his clergy.⁴⁵

The Russian government also began to use its political influence to promote the canonical authority of the Catholicosate among Armenians outside the Russian Empire. In İstanbul, for example, the Russian legation called for normalization of relations, which had been in suspension for many years, between Echmiadzin and the various branches of the Armenian Church in the Ottoman Empire. Specifically, the legation wanted all Ottoman Armenians to commemorate the catholicos in their liturgies, receive Holy Chrism [*muron*] from him, and accept the presence of a permanent nuncio, or *vekil*, to represent the catholicos in the Ottoman Empire.⁴⁶ The Sublime Porte was rightly suspicious of Russia's sudden interest in Armenian ecclesiastical affairs, but it nevertheless allowed the legation to broker an agreement in 1838 restoring the nominal supremacy of Echmiadzin over Ottoman Armenians. Russia only achieved this, however, by conceding de facto independence to the Armenian Patriarchate of Constantinople and promising that the catholicos would appoint no permanent representative to represent it in the Ottoman capital.⁴⁷

The new arrangement pleased no one. On the one hand, it fell far short of the ecclesiastical integration that the Russian government had hoped for, while on the other, it was much more than the Sublime Porte could accept. The Porte allowed the agreement to stand, but it surreptitiously encouraged factions within the Armenian Church that were hostile to Russia.[48] In London, the British Foreign Office considered even the nominal submission of Ottoman Armenians to Echmiadzin dangerous, and it vigorously opposed any rapprochement between the various branches of the Armenian Church. In April 1836, for example, Ambassador John Ponsonby expressed strong concerns in his dispatches to London about the formal links that the Russian government was forging with the Ottoman Armenian community. These ties would, he predicted, produce "evil consequences" for the Ottoman Empire and its friends. The foreign secretary of the day, Lord Palmerston, agreed and he instructed Ponsonby to advise the Porte that it should insist on total separation between the churches of Constantinople and Echmiadzin. Palmerston specifically urged the Porte not to permit any special commemorations of either the tsar or the catholicos.[49]

The British embassy in İstanbul never reconciled itself to these various liturgical reminders of Russia's "special relationship" with Ottoman Christians, and it would periodically renew its objections. In 1850, for example, the Chiote journalist and author Iakovos Pitzipios submitted a comprehensive memorandum on Ottoman Christian affairs to the British embassy that helped revive the interest of Blunt's superior, Ambassador Stratford Canning. Most of Pitzipios's proposals to counteract Russian influence were wildly impracticable, but he struck a chord in the ambassador with his argument that religion was "the principal organ of [Russia's] projects" in the Near East and that the other European powers must fight fire with fire.[50] As an example of the need to use religious means to combat Russian influence, Pitzipios singled out the fact that the Ottoman government took no interest in the prayers read in Orthodox churches. This lack of censorship, he argued, was a strategic oversight that allowed Russia to introduce all sorts of inappropriate prayers.[51]

The private journals of William Palmer, an Anglican deacon visiting İstanbul in the summer of 1850, show that these arguments made an impression on the British ambassador. During an embassy dinner, Canning expounded to his guest on the dangerous situation that the Porte had created by its negligence of Eastern Christian affairs. Palmer noted in his diary:

Sir Stratford Canning asserted very strongly that the Russian Government caused to be printed at Moscow and then circulated throughout the East books designed to excite in the Christian subjects of the Porte a spirit of disaffection to their Governors. Such books had been brought to him, and though he could not read them himself, the places had been marked for him, and the more important passages translated into French. I expressed some curiosity to see the books: so he took me aside into another room and produced a copy of the Psalter in Slavonic and another of the *Trebnik* or Book of Offices. At the beginning of each was a notification: that "This book is printed at Moscow, in such a year, to the glory of Almighty God, by the command of H. I. M. the Emperor Nicholas Paulovich of all the Russias etc. etc. and by command of the M. H. Synod." . . . Then in the matter at the end among the daily prayers and intercessions to be said by monks and others there is one to this effect: "The infidel and abominable empire of the Hagarenes do Thou o God speedily destroy, and transfer it to Orthodox Sovereign; and lift up the horn of Christendom and subdue our enemies under our feet." While in the office book there was a form for the reception of Turks etc as proselytes wherein the proselyte is made to renounce "the impious Koran of Mahomet and all the unclean and wicked doctrines of Mahometanism." What [concluded Canning] could be plainer?[52]

Palmer—an admirer of the Eastern Churches—disagreed. He argued that the prayers in question were ancient and therefore long predated any Russian designs on the Turkish Straits. He was sure, moreover, that the Russian ambassador could cull dozens of similar statements from Anglican prayer books. Palmer's objections made no impression on the ambassador. Canning insisted that the inclusion of *these* particular prayers in a book printed in Russia for circulation in the Ottoman Empire must have an ominous significance. It was, he insisted, "most reprehensive" of the Russian government to "countenance such intolerance . . . and must shew a political design." Canning admitted that he had been urging the Porte privately to order the suppression of all such litanies and special prayers commemorating the Romanovs, whether among the Orthodox or the Armenians.[53]

Appointment and Removal of Hierarchs

European attempts to intervene in the appointment and dismissal of Orthodox clergymen provide further evidence of the increasing politicization of Ottoman Christian affairs during the 1840s and 1850s. Such involvement was not entirely new for Russia, which had exercised some influence on the election and removal of Orthodox patriarchs since at least the early 1700s and over the election of the catholicoi of Echmiadzin since 1800. Russia had exerted this influence through informal channels and subsidies, however, rather than by more overt means. In particular,

Russia had cultivated a network of friends and clients among the Ottoman Christian elites who dominated the affairs of their respective communities. Powerful members of these elites had then promoted or removed clergymen based on a convergence of interests with those of the Russian legation, rather than simply at the direction of the latter. Russian involvement in Near Eastern ecclesiastical politics had thus been effective, but diffused and subsumed within its broader "special" relationship with Ottoman Orthodox society.

Representatives of the other European powers, and especially Britain, began to challenge this informal Russian monopoly over Ottoman ecclesiastical affairs in the late 1830s for political, humanitarian, and strategic reasons.[54] As a matter of good governance, the European diplomatic corps were virtually unanimous that the extensive temporal powers enjoyed by the upper clergy in the Ottoman Empire ought to be curtailed. In practical terms, moreover, the close association between Russia and the Orthodox faith made it seem inevitable that the powers of the clergy would always be used to promote Russian interests at the expense of all other states. As the French ambassador to İstanbul in the late 1850s observed to his superiors regarding the situation that confronted French diplomacy prior to the Crimean War: "The power of the [Orthodox] clergy was at the same time a cause of their own debasement and the strongest obstacle to the influence of Western ideas among the populace. It served as a species of rampart that separated the Christians of the East not only from the Turks but also from Europe and delivered them over, as if in a closed field, to the exclusive activity of Russia. Whatever future is reserved for the Ottoman Empire . . . our political interests require the toppling of that barrier."[55]

Western statesmen were rarely so forthright in enunciating a formal policy toward the Orthodox Church, but they engaged in a clear pattern of interference over the course of the 1840s. Western diplomats began, for example, to call for the censure and removal of individual hierarchs they considered abusive. The British embassy blazed the way in 1840 by becoming the first European state publically to demand that the Porte remove a reigning Orthodox patriarch of Constantinople. Grigorios VI Fourtouniadis had repeatedly courted trouble by criticizing the British colonial administration on the Ionian Islands ex cathedra. Most daringly, in 1839 the patriarch called on Christians to disobey recent changes to the Ionian law code that violated Orthodox canon law. Rather than treat the patriarch as a conscientious objector, the British government insisted that the patriarch had committed a political offense, and that the Porte must either punish him or share in his guilt. Ambassador John Ponsonby accused the patriarch of "sedition," "improper and criminal conduct," and of "creating discord and confusion in a friendly state under the pretext of Religion." After several months of such official complaints, the Sublime Porte finally agreed to remove Grigorios.[56] Over the next decade, the British embassy would apply varying degrees of pressure on the Ottoman government to remove two other patriarchs of Constantinople, Anthimos IV and Yermanos IV. It also intervened in at least three other patriarchal elections to ensure that the Porte prevented the selection of candidates Britain deemed objectionable.[57]

In the provinces of the Ottoman Empire, British, French, and Austrian consuls all began during the 1840s and 1850s to complain in the strongest terms about the general character of the Orthodox clergy and to call for the removal of bishops they deemed unfit for office.[58] In Thessaloniki, for example, Consul Blunt was a particularly vociferous critic of the local hierarchy; he singled out for censure at least ten individual bishops in his reports over the decade. Blunt repeatedly expressed the opinion during his long stint as British consul in Thessaloniki, from 1835 to 1856, that the oppressions carried out by the Orthodox episcopate were "far more onerous to the *Rayjahs* [i.e., *ordinary Christians*] than any acts of the Turks."[59] The first act of a new bishop, he complained in a report from 1839, "after his arrival at his post, is plunder! I believe My Lord that I do not advance what can be subject to the slightest taxation as to veracity, when I state that the present System of the Greek Church does far more injury to the *Rayjahs*, then all the real and supposed oppressions of the Turkish Authorities."[60]

In Larnaca, Consul Niven Kerr complained so bitterly and repeatedly about the primate of the Church of Cyprus, Ioannikios II, that the British embassy requested that archbishop's removal in 1847 on the following grounds: "[He is] ignorant in the extreme, depraved, licentious, and void even of the external decency and decorum which is expected from the ministers of religion, he only makes use of his sacred trust to pillage and impose upon the superstitious and priest ridden *Rayah* population."[61] When the Porte refused to comply, the British embassy insisted that the Ottoman government must at the very least appoint a special commissioner to investigate Kerr's complaints against Ioannikios.[62]

Western criticism of the Orthodox clergy did not stop at individual hierarchs but led directly to calls for a sweeping reform of the structure and powers of the Orthodox Church. Consuls like Blunt reiterated in their communications with both Ottoman officials and their own superiors in Whitehall that punishment of individual clergymen would change nothing so long as the overall structure of Ottoman Christian society remained the same. "If the Porte is sincere," Blunt wrote in 1843, "in its intentions towards the Christian Subjects of the Sultan, it would be greatly to their advantage, for the Porte to take the conduct of the Greek Bishops *in general* [emphasis in the original] into its most serious consideration, and put some check upon their well known rapacity."[63] By the early 1850s, British, French, and Austrian statesmen also generally agreed on the specific measures necessary to effect such a reform: the Porte should limit or abolish the temporal powers of the clergy, it should replace the existing system of tithes and fees with regular clerical salaries, and it should establish a more effective and stringent system of state supervision over religious affairs generally.

Two common threads thus ran through virtually all Western policies toward the Orthodox Church in the 1840s and 1850s. The first was a desire to displace Russian influence over Ottoman Christians. The second was a conviction that the Ottoman government must take a more active and interventionist role in Christian religious affairs. Both considerations pointed to the need for a systemic reform of the non-Muslim communities and churches. In September 1840, for example, the chargé d'affaires of the French Embassy recommended that his government actively encourage the Porte to carry out a wholesale reorganization of the Orthodox community. A reduction in the powers of the Orthodox clergy, he argued, would hobble Russian influence and clear the way for French and Catholic expansion in the region. "In order for the new order of things to be a success for France," he concluded, "it must intervene in the regulation of these [ecclesiastical] questions."[64]

The reforming faction within the Ottoman bureaucracy associated with Mustafa Reşid Paşa was most likely to cooperate in such a recasting of religion. Even without Western prompting, Reşid and his circle had already concluded by the 1830s that the entire system of clerical privileges had outlived its usefulness. In centuries past, it had been convenient for the Ottoman state to share its powers and responsibilities with a range of intermediaries, from tax farmers and clergymen to local warlords. Under Mahmud II and Abdülmecid I, however, the Ottoman administration had begun to re-create itself along modern European lines. This meant an ambitious program of reclaiming the powers and responsibilities that in the past it had devolved onto others. Reformist proclamations such as the Hatt-ı Şerif of Gülhane, drafted by Mustafa

Reşid in 1839, looked forward to a state that ruled directly and equally over all its subjects. Clearly, the existing powers and independence of the Orthodox clergy fit awkwardly with such plans.

Ottoman statesmen were also just as concerned as their British and French counterparts about the special ties between Russia and the sultan's Eastern Christian subjects. In 1846, for example, the Austrian internuncio noted that Reşid Paşa was "not very happy with the Russian Mission," regretting in particular "the constant influence that the Russians [sought] to exercise over all that concern[ed] the Greek subjects of the Porte and the exercise of their cult."[65] The following year, Reşid complained to Sultan Abdülmecid that every time the Porte had a dispute with the Orthodox Patriarchate of Constantinople, the latter sought to embroil the Russian legation. Reşid considered such reliance on the support of a foreign power unacceptable, and he warned the sultan that the Orthodox upper clergy would become completely unmanageable if the government did not act. The Orthodox clergy must be taught, he concluded, "that they cannot make laws for themselves in this country."[66]

Reşid Paşa contemplated measures as early as the summer of 1840 to reduce the secular powers of the clergy and to replace ecclesiastical fees and taxes with a regular salary paid by the state. Mathurin-Joseph Cor, whose testimony is all the more valuable for his having worked previously as Reşid's personal secretary, hailed the news:

> The actual state of Christians and their administration will soon be modified. Force of circumstances will make the Turkish Government take measures to introduce the most complete religious liberty before long, such as the adoption of a system of fixed salaries for the members of the clergy and the nomination of lay chiefs for the administration of the temporal affairs of the diverse non-Muslim communities and their relations with the Ottoman Government, etc. etc. . . . This division of the temporal from the spiritual had never before appeared, in theory, a good measure to recommend; but today it is a profitable idea, and this is what makes me think that it will not be long before it is taken in hand.[67]

Rumors that the Porte was considering such reforms spread quickly to the provinces. In Thessaloniki, for example, Blunt reported with obvious approval in 1841 that it was widely reported the Porte intended "to take under its immediate consideration the state of the Greek Clergy, and that they [would] henceforth have fixed salaries." These reports apparently caused panic among the local Orthodox hierarchy, who raised their fees sharply in order to reap the maximum profit while they still had the ability to do so.[68]

Between 1843 and 1853, the Porte made several attempts to initiate a formal process of reform within the Orthodox and Armenian communities. A confluence of circumstances, however, including the determined resistance of the Orthodox clergy and disagreements within the Ottoman political elite, delayed these reforms until the end of the Crimean War. The single most important factor in this delay, however, was the well-founded fear among Ottoman statesmen that any attempt to impose reforms on the Orthodox and Armenian communities would lead to a serious confrontation with Russia. In the spring of 1843, for example, the Grand Vizier Mehmed Emin Rauf Paşa reported to the sultan that he wished to remove the current patriarch, Yermanos IV, and that concrete steps were urgently needed to rectify the disordered state of Orthodox affairs.[69] In a very telling admission, however, Rauf tempered this call for action by noting that his government had to proceed with extreme caution because of the jealous vigilance that Russia exercised over all such questions. The Porte therefore could not remove Yermanos immediately; it would have to wait for a credible excuse. Similarly, the Ottoman government believed it had to introduce changes to the structure of the Orthodox community surreptitiously and piecemeal or risk a direct confrontation with Russia.

The resulting Ottoman policy of chipping away at the power and independence of the Orthodox clergy was wholly unsuccessful, failing either to bring about the desired changes or to avoid an imbroglio with Russia. On the contrary, the Russian legation expressed mounting anger over the Porte's clumsy attempts to meddle in patriarchal affairs—and the appearance of Western connivance in those attempts. In 1845-46, for example, the patriarchal throne changed hands three times in rapid succession. Each time there was clear evidence of irregular interference by the Ottoman state. The Porte had first pressured Yermanos IV into submitting his "voluntary" abdication and had then issued directives illegally excluding several Russophile hierarchs from standing for election.[70] In the elections of December 1845, the Porte further sought to intimidate the synod by adopting the innovation of sending the dragoman of the Porte, Mehmet Fuad Paşa, to attend its meetings as an "official observer." What little legitimacy remained to the electoral process was destroyed by the revelation that the winning candidate, Anthimos VI, had purchased his victory at the cost of an enormous bribe (reportedly five million piastres) to the sultan's chamberlain.[71]

The Russian minister, Vladimir Pavlovich Titov, angrily condemned these proceedings in his reports to St. Petersburg as "tumultuous, disorderly, and scandalous." What was worse was that in each case the Porte seemed to have intervened explicitly to side with Russia's enemies. It was notorious, for example, that the majority of the Orthodox faithful desired the reelection of Grigorios VI, but that the British embassy had warned the Porte it would take the restoration of this pious, popular clergyman as an insult. The Porte had therefore resorted to illegal exclusions, intimidation, intrigues, and bribery to bring about the elevation of a candidate acceptable to its British allies.[72] It was urgent, Titov insisted in his reports, that Russia protest against such abuses, or they would proliferate "in a manner at once impudent and dangerous."[73] Tsar Nicholas I agreed with this evaluation and ordered Titov to address a formal note of complaint to the Ottoman government.[74] In the resulting letter, dated 6 March 1846, Titov complained at length of "the abuses that accompany the elections of the ecumenical patriarch" and of "the grave inconveniences that result from the frequent changing of the personages invested with that high ecclesiastical dignity."[75] Recent developments, he added in an uncharacteristically menacing tone, had profoundly troubled the tsar and the latter could not "view such a state of affairs with indifference." The ministers of the sultan must take steps, Titov continued, "to prevent the repetition in the future of similar irregularities and of such deplorable malversations. The election of the patriarch must be completely free and the Porte, far from intervening, must avoid indicating any preferences or exclusions, which accord neither with canon law nor with the freedom of action that constitutes . . . one of the immunities accorded to the [Orthodox] nation and the clergy."[76] The traditional rights and privileges of the church were, Titov concluded, "the essential and invariable precondition" upon which the loyalty of the Sultan's Orthodox subjects was based. The Porte invited perilous political consequences "by permitting these privileges to be violated or evaded."[77]

The cases reviewed here demonstrate the intimate connections that had developed between the Eastern Question and Ottoman Christian religious affairs by the mid-nineteenth century. By 1853, matters such as the possession of a relic, the elevation of a hierarch, or control over a shrine in the Ottoman Empire were no longer purely domestic or spiritual affairs. They had instead acquired a distinctly international dimension as matters directly affecting British, Russian, or French interests in the region. Politicization and internationalization of the *res sacrae* of the East was most obvious in Palestine, where one might expect European states to take an interest in shrines common to all Christians. In most other cases, however, Western statesmen invested considerable energy in influencing the regulation of religious matters that the general public in London or Paris considered embarrassingly obscure and inappropriate.

In part, the heightened politicization of Christian religious life in the Ottoman Empire was a product of the structure of Ottoman society itself. In particular, the division of Ottoman subjects into a hierarchy of confessional communities encouraged non-Muslims to improve their status by identifying with powerful foreign coreligionists. At the same time, the system rewarded European states that cultivated these connections and put at their disposal all the extensive powers wielded by the non-Muslim clergy. In a sense, religion became the site of a strategic exchange as Ottoman Christians and European states attempted to trade patronage for entrée into Ottoman domestic affairs. The Ottoman government underwrote this exchange by accepting the principle that foreign states could legitimately exercise jurisdiction over individuals, places, and religious groups or organizations within Ottoman imperial space on the basis of little more than a shared religion and outdated capitulations.

Given these features of Ottoman rule, it was only natural that states already possessing recognized *protectorats religieuses* like France, Spain, and Austria would seek to expand their scope. As it seemed unlikely that Ottoman Christians would ever convert to Catholicism en masse, these states sought new means of cultivating clients across several religious communities. Why, as Édouard Thouvenel observed, should France settle for a protectorate over just Catholics when it might multiply its influence many times over by posing as the "solicitous and benevolent patron of the Christian subjects of the Sultan, without consideration of rite"?[78] States like Russia and England that did not enjoy clearcut legal rights of religious protection just as naturally sought parity with those that did. Russia at least had the advantage of being able to claim a religious protectorate over the Orthodox Church on the basis of the 1774 Treaty of Kuchuk Kainardji and long-standing economic, religious, and cultural ties with the "Orthodox East." In private, the upper clergy and the Russian legation often had their differences, but to the rest of the world the two sides presented an appearance of monolithic pan-Orthodox solidarity.[79] Russia thus enjoyed a degree of influence over the largest non-Muslim community in the empire that was the envy of other European states and of the Porte itself. Like France, however, Russia saw no reason to limit itself to a special relationship with just one community. As Eileen Kane, Robert Crews, Paul Werth, Daniel Brower, and others have demonstrated, the Russian state was also eager to be considered guardian of the Armenian Catholicosate, of the Ethiopian and Syriac Orthodox churches, and of the many thousands of Jews and Muslims who traveled from the Russian Empire to the Holy Land as emigrants or pilgrims.[80]

Britain had been dealt the worst hand in any contest for religious influence as it possessed neither substantial numbers of Ottoman co-religionists nor any treaty rights of protection. This left the British embassy in İstanbul with only two cards to play: it could claim a dubious "natural guardianship" over the small communities of Ottoman Protestants, Jews, and Druze, or—more promisingly—it could seek to level the playing field by undermining the political significance of religion altogether. As Ann Pottinger Saab has observed, circumstances dictated that Britain must seek as much as possible to secularize the structure of Ottoman society in order "to minimize the importance of religious ties except as a purely personal attribute, and to replace the corporate structure of the Ottoman state with an individual, strictly political bond between Sultan and subject."[81]

By the 1850s then, British, Ottoman, French, and Austrian statesmen were separately moving toward a similar conclusion: that the Porte should carry out a thorough reorganization of the religious and communal life of Ottoman Christians. The necessary reforms ought to curb the arbitrary power of the clergy, encourage civic equality, and make the various communities more responsive to central state control. These developments, in turn, would undermine Russian influence and open the Eastern Christian communities up to greater Western influence. As in so many other areas of Ottoman life, one of the major effects of the Eastern Question on Ottoman society was thus to encourage the dissolution of established monopolies and privileges—in this case by making the non-Muslim communities of the empire into something of an open market for great powers in search of clients.

The opening up of Ottoman religious affairs to foreign competition produced an appreciable escalation in tensions both internationally and within the empire. The cases examined here illustrate this trend and prefigure many of the fatal dynamics that would reappear in 1852–53 during the holy places dispute and the Menshikov mission. Mustoksidi's uncomprehending reaction to the "Grail affair," for example, was symptomatic of the larger failure of Russian diplomacy to defuse the suspicions that its special relationship with Orthodox Christendom aroused in rival states. Mustoksidi clearly understood that acquisition of the Potirion would be advantageous for Russia, yet he was strangely oblivious to how his efforts might be interpreted by Ottoman and British observers. In a pattern that would be repeated by other Russian diplomats, Mustoksidi acted within what he confidently assumed were the natural and legitimate bounds of Russia's special relationship with Orthodox Christians, only to be nonplussed by accusations that his actions represented new and dangerous pretentions.

In the eyes of the Russian government, any suggestion that it was disrupting the status quo was ludicrous. Russia's rulers saw themselves as paragons of conservatism and they could not understand how anyone could misconstrue their solicitude for Eastern Christians. What Russia claimed, as Nesselrode protested during the crisis of 1853, was nothing more than the "religious patronage ... that [they had] always exercised in the East."[82] Nor did the Russian government believe that it demanded anything radically different from the sort of religious protectorates exercised by other powers or even by the Ottoman sultan himself, given the latter's standing claim to be caliph of Sunni Muslims everywhere.[83]

While the Russian ministry thus excused its own interventions in Orthodox affairs, it reacted with fury to any attempt by the Ottoman government or its Western allies to do the same. Russia particularly objected to the Porte's projects for reforming the non-Muslim communities, believing that these changes were intended to undermine Russian influence in the region. In truth, there were good reasons for thinking this. In 1847, the Russian chargé d'affaires in İstanbul glumly reported that his spies had intercepted documents establishing beyond any reasonable doubt the grand aims of British and French foreign policy in the eastern Mediterranean. These two powers intended, he declared, "if not openly, then at least by all the underhanded means in their power ... to sap as much as possible and everywhere among the Christian populations of the Ottoman Empire their ancient and profound sentiments of devotion to Russia, in order to replace them with contrary dispositions of hostility and mistrust."[84] In Russian eyes, then, the British and French embassies were willfully leading the ministers of the Ottoman Porte down dangerous byways to promote their own interests. They did so at the expense of Russia, of Orthodoxy, and—ultimately—against the best interests of the Ottoman Empire itself. There was thus a growing sense of grievance among Russian diplomats in the early 1850s at the emerging pattern of systematic interference in Orthodox religious affairs.

The mounting sensitivity of the Russian government on this point is critical to understanding its reactions to the renewal of Catholic claims at the holy places during the early 1850s. Notoriously, the debate over who owned or had precedence at the most sacred shrines in Christendom had limped along for centuries without engaging the interests or energies of European governments. Certainly, no one had been willing to go to war over the issue since the Middle Ages. This impasse acquired fresh political significance in 1850, when the French government decided to throw the full weight of its influence behind Catholic claims, and the Ottoman government appeared ready to acquiesce. As Nesselrode insisted to his ambassador in Paris in the summer of 1853, it had become clear to the tsar that the weakness of the Porte in this case was not an isolated event but rather the *culmination* of "a series of similar acts, which demonstrate[d] a systematic malevolence on the part of the Turkish Government against the rite [Russians] profess[ed] and an obvious partiality for the other Christian communions."[85] The tsar had no choice, the chancellor added, but to arrest a trend that became "day by day more pronounced" and that threatened the peace of Europe and the domestic stability of the Ottoman Empire. Russia could tolerate no more attempts on its influence either in the Near East or on the Orthodox Church.

When Nicholas I dispatched Prince Aleksandr Sergeyevich Menshikov to İstanbul as his special envoy in the spring of 1853, it was therefore with instructions to resolve all ambiguities and to retrace in bold the lines that the Porte and its Western provocateurs had blurred. In particular, Menshikov was to secure formal engagements from the sultan recognizing Russia's special relationship with Ottoman Orthodoxy and drawing a protective barrier around the internal affairs and privileges of the church.[86] Among the long list of related objectives, Prince Menshikov was specifically directed not only to reject Catholic claims at the holy places but also to demand such telling concessions as the reinstatement of Patriarch Grigorios VI—the same hierarch who had been removed in 1840 and barred from reelection thereafter at British insistence. In order to prevent future scandals, Abdülmecid was to sign a formal agreement promising that all patriarchs would henceforward "remain irremovably at their posts for life."[87] The Porte was also to do something about the manner in which Orthodox liturgical books were "arrested, confiscated, and lacerated [i.e., by removal of the prayers for the imperial family, anathemas against Islam, etc.] ... to such a degree as to render them completely unsuitable for their purpose."[88]

These demands were not trivial addenda to Menshikov's mission; rather, they were its very essence and most contentious aspect. As Nicholas and Nesselrode had feared, the Porte proved ready to give complete satisfaction regarding the holy places but stubbornly refused to provide binding guarantees for the rights and independence of the Orthodox Church. When Menshikov announced the formal termination of his mission on 18 May 1853, he singled out the Porte's failure to give any meaningful guarantees as *the* issue that had disrupted Russian-Ottoman relations. This failure, he declared, proved that the Russian government was right to have "serious apprehensions ... for the security and maintenance of the ancient rights of the Eastern Church."[89]

The evidence presented here is insufficient to vindicate all of Russia's complaints in 1853, but it does justify a serious reevaluation of them. As Blunt's letter of 8 October and many other examples show, the Porte and the Western powers were indeed intervening to an unprecedented extent in Orthodox religious life. They did so, moreover, with a deliberately anti-Russian agenda. The policies of the Porte and its Western allies could also be construed as broadly anti-Orthodox inasmuch as they sought to undermine the position of the clergy and to subordinate it as thoroughly as possible to Ottoman state control. The evidence contained in Ottoman, British, and French state archives make it difficult to escape the conclusion that these governments were—at best—ill-informed about the actions of their own agents when they issued formal denials of Russia's complaints in 1853-54. Stratford Canning, whose officious meddling in Orthodox affairs over the previous decade had done so much to aggravate the situation, tacitly admitted in a letter to Clarendon that his central objection to Russian demands was not that they required anything new. It was precisely that they would have frozen in place a status quo that the British embassy found objectionable and was working to overthrow. "In Turkey," he explained, "the dignitaries of the Greek or Orthodox church exercise in some degree the powers of civil magistrates. ... The abuses of the Greek hierarchy, as well in the exercise of civil authority as in the management of temporalities, are notorious; but if the pretensions of Russia were placed under the sanction of international law, *all prospect of improvement would be lost* [emphasis added]. Privilege and abuse would be bound up together in scandalous perpetuity."[90]

Russia's failed attempts to obtain a fragment of the Grail, to prevent the "laceration" of Orthodox prayer books, and to safeguard the independence of Orthodox patriarchal elections were thus separate instances of a larger problem. Together, they reveal a pattern of deliberate challenges to Russian hegemony over the Orthodox community during the 1840s and 1850s as European imperial rivalries were translated into an escalating engagement in the minutiae of Ottoman Christian religious life. This competition reached its tragic denouement in 1853 when Russia's claim to be the champion of Orthodoxy was forced from the realm of rhetoric and onto the battlefield. The frustrations of Russian statesmen in each case were symptomatic of a wider failure to prevent Orthodoxy, ostensibly Russia's greatest advantage in the Near East, from becoming its Achilles heel—a source of tribulation, embarrassment, and ultimately of national disaster. Whether or not the ailing and recently widowed Alexandra Fedorovna obtained her fragment of the Ayion Potirion in 1856, the figurative holy grail of a stable and recognized hegemony in the Near East continued to elude her adopted country.

NOTES

1. Timothy Samuel Shah and Daniel Philpott, "The Fall and Rise of Religion in International Relations: History and Theory," in *Religion and International Relations Theory*, ed. Jack Synder (New York: Columbia University Press, 2011), 24.

2. Philip Gorski, *The Disciplinary Revolution: Calvinism and the Rise of the State in Early Modern Europe* (Chicago: University of Chicago Press, 2003), 158. For some exemplars of what is now a very extensive body of work, see Daniel Philpott, *Revolutions in Sovereignty: How Ideas Shaped Modern International Relations* (Princeton, NJ: Princeton University Press, 2001); Adrian Hastings, *The Construction of Nationhood: Ethnicity, Religion and Nationalism* (Cambridge: Cambridge University Press, 1997); Armando Salvatore, *The Public Sphere: Liberal Modernity, Catholicism, Islam* (New York: Palgrave Macmillan, 2007); Derek Beales, *Prosperity and Plunder: European Catholic Monasteries in the Age of Revolution, 1650–1815* (Cambridge: Cambridge University Press, 2003); Ivan Strenski, *Contesting Sacrifice: Religion, Nationalism and Social Thought in France* (Chicago: University of Chicago Press, 2002); Steven Merritt Miner, *Stalin's Holy War: Religion, Nationalism and Alliance Politics, 1941–1945* (Chapel Hill: University of North Carolina Press, 2003); Robert Alvis, *Religion and the Rise of Nationalism: A Profile of an East-Central European City* (Syracuse: Syracuse University Press, 2005).

3. For example, see Marc D. Baer, *Honoured by the Glory of Islam: Conversion and Conquest in Ottoman Europe* (New York: Oxford University Press, 2008); David D. Commins, *Islamic Reform: Politics and Social Change in Late Ottoman*

Syria (New York: Oxford University Press, 1990); Selim Deringil, *The Well-Protected Domains: Ideology and the Legitimation of Power in the Ottoman Empire, 1876-1909* (London: I. B. Tauris, 1999); idem, *Conversion and Apostasy in the Late Ottoman Empire* (New York: Cambridge University Press, 2012); Suraiya Faroqhi, *Der Bektaschi-Orden in Anatolien: Vom späten fünfzehnten Jahrhundert bis 1826* (Vienna: Verlag des Institutes für Orientalistik der Universität Wien, 1981); Kemal Karpat, *The Politicization of Islam: Reconstructing Identity, State, Faith, and Community in the Late Ottoman State* (New York: Oxford University Press, 2001); Ussama Makdisi, *The Culture of Sectarianism: Community, History, and Violence in Nineteenth-Century Ottoman Lebanon* (Berkeley: University of California Press, 2000); idem, *Artillery of Heaven: American Missionaries and the Failed Conquest of the Middle East* (Ithaca, NY: Cornell University Press, 2009); Dimitris Stamatopoulos, *Metarrythmisi kai enkosmikefsi: Pros mia anasynthesi tis istorias tou Oikoumenikou Patriarcheiou ton 19o aiona* (Athens: Alexandreia, 2003); Itzchak Weismann, *Taste of Modernity: Sufism, Salafiyya, and Arabism in Late Ottoman Damascus* (Leiden: Brill, 2000).

4. See the proclamations of 14 June and 26 September [OS] in *Journal de Constantinople*, 9 October 1853, 1. All dates in this chapter according to the Gregorian calendar, except for those identified in square brackets as either [OS]—Old Style/Julian calendar—or [AH]—anno Hegirae/Hijri calendar.

5. *Moskovskiia Vedomosti*, 18 June [OS] 1853, 1.

6. Cabinet Memorandum, 18 February [OS] 1854, in *Le Nouveau Portfolio: Question d'Orient; Documents* (Berlin: F. Schneider, 1854), 4-6.

7. *Journal de Constantinople*, 9 October 1853, 1.

8. Clarendon complained to the British ambassador in St. Petersburg in July 1853: "Russia claims for her 'co-religionnaires' in the East the strict *status quo*, and the maintenance of the privileges they have enjoyed under the protection of their Sovereign; but Count Nesselrode entirely omits to show how that *status quo* has been disturbed, how those privileges have been curtailed, what complaints have been made, what grievances remain without redress?" G. F. W. Villiers, Earl Clarendon to Hamilton Seymour, 16 July 1853, TNA FO 352/61, folder 5.

9. From the House of Commons debates of 20 February 1854, in *Hansard's Parliamentary Debates* (London: Hansard, 1854), 1037.

10. *Journal de Constantinople*, 9 October 1853, 1. For a similar rationalization, see the British declaration of war in A. L. Macfie, *The Eastern Question, 1774-1923* (London: Longman, 1989), 97-100.

11. Clarendon to Seymour, 15 June 1853, in *Correspondence respecting the Rights and Privileges of the Latin and Greek Churches in Turkey* (London: Harrison and Sons, 1854), 288.

12. For a representative (but hardly exhaustive) sample of historiography on the origins of the war, see Alexander Kingslake, *The Invasion of the Crimea: Its Origin, and an Account of Its Progress down to the Death of Lord Raglan* (London:

Blackwood, 1863); Aleksandr Genrikhovich Jomini, *Étude diplomatique sur la guerre de Crimée (1852 à 1856) par un ancien diplomate* (Paris: Ch. Tanera, 1874); Edmond Bapst, *Les origines de la guerre de Crimée* (Paris: C. Delagrave, 1912); Vernon J. Puryear, *England, Russia, and the Straits Question* (Berkeley: University of California Press, 1931); Harold Temperley, *England and the Near East: The Crimea* (London: Longmans, 1936); M. S. Anderson, *The Eastern Question, 1774–1923: A Study in International Relations* (London: Macmillan, 1966); Paul Schroeder, *Austria, Great Britain, and the Crimean War: The Destruction of the European Concert* (Ithaca, NY: Cornell University Press, 1972); Ann Pottinger Saab, *The Origins of the Crimean Alliance* (Charlottesville: University Press of Virginia, 1977); Norman Rich, *Why the Crimean War? A Cautionary Tale* (Hanover, NH: University Press of New England, for Brown University, 1985); David Wetzel, *The Crimean War* (Boulder, CO: East European Monographs, 1985); Winfried Baumgart, *The Crimean War, 1853–1856* (London: Arnold; New York: Oxford University Press, 1999).

13. Brison D. Gooch, "A Century of Historiography on the Origins of the Crimean War," *American Historical Review* 62, no. 1 (1956): 33.

14. See John Sheldon Curtiss, *Russia's Crimean War* (Durham, NC: Duke University Press, 1979); David Goldfrank, *The Origins of the Crimean War* (London: Longman, 1994); Mara Kozelsky, *Christianizing Crimea: Shaping Sacred Space in the Russian Empire and Beyond* (DeKalb: Northern Illinois University Press, 2010); Orlando Figes, *The Crimean War: A History* (New York: Metropolitan Books, 2010).

15. As Candan Badem notes in *The Ottoman Crimean War (1853–1856)* (Leiden: Brill, 2010), 65, it remains a commonplace among historians outside Russia "that the question of the holy places was no more than a pretext for the Crimean War."

16. Charles Blunt to Stratford Canning, 8 October 1850, TNA FO 195/293.

17. Andrei N. Murav'ev, *Pis'ma s Vostoka v 1849–1850 godakh*, 2 vols. (St. Petersburg: V Tipografii III Otdeleniia Sob. E.I.V. Kantseliarii, 1851), 1:389.

18. Angel Mustoksidi to Vladimir Titov, 7 June [OS] 1850, AVPRI, f. 180, op. 517/1, d. 1315, ll. 90–92. Pictures, historical discussion, and a detailed description of the relics are in Yeoryios Stoyioglou, *Monastiria tis Makedonias: A' Monastiria tis Thessalonikis* (Thessaloniki: Ekdotikos Oikos Adelfon Kyriakidi, 1990), 139–49.

19. S. Z. Baikulova, Ia. Iu. Matveeva, and A. L. Bauman, *Rukovoditeli Sankt-Peterburga* (St. Petersburg: Neva/Olma Press, 2003), 198–99.

20. Mustoksidi to Titov, 24 May [OS] 1850, AVPRI, f. 180, op. 517/1, d. 1315, l. 79. For the biography and career of Mustoksidi, see, Lucien J. Frary, "Russian Interests in Nineteenth-Century Thessaloniki," *Mediterranean Historical Review* 23, no. 1 (2008): 15–33.

21. Mustoksidi to Titov, 7 June [OS] 1850, AVPRI, f. 180, op. 517/1, d. 1315, l. 92.

22. Mustoksidi to Titov, 24 May [OS] 1850, AVPRI, f. 180, op. 517/1, d. 1315, ll. 79–80.

23. When Grand Duke Konstantin Nikolaevich visited Jerusalem in 1858, for example, he wrote in his diary that Patriarch Kyrillos showered the imperial party with Holy Land souvenirs. At the end of one mass in the Holy Sepulcher, "the patriarch called us to the altar, where he cut off and gave us [fragments of] the relics of: 1) Emperor Constantine, 2) Empress Alexandra (for Zhinkov and Mama), 3) Basil the Great, and 4) Mary Magdalene." See Nikolai N. Lisovoi, *Rossiia v Sviatoi Zemle: Dokumenty i Materialy*, 2 vols. (Moscow: Mezhdunarodnye Otnosheniia, 2000), 1:134.

24. Mustoksidi to Titov, 19 September [OS] 1850, AVPRI, f. 180, op. 517/1, d. 1315, ll. 144–45.

25. Blunt to Canning, 8 October 1850, TNA FO 195/293.

26. Ibid.

27. Ibid.

28. Mustoksidi to Titov, 27 September [OS] 1850, AVPRI, f. 180, op. 517/1, d. 1315, l. 154.

29. It is not clear to which *firman* the governor was referring. For more on Ottoman policies regarding protection of antiquities, see Hüseyin Karaduman, "Belgelerle İlk Türk Asar-ı Atika Nizamnamesi," *Belgeler: Türk Tarihi Belgeler Dergisi* 25, no. 29 (2004): 73–92. I am indebted to Michael Walsh for this reference. See also Zainab Bahrani, Zeynep Çelik, and Edhem Eldem, eds., *Scramble for the Past: A Story of Archaeology in the Ottoman Empire, 1753–1914* (İstanbul: SALT, 2011); and Izabella Donkow, "The Ephesus Excavations 1863–1874, in the Light of the Ottoman Legislation on Antiquities," *Anatolian Studies* 54 (2004): 109–17.

30. Blunt to Canning, 8 October 1850, TNA FO 195/293.

31. For examples of Mustoksidi's letters on the matter to Titov, see 6 September [OS] 1850, AVPRI, f. 180, op. 517/1, d. 1315, l. 141; 2 September [OS] 1850, AVPRI, f. 180, op. 517/1, d. 1315, ll. 150–51; 27 September [OS] 1850, AVPRI, f. 180, op. 517/1, d. 1315, l. 154; 17 October [OS] 1850, AVPRI, f. 180, op. 517/1, d. 1315, l. 161.

32. Mustoksidi to Titov, 27 September [OS] 1850, AVPRI, f. 180, op. 517/1, d. 1315, l. 154.

33. Mustoksidi to Titov, 13 December [OS] 1850, AVPRI, f. 180, op. 517/1, d. 1315, l. 177.

34. Stoyioglou, *Monastiria tis Makedonias*, 145.

35. Ibid., 143–45.

36. Ibid., 139; Mustoksidi to Titov, 7 June [OS] 1850, AVPRI, f. 180, op. 517/1, d. 1315, ll. 90–92.

37. Mustoksidi to Titov, 7 June [OS] 1850, AVPRI, f. 180, op. 517/1, d. 1315, l. 91.

38. In Russia, commemoration of the reigning prince dated from at least the twelfth century. John Meyendorff, *Byzantium and the Rise of Russia: A Study of Byzantino-Russian Relations in the 14th Century* (Crestwood, NY: St. Vladimir's Seminary Press, 1989), 255. For a concrete Serbian example of prayers from the 1830s mentioning "our pious Lord and Prince Miloš [Obrenović]," see *Kniga się Trebnik* (Belgrade: Typ. Knęzhesko-Serbskoĭ, 1836), l. 16v.

39. *Eucholoyion to Mega, en o Periechondai kata Taxin ai ton Epta Mystirion Akolouthiai* (n.p.: Patriarcheio tis Konstantinoupoleos Typ., 1803), 36. For other examples of the same text, see Jacques Goar, *Euchologion sive Rituale Graecorum Complectens Ritus et Ordines Divinae Liturgiae* (Venice: B. Javarina, 1730), 52; *Eucholoyion to Mega* (Venice: Nikolaos Glykis, 1767), 39.

40. *Eucholoyion to Mega* (1803), 388.

41. "Typos peri tou pos prepei na mnimonevondan ta tis Aftokratorikis Oikoyeneias onomata eis tas Ieras Akolouthias," Princeton University Library, Constantinople Records of the Orthodox Patriarchate of Jerusalem, C0692, box 3.

42. From the priestly prayers during the Holy Anaphora of St. John Chrysostom. *Eucholoyion to Mega* (1803), 50.

43. Paul Werth, "Imperial Russia and the Armenian Catholicos at Home and Abroad," in *Reconstruction and Interaction in Slavic Eurasia and Its Neighboring Worlds*, ed. Ieda Osamu and Uyama Tomohiko (Sapporo: Slavic Research Center, Hokkaido University, 2006), 204. See also Eileen Kane, "Pilgrims, Holy Places and the Multi-Confessional Empire: Russian Policy towards the Ottoman Empire under Tsar Nicholas I, 1825–1855" (PhD diss., Princeton University, 2005), chap. 5.

44. Kane, "Pilgrims, Holy Places and the Multi-Confessional Empire," 128.

45. See the letter of the viceroy of the Caucasus, Baron Gregor von Rosen [Russian: Grigorii Vladimirovich Rozen] to Counselor Dmitrii Nikolaevich Bludov, dated 27 July [OS] 1833, and Article 21 of the *Polozhenie* in *Russia and the Armenians of Transcaucasia, 1797–1889: A Documentary Record*, ed. and trans. George A Bournoutian (Costa Mesa, CA: Mazda, 1998), 330, 353.

46. Von Rosen to Apollinarii Petrovich Butenev, 28 June 1834, in *Russia and the Armenians of Transcaucasia*, 344.

47. Werth, "Imperial Russia and the Armenian Catholicos," 208.

48. Kane, "Pilgrims, Holy Places and the Multi-Confessional Empire," 145–46.

49. See the exchanges between John Ponsonby and Palmerston of 22 April and 13 June of 1836, TNA FO 197/6.

50. "Mémoire sur la politique Russe dans l'Orient," Iakovos Pitzipios to Stratford Canning, 18 July 1850, TNA FO 352/33B, folder 9, 44–46.

51. Journal entry for 30 September 1851, Palmer Journals, Lambeth Palace Library, MS 2829, Palmer Papers, 391.

52. Journal entry of 5 June 1850, Palmer Journals, Lambeth Palace Library, MS 2826, Palmer Papers, 94–96. It is difficult to identify precisely the publications that Palmer cites, but he appears to be paraphrasing from a copy of the Great Euchologion (Velikii Trebnik), which contains an intercessory service (*moleben*) for "the Release of Those under Bondage and Captivity to the Hagarenes, and for the Destruction of These Christ-hating Authorities" as well as a formula for converts from Islam to renounce "the Impious Wickedness of the Saracens, that is to say, Turks." See *Trebnyk Mytropolyta Petra Mohyly: Kyiv 1646*, 3 vols. (Kyiv: Informatsiyno-Vydavnychyi Tsentr Ukrainskoi Pravoslavnoi Tserkvy, 1996), 1:93; 3:116–35.

53. Journal entry for 30 September 1851, Palmer Journals, Lambeth Palace Library, MS 2829, Palmer Papers, 391.

54. There were precedents for this behavior inasmuch as Western embassies had interfered forcefully in Orthodox affairs before the 1800s. See Gunnar Hering, *Ökumenisches Patriarchat und europäische Politik, 1620–1638* (Wiesbaden: Franz Steiner Verlag, 1968); and George A. Hadjiantoniou, *Protestant Patriarch: The Life of Cyril Lucaris (1572–1638) Patriarch of Constantinople* (Richmond, VA: John Knox Press, 1961).

55. Édouard Thouvenel to Alexandre Colonna Walewski, 21 February 1856, AHMAE, Correspondance Politique, Turquie, vol. 324.

56. For a more thorough account, see Jack Fairey, "'Discord and Confusion . . . under the Pretext of Religion': European Diplomacy and the Limits of Orthodox Ecclesiastical Authority in the Eastern Mediterranean," *International History Review* 34, no. 1 (2012): 19–44.

57. Jack Fairey, "The Great Game of Improvements: European Diplomacy and the Reform of the Orthodox Church" (PhD diss., University of Toronto, 2004), 166, 262.

58. Palmerston to Canning, 13 April 1849, TNA FO 78/769, l. 26.

59. Blunt to Ponsonby, 11 September 1840, TNA FO 195/176.

60. Blunt to Ponsonby, in *Britanski Dokumenti za istorijata na Makedonskiot Narod*, 2 vols., ed. Hristo Andonov-Poljanski (Skopje: Arhivna Makedonija, 1968), 1:287.

61. Niven Kerr to Henry Wellesley, Earl Cowley, 22 November 1846, TNA FO 78/677. A copy of Kerr's charges can also be found in the BOA, Hariciye Nezareti Siyasi Kısım, Gömlek, 6.

62. Cowley to Palmerston, 15 January 1847, TNA FO 78/677; and Kerr to Cowley, 31 December 1847, TNA FO 78/715.

63. Blunt to Canning, 2 September 1842, TNA FO 195/176. For similar observations by Blunt's colleague at the French consulate, see Edouard Grasset to Quai d'Orsay, 24 December 1850, AHMAE, Correspondance Politique, Turquie, Consulats Divers, Salonique 1841–47, 1848–59, fols. 22–23.

64. Cor to Pontois, September 1840, AHMAE, Mémoires et Documens, vol. 56, l. 119.

65. Baron Bartholomäus von Stürmer to Prince Clemens von Metternich, 23 September 1846, HHSA, Staatenabteilungen Türkei VI, Karton 95, l. 243v.
66. Reşid Paşa to Sultan Abdülmecid, 20 June 1847, BOA, Mesail-i Mühimme İrade, 922.
67. Cor to de Pontois, September 1840, AHMAE, Mémoires et Documens, vol. 56, fols. 108, 117–18.
68. Blunt to Ponsonby, 15 March 1841, TNA FO 195/176.
69. Mehmed Emin Rauf Paşa to Sultan Abdülmecid. The document is undated and unsigned, but internal evidence indicates the spring of 1843. BOA, Mesail-i Mühimme İrade, 916.
70. For the abdication of Yermanos, see Canning to Aberdeen, 17 May 1845, TNA FO 78/597. For the irregular exclusions, see Vezieral *buyuruldu* to the Patriarchal Synod, 14 Zilhicce 1261 [AH], enclosed in Titov's report to Count Ivan Illarionovich Vorontsov-Dashkov, 4 December [OS] 1845, AVPRI, f. 180, op. 517/1, d. 192, ll. 313–15.
71. Titov to Vorontsov-Dashkov, 24 December 1845 [OS], AVPRI, f. 180, op. 517/1, d. 192, l. 363.
72. Titov to Vorontsov-Dashkov, 4 December [OS] 1845, AVPRI, f. 180, op. 517/1, d. 192, l. 311.
73. Titov to Nesselrode, 12 December [OS] 1845, AVPRI, f. 180, op. 517/1, d. 192, l. 338.
74. Instructions of Titov to Prince Handjery [Tilemachos Chatzeris], 22 February [OS] 1846, AVPRI, f. 180, op. 517/1, d. 194, l. 148; Titov to Vorontsov-Dashkov, 24 February [OS] 1846, AVPRI, f. 180, op. 517/1, d. 194, l. 147.
75. Titov to Reşid Paşa, 22 February [OS] 1846, AVPRI, f. 180, op. 517/1, d. 194, ll. 149–51. A copy exists in BOA, Hariciye Nezareti Siyasi Kısım, Dosya 1786, Gömlek 3.
76. Ibid.
77. Ibid.
78. Thouvenel to Walewski, 8 November 1855, AHMAE, Correspondance Politique, Turquie, vol. 323.
79. For a discussion of these problems, see Nikolai N. Lisovoi, *Russkoe dukhovnoe i politicheskoe prisutstvie v Sviatoi Zemle i na Blizhnem Vostoke v XIX–Nachale XX v.* (Moscow: Indrik, 2006), 309–11.
80. See D. Brower, "Russian Roads to Mecca: Religious Tolerance and Muslim Pilgrimage in the Russian Empire," *Slavic Review* 55 (1996): 567–84; R. Crews, *For Prophet and Tsar: Islam and Empire in Russia and Central Asia* (Cambridge, MA: Harvard University Press, 2006), 50–51, 71–74, and 325; and Kane, "Pilgrims, Holy Places and the Multi-Confessional Empire," chap. 2.
81. Saab, *Origins of the Crimean Alliance*, 6.
82. Circular of Nesselrode to all Russian ministers and diplomatic agents, 20 June 1853, in *Journal de Constantinople*, 19 July 1853.
83. When Russia annexed the Crimean khanate in the late 1700s, for example,

the Ottomans had insisted on writing into the terms of the 1774 Treaty of Kuchuk Kainardji that the sultan would continue to act as caliph and supreme religious leader of Crimean Muslims. The Treaty of Constantinople on 8 January 1784 would later rescind this clause. See the third article of the Treaty of Kuchuk Kainardji in *Treaties, &c. between Turkey and Foreign Powers, 1535-1855* (London: HMP, 1855), 465.

84. Mikhail Mikhailovich Ustinov to Nesselrode, 20 January [OS] 1847, AVPRI, f. 180, op. 517/1, d. 197, l. 83.

85. Dispatch from Nesselrode to Nikolai Dimitrievich Kiselev, 1 August 1853, in *Le Nouveau Portfolio: Question d'Orient; Documents* (Berlin: F. Schneider, 1854), 56-58.

86. Tsar Nicholas I to Sultan Abdülmecid I, 24 January [OS] 1853, in A. M. Zaionchkovskii, *Vostochnaia Voina 1853-1856 gg. v sviazi s sovremennoi ei politicheskoi obstanovkoi*, 2 vols., 3 suppl. (St. Petersburg: Ekspeditsiia Zagotovleniia Gosudarstvennykh Bumag, 1908), 1:386; and Nesselrode's instructions to Menshikov, 28 January [OS] 1853, in Zaionchkovskii, *Vostochnaia Voina 1853-1856*, 1:377.

87. Article III, *Project d'une Convention avec la Porte Ottomane*, in Zaionchkovskii, *Vostochnaia Voina 1853-1856*, 1:383-84.

88. "Notice sur quelques questions spéciales à traiter avec la Porte," AVPRI, f. 5, op. A2, d. 523, ll. 443-44.

89. Menshikov to Reşid Paşa, 6 May [OS] 1853, copy annexed to Klezl's report of May 19, 1853, HHSA, PA.XII, karton 46.

90. Redcliffe to Clarendon, 22 May 1853, TNA FO 78/932/57.

The Crimean War and the Tatar Exodus

MARA KOZELSKY

In the years following the Crimean War (1853–56), nearly two-hundred thousand Crimean Tatars fled their native peninsula en masse to resettle in the Ottoman Empire. They abandoned their homes and livestock; sold their property at devastatingly low prices; gave up their *poddanstvo*, or subjecthood in the Russian Empire; and bid farewell to the country that had been their home for centuries.[1] Beginning in a steady trickle in 1855, the number of refugees per year increased after the Treaty of Paris (1856), which guaranteed Muslims safe passage to the Ottoman Empire. By the time the emigration ran its course, about two-thirds of Crimea's native population had fled their native lands. The Crimean Tatar departure plunged the peninsula, already wasted from the war, into the deepest crisis of its history since the Russian annexation of the region in 1783.

With the most concentrated out-migration occurring in the summer of 1860, Crimea's struggling postwar economy came to a standstill. The new technologies of the steamship, which could rapidly transport the Tatars across the Black Sea to İstanbul, made their departure starkly immediate and dramatic. Crimeans mourned the loss of the landscapes of their childhoods and wept as their neighbors and friends traveled in

Burning of the Government Buildings at Kertch. (from the personal collection of Mara Kozelsky)

convoys to ships waiting to carry them to their new lives. Goods waited at the docks for Tatar drivers and horses that never came. Fruit rotted on the vine, and wheat withered on the stalks. Landowners, many of whom had previously tormented the Tatar population, panicked at the absence of agricultural laborers to gather the harvest. An observer of the migration reflected, "Emigration of an entire population always impoverishes the country, and in this case indelible traces will remain for decades."[2]

Migration of the Crimean Tatars constituted one of the largest internal mass migrations of nineteenth-century Europe.[3] Recent scholarship on migration during the nineteenth century has tended to focus on Western European labor movements and mass urbanization and ascribe violence-inspired migration to the provenance of the twentieth century.[4] Researchers working on the population exchanges along the Russian-Ottoman frontier, however, have long recognized the role of violence in migration. Soviet historians E. I. Druzhinina and V. M. Kabuzan, for example, traced the waves of refugees that streamed into New Russia after the multiple Russian-Ottoman wars between 1774 and 1878.

Greeks, Bulgarians, Serbs, and Armenians who had taken arms against the Ottoman Empire sought asylum in the empire of the tsars.[5] Odessa, a Greek city from its inception, served as a beacon for thousands of Ottoman Christians previously engaged in the uprisings against the sultan.[6] For this reason, Greeks from refugee families dominated the first decades of historical scholarship of New Russia, and their work naturally emphasized the relationship between war, refugees, and regional development.[7]

Focusing on the opposite pattern of population movement, Kemal Karpat has examined the waves of migration into the Ottoman Empire that accompanied different Russian-Ottoman wars in his groundbreaking study of the Ottoman population. He estimates that millions of Muslims from Russia, the Balkans, and the Caucasus immigrated to the Ottoman Empire during the nineteenth century through the First World War, including nearly 1,800,000 Tatars.[8] Examining the population exchange of Tatars and Bulgarians between the Ottoman and the Russian Empire at the end of the Crimean War, Mark Pinson is one of the few scholars to explicitly portray the violence inherent to the population exchange and describe the phenomenon as "demographic warfare."[9] Following the studies of Karpat and Pinson, Alan W. Fisher and Bryan Glyn Williams have emphasized that violent upheaval and hostile state policies characterized the Muslim migrations from Balkans and the Russian Empire.[10]

This chapter contributes to the scholarship on the Tatar migration by examining local war conditions that precipitated the Tatar exodus as well the local and imperial response to Crimea's sudden population loss. Research based on previously untapped archival materials, including Tatar petitions and government reports at local and imperial levels, suggest that many Russian officials actively encouraged Tatar outmigration.[11] Other officials who may have been sympathetic to Tatars, such as Prince Mikhail Gorchakov, the head of Military Command in Crimea from 1855, made ad hoc policy decisions throughout the war and recovery period that reduced the Tatars' access to resources, making survival in Crimea untenable. Much worse, Russian officials such as the military governor of Tauride, Count Nikolai Adlerberg, and his direct superior, the military general governor of New Russia, Count Andrei Stroganov, blamed the Tatars for Crimea's prewar economic stagnation and suspected Tatars en masse of collaborating with the enemy during the war. These men engineered the forcible relocation of some ten thousand coastal Crimean Tatars during the war and called for an ethnic cleansing of the peninsula after the war. In this sense, the Crimean exodus should be seen as a forced rather than a voluntary migration, a point I have argued elsewhere.[12]

Although this chapter principally analyzes the local causes of the Crimean migration, I also argue that the migration must be understood fundamentally as a product of the Eastern Question. Thus, the Tatar migration following the Crimean War is the largest of many migrations connected to the Eastern Question in the nineteenth century. The connection to the Eastern Question is particularly evident in the Allied intention to stir up Tatar nationalism; the holy war rhetoric that permeated discourse of all belligerents; and the sanctioning of population exchange in the Treaty of Paris (1856). In Crimea, local officials formulated policy directly in response to international developments. The Eastern Question, as I argue, transformed the Crimean Peninsula, both in terms of the destruction created by war, and the demographic shift that followed on its heels.

The Crimean War began in October 1853 as a localized dispute between the Russian and the Ottoman Empire over Russian concerns about the treatment of Ottoman Christians.[13] England and France joined forces with the Ottoman Empire against Russia in the winter of 1854, when a Russian victory over the Ottoman Empire seemed imminent. The war moved to Crimea in the fall of that same year.[14] Although the siege of Sevastopol became the most notable battle of the war, apart perhaps from the Battle of Balaklava (better known for the Charge of the Light Brigade), tentacles of violence spread throughout the entire peninsula. The Allies occupied Evpatoria in the west and entered the Sea of Azov, bombarding Kerch-Enikale and Genichesk in the east. Allied soldiers sortied into remote Tatar villages nestled in Crimea's interior mountains, conscripted Tatar laborers, and stole their goods. Russian troops commandeered the heart of the peninsula, turning houses and public buildings into barracks and hospitals. The peninsula became a war zone; every civilian who did not flee lived the war.

The conditions of the Tatar exodus were thus set on the first day of the Allied invasion of Crimea. From the moment that Allies disembarked in Evpatoria on 1 September 1854, continuing through October as they cemented their advance in Sevastopol, the peninsula entered a period of what contemporaries described as "the chaos." The "chaos" began when Prince Alexander Menshikov, the first head commander of the Russian military, concentrated forces at Sevastopol. He pulled all Russian forces from the other regions of the peninsula to post at the naval city, leaving the long Crimean coast undefended. Crimeans watched in horror as Russian troops packed up and moved out while enemy warships menaced their seaside villages.

As Menshikov focused on supporting Sevastopol, Tauride governor Vladimir Ivanovich Pestel ordered all government offices and personnel to relocate into Tauride's northern districts.[15] As bureaucrats packed up their offices for transfer on a day's notice, they also demanded the destruction of town and village bread reserves that could fall into the hands of the enemy.[16] Local bureaucrats commissioned carriages and postal stations and made no provisions for the evacuation of civilians.[17] Those people who had the means evacuated with the clothes on their backs and what small amounts of food they could carry. Many slept in the open air as they made their way north into the interior of the peninsula and the Russian provinces.[18] Most peasants, the majority of whom were Tatars, could not afford to leave their homes and so were left, unprotected, to face the enemy invasion and to watch their own government waste a supply of bread that could have carried them through several years.

Waves of robbery accompanied the frenzied evacuation in the first days of September; peoples of all nationalities, whether Greeks, Armenians, Russians, Tatars, or Jews, ransacked abandoned houses.[19] Allied foragers pillaged estates and villages and stole food, livestock, and whatever movable property they could carry.[20] People were murdered, some in broad daylight.[21] Russian attempts to calm the chaos only made it worse. Prince Menshikov called on irregular units of Don Cossacks to reestablish order in Crimean cities and villages. Cossacks streamed into the peninsula, joined the plunder, and terrorized frightened residents already suffering under Allied occupation.[22] The Cossacks, along with their Russian counterparts, subjected Tatars to baseless arrests and corrupt requisitioning.[23]

Selim Telersh Oglu, who lived near the Mackenzie foothills outside Sevastopol, for example, testified after the war that Cossack militia arrested him in September 1854 without cause. Cossacks arrived in his village and asked for information about passing French troops. Selim Oglu did not personally witness the troop movement but was able to lead the Cossacks on horseback through trails that the French were rumored to have taken. On their return, the Cossacks presented their

Tatar guide to Prince Menshikov, who interrogated him further. When Selim Oglu could give no additional information about French whereabouts, Menshikov ordered him to be thrown into prison in Simferopol, where he remained for eight months. Subsequently, authorities removed him from Kherson in 1855 and then to Voronezh, where he remained until 1859, when he was freed to settle in Kherson.[24] Many Tatars shared Selim Oglu's fate. Stories like his quickly circulated the peninsula, fueling Tatar distrust of the Russian government and Cossacks in particular.

As Russian bureaucrats evacuated and Russian forces streamed into Sevastopol, Allies entered many towns on the Crimean coast without any resistance at all. They immediately occupied Evpatoria, one of the larger Crimean cities and the busiest port, and used it as a base of operations throughout the war. Thus another element of "the chaos" involved confusion over the occupation of Evpatoria, ensuing outbreaks of sectarian violence between Tatars and Russians in Evpatoria, and uncertainty over whether the Tatars supported the Allies or were imprisoned by them.

The only two surviving memoirs of this invasion, both written by Russians, describe the arrival of thousands of Tatars from the city and surrounding villages to greet the Allies on the Evpatoria quay. These men, a Russian bureaucrat, V. S. Rakov, and an Orthodox priest, whose name is indecipherable, lived in Evpatoria at the time. Both men believed that the Allies actively sought to incite mutiny among the Tatars by whipping up dreams of independence and nationalist sentiments.[25] The few studies that do exist on this topic suggest that the Allies did indeed send Ottoman Tatar agents and Polish rebels among Muslim tribes in Crimea and the Caucasus, but more work needs to be done to fully understand the level of Allied involvement.[26] In any case, by mid-October Russian officials estimated that fourteen thousand Tatars living in Evpatoria and surrounding villages had joined the Allies.[27] Many of these Tatars immigrated to the Ottoman Empire before the war's conclusion, and for the purposes of this chapter, can be seen as the first wave of migration.

The period of chaos had run its course by the beginning of November 1854 as the Allies and the Russians settled into their battle positions. As fall turned to winter and inclement weather forced a pause in the fighting, the imperial government changed the peninsula's ruling authorities. Count Nikolai Adlerberg, who fought in the Caucasus in 1841–42 and served in Hungary in 1849, became the military governor of Tauride and Simferopol, replacing Pestel, who had fallen into disfavor for evacuating the peninsula.[28] Count Andrei Stroganov, who had fought in the Napoleonic Wars and suppressed the Polish uprising of 1831, replaced Prince Mikhail Vorontsov as the governor general of New Russia and Bessarabia, a post he occupied from 1854 to 1861.[29] Finally, Prince Mikhail Gorchakov replaced Prince Menshikov as head commander of the Russian forces in Crimea. This change of personnel meant the imposition of martial law in Crimea. As opposed to the outgoing civilian administrators, who built careers on managing Tauride's complex ethnic and religious diversity, military authorities were principally interested in managing the war to a successful conclusion.[30] Thus, Adlerberg, Gorchakov, and Stroganov worked to extract resources for the Russian military from Crimea and the surrounding regions of New Russia. They also settled social unrest through heavy-handed measures, including the exile of Tatars to the interior of the peninsula. Despite the fact that the majority of Tatars remained loyal to the state, Menshikov, Adlerberg, and Stroganov particularly blamed the Tatars for Russian losses following the uprising in Evpatoria.[31]

Rumors of government proposals to relocate the Tatars en masse during the war became one of the most important causes of the Tatar migration. As early as October 1854, only one month after the Allied invasion, Russian military authorities posted in Crimea, particularly Count Adlerberg, began to advocate for the relocation of Crimean Tatars to the interior of the peninsula. The evacuation was punitive in nature, designed to prevent the Tatars from colluding with the enemy, sharing their food and livestock, or providing information about strategic points.[32] After the appearance of Tatars supporting the Allies in Evpatoria, military authorities placed the whole ethnic group under suspicion and viewed "cleaning the shore" of Tatars as necessary to protect imperial war aims. They also arrested groups of Tatars for betraying the Russian state and dispatched them to Kursk, Kherson, and Ekaterinoslav.[33] By May 1855, the Russian military had relocated 4,279 men and 3,090 women to Simferopol and Perekop, where some were given strips of land and remained until the war's conclusion.

Removed from their sources of food and their livelihood, many of the Tatars suffered starvation during the war and impoverishment afterward. Others found that landlords had seized their estates during their absence. Authorities contemplated a much wider mass relocation of all those Tatars living within twenty-five kilometers of the sea in February 1856. Fortunately, the war came to a conclusion before this larger resettlement came to pass.[34] Still, the relocation of ten thousand Tatars and the continuation of similar proposals made lasting impressions on the Tatar population.

Conditions for Tatars worsened as the war moved forward. Prince Gorchakov, who consistently discouraged baseless arrests of Tatars and often opposed relocating them, nevertheless instituted a relentless policy of requisition. In the minutes of a postwar commission established to calculate regional losses, Gorchakov revealed that as a matter of course, the Russian army took what it needed from Tatar villages without fair compensation. When the military occupied the village of Tash-Basty (now Bol'shoe Sadovoe) in the fall of 1855, it razed an orchard. Gorchakov initially planned to pay the Tatars fair value for materials, he said, because he recognized that "the trees composed a chief source of income for the people."[35] A deputation of citizens and officers estimated village losses at 30,550 rubles. As rumors of the proposal for Tash-Basty spread, however, other villages came forward demanding fair compensation for losses they had suffered at the hands of the Russian military. Gorchakov concluded that if the measures for Tash-Basty were to be followed, the minimum compensation would "be a huge expenditure for the treasury." Subsequently, he rescinded his initial offer and gave the residents from Tash-Basty only 3,000 rubles toward the full value of their losses. Gorchakov promised further compensation only if their "behavior demonstrated sincere respectful attention to their government."[36] In practice, this meant that in the best of circumstances the army compensated Tatars for one-tenth of the estimated value of their losses. In the worst of circumstances, such a policy implied that Tatars who attempted even the mildest of resistance to army requisitioning would receive nothing during or at the end of the war.[37]

In addition to harmful Russian policies, widespread devastation from battle and ceaseless pillaging prompted many Tatars to abandon their homes. Within a year, most Crimean cities had been bombarded to ruins or completely emptied of consumable goods. Nearly all private property in Crimea had been stolen or damaged by Russian and Allied forces or local pillagers. Orchards and vineyards, like those in Tash-Basty, had been cut to the ground. The Tatars, who composed the majority population living along the Black Sea coast, felt the astounding losses most sorely. The war governor in Crimea, Count Adlerberg, reported, "132 landed estates and 105 Tatar villages have been completely ruined, not speaking of the cities and the surroundings, which were occupied by the enemy (Sevastopol, Balaklava, Evpatoria, and Kerch with Enikale)." Allies and Russians established 187 cemeteries in civilian gardens, fields, and pastures for the bodies of more than 120,000 men. Only fourteen houses remained intact in Sevastopol, and on the opposite side of the peninsula, only 380 of 1,940 homes still stood in Kerch.[38] Russian officials further estimated that by the war's conclusion, "not more than one-fourth the work animals remain[ed]," and noted that "the fall sowing of 1855, and the spring of the present year ha[d] been completely destroyed."[39] The war plunged the entire peninsula into poverty, and many Crimeans—Tatars, Russians and Greeks alike—suffered starvation.

The general governor of New Russia, Count Stroganov, whose entire province bore the brunt of war from Izmail to the Caucasus, repeatedly emphasized that Crimea suffered the most sustained damage. Calculating the per capita losses of the different regions of the empire during the war based on "a few different sources of data," Stroganov concluded that on average subjects in Bessarabia lost 10 rubles per person; in the southern districts of Kherson and Ekaterinoslav province up to 15 rubles per person; and in "the Northern districts of Tauride, particularly in Dneprovsk, Melitopol and Perekop, up to 25 rubles per male," with a total for all three regions approaching 12,600,000 rubles in silver.[40]

He could not provide a figure, however, for Crimea. The massive damage there was unprecedented in Russian history, exceeding even that which Russia had experienced during the Napoleonic Wars.[41] Such widespread destruction made it impossible, Stroganov argued, to calculate "the value of the losses." Crimea "was deeply damaged not only from the activities of the enemy" but also from evacuations of residents along the seashore, which meant the absence of regular farm labor for more than a year. "Extreme congestion of the military" created highly unsanitary conditions, ruined residences, and infected water supplies. The mountainous part of the peninsula better survived direct bombardment and occupation, but still "many localities were destroyed and orchards and vineyards were desolated." Residences and "all property," Stroganov emphasized to the central government in St. Petersburg to which he had turned for state aid, "suffered complete ruin."[42] The devastation of agriculture and unsanitary conditions caused by military congestion and mass graves meant that by 1855, Crimean Tatars were suffering typhus, cholera, dislocation, and starvation.

Peace did little to improve circumstances for the Tatars, and unfair policies continued. With no end in sight, many Tatars must have seen little future for themselves or their families in Crimea. Many Russians blamed the Tatars for losses in the war, and others sought to gain from Tatar misfortune. Crimean landlords of Russian and European heritage moved quickly to absorb Tatar property into their estates, including the property of Tatars who had been forced into the interior of the province. In the village of Chorgun, for example, more than forty Tatars petitioned the Simferopol district authorities to protest the seizure of their land by the noblewoman Mavra Mikhailii during the war. Three years after the war's conclusion, she still had not returned their land. Instead, she had settled it with Russian families.[43]

Settling confiscated Tatar lands around the war zones with German and Russian colonists quickly evolved into a de facto policy supported by authorities in Tauride. In his annual report for 1855, the military governor of Simferopol and Tauride, Count Adlerberg, argued that "experience ha[d] shown [Tatars] as incapable of being successful agriculturalists." In their place, he recommended settling German and Mennonite colonists on half of this territory "due to the real advantage they [would] bring to agriculture in the northern districts."[44] On the other half, he proposed settling veterans of the war, who showed "particular zeal and devotion to the government."[45] The representative of the nobility in Evpatoria shared Adlerberg's sentiment. In a proposal discussing how to reestablish agricultural production after the war, the nobleman argued that agricultural estates not only could be restored to their former value but also could increase in price following the departure of the Tatars. "The transfer of land from Tatars to Russian owners will strengthen grain harvesting," he wrote, as well as "improving agriculture and the raising of livestock."[46]

Such racialized notions of labor dated to the era of Catherine II, when the state fixed upon German colonists as a solution to settling the sparsely populated regions conquered during the Russian-Ottoman wars. Alexander I and Nicholas I expanded the racialized approach to labor by including Russian Old Believers and sectarian groups, deemed more productive and skilled than natives in colonized areas.[47] In Crimea, such views also acquired a religious and political cast, as many of the foreign settlers included Christian refugees from the Ottoman Empire, who brought their political resentments with them.[48] The Crimean War had the effect of calling into action the most cynical of racialist settlement schemes.

Stroganov supported Adlerberg's desire to replace the native Tatar population with foreign settlers, and in April 1856, he forwarded a proposal to the Ministry of State Domains in St. Petersburg. Because the Ministry of State Domains oversaw the affairs of state peasants, including Tatars, and had established lawful practice for relocating state peasants, Stroganov sought cooperation from this particular imperial body. Despite its rich natural gifts, he wrote in his proposal, Crimea "remained for seventy years in the same state of wilderness, due in large part to the inability of the Muslim population to work hard." Stroganov emphasized the recent history of Tatar mutinies, arguing that "during the war, the Tatars demonstrated readiness to do harm" to the Russian state. Pointing to Crimea's significant salt industry and the importance of the Azov Sea to accessing Russia's interior and the Caucasus, Stroganov asserted that the peninsula was too strategically important to leave to a non-Russian population. He advocated populating Crimea with "pure Russian tribes, even without taking German colonists." Stroganov maintained that such a plan needed to be "attentively thought out, founded upon sensitive study of the details of practical accomplishment."[49]

In July 1856 the ministry approved Stroganov's proposal to settle Crimea with Russian populations but recommended limiting settlement to those territories from which Tatars had already been expelled or whose land had been confiscated by the state following proven mutiny.[50] The ministry further suggested that the state acquire Tatars' private property as it came up for sale in the shore regions, for resale exclusively to Russian peasants. Count Stroganov responded that the "ability to clean [*ochistit'*] Crimea of Tatars by degrees through the state acquiring private lands for Russian settlers could be successful," but such would "require significant capital." Purchasing lands, Stroganov complained, would not happen quickly because "the lazy and useless Tatars would not leave Crimea voluntarily." Instead, one would have to "forcibly evict them."[51] To be sure, the Russian policy to relocate Tatars in 1856, particularly the emphasis on "cleaning" the territory, calls to mind Stalin's genocidal deportation of the Tatars and other ethnic groups in Crimea nearly one hundred years later. For the purposes of this discussion, it bears emphasizing that the 1856 proposal for the Tatar relocation originated in the confluence of Eastern Question violence and Russia's long history of racialist settlement policies that began in the eighteenth century with the Russian conquest of the northern Black Sea littoral.

The Tatars left little written record explaining their exodus, no lengthy epistle to the Russian government, no statement regarding the reasons for their departure. There can be little doubt, however, that the terrible conditions of war, whether the forcible relocation of Tatars into the interior, the requisitioning and destruction of Tatar property, or rumors of an impending forced migration prompted the first wave of emigration. Apart from the migrations of the Tatars from Evpatoria, which began with the Allied occupation in September 1854, Russian officials first observed Crimean Tatars leaving their homes in the spring and summer of 1855.[52] On 30 June 1855, a Simferopol administrator reported to Adlerberg that a local aristocrat by the name of Abdulla Murza Dzhaniiskii, together with thirteen members of his family, gathered at their property and "went to the enemy [Ottoman Empire]."[53] Later, in December 1855, forty-six men and fifty women abandoned their homes in the village of Kuchuk-koi.[54]

Concerned local officials referred the matter to regional authorities, who in turn forwarded the question of emigration to Tsar Alexander II, asking whether they should prevent the future departure of Tatars. Alexander II, who had assumed the throne after Nicholas I died in March 1855, responded that there was no reason to prevent relocation of Tatars, stating, "it would be advantageous to rid the peninsula of this harmful population."[55] Subsequently, the tsar's statement was forwarded to all of Crimea's districts, including those most affected by the war: Perekop, Yalta, Theodosia, and Evpatoria.[56] Stroganov interpreted the tsar's words strictly and communicated to regional officials in Crimea: "His Imperial Highness [had] ordered that it was *necessary* [my emphasis] to free the region of this harmful population."[57] Here under Stroganov and Tsar Alexander II, the state officially encouraged Tatar emigration, which gathered speed as the war came to its conclusion.

On 22 April 1856, 4,500 Tatars left Balaklava for Constantinople, with their right to leave guaranteed in the Treaty of Paris.[58] As in previous conflicts with the Ottoman Empire, conquered peoples of both empires sided with the enemy. In the Crimean War, regiments of Ottoman Bulgarians and Greeks fought for Russia, just as Evpatorian Tatars formed a militia unit to fight for the Ottomans. To prevent Russia and the Ottoman Empire from taking retributive measures against these groups, the Treaty of Paris provided for their safe passage. Thus, according to point 5 of this treaty, all warring nations had to "give full pardon to those of their subjects who appeared guilty of actively participating in the military affairs of the enemy." The treaty further required that "each of the warring powers give full pardon to those who served for another warring power during the war."[59] In the larger view, such stipulations produced a religiously tinged population exchange, as Muslim Tatars fled Russia and Christian Bulgarians fled the Ottoman Empire, taking up new residence in the state of their coreligionists.

Tatars continued to trickle out of Crimea toward the end of the 1850s. Their numbers remained sufficiently steady and small enough that their departure attracted little attention. Suddenly, however, in the fall of 1859, a new, much larger wave of migration gathered momentum. Stunned Russian officials attributed their migration to a religious motivation, writing the central government in St. Petersburg that emissaries from Turkey had circulated a proclamation exhorting Crimean Tatars to relocate there.[60] A translation of the document attached to official correspondence and preserved in Russian archives offers a rare glimpse into Islamic aspects of the migration. It states: "God said: 'my land is wide: where one wants, there one can live.' And the Prophet said: 'yes, be with them in peace!' If you cannot freely fulfill the Sharia (the Muslim law and all its religious-civil practices and religious civil rituals) then settle in another (Muslim) country, be careful doing this, not losing time to resettle to our country. Who does not settle, then they will be shamed, and will not receive help in the future life [material in parentheses from the Russian original]."[61] The proclamation exhorted Tatars to live under a Muslim power in order to freely practice their faith, to dwell alongside their coreligionists. In particular, the proclamation strongly impressed upon Crimea's Tatars the need to fulfill sharia. Among other things, it is interesting that the local Russian translator felt the need to define sharia for officials in St. Petersburg.

Whether religion inspired the Tatar migration remains an important question in the scholarly literature. If Tatars migrated due to sympathies with their coreligionists, such would suggest that the Tatars left Russia voluntarily rather than being pushed out by Russian policy. For any historical question, the role of religion in motivating behavior is extremely difficult to assess and is particularly so in Crimea when religious rhetoric penetrated all sides of the conflict.[62] Although historians have recently turned their attention to religion in the Crimean War, they have yet to sift through the rhetoric and separate cynical nationalist discourse from authentic belief. Moreover, as scholars of religion and violence have noted, separating materialist conditions from spiritual ones can be challenging.[63]

According to Kemal Karpat, the Ottoman government did invite Tatars to settle in the Ottoman Empire and published an official invitation in March 1857 offering potential immigrants land and tax incentives in the eastern portions of the southern Balkan Peninsula. Karpat notes, however, that Ottoman officials intended foreign settlement to resolve labor shortages and did not aim this offer specifically at Muslim populations.[64] Still, the role of religion should not be dismissed out of hand. It is indeed quite possible that a desire to live under a Muslim government held an attraction for Tatars, and it is also quite possible that living under a state infused with Orthodox nationalism had grown too burdensome. In any case, Russian officials like Count Stroganov who already agitated for pushing the Tatars out of Crimea seized the opportunity to encourage Tatar migration.

Count Stroganov wrote officials in St. Petersburg that in religious meetings and night prayers, "Muslims were convinced to leave the land of the unbelievers" and "were reminded of the approaching Judgment Day." Agitators warned Tatars that they would not find salvation in the land of the Russian unbelievers and explained clauses in the Paris Treaty of 1856, which allowed emigration to Turkey. These Turkish emissaries promised money and livestock upon the Tatars' resettlement in Turkey but first demanded one thousand silver rubles per person to "sign up those desiring to settle, to find a seat on the ship, and necessary shelter in Constantinople." Stroganov argued that the emissaries, or as he implied, charlatans, did everything they could to incite Tatar emigration, including spreading rumors that the new diocese was established to "Christianize all the Tatars," and that the government planned to resettle all Tatars in the northern provinces.[65] Here he depicted the rumors of government relocation to the interior as if such were a dark Tatar fantasy rather than a real product of his own ambition. With his prodding, Russian officials decided to permit Tatar emigration to Turkey on the foundation established by Tsar Alexander II three years earlier.[66]

By August 1860, officials recorded 89,190 people of both sexes who had either left for Turkey or applied for passports.[67] By mid-November 1860, reports indicated that 28,000 Nogai Tatars and 57,000 Tatars from the steppe and mountain region had already immigrated to Turkey. Of this latter group, 13,500 Tatars lived on state lands, 43,500 lived on estates and private lands (i.e., were not state peasants), 12,000 came from the steppe, 23,000 from the mountains, and 8,800 from the coast.[68] The departure of nearly 90,000 people in just a few months dramatically changed Crimean landscapes. Already severely damaged by war, with an economy in tatters, Crimea was sent deeper into shock by the sudden population loss. Those left behind feared for Crimea's total collapse.

Pessimists anticipated the total ruin of Crimean agriculture without the experienced labor of the Tatars and an end to Crimean crafts and industry, including the wool and silk trades, the manufacture of Turkish-style carpets, and other handiwork. The collapse of Crimean cities and postwar urban recovery seemed imminent without Tatar tax revenues and labor for reconstruction. One observer wrote, "There is no sadder vision than in the steppe part of Crimea, in which now entire empty villages and fields remain without workers and [the land goes] unsown. Deeper in the country, the more remote roads and the surrounding landscape are completely empty; one hears only the howls of despondent packs of Tatar dogs left behind."[69] It remains to be determined, the writer continued, "from grain harvest or sowing, from crafts to factories, what in Crimea will be touched in consequence of this exodus. How various interests will be defeated by this sudden event—what will fall into disrepair and what will be lost—is much more significant than might have been seen at first glance."[70] Bureaucrats, noblemen, landed proprietors, townspeople, and merchants entered into a protracted heated debate about why the Tatars fled and how to restore the peninsula to a prosperous course.

Alarm over the rapid Tatar migration originated in Crimea and emanated outward. Even in Minsk, Khatib Aleksandr Usmanov Bogdanovich asked the Tauride Muslim Spiritual Assembly about the emigration. Lithuanian Tatars, he wrote, had heard that "many Crimean Tatars . . . had completely abandoned their Russian estates to enter Turkey."[71] The Committee of Ministers in St. Petersburg shared Bogdanovich's concern. It initiated an official inquiry into the Tatar emigration, which it assigned to the general adjutant Prince Viktor Ilarianovich Vasil'chikov.[72] Prince Vasil'chikov had earned distinction during the siege of Sevastopol for reestablishing order in the notoriously corrupt Military Intendancy. Immediately after the war, Prince Gorchakov assigned Vasil'chikov to investigate and prosecute the corruption.[73] Vasil'chikov was thus a logical choice for the Committee of Ministers: he had successfully concluded a major corruption case and had firsthand experience with Crimean affairs. For his assignment on the Crimean Tatars, Vasil'chikov gathered hundreds of pages of government reports by local and imperial officials and various ministries as well as Tatar petitions, the latter of which are unfortunately lost.[74]

Vasil'chikov's investigation uncovered a host of different causes behind the Tatar emigration. In addition to building an archive of all significant local and central correspondence on the question, Vasil'chikov canvassed Crimean landowners for their perspectives and sent the engineer Eduard Totleben to Tauride as his personal agent to research the migration. Totleben, one of the most widely celebrated heroes of the siege of Sevastopol, organized the rebuilding of the bastions at the height of the bombardment. Many credited him with Russia's ability to withstand the siege as long as it did, and he held the respect of the Committee of Ministers and the Russian tsar. Totleben's damning exposé of the disgraceful treatment of the Tatars during the war, the peculation of local landowners, and the complicity of Russian bureaucrats provoked shock when it circulated among St. Petersburg's ministers. It became a cornerstone of Vasil'chikov's report.

The mutiny of a few Tatars during the war, Totleben argued, convinced local authorities that "Tatars as unbelievers [*inovertsy*] were harmful for Russia." Many Russians began to believe that the Tatars would endanger the success of Russian forces and because of fanatical religious beliefs would forever stall Crimean development. Such views, Totleben implied, were themselves fanatical, as the Tatars had "altogether only weak influence on [Russia's] lack of success, which as [was] known, resulted from many other, better-known existing causes."[75] Harsh wartime abuse by Cossacks and the relocation of Tatars into the interior of the province had left many Tatars "afraid of their own government." Totleben also identified illegal and immoral Russian absorption of Tatar lands as another cause of Tatar migration. "Not knowing the Russian language and not having Russian laws translated into the Tatar language," Tatars had little defense against self-interested government agents or property owners. Some Tatars signed contracts without fully understanding the contents and quickly lost legal rights to the property that had been in their families from time immemorial.[76] The war only accelerated this process as neighboring landowners seized Tatar land during their exile.

The leader of the nobility in Perekop, Ivan Lampsei, shared Totleben's bleak assessment of the Tatars' position on the peninsula. Only a people in despair, Lampsei argued, would leave their "natural land, the graves of their fathers" to gamble on a distant, unknown location in an unfamiliar country. Lampsei emphasized the harsh conditions of war, particularly the dangerous "conviction that the Tatars were a harmful people for [the Russian] government," and the subsequent plans to remove Tatars from the coast. It must have been terribly difficult, he wrote, for the Tatars during the war, "seeing the exile of [their] brothers in faith to the Great Russian Provinces from where they still [had] not returned."[77]

Lampsei also shared many of Totleben's criticism of landlord abuses and pointed out that after the war, when the Tatars continued to suffer from exhaustion and years of poor harvests, landlord obligations increased and Russian administrators like Stroganov agitated for the Tatars' removal.[78]

After reading these reports and others, Vasil'chikov concluded that religion little entered the equation. Rather, "various persecutions" and wartime prejudices prompted the Tatars to leave. Specifically, Vasil'chikov cited collusion between landholders and the Ministry of State Domains to seize Tatar lands after the war, the growth of land-labor requirements, and the increase in state taxes to fund war recovery. "Taking into account that this version of events corresponds with the report submitted by Totleben on the affair of resettlement of the Crimean Tatars," the centralized Committee of Ministers concluded that the policies of the Ministry of State Domains and Count Stroganov contributed to the causes of Tatar migration.[79] The committee professed that it would have ordered an official review of Stroganov's office, but "war circumstances" made a formal review impractical.[80] In bypassing the standard procedure of the senatorial review, the committee proposed several changes, including the dismissal of Stroganov, who left office by 1862.

First, the committee tasked the general governor with moving Tatar land disputes more quickly through Russian courts. Quite often, Tatar petitions against landlord encroachment went through procedures at the district, the regional and the provincial levels, only to be sent back again to the district, where the process was repeated again. Such a lengthy trial process, the committee noted, served the interests of wealthy landlords, who better knew Russian laws and had the money and time to wait out poor Tatar peasants, who were more likely to give up on cases before decisions had been reached.[81]

The committee next advocated "compensating Tatars" who had suffered during the war and establishing a three-member committee to "formally research the level of abuse and disorder of the [Ministry of] State Domains." Such a committee would develop a plan for improving Tatar conditions and guard against "future abuse and disorder."[82] The committee was to pay particular attention to reducing the labor debt for spring planting and paring down transportation obligations, as custom required Tatar villages to provide transit for government officials.[83] Finally, the Committee of Ministers ordered local officials to prevent further migration as much as possible without violating the Treaty of Paris.[84]

The Committee of Ministers acted too late to rectify conditions for the Tatars. The Tatars continued to migrate, albeit with a few more obstacles, through the mid-1860s. By 1867, the Tauride Statistical Committee concluded that in all, 104,211 men and 88,149 women had emigrated from Russia to the Ottoman Empire.[85] They left hundreds of villages completely vacant, including 68 in Berdiansk, 9 in Melitopol, 278 in Perekop, 24 in Simferopol, 67 in Feodosia, and 196 in Evpatoria. To resolve the population crisis, the local government with the imperial government's permission moved forward with the foreign and internal settlement program. Russian peasants continued to settle vacated lands; more than sixteen hundred families had been summoned from Chernigov, Poltava, Voronezh, Kursk, and Tambov provinces even before the Committee of Ministers finished its review.[86] By 1864, local officials concluded that 437,327 *desiatin* of land were available for settlement by Montenegrins, Greeks, Mennonites, and Bulgarians, who could settle in the Russian Empire in accordance with the Treaty of Paris.[87] The dreams of those officials who wished to repopulate Crimea with Christians had come true, and Russians, Armenians, Greeks, and Bulgarians soon overwhelmed the Tatar population that remained.[88]

In just ten years, from 1854–63, Crimea underwent dramatic, rapid change. Its landscape was ruined, its buildings destroyed, and its population decimated. The mass migration of Crimean Tatars was as meaningful a consequence of the Crimean War as the more often discussed Russian retrocession of Bessarabia to the Ottoman Empire or Russia's restrictions in the Black Sea. Yet this momentous event has received comparatively short shrift in the literature. Writing 150 years later, Crimean Tatar author and activist Gul'nara Abdulaeva reflects: "It is not hard to imagine what prompted the native population to abandon its homeland. Hunger and ruin ruled together. Crimean Tatars were of interest to belligerents only for the ability to supply provisions, carriages, and portage. Russian bureaucrats ran at the beginning of the war, leaving the Tatars to their fate."[89] As Abdulaeva suggests, Russian policy and the war itself created inhospitable conditions for Crimea's native population.

To a large degree, Tatar emigration to Turkey stemmed from Russian colonial administration and wartime policy, neither of which can be said to be monolithic. Instead, Russian population policy was a fluid process, a constant interplay between subject and colonizer, center and periphery, and conflict among individuals with different philosophies of rule.[90] The trend toward Russian erosion of the Tatars' position in their native land was neither a uniform nor a consistent goal of Russian imperial governance. That said, the notions that the Tatar migrations, including the exodus of Muslims from the Caucasus, constituted exceptional cases, and that the Russian government actively sought to retain its Muslim population, as scholars have recently suggested, can hardly be the case.[91] Alan Fisher shows that along with the Crimean Tatar emigration, several hundred Circassians left following the Russian capture of Shamil, while Candan Badem's essay in this volume demonstrates a concerted Russian effort to encourage Muslim migration from the Kars-Batum province after the Russian-Ottoman War of 1877–78.[92] In other words, Russian policy toward Muslim populations bordering the Ottoman Empire appears consistently hostile.

It is also important to consider the Crimean Tatar migration in relation to the larger picture of genocide and forced migrations in the Russian Empire. In his comparative analysis of twentieth-century genocides, Norman Naimark has argued that the level of violence associated with twentieth-century migrations and genocide was unique, a product of the modern state.[93] While the twentieth-century was unusually brutal, the tendency of scholars to view forced migration and genocide through the lens of the Second World War obscures the continuity of violence between the nineteenth and the twentieth century. In this case, the state's willingness to forcibly relocate Tatars at the height of the Crimean War strikes a resonant note with later deportations of Tatars under Stalin.[94] Most relevant for this volume, however, the emphasis on twentieth-century episodes of population displacement obscures the long history of violent migration between the Russian and the Ottoman Empire. In this sense, the international political climate of the Eastern Question framed the Tatar migration as well as Russian colonial settlement policies. A pattern of Muslim-Christian population exchanges predated the Crimean War and continued well afterward. During the war itself, Allied occupation of Tatar villages and concurrent attempts to incite rebellion made Tatar departure in many cases a necessity. Finally, the provisions of the Treaty of Paris for population exchanges between the Russian and the Ottoman Empire legalized the process and set a precedent for future population exchanges following the First World War.

NOTES

1. Russian sources on Tatar migration frequently note that Tatars gave up their *poddanstvo*, a term today defined as "citizenship" but more accurately as

"subjecthood" for the imperial period. For the positive as well as negative elements of "subjecthood," see Valerie Kivelson, "Muscovite 'Citizenship': Rights without Freedom," *Journal of Modern History* 74, no. 3 (September 2002): 465–89; and Eric Lohr, *Russian Citizenship: From Empire to Soviet Union* (Cambridge, MA: Harvard University Press, 2012).

2. Anon., "Zapiska vyselenii tatar iz Kryma," unsigned report addressed to S. S. Lanskoi, 20 November 1860, RGIA, f. 1287, op. 6, d. 1710, "O pereselenii Krymskikh tatar za granitsu i o kolonizatsii vladelicheskikh v Krymu imenii," 30 May 1860–16 January 1864, l. 70.

3. Specifically here I am referring to migration within Europe, not the mass out-migration from Europe to the United States, Africa, and Asia.

4. See, for example, the classic migration study by Leslie Page Moch, *Moving Europeans: Migration in Western Europe since 1650*, 2nd ed. (Bloomington: Indiana University Press, 1992). Works devoted to war-related migration in the twentieth century are too numerous to count. Recent studies include Peter Gatrell, *A Whole Empire Walking: Refugees in Russia during World War I* (Bloomington: Indiana University Press, 1999); Nick Baron and Peter Gatrell, *Homelands: War, Population and Statehood in Eastern Europe and Russia, 1918–1924* (London: Anthem Press, 2004); Pavel Polian, *Against Their Will: The History and Geography of Forced Migrations in the USSR* (Budapest: Central European University Press, 2004); and Norman Naimark, *Fires of Hatred: Ethnic Cleansing in Twentieth-Century Europe* (Cambridge, MA: Harvard University Press, 2001).

5. See Vladimir Maksimovich Kabuzan, *Zaselenie Novorossii (Ekaterinoslavskoi i Khersonskoi gubernii) v XVIII–pervoi polovine XIX veka (1719–1858)* (Moscow: Nauka, 1976); Elena Ioasafovna Druzhinina, *Severnoe prichernomor'e v 1775–1800* (Moscow: Nauka,1959); idem, *Iuzhnaia Ukraina v 1800–1825* (Moscow: Nauka, 1970); and *Iuzhnaia Ukrainia v period krizisa feodalizma, 1825–1860* (Moscow: Nauka, 1981). For a more recent study of the settlement of New Russia, see Willard Sunderland, *Taming the Wild Field* (Ithaca, NY: Cornell University Press, 2004).

6. For works that pay particular attention to the Eastern Question migrations between Greece and Russia, see Gregory L. Bruess, *Religion, Identity and Empire: A Greek Archbishop in the Russia of Catherine the Great* (Boulder, CO: East European Monographs, 1997); John Mazis, *The Greeks of Odessa: Diaspora Leadership in Late Imperial Russia* (Boulder, CO: East European Monographs, 2004); Theophilus Prousis, *Russian Society and the Greek Revolution* (DeKalb: Northern Illinois University Press, 1994); M. A. Aradzhioni, *Greki Kryma i priazov'ia izucheniia i istoriografiia etnicheskii istorii i kul'tury (88-e gg XVIII v. 90-e gg XX v.)* (Simferopol: Amena, 1999); for Eastern Question migrations featuring Armenians and Bulgarians, see Vardges Aleksandrovich Mikaelian, *Na krymskoi zemle: Istoriia armianskikh poselenii v Krymu* (Erevan: Aistan, 1974); Nina Noskova, *Krymskie bolgary v XIV–nachale XX v.: Istoria i kul'tura* (Simferopol: SONAT, 2002).

7. Russian intelligentsia of Greek origin including Mikhail Paleologos, Zakharii Arkas, and refugees from other European areas of the Ottoman Empire like Alexandru Sturdza dominated the early formation of the Odessa Society of History and Antiquity. See the contributor pages for the journal *ZOOID* (Odessa, 1844-1914).

8. Kemal H. Karpat, *Ottoman Population, 1830-1914: Demographic and Social Characteristics* (Madison: University of Wisconsin Press, 1985), 66.

9. Mark Pinson, "Demographic Warfare—an Aspect of Ottoman and Russian Policy, 1854-1866" (PhD diss., Harvard University, 1970).

10. Alan W. Fisher, "Emigration of Muslims from the Russian Empire in the Years after the Crimean War," *Jahrbücher für Geschichte Osteuropas* 35, no. 3 (1987): 356-71; idem, *The Russian Annexation of Crimea, 1772-1783* (Cambridge: Cambridge University Press, 1987); Bryan Glyn Williams, "The Hijra and Forced Migration from Nineteenth-Century Russia to the Ottoman Empire: A Critical Analysis of the Great Crimean Tatar Emigration, 1860-1861," *Cahiers du monde russe* 41, no. 1 (2000): 79-108. See also Willis Brooks, "Russia's Conquest and Pacification of the Caucasus: Relocation Becomes a Pogrom in the Post-Crimean War Period," *Nationalities Papers* 23, no. 4 (1995): 682-83. One of the earliest studies, on which Fisher, Pinson, and Williams based their research, was composed by the Soviet historian Arsenii Markevich, "Pereseleniia krymskikh tatar v Turtsiiu v sviazi s dvizhennem naseleniia v Krymu," *Izvestiia Akademii nauk SSSR*, seriia 8, otdelenie Gumanitarnykh nauk, nos. 4-7 (1928): 375-405. For Markevich's reference to the limitations of his research, see "Pereseleniia krymskikh tatar v turtsiiu," 395; see also B. M. Vol'fson, "Emigratsiia krymskikh tatar v 1860 g.," *Istoricheskie zapiski* 9 (1940): 186-97; G. I. Levitskii, "Pereselenie tatar iz Kryma v Turtsiiu," *Vestnik Evropy* 17, no. 5 (1882): 596-639.

11. Material from the personal *fond* of Prince Viktor Ilarionovich Vasil'chikov, the man tasked by the Russian Committee of Ministers to investigate the causes of Tatar migration, figures centrally in this analysis. The collection of documents about the Tatar migration stored in the archives of the Ministry of State Domains, to which the Russian government legally attached Tatar state peasants, offers additional sources indispensable for understanding how the war transformed the peninsula and led to the exodus of the Tatars. See RGIA, f. 651, op. 1, d. 468, "O pereselenii Krymskikh tatar za granitsu"; and RGIA, f. 1287, op. 6, d. 1710, "O pereselenii krymskikh tatar za granitsu i o kolonizatsii vladelicheskikh v Krymu imenii," 30 May 1860-16 January 1864. Henceforth these sources will be referred to by their *fond*, *opis*, and *delo* numbers only. Vasil'chikov mentions the existence of hundreds of pages of Tatar petitions, which would have been stored in RGIA, f. 383, op. 17, d. 21728. Unfortunately, d. 21728 has been marked as "vybylo" (a word used to describe files that have been transferred, lost, censored or destroyed) in RGIA records.

12. See Mara Kozelsky, "Casualties of Conflict: Crimean Tatars during the Crimean War, 1853-1856," *Slavic Review* 67, no. 4 (Winter 2008): 866-91.

13. For the most comprehensive analysis of the causes of the Crimean War to date, see David Goldfrank, *The Origins of the Crimean War* (New York: Longman, 1994); and Winfried Baumgart, *The Crimean War: 1853-1856* (London: Oxford University Press, 1999). For an analysis of religious causes of the Crimean War from the Russian side, see the chapter by Jack Fairey, this volume.

14. The best treatment of the major events of the Crimean War remains E. V. Tarle's, *Krymskaia voina*, 2 vols. (Moscow: Voenmorizdat, 1941; repr., 2003).

15. For a brief biography that includes the controversy over his evacuation of Crimea, see M. S. Leonidov, "Pestel, Vladimir Ivanovich," in *Russkii biograficheskii slovar* (St. Petersburg: I. N. Skhorokhodova, 1902), 13:591-92.

16. The destruction of bread reserves, livestock, and other foodstuff proved devastating to the civilian population. Multiple files about the food requisition exist in Russian and Crimean archives. For examples, see "O raskhodakh na unichtozhenie zapasov khleba v Evpatorii, pri vtorzhenii v onuiu nepriiatelia," RGIA, f. 1287, op. 6, d. 1184, ll. 1-12; "Ob unichtozhennoe ili vyvoz v otdalennoe ot berega moria zapasov drov v Ialtinskom i Feodosiiskom uezdakh," GAARK, f. op. 1, d. 19778, ll. 1-28. For requisitioning later in the war, see "O perevozke iz raznykh punktov do 63,000 chetvertei i provianta i furazha dlia voisk . . . ," GAARK, f. 26, op. 1, d. 20096, ll. 1-32.

17. Nikolai Mikhno, "Iz zapisok chinovnika o Krymskoi voine," in *Materialy dlia istorii krymskoi voiny i oborony sevastopolia: Sbornik', izdavaemyii komitetom po ustroistvu sevastopol'skago muzeia, vypusk III* (St. Petersburg, 1872), 7; and V. S. Rakov, *Moi vospominaniia o Evpatorii v epokhu Krymskoi voiny, 1853-1856* (Evpatoria: Tip. M. L. Murovanskago, 1904), 30-37.

18. Although Crimean archives contain evidence regarding pillaging and plunder during the evacuations when authorities made arrests, very little archival information exist about the experience of the evacuees themselves.

19. On 3 October 1854, for example, the head officer of the Cossack Ulan division wrote local authorities in Evpatoria that "Greeks, Armenians and even a few *chinovniki*" robbed abandoned Tatar villages; the authorities responded that Cossacks were also involved in the plunder. "O sokhranenii imushchestva ostavlennago tatarami bezhavshimi k nepriateliu," GAARK, f. 26, op. 1, d. 20024, ll. 1-10; here ll. 2, 4.

20. Abundant reports of Crimean residents who lost property to Allied plunder, fire, and bombardment exist in Crimean archives. The largest collections are stored in GAARK, f. 128 and f.165, both with hundreds of files about losses in the Simferopol and Kerch districts respectively.

21. For example, two Tatars were implicated by local villagers in the murder of two Karaim merchants. "Ob ubiistve bliz der. Urkusta dvukh Karaimov," GAARK, f. 26, op. 1, d. 20079, ll. 1-15.

22. Cossacks were also guilty of robbing landowner estates. "Po ob'iavleniiu Shtab Rotmeistura Revelioti ob ograblenii ego v d. kontugan Donskimi

Kazakami," 27 November 1854, GAARK, f. 26, op. 1, d. 20065, ll. 1-7; the attacks on the villagers increased again as troops pulled out. See also "Po raportu Simferopol'skogo Zemskogo Ispravnika O bez poriadke proisvedavshikh v der. Uppy," GAARK, f. 27, op. 1, d. 6649.

23. For an order prohibiting baseless arrests, see "O vpospreshchenii soldatam brat' pod arrest Tatar' bez prichiny," GAARK, f. 26, op. 1, d. 19726.

24. "O dozvolenii Tatarinu Seliamet Memirsh Olgu vozvratit'sia v Krym na vremia prodazhi ego imushchestva," GAARK, f. 26, op. 2, d. 66, l. 16.

25. Rakov, *Moi vospominaniia*, 6. For his involvement in Tatar arrest and exile, see "O Vysyl'ke v Voennosudnuiu Kommissiiu tatar, izmenivshikh Russkomu Prestolu," GAARK, f. 26, op. 1, d. 19999, l. 88. The memoirs of the parish priest about the enemy invasion of Evpatoria were written in 1856 and are stored without title or clear signature in OR RNB, Archbishop Innokentii Borisov, 1847-1857, f. 313, op. 1, d. 44, ll. 724-40.

26. The Allied relationship to the Tatar insurrection awaits extended research. One exception includes an article by Hakan Kirimli about the French use of Mussad Giray (a descendent of the Crimean khans who had been living in the Ottoman Empire) in Evpatoria. See "O Krymskotatarskikh voiskakh v sostave Osmanskoi armii v period Krymskoi voiny," *Golos Kryma*, 31 October 2003), 7; idem, "Krymskie tatary i Osmanskaia imperiia vo vremia Krymskoi voiny," in *Crimean War 1853-1856: Colonial Skirmishes or Rehearsal for World War*, ed. Jerzy W. Borejsza (Warsaw: Wydawnictwo Neriton Instytut Historii PAN, 2011), 333-50; and Rakov, *Moi vospominaniia*, 32, which describes a Polish insurrectionist by the name of Tokarskii who incited unrest among the Tatars. For Allied activity among Muslim tribes in the Caucasus, see A. D. Panesh, *Zapadnaia Cherkesiia v sisteme vzaimodeistviia rossii s turtsiei, angliei, i imamatom shamiilia v XIXv (do 1864)* (Maikop: Adygeiskii respublikanskii institut gumanitarnykh issledovanii im. T. M. Kerasheva, 2007).

27. The Ministry of State Domains to Tauride General Governor Pestel, 14 October 1854, "O pereselenii Tatary iz Kryma vnutri Rossii," GAARK, f. 26, op. 1, d. 20004, l. 18.

28. He stayed in this position from November 1854 through May 1856. See anon., "Adlerberg, Count Nikolai Vladimirovich," in *Russkii biograficheskii slovar*, 1:78; and anon., "Adlerberg, Count Nikolai Vladimirovich," in *Voennaia Entsiklopediia* (Moscow: V. F. Novitskago,1911), 1:145.

29. "Andrei Grigorievich Stroganov," *Russkii biograficheskii slovar*, 19:484-85.

30. For an extended treatment of Russian policy toward Tatars before the Crimean War, see Kelly Ann O'Neill, "Between Subversion and Submission: The Integration of the Crimean Khanate into the Russian Empire, 1783-1853" (PhD diss., Harvard University, 2006).

31. Many Tatars received commendations for their service in Crimea during the war. See, for example, "O nagrazhdenii Tatarina [Bey Namer Selimsha]

Oglu serebrianoiu medaliu," RGIA, f. 560, op. 38, d. 146, l. 1859; and "Chinovniki nagrazhden serebrianoi medaliu dlia sluzhby v Sevastopole," GAARK, f. 27, op. 1, d. 6628, l. 50.

32. "O pereselenii Tatary iz Kryma vnutri Rossii," GAARK, f. 26, op. 1, d. 20004, ll. 1-40. Before the Allies landed, the Tauride government had discussed the evacuation of the shore regions in July, but such conversations took a much more ominous tone in September, after the Tatars in Evpatoria mutinied. By mid-September, Prince Alexander Menshikov and Tauride general governor Pestel exchanged several pieces of correspondence strategizing Tatar evacuation, but other officials, including those in the Ministry of State Domains, to which Tatar peasants were legally assigned, objected and encouraged Menshikov and Pestel to wait until spring. In March and April 1855, the question of Tatar evacuation from coastal regions reemerged, this time under the military governor of Tauride and Simferopol, Adlerberg, and the new head commander of the Russian military, Gorchakov. Under their leadership, evacuation of Tatars commenced but was not completely carried out due to objections from some local landlords, officials in the Ministry of State Domains, the shortage of manpower in the military to conduct the evacuation safely, and Gorchakov's own reservations (ibid., ll. 60-129).

33. Crimean archives contain a number of files about the arrest of Crimean Tatars. See Kozelsky, "Casualties of Conflict," 866-91.

34. M. Murav'ev, untitled Ministry of State Domains report, no. 2292, 21 November 1860, RGIA, f. 651, op. 1, d. 468, ll. 144-46.

35. Prior to this point, provincial officials and officers were to issue residents receipts for everything requisitioned, for reimbursement after the war. As fighting in Crimea continued and food grew scarce, Gorchakov implemented the plan in Tash-Basty in part to "inculcate[e] in the people a trust for the government's justice." See the limited publication of meeting minutes and reports from the Russian Ministry of the Interior, December 1856, no. 1518, *Vsopomozheniiakh Novorossiiskomu Kraiu i voobshche o merakh k vozstannovleniu onago posle voinyi* (St. Petersburg: Ministerstvo Vnutrennikh Del/ Khoziaistvennyi otdel, 1857), 13.

36. Ibid., 13-14.

37. After the war, the government took several measures to aid in Crimea's recovery, including the distribution of eight thousand oxen and hundreds of horses to Crimean peasants. This distribution met mixed success, with some villages fairly allotting the livestock and others suffering exploitation. See "O vspomoshchestvovanii Obyvateliam Tavricheskoi Gubernii ot kazny 3,000 para volov," GAARK, f. 26, op. 1, d. 20982.

38. Untitled summary report from the meeting of the Ministry of Internal Affairs, 22 December 1856, "O darovanii posobii Novorossiiskomu kraiu i Bessarabskoi oblasti, po sluchaiu nyneshnykh voennykh obstoiatel'stv," RGIA, f. 560, op. 12, d. 346, 1860, l. 159.

39. Ibid., l. 159.
40. Ibid., Count Stroganov to Alexander II, 17 June 1856, RGIA, f. 560, op. 12, d. 346, 1860, l. 55.
41. Ibid., ll. 55-56.
42. Ibid., Count Stroganov to Alexander II, l. 56. As the Committee of Ministers debated what measures to take in order to aid Crimea's recovery, it concluded that those measures established for the Napoleonic Wars fell short of the need in New Russia and particularly in Crimea.
43. "O vospreshchenii Pomeshchitse Mavromikhaili zakhvatyvami ostavshiesia posle uchedshikh za granitsu tatar," GAARK, f. 26, op. 2, d. 52, ll. 1-5.
44. Russian administrators from the era of Catherine II compared the agricultural practices of Germans and Mennonites favorably with those of Russian serfs and other ethnic groups. For a good synopsis of Russian attitudes toward German settlers, see Detlef Brandes, "A Success Story: The German Colonists in New Russia and Bessarabia, 1787-1914," *Acta Slavica Iaponica* 9 (1991): 32-46.
45. "Otchet gubernatora Simferopolia i Tavricheskago Grazhdanskago Gubernatora, o sostoianii Tavricheskoi gubernii za 1855," RGIA, f. 1263, op. 1, d. 2552, l. 51.
46. Report about establishing property prices in Evpatoria district for mortgage transfers from the Treasury, "Ob uchrezhdenii komiteta po sozdaniu zakonov stoimost' zemli razrushen nepriiatelia," GAARK, f. 327 op. 1, d. 999, l. 13.
47. For a discussion of state settlement policies, see Brandes, "Success Story"; Sunderland, *Taming the Wild Field*; Kabuzan, *Zaselenie Novorossii*; Druzhinina, *Iuzhnaia Ukrainia v period krizisa feodalizma*; and Nicholas Breyfogle, *Heretics and Colonizers: Forging Russia's Empire in the South Caucasus* (Ithaca, NY: Cornell University Press, 2005).
48. See Mara Kozelsky, *Christianizing Crimea: Shaping Sacred Space in the Russian Empire and Beyond* (DeKalb: Northern Illinois University Press), 67-78.
49. Murav'ev, untitled report to Ministry of State Domains, RGIA, f. 651, op. 1, d. 468, ll. 146-47.
50. Most likely, the ministry exercised this limited caution, because Prince Gorchakov had intervened in earlier exchanges among local officials about what to do with Tatar land vacated during wartime. When Yalta and Evpatoria district officials recommended reassigning vacant Tatar land to the state in 1855, Gorchakov warned officials first to determine whether the "empty lands" belonged to mutinous Tatars, Tatars who had been forcibly evacuated, or Tatars who had been taken captive. See RGIA, f. 1263 op. 1, d. 2552, l. 51.
51. Murav'ev, untitled report to Ministry of State Domains, RGIA, f. 651, op. 1, d. 468, l. 148.
52. The following two paragraphs about Tatar migration consist of modified material from Kozelsky, "Casualties of Conflict," 884-86.
53. GAARK, f. 26, op. 4, d. 1495, 1. 11.
54. GAARK, f. 26, op. 4, d. 1579, l. 4.

55. "O tatarakh peredautsikhsia taino nepriiateliu i vyezhantsiikh za granitsu," GAARK, f. 26, op. 4, d. 1605, l. 1.

56. Ibid., l. 3.

57. "O osvobozhdenii iz pod aresta iz ot suda lits zamechennnykh v snoshenii s nepriiatelem," GAARK, f. 26, op. 4, d. 1685, l. 65.

58. Winfried Baumgart's monograph on the Peace of Paris, the only full-length study in English, does not discuss the refugees from the war, a question that was in fact very important in the peace process and the war's aftermath. See Baumgart, *The Peace of Paris, 1856: Studies in War, Diplomacy, and Peacemaking*, trans. Ann Pottinger Saab (Oxford: Oxford University Press, 1981).

59. "Traktat zakluchenyi v parizhe 18 (30) Marta 1856," in Tarle, *Krymskaia voina*, unpaginated appendix.

60. Untitled report in the Ministry of State Domains, 21 November 1860, no. 2401, RGIA, f. 651, op. 1, d. 468, l. 150.

61. Untitled report in the Ministry of State Domains, 12 November 1859 (original date) and 15 December 1860 (copy), no. 2401, RGIA, f. 651, op. 1, d. 468, l. 3.

62. For an exploration of Christian religious rhetoric about the Crimean War, see Kozelsky, *Christianizing Crimea*; for Ottoman jihad rhetoric, see Candan Badem, *The Ottoman Crimean War (1853-1856)* (Leiden: Brill, 2010), 91-100. For a sweeping synthesis of research on religion and the Crimean War, see the first two chapters of Orlando Figes, *The Crimean War: A History* (New York: Metropolitan Books, 2011).

63. The theoretical literature on religion and violence is quite large. Principle works include Regina Schwartz, *The Curse of Cain: The Violent Legacy of Monotheism* (Chicago: University of Chicago Press, 1997); Mark Juergensmeyer, *Terror in the Mind of God: The Global Rise of Religious Violence* (Berkeley: University of California Press, 2000); J. Harold Ellens, ed., *The Destructive Power of Religion: Violence in Judaism, Christianity and Islam*, 4 vols. (Westport, CT: Praeger, 2004); Charles Kimball, *When Religion Becomes Evil* (San Francisco: Harper Collins, 2003); and Charles Selegnut, *Sacred Fury: Understanding Religious Violence* (Lanham, MD: Altamira, 2003).

64. Karpat, *Ottoman Population*, 62.

65. The General Governor of New Russia and Bessarabia to the Minister of Internal Affairs from 10 August 1859, report no. 7704, RGIA, f. 651, op. 1, d. 468, l. 235.

66. From the Ministry of State Domains, RGIA, f. 651, op. 1, d. 468, ll. 9-10.

67. New Russian and Bessarabian General Governor to the Minister of State Domains, September 9, 1860, f. 1287, op. 6, d. 1710, l. 4.

68. Anonymous report to the Minister of the Interior S. S. Lanskoi, RGIA, f. 651, op. 1, d. 468, l. 161.

69. "Zapiska vyselenii Tatar iz Kryma," unsigned and undated, RGIA, f. 1287, op. 6, d. 1710, l. 70.

70. Ibid.

71. RGIA, f. 651, op. 1, d. 470, "Raport—musul'manskogo sviashchenosluzhitelem Aleksandr Usmanov Bogdanovich v Tavricheskoe Magometanskoe Dukhovnoe Pravlenie o zaprosom o prichinakh pereselenie tatar Krymskoe polustrove v Turtsiiu," June 1860, l. 1. RGIA files have preserved only Bogdanovich's request, and not the answer.

72. "O vyselenii Tatar' iz Kryma," an unsigned report from the Ministry of the Interior, stored in the Ministry of State Domain files, 22 November 1860, RGIA, f. 1287, op. 6, d. 1710, l. 83.

73. The Vasil'chikov family collection in RGIA contains multiple files about V. I. Vasil'chikov's inquiry into the intendancy. See, for example, "Perepiska po delu o zloupotrebleniia v intendantstve iuzhnoi armii," RGIA, f. 651, op. 1, d. 416.

74. The Committee of Ministers ordered that the Tatar petitions gathered by Vasil'chikov be transferred to the Ministry of State Domains. These reports appear to have been stored in RGIA, f. 383, op. 17, d. 21728, which according to RGIA records, no longer exists.

75. Eduard Totleben to Prince Vasilii Andreevich Dolgorukov, 15 November 1860, RGIA, f. 651, op. 1, d. 468, ll. 106, 112. Totleben's notes were published three decades later in *Russkaia Starina*, and this chapter draws from both the archival and the published form. See Eduard Totleben, "O vyselenii tatar iz Kryma v 1860 gody," *Russkaia starina* 78 (1893): 531-50.

76. Totleben, "O vyselenii tatar iz Kryma v 1860 gody," 535.

77. Ivan Lampsei to Viktor Iliarionovich Vasil'chikov, RGIA, f. 651, op. 1, d. 471, "Zapiska perekopskogo uezdnogo predvoditelia dvorianstva Simferopol'," in "O prichinakh pereseleniia Krymskikh tatar v Turtsiiu (1861)," February 1861, l. 2.

78. Specifically, Lampsei attributed the Tatar exodus to the pillaging of bread reserves as well as the general abuse of villages during the war by the police and the local Ministry of State Domains. After the war, Tatars lost in the redistribution of land and livestock, the latter of which was intended to help the poorest of Crimean villagers but often went to the wealthiest. After the war, the tax burden increased for Tatars, who as the majority population on the peninsula, paid for the peninsula's rebuilding and for the sustenance of the Crimean Tatar Squadron. Finally, Lampsei pointed to the general corruption that pervaded local government during and after the war. Lampsei to Vasil'chikov, February 1861, RGIA, f. 651, op.1, d. 471, l. 3.

79. Komitet Ministerstva, "Zapiski iz zhurnala Komiteta Ministerstva," 30 May, 6 and 20 June 1861, " RGIA, f. 1287, op. 6, d. 1710, ll. 104-23, esp. 104-5.

80. For analysis of the importance of senatorial reviews for restoring order to provincial administration, see A. N. Biktasheva's *Kazanskie gubernatory v dialogakh vlastei: Pervaia polovina XIX veka* (Kazan: Natsional'nyi muzei respubliki Tatarstan, 2008). Biktasheva argued in her study of senatorial reviews of the

Kazan province that official reviews typically resulted in the dismissal or disciplining of regional governors.

81. Komitet Ministerstva, "Zapiski," ll. 107-8.
82. Ibid., l. 110.
83. Ibid., ll. 113.
84. Ibid., ll. 115-23.
85. Kozelsky, "Casualties of Conflict," 889.
86. Letter from Acting State Councilor Gengros to the Minister of State Domains, 15 September 1860, GAARK, f. 1287, op. 6, d. 1710, ll. 8-10.
87. "Vysochaishe utverzhdennoe pravila o zaselenie Kryma i Tavricheskoi Gubernii Russkii i inostrannymi pereselentsami 1860," GAARK, f. 26, op. 1, d. 24129, ll. 63-64.
88. Kozelsky, *Christianizing Crimea*, 152-55.
89. Gul'nara Abdulaeva, "Krymskie tatary v Vostochnoi (Krymskoi) voine," *Advet*, 22 January 2007, 11.
90. Kozelsky, "Casualties of Conflict," 889.
91. See Robert D. Crews, *For Prophet and Tsar: Islam and Empire in Russia and Central Asia* (Cambridge, MA: Harvard University Press, 2006), 300-311; and James Meyer, "Immigration, Return, and the Politics of Citizenship: Russian Muslims in the Ottoman Empire, 1860-1914," *International Journal of Middle Eastern Studies* 39 (2007): 15-32.
92. Fisher, "Emigration of Muslims from the Russian Empire," 356. See also Candan Badem's chapter in this volume.
93. See Naimark, *Fires of Hatred*.
94. Some Tatar historians have thus described the deportation of Tatars under Stalin as "fulfilling the eternal dreams of the Russian tsars." See for example, Ibraim Abdullaev, "Torg s istoriei ne umesten!," *Golos Kryma* no. 28, 7 July 2006; and V. E. Vozgrin, *Istoricheskie sudby Krymskikh tatar* (Moscow: Mysl', 1992), 324-30.

Russia, Mount Athos, and the Eastern Question, 1878–1914

LORA GERD

Beginning in the seventeenth century, Russia turned its political aspirations toward the Black Sea and the Straits of the Bosporus and Dardanelles. The desire for a free exit to the Mediterranean for its trade, and from the eighteenth century onward a safeguard for its southern frontier, generated a more assertive Russian foreign policy in its southwestern borderlands. The only possible way to guarantee these economic and security requirements was the possession of the Turkish Straits and Constantinople. The many times revised theory of Russian domination in the Eastern Christian world continued to provide the ideological background for this strategy, for after the fall of Constantinople in 1453, Russia remained the only free and strong Orthodox state in the world. As the self-proclaimed heir of Byzantium and the protector of the Orthodox world, Russia sought to add legitimacy to its foreign policy objectives through religious backing until the revolution of 1917. By the late eighteenth century, imperial Russian foreign policy departed from this general line, but after the defeat in the Crimean war (1853–56), Russian policy makers returned to the ecclesiastical trend when formulating strategy in the Near East.

Russian Skete of St. Andrew. The diplomat B. S. Serafimov and Archimandrite Hieronym to his right, 1913. (from the Photograph Archive, Simonopetra Monastery)

Russia's spiritual enterprise in the Ottoman Empire aimed at achieving closer contacts with the Orthodox population while strengthening tsarist influence in the eastern Mediterranean as a whole. Mount Athos, a collection of monasteries situated on a small peninsula in the north of the Aegean, played a leading role in this process. Unlike the Russian foundations in Palestine, the Russian monastic community on the holy mountain had a long history outside government initiatives. Rather, the spiritual aspirations of common people (*narod*) supported by the tsars and governing elite provided the material foundation for Russia's presence on Athos. This chapter explores how Russian policy between the Russian-Ottoman War of 1877–78 and the First World War harnessed popular spirituality for geostrategic purposes. Stated differently, this chapter considers the possible subordination of the general line of Russian strategic aims in the Balkans and the Near East to purely spiritual concerns. It argues that debates surrounding monasticism on Mount Athos crystallized the tensions between Russia and Greece over political interests in newly independent regions of the former Ottoman Empire. The case of Athos further demonstrates the continuing relevance of religion in the Russian-Ottoman-Balkan relationship. Finally, the case of Mount Athos suggests ways in which popular spirituality could influence Eastern Question diplomacy.

The Russian-Ottoman War of 1877-78 changed the map of the Balkans. The Treaty of San Stefano finalizing the war sanctioned the creation of an independent Bulgarian state, covering a large territory in the Balkan peninsula. Unsatisfied with the results of the peace, Britain and Austria-Hungary intervened to thwart the Russian quest to create a large Slavic buffer state on the road to Constantinople. The Berlin Congress convened in June 1878 by the German chancellor Otto von Bismarck, who acted the "honest broker," partly revised the terms of the San Stefano Treaty. The semi-independent Bulgarian Principality was limited to the area between the Danube and the Balkan mountains. Eastern Rumelia remained subordinate to the sultan, and a vaguely defined region called Macedonia with a large Slavonic population stayed within the borders of the Ottoman Empire as well. This compromise decision led to further confrontations in the turbulent Balkan region.

The project of "Great Bulgaria" proposed by the Russian ambassador to the Sublime Porte, Count Nikolai Ignat'ev, therefore failed. Despite the general disappointment with the results of the Congress of Berlin, Russian diplomacy insisted on including an important article, number 62, which provided diplomatic patronage for the non-Greek monks on Athos. This crucial point guaranteed the autonomous existence of a Russian community in Ottoman territory under Russian state protection. In the following decades preceding the First World War, the center of the Eastern Question remained the straits, Constantinople, and the adjacent territory. Mount Athos, due to its important geographical location on the southern coast of Macedonia and its spiritual significance for the Eastern Orthodox world, was a center of attention for all the states interested in the future division of the Ottoman legacy.[1]

As the Ottoman Empire withdrew from southeastern Europe, Russia quickly moved to consolidate its influence in the vacated territories through diplomatic means and grassroots agitation. The Russian Foreign Ministry deployed specially prepared agents from St. Petersburg to work among the local population. The traditional supporters of Russian policy in the Balkans and the Near East were the Orthodox peoples of the Ottoman Empire, including Greeks, Bulgarians, Serbs, and Arabs. These peoples formed a "state within a state" in the sultan's domain, enjoying a large degree of semi-independence, thanks to their special position within the *millet* system. On their way to the west during the years of conquest in the fourteenth century, the Ottoman sultans formed separate communities from the non-Muslim population called *millets*. Inside the *millets*, the Christians or Jews could follow their religion and live according to their own juridical norms. Until the reforms in the middle of the nineteenth century known as the Tanzimat, religion, not nationalism, formed the guiding principle for the *millet* system. The term *millet* acquired new meaning only with the rise of Balkan nationalism and especially in connection with the Bulgarian ecclesiastical question by the 1870s.[2]

As the leaders of the Orthodox *millet*, the religious authorities in these Christian communities played the role of political administrators. This is one reason why the church was so important in Russian foreign policy formulation in the Near East and the Balkans. The shared Orthodox faith gave Russian policy makers in St. Petersburg and in consular posts throughout the region a strong ideological weapon, which was an essential advantage over the Western great powers. This direction of Russian Near Eastern policy was traditional since at least the sixteenth century, when Russia declared itself the successor of Byzantium in the Orthodox world. Philanthropic donations to Eastern monasteries and churches, and general support of Orthodoxy in the Ottoman Empire, combined with political aspirations formed the basis of Russian policy in the region. In the nineteenth century, a new modification of the same theory of the Third Rome in modern conditions emerged.

One of the main obstacles for Russian activities in the Balkans in the second half of the nineteenth century was the Bulgarian schism, proclaimed by the Patriarchate of Constantinople in 1872.[3] The struggle of the Bulgarian people for national independence led to the establishment of a region of church autonomy in 1870, called the Bulgarian Exarchate. The Pan-Slavic-oriented Russian government of the 1860s and 1870s strongly supported the Bulgarian movement for church independence. The fact of the schism, however, put Russia in a very difficult position. On one hand, Russia did not stop supporting the Bulgarians, yet it could not allow itself to ignore the patriarchal council of 1872. Russia had no opportunity to support the Bulgarians openly in order to avoid a conflict with the Ecumenical Patriarchate. Therefore, St. Petersburg maintained a passive position by tacking between the two sides. In fact, Russia was aware of the dangerous complications of unilateral action and generally rejected opportunities to take an active part in the major political events in the Balkans during this period. The Russian Holy Synod continued sending money and other forms of aid to

Bulgarian monasteries and churches, and scores of Bulgarian youths continued to study in Russian theological academies on imperial scholarships. However, official relations between the Russian and the Bulgarian churches ceased for many decades, until the final abandoning of the schism in 1945. In 1878 and afterward, the Bulgarian Exarchate became the banner behind which the Bulgarian nationalist movement waged the struggle against the Greeks in Macedonia. During this broiling conflict, Russia tried to play the role of peacemaker and withdrew its support from either side.[4]

As the controversy surrounding Bulgarian ecclesiastical independence gained momentum, Russian relations with the independent Kingdom of Greece remained rather cool. In the 1880s during the tenure of Prime Minister Charilaos Trikoupis, who kept Greece closely aligned with Great Britain in Near Eastern affairs, there could be no question of active ecclesiastical and political cooperation between Russia and Greece. In Constantinople, the "second center of Hellenism" according to the majority of Greek observers, Russia tried to support the moderate bishops, who were mostly natives from the Ottoman regions of the Balkans and Asia Minor. These hierarchs, if not friendly, at least tolerated Russia's ambitions in ecclesiastical questions. The diplomatic slogan of the times was "to elevate the Greek Eastern clergy in its own eyes" and to divest it of the nationalistic influence of Athens. Russian agents were instructed to inspire a "true ecumenical spirit," free from nationalist aspirations.[5] A united, peaceful Orthodox world under Russian direction, the final goal of Russian church policy, could be formed only on a supernational basis. At this point, the Russian imperial idea of an ecumenical Orthodox community contradicted the Greek irredentist Great Idea (Megali Idea), which aimed at the liberation and unification all historic Greek lands with Constantinople as the natural center. The rivalry of these two ideas determined relations between Russia and the Greek world in the nineteenth and at the beginning of the twentieth century.

The center of ecclesiastical relations between Russia and the Orthodox population of the Ottoman Empire was the Ecumenical Patriarchate of Constantinople. The turbulent world of the patriarchal synod and the Mixed Council (Mikton Symbouleion) was a constant object of attention for the Russian embassy in Constantinople. At the same time, Russian agents could use ecclesiastical politics as an avenue for exercising influence and pressure. Patriarch Joachim III (first patriarchate, 1878-84) was the most suitable person through whom Russia could pursue such a policy of balance and maneuver in the region. Joachim kept a moderate pro-Russian position and had great authority among the Greek population of Turkey. In contrast, his successors, Joachim IV (1884-86), Dionysios V (1887-90), Anthimos VII (1895-97), and Constantine V (1897-1901), pursued an anti-Russian line during their tenures on the patriarchal throne. During his second term as patriarchate (1901-12), Joachim III was initially supported by Russia but did not meet the Russian aims to the degree that was expected; he preferred to listen to advisers from Athens and became a strong supporter of the Megali Idea.

The first decade of the twentieth century was a period of stagnation in Russian Balkan and Near East policy.[6] On one hand, a series of treaties with Austro-Hungary (first of all, the Murav'ev-Goluchwski agreement of 1897), designed to preserve the status quo in the Balkans, limited the flexibility of Russia's policy. On the other, Russia was too busy in its war with Japan and later the revolutionary events of 1905-7 to pay much attention to the Near East. The "Diplomatic Tsushima" of the Bosnian crisis of 1908-9, which led to further humiliation of Russia, was followed by an attempt to review the reactive policy of the previous decades. It was only in the second decade of the twentieth century that St. Petersburg again adopted a more active policy in the region. In 1911-12, Russia provided strong diplomatic support for the Balkan Alliance (including Greece, Serbia, Bulgaria, and Montenegro). Usually regarded as the most important aspect of Russia's Balkan foreign policy in this period, the formation of the Balkan Alliance may be St. Petersburg's only serious success at the beginning of the twentieth century. As one of the conditions of support for the alliance, Russia demanded the mending of the Bulgarian schism. Nevertheless, the Balkan Wars (1912-13) did not bring the results that Russia expected. The new map of the Balkans failed to satisfy the Balkan nations, especially Bulgaria, which lost in 1913 most of the territorial gains won in the preceding year. Neither could the ecclesiastical problem be solved. Thus, on the eve of the First World War, the political and ecclesiastical situation in the Balkans remained tense and dangerous.[7]

In this complicated international setting, the Russian Foreign Ministry, limited in its military and political activities, paid more attention to its ideological instruments. Mount Athos played a primary role, due to its geographical situation in Macedonia and because of its unique, outstanding position in the Aegean and proximity to the Straits of Constantinople. Beginning in the tenth century, Athos, the eastern part of the Chalkidiki peninsula, was one of the most important spiritual centers of the Eastern Christian world. It was a unique monastic republic: every Orthodox people (besides the dominant Greeks, then Georgians, Bulgarians, Serbs, Rus/Russians, and later Romanians) had its own monastery on Athos. As Byzantium was an empire of Greek culture and language and the ecumenical patriarchs were usually of Greek origin, most of the monasteries belonged to the Greeks. The high spiritual authority on Athos was the patriarch of Constantinople. All the monasteries were under the protection of the Byzantine emperors and the monarchs of the Orthodox states. Athos thus presented a spiritual model of the Eastern Christian world, reflecting all political and cultural processes within it. The privileged and isolated position of Athos due to the so-called *abaton* (the prohibition of access for women and alien persons) and the rich donations contributed to the self-government of the holy mountain and made the monasteries very influential spiritual and cultural centers. The sultans preserved these privileges after the Ottomans conquered Athos in 1423-24.

Though the position of the church in the Muslim state was principally different, Athos continued to be the symbol of the aspirations of all Orthodox Christians. During the sixteenth and seventeenth centuries, the monasteries of the holy mountain received huge sums from the *hospodars* of Moldavia and Wallachia and from the Russian tsars. However, they also became victims of robbery and the despotic actions of Ottoman authorities. Step-by-step, the non-Greek monasteries fell into the hands of Greek monks, a process that reflected the situation in the Orthodox Church in the whole territory of the Ottoman Empire.[8]

In the eighteenth century, according to the account of the traveler Vasilii Barsky, only a few Russian monks could be found on the holy mountain.[9] The Russian monastery of St. Panteleimon and the two *sketes*—the Holy Prophet Ilias and the Holy Apostle Andrew—rose in the middle of the nineteenth century. The prosperity of Russian monasticism on Athos in the late nineteenth and early twentieth centuries is usually connected with two major figures, the confessor of the Russian monastery Hieronym and its abbot, Makarii Sushkin.[10] After the Russian-Ottoman War of 1877-78, due to the protection of high diplomatic and governmental officials and increasing interest among the Russian people, the Russian monastic communities grew rapidly. In fact, they soon became the richest and most populated on the rocky peninsula.

This spiritual flourishing inspired admiration among Russian pilgrims and travelers, who began to flock to the region in large numbers. The former patriarch Joachim III, who lived on Athos in 1886-1901, stressed the contrast between the Russian institutions and the Greek ones. "The spiritual power on Athos doesn't matter at all," he wrote to the Russian consul in Thessaloniki, Ivan S. Iastrebov. "You can notice disobedience everywhere. The Greek monasteries are at odds and are trying to surpass each other in willfulness. On the contrary, order dominates in the Russian communities; everybody follows the voice of the abbot, they are working with humility and are self-denying, and they don't interfere in lay affairs."[11]

The prosperity of the Russian monasteries and *sketes* provoked discontent and envy among the Greeks, whose monasteries at the same time suffered lack of financial support. The general adverse conditions in the Balkans, the intensity of nationalist passions, and anti-Slav prejudices promoted hostility on the holy mountain. The government of Athens repeatedly undertook measures against the Russian monastics. In 1883, a delegation of two theologians and historians, professors N. Damalas and P. Pavlidis, arrived from Athens. They proposed several steps to strengthen the Greek positions on Athos. Primarily, they advocated convincing the patriarch to resist the pressures of Russian diplomacy and to act independently. They also proposed strengthening Greek education on the holy mountain to encourage the monks to protect the rights of the Greeks and sending a Greek consul from Macedonia to Athos at least once a year to support the national feelings of the monks. The Greek delegation further sponsored the plan of organizing Greek pilgrimages to Athos, to counter the Russian ones, which included as many as four thousand pilgrims a year. Finally, the project proposed a scheme to grant Athonite monks British citizenship so that they would benefit from British protection. If this latter point would be difficult, continued Damalas and Pavlidis, "we should encourage the arrival of more monks who are English citizens, for example from Cyprus."[12] Though this project was not fulfilled, it testifies to Greek concern about Russian influence on Athos as well as the British influence on Greek policy at this time.

The Greek consul in Thessaloniki, G. Dokos, who visited Athos in 1887, wrote a lengthy report to the Greek foreign minister, Stephanos Dragoumis, which analyzed the situation on the holy mountain from the viewpoint of Greek national interests. In his report, Dokos paid special attention to the Russian threat and suggested that leasing buildings in the Athos capital, Karea, should be prohibited. He also considered the opening of diplomatic representatives there expedient. "We must have able people in every monastery," stressed Dokos. "By systematic work from one center, we can neutralize the activities of the Russians, who are under strong protection. They are working with one purpose: they are organized with military discipline and submit to political centers abroad."[13] It is interesting to note that among the measures that could be used against the Russians, Dokos did not exclude help from even the Roman Catholic states. In fact, he observed that the Austrian consul in Thessaloniki showed interest in the former Italian monastery of the Amalfitani, known as Morfanou. The consul was curious to find some documents concerning this monastic settlement, which had ceased to exist centuries earlier. Dokos believed that establishing a Catholic monastery on Athos was hardly possible, but the support from a representative of a great power like Italy could be used against the Russians.[14]

As the reports indicate, Greek diplomats feared that the Russian government was interested in Athos as a political and even a military base. Indeed, St. Petersburg spared no expense for strengthening the Russian element there. The real position of the Russian government regarding the Greek clergy and Russian monasticism can be gleaned from a report composed by an employee of the Russian embassy in Constantinople, A. E. Vlangali, in late December 1883. Vlangali wrote: "Under the general name 'Greeks,' we mean the Athens government, the inhabitants of Turkey of Greek origin, the patriarchate and the clergy, and at last the Greek monks of Athos. . . . Our duty is to protect as possible the rights and independence of the Eastern Church. But we must draw a strict line of demarcation between the interests of this church and the national interests of the Greeks of Athens, because the Ecumenical Patriarchate is not called at all to serve as a stronghold of Hellenism."[15]

Thus it appears that the general aim of Russian church policy in the Near East at this time was to pacify and reconcile the Orthodox peoples under the power of a supranational Ecumenical Patriarch. The Greek monks on Athos are regarded here as an element of the general term "Greeks" in the Ottoman lands, and according to the sense of the report they should not serve as a weapon of the political ambitions of the Athens government. In fact, the Russian diplomats distinguished well enough between the Greek monks of Ottoman origin, who usually were more open to supernational ecumenical views, and those who had come from the Greek kingdom and were typically influenced by extreme nationalism.

The increasing number of Russian monks and pilgrims on Athos prompted the Russian government to appoint a representative to control the situation. Until 1889, Abbot Makarii fulfilled this role, but after his death, the question about appointing a leader to supervise the flood of pilgrims appeared again. Government officials in St. Petersburg, who were afraid of creating on Athos the same conflict and complicated situation that they had with the Russian spiritual mission in Jerusalem, did not support ideas of opening a Russian consulate on Athos or sending an ecclesiastic representative there.[16]

Based on the inconsistent instructions of the Russian Foreign Ministry, one can see that the Russian government had no clear policy toward Athos; it exhibited no definite position regarding the usefulness of the Russian presence there at all. The Russian embassy in Constantinople as well as the consulate general in Thessaloniki sent numerous inquiries to the Russian Foreign Ministry concerning Athos but never received concrete answers. Many of the diplomats expressed a strong objection against the further progress of Russian Athos (an idea earlier proposed by the metropolitan of Moscow, Filaret Drozdov) because of the outflow of Russian money abroad.[17] They argued that such resources would be better used in the peripheries of the Russian Empire itself. Realizing the desirability of a concrete decision, the Russian ambassador to the Sublime Porte, Alexander I. Nelidov, regretted that he could not point a way out, because nobody would donate such sums of money for the recently founded monastery of New Athos in the Caucasus.[18] "We have only physical data that demonstrate the deep reverence of the Russian people for the holy mountain and cannot weigh the moral advantages of this veneration or to what degree Athos is useful for us from governmental point of view. . . . We must deal with an unknown area, the independent and mighty national force," wrote Nelidov.[19] Nelidov supposed that the Russian government should refuse to have exclusive influence on Athos and should avoid coordinating the popular movement there. Nevertheless, St. Petersburg consistently tried to limit the stream of money collected all over Russia by Russian monks, most of whom were *kelliotes* (inhabitants of the small cells that belonged to the big monasteries and could never be regarded as Russian property).

The juridical status of the Russian monks on Athos remained uncertain as the surge in pilgrimages coincided with major political and judicial changes taking place in the Ottoman Empire at this time. The movement of Tanzimat in Turkey covered a period of several decades after the Crimean War. Its general goal was the secularization and modernization of the government and the administrative system of the Ottoman Empire. As for the church, the reforms aimed at state control of it.[20] According the Athos Regulations (Kanonismos) of 1876 (included in the Turkish law code), all Athos monks irrespective of their nationality were considered Ottoman citizens. They were given a document called in Turkish a *nufus* (a sort of residence permit), but in fact their Turkish citizenship remained nominal. The Russian monks preserved their Russian passports and enjoyed the protection of the diplomatic authorities according to Article 62 of the Berlin Treaty of 1878. Russian laws stipulated that a person could lose his or her nationality by serving a foreign state without the permission of the person's government and by refusing to return to Russia on the call of the government. However, according to the edict of the Russian Holy Synod of 13 July 1816, Russian subjects who became monks abroad were not recognized as monks inside Russia. Furthermore, Tsar Alexander I amended another law that allowed Russian citizens to become monks abroad on the condition that they would never return to their motherland.[21] Later persons who had become monks abroad were adopted into Russian monasteries after spending three years as novices; in every case, permission from the Holy Synod was necessary. The dual status of the Russian monks on Athos gave them an opportunity to act in Russia with their former social rank; on the other hand, it was convenient for governmental officials to protect them only when they found it reasonable to do so. If a certain monk was regarded as "unreliable," the formula "such person, calling himself a hieromonk," was employed; in some cases, Russian diplomats did not hesitate to send away the most importunate applicants because they were "Turkish citizens."[22]

The Turkish authorities undertook many attempts to recognize the Russian monks as Ottomans, but these efforts always found counteraction from Russian diplomacy. During the census of the Athos population in 1905, for example, the Turkish authorities tried to confiscate the passports of Russian monks. The demand of the officials, however, met resolute refusal from all Russian monasteries. Rather than create an international scandal, the Turkish authorities did not insist. Only the monks of the Georgian cell of St. John the Theologian surrendered their passports, but after the protest of Russian representative in Thessaloniki, Nikolai V. Kokhmanskii, the *vali* (governor) of the city promised their return.[23] After a new wave of confiscations of Russian monks' passports by the Young Turk government in 1909, Kokhmanskii composed a note on this subject, in which he again stressed that the Russians on Athos were regarded as temporarily outside Russia and had never lost their citizenship. Unwilling to clash with the Ottoman authorities, the Russian consulate in Thessaloniki decided to issue new passports in place of the confiscated ones, as if their owners had lost them. The Ottoman authorities did not object.[24]

By the beginning of the twentieth century, the main tendencies connected with the Russian presence on Athos continued. The fears concerning Russian expansion on the holy mountain and its final transition into Russian hands are reflected in the report of the Bulgarian agent in Thessaloniki, Atanas Shopov:

> I traveled from monastery to monastery around the whole Athos peninsula, and it seemed to me as if I were traveling around Russia. Continually on the quays, in the monasteries, in the cells, in the centre of the *kaza* (the administrative district of Athos), in forests and on roads you meet Russians and Russians, both monks and laity. Their number is increasing from day to day. . . . In five or six years, the number of Russians will be two or three times more. Nobody doubts that in few years only Russians will inhabit the entire holy mountain. First the Russians and after them the Greeks and Bulgarians suppose that soon the Athos peninsula will become politically Russian as well. Economically it has been in Russian hands for a long time. All the rich Greek monasteries receive their incomes from Russia under the control of the government.[25]

In 1898, the Russian consul in Thessaloniki, N. A. Ilarionov, visited the Serbian Hilandar monastery. Hilandar, one of the oldest monasteries on the holy mountain, had huge debts and a very small monastic population. The Serbs there were few, and most of the monks were Bulgarians from Macedonia. The Russians had kept an eye on this monastery and proposed to pay its debts in order to settle one or more Russians into the brotherhood; in this way step-by-step the monastery could pass to the Russians.[26] The Serbian government, for its part, undertook measures to strengthen the Serbian element at Hilandar. In 1900, an agreement was made according to which Belgrade paid the debts of the monastery and granted it an annual sum of one thousand Ottoman liras.[27] The Russian consul decided to support the Serbs in Hilandar, which was consistent with the general policy of the Russian government in Macedonia during these years of supporting the Serbs against the Bulgarians.

The Russians occupied several cells belonging to Hilandar; the biggest one being the cell of St. John Chrysostom. In 1902, an agreement was signed between the abbot of the cell and the Serbian metropolitan of Rashka and Prizren. According to this act, the metropolitan passed authority over the historically Serbian Lavra of Dechani to the Russians for a number of years. In exchange, the Russians agreed to organize a strict monastic order, to restore the buildings, and to protect the monastery from attacks by Albanian brigands. While for the Serbian ecclesiastical authorities this measure was the only way to save the monastery, for the Russian monks it was an opportunity to found a new Russian monastery in the Balkans. The Russian abbot aimed at organizing the settlement as a department of the cell of St. John Chrysostom, which would not be limited in the number of monks and building initiatives.

In the following years, about twenty Russian monks were installed in Dechani. Since the Russian government regarded this project as complementary to its general line of protecting the interests of Orthodoxy in the Near East, it accorded the Dechani monastery an annual subsidy of ten thousand rubles. Later, however, the matter provoked great resistance from the Serbian government and church, which feared the aggressive Russian incursion. The Russian government also expressed doubts regarding the necessity of maintaining control over the monastery.[28] Despite the government subsidy and the incomes of the cell, Dechani suffered because of the complicated political situation in Albania and the necessity to pay large sums to Albanian chieftains. The Russian monks refused to leave Dechani on conditions other than turning their cell on Athos into an independent monastery, which would be an inalienable Russian possession. They hoped that the Serbian government would press the Hilandar monastery to fulfill their desire. The situation remained the same until 1916, when the Austrians deported the monks.

Simultaneously, Russian monks from Athos explored another direction for their creative activities, namely, Palestine and Syria. Many neglected small monasteries existed in this region that could be easily bought by the rich Russian *kelliots*. In 1903, the abbot of the Russian cell of the Holy Cross on Athos, Panteleimon, purchased the ancient Lavra of St. Chariton, eight kilometers from Jerusalem, and settled seven monks there.[29] This act provoked the patriarch of Jerusalem, Damianos, to object that it was an uncanonical interference into the affairs of another church, but the patriarch's letter of protest remained unanswered. On 12 July 1912 in Damascus, the patriarch of Antioch, Gregory, and the representative of the cell of the Holy Cross on Athos, Gennady, signed an agreement that enabled Russians to lease the patriarchal monastery St. Ilias Shuaya in Lebanon. The Russian abbot of the cell was appointed abbot of the monastery. According to the agreement, the Russian brotherhood became forever owners of all the movable and immovable properties of the monastery and had to pay the patriarch a graduated payment of two hundred to four hundred French napoleons a year. The Russian consul in Damascus considered this arrangement as favorable both for the strengthening of Orthodoxy in Syria and for the Russian convent.[30]

Irrespective of the political significance of such initiatives, the main reason for the Russian monks' interest in Palestine was the lack of space and opportunities for development on the Athos peninsula. The abbots of the richest Russian cells had enough money to receive a greater number of monks and to build large monasteries, but Athonite regulations strictly forbade this activity. The challenge led to constant conflicts between Russians and Greek church authorities. The *kelliots* posed one of the main problems associated with the Russian presence on Athos at the beginning of the twentieth century, for both Greek and Russian diplomacy. Officially, no more than three monks could live in each cell, one senior and two younger. But in practice, within a few years the senior monk often gathered money to take on more novices and rebuild the cell into a more substantial and prosperous settlement. The population of such cells sometimes grew to more than one hundred persons, who built magnificent churches and houses. This development made the dependent cells, the inhabitants of which were no more than tenants, and de facto monasteries sometimes richer than the primary one.

In 1896, the Athos *kelliots* united and founded an organization, "The Brotherhood of Russian Kelliots."[31] The organization aimed to protect the rights of the *kelliots* in their struggle with the Greek chief monasteries. Soon the brotherhood managed to draw favorable attention of the tsar's family and support from the ambassador in Constantinople, Ivan A. Zinoviev, as well as the influential director of the Russian Archaeological Institute in Constantinople, Feodor I. Uspenskii. The brotherhood kept a hospital in Thessaloniki and a monastic school in the Ottoman capital.

Although the *kelliots* enjoyed sympathy from some diplomats and high officials, the Russian Holy Synod was not inclined to support them. It was easier for church authorities to deal with the big monasteries than with independent settlements. The legal disputes between the smaller Russian settlements and the large Greek monasteries could continue for decades and provoke serious difficulties. The Russian Holy Synod therefore prepared several decrees against the *kelliots* and monks' letters for economic support, which had been spread to all corners of Russia.[32] The large Russian monasteries and some public authorities supported the position of the Russian synod. For example the famous liturgist professor of the Theological Academy in Kiev, Alexei Dmitrievskii, wrote a passionate article against the *kelliots'* activities.[33] Obviously, such criticism toward a large segment of the Russian monks could not contribute to the stability of the Russians on the holy mountain as a whole. Dmitrievskii's article also caused a sensation in Greece after being translated by the secretary to Meletios Metaksakis, the archbishop of Cyprus and later patriarch of Alexandria and of Constantinople, who used it in his extreme Russophobic book.[34] Encouraged by the position of the Russian synod, the patriarch of Constantinople issued a decree limiting the power of the *kelliots* and their number on Athos.[35] Despite these measures, the *kelliots* continued their activities.

In the dangerous and stormy situation in the Balkans in the first decades of the twentieth century, the rich Russian monks, who lived without any guard, increasingly became victims of thefts and robbery. The Russian diplomats during their frequent visits to the holy mountain tried to protect the *kelliots*. The reports of the employees of the embassy and the consulate in Thessaloniki indicate that they usually sympathized with the *kelliots* and stressed that with rare exceptions they were pious people who cared only about saving their souls.[36] This provides an example of the contrast between the actions of the Russian Foreign Ministry and the Holy Synod; here, the Russian government proved more supportive of monks on Athos than did the Russian Orthodox Church.

A new period in the life of Athos began with the Balkan Wars. In November 1912, the Greek military annexed the holy mountain. A Greek army detachment of eight hundred soldiers formed a garrison; the Bulgarians also sent seventy soldiers to protect their monastery. While the Greek inhabitants of Athos regarded the liberation as a true resurrection, the Slavs were rather anxious about their future. The question about the status of Athos was a matter of international discussion at the London Conference of 1912–13. Russia categorically insisted on the internationalization of Athos under the protectorate of the six Orthodox states (Russia, Greece, Serbia, Romania, Montenegro, and Bulgaria). The first goal was to neutralize Greek supremacy; the second was the protection of the rights of the monks, native from each Orthodox state. Had the Greeks succeeded in dominating Athos, all the controversial questions would have been resolved in favor of the Greeks and not the Russians. In the Russian plan, unsurprisingly, international control of the Orthodox states over the holy mountain provided for the domination of Russia.

Russian diplomats proposed several projects concerning jurisdiction. According to the proposal of the consul in Thessaloniki, Alexei K. Beliaev, each of the six Orthodox states had to appoint one representative, who would have his seat in Karea, the administrative center of Athos. The delegates would comprise an official council with the Russian representative as chairman. This council would be the only representative of Athos in its international contacts. The functions of the delegates would be the same as of the consuls of the great powers in the Ottoman Empire. Thus Beliaev's plan made the Athos monastic population dependent politically on the Russian Foreign Ministry. The spiritual authority of the patriarch of Constantinople and the self-government of Athos in its internal affairs would remain as previously.[37] The second proposal, written by the Russian consul in Monastir, A. M. Petriaev, in general repeated the main points articulated by Beliaev.[38]

The proposal written by Boris S. Serafimov, the adviser on ecclesiastical affairs of the Russian embassy in Constantinople, further enhanced the degree of tsarist protection.[39] Serafimov stressed that since the non-Russian monasteries existed due to incomes from their estates in Russia or the collection of money there, without Russian aid they should soon be reduced into desolation. He emphasized the number of Russian monks in 1909–11, which was 4,250, without considering the *metochs* (farmsteads) and advocated expanding Russian influence there. "One can hope that with the change of political circumstances the present situation will change as well. In due course many of the 17 Greek monasteries will become Russian, as had happened with the monastery of St. Panteleimon, and then our monks will feel themselves in better conditions," he wrote.[40] Russia itself would deal with all Athos affairs, giving the monks the opportunity for internal self-government according to the ancient rules. The representatives of the other Orthodox states would also send their representatives in turn. One can notice that this proposal was written in haste and was not free of political romanticism.

The legal adviser of the Russian embassy in Constantinople, Andrei N. Mandelshtam, discussed the juridical side of the question in detail. He advocated either designating Athos as a neutral territory under the protectorate of the six Orthodox states or making it a neutral territory under common sovereignty of these states.[41] In his opinion, the creation of a neutral territory was preferable for Russian interests, because on such a territory Russian laws could be applied. Mandelshtam maintained that in either case a strong governmental power was obligatory in order to stop the national disagreements on the holy mountain. The national contradictions between the Russians and the Greeks, the Greeks and the Bulgarians, the Greeks and the Georgians were a reflection of the general Greek-Slav (and Greek-Georgian) tension in the Balkans in those years. The Second Balkan War and the defeat of Bulgaria had made the situation on Athos more acute.

When the Athos monks learned of Russian proposals for internationalization and condominium, the seventeen Greek monasteries sent their delegates to the Athens government and to the London conference with a petition to unite Athos with the Greek kingdom. At the same time, the Russian monks on 12 May 1913 addressed another petition to the representatives of the powers in London demanding the neutralization of Athos under the protectorate of Russia and the Balkan states. The petition argued for sending a representative from every 250–300 monks to the central council; separation of the civil and criminal matters from the spiritual; and cancelling the present rules on possession of landed estates and the privatization of these estates by the owners who had bought them.[42]

The question of the international status of Athos was not solved during the deliberations of the great powers in London. The London Treaty of 17 May 1913 only postponed the decision regarding the holy mountain. In July–August 1913, ambassadors of the great powers held a meeting about the consequences of the Balkan Wars in London, and the status of the holy mountain numbered among the issues of discussion. The Russian proposal for neutralization met strong resistance from the Austro-Hungarian representative. This opposition can be understood if one examines the activities of Austria-Hungary toward the Thessaloniki region during several decades before 1914. At this time, the Habsburg Empire more than the other powers was interested in southern Macedonia. As a result, only the first part of the proposal was adopted, concerning the preservation of the spiritual subordination of Athos to the patriarch. As for the second part of the proposal, the common protectorate, it was postponed due to irreconcilable disagreements. The Treaty of Bucharest signed on 26 August 1913 also did not resolve the problem.

The Second Balkan War and the defeat of Bulgaria buried all hopes for a union of Orthodox states or of Slavic states under a Russian protectorate. The Bulgarian ecclesiastical schism could not be mended, and a common protectorate on Athos was unlikely. The resistance of the Western powers was not the only obstacle. In June–July 1913, another internal problem arose on Athos, namely, the Name Worshipers (Imiaslavtsy, or Imiabozhniki) movement. The followers of the movement accepted the idea that "the name of God is God himself." The roots of this concept lay in the traditions of the Byzantine mysticism of Symeon the New Theologian and *hesychasts* lead by St. Gregory Palamas. The constant repeating of the Jesus prayer was a long-held tradition of the Athos monks. Thus it was not a modern heresy but just an interpretation of the old tradition.[43] This movement, being purely spiritual, split the Russian monastic population into two parties. The Russian government, weary of further complications in the Balkans, mistook the disturbances for something more political. The Greek monasteries and the patriarch, who desired the deportation of a part of the Russian monastic community, supported the Russian ecclesiastical and civil authorities, who regarded the movement as a rebellion. As a result, in July 1913 more than eight hundred Russian monks were forcibly removed to Russia. This action marked the beginning of the weakening of the Russian element on Athos.

As the international status of Athos remained uncertain, in September 1913 a representative of the Russian embassy in Constantinople, Boris S. Serafimov, arrived on a special mission. The aim of his visit was to inform the embassy about the situation, to protect the monks from violations, and to contribute to the pacification of the holy mountain. In the same month, the metropolitan of Cyprus, Meletios Metaksakis, arrived in Athos to incite agitation among the Greek monks and support their national feelings. The presence of Serafimov (who despite his incognito was regarded as a Russian consul) irritated the Greek monks to a remarkable degree. At the end of September 1913, the Kinot (the Athos administration body) decided to move him from the Skete of St. Andrew. This decision was not carried out because of the uncertain position of the Vatopedi monastery, which was afraid to lose income from its estates in Bessarabia. Meanwhile, the Greek press printed angry articles against Serafimov in its sections on recent news.[44]

In October 1913, the Kinot of Athos together with Metropolitan Meletios wrote a petition to the Greek king Constantine expressing the will of the holy mountain to be included in the territory of the Greek kingdom so that no civil authority could interfere in its affairs.[45] The representatives of the Bulgarian and Serbian monasteries, intimidated by the Greeks, also subscribed to the petition. Only the representative of St. Panteleimon Monastery refused. The announcement of this document on 3 October, a great national holiday for the Greeks, was accompanied by a ceremony and prostration before the icon Aksion Esti, claims of "Long live Greece!" and a passionate patriotic speech by Metropolitan Meletios.[46] A delegation of five representatives visited King Constantine and Prime Minister Eleftherios Venizelos. The latter assured the monks, "As the holy mountain has kept and keeps all the Byzantine rites, has kept for us our language during the long ages of slavery, it is of great importance for Hellenism. Be sure, fathers, that the government will do its best to preserve on Athos its structure, both ecclesiastical and political."[47]

Despite of the pending rift between the king and the prime minister, both of them were ready to support the desire of the Greek monks on Athos. During his stay on Athos, Serafimov continued to concentrate on the future international status of Athos. Metropolitan Meletios proposed that Russia should abstain from the project of internationalization, while Greece should guarantee all the Russian monks the rights and privileges that they had previously. In the present situation, Serafimov was inclined to adopt this proposal, because the establishment of an association of Orthodox states would be impossible without violent measures and Greek petitions to the powers. Meanwhile, the Bulgarian schism continued, and Serbia began acting in unison with Greece against Russian interests. Romania had only two *sketes* and several cells on Athos (which were hostile to the patriarchate), and Montenegro had no interests on the holy mountain. The protests of the Athos Greek *kinot* would result in the limitation of Russian penetration toward the archipelago and the Mediterranean and would end the Russian project. The latter would mean a catastrophe for the Russian monasteries, while the adoption of Meletios's proposal could "give [them] the opportunity to reach [their] intended results."[48]

Serafimov also presented the conditions under which, in his opinion, the Russian-Greek agreement could be signed. Serafimov proposed that the Athos religious community remain under the spiritual power of the ecumenical patriarch, and that all actions on Athos would be undertaken only after their approval by both Russian and Greek authorities. According to his proposal, a guard formed by both Greeks and Russians would replace the Greek military detachment, and the Greek government should not confiscate monastic properties off the peninsula (mainly in Macedonia and Thrace). The latter point, stressed Serafimov, had special significance for Russia regarding the estate "Nuzla," belonging to the Russian Skete of St. Andrew, in the Gulf of Kavala, which could be used as an excellent naval-military base.[49] The proposal of Serafimov, though very favorable for the Russian side, was not adopted by the Russian Foreign Ministry. Meanwhile, the position of the Russian representative on Athos became increasingly difficult and even dangerous. In December 1913, he left the holy mountain.

The question of the status of Athos continued to be discussed in 1914. The artful and flexible diplomat Venizelos, who desired Russian support, was ready to make concessions. In May 1914, the Russian ambassador in Constantinople, Mikhail N. Giers, handed the Greek representative the plan concerning the international status of Athos and expressed his readiness to start negotiations. The conditions of the agreement borrowed from Serafimov's plan and their general sense came to the same two main points: the spiritual subordination of Athos to the ecumenical patriarch and Russian control over the political administration of the monastic foundations.[50] The Greek government put forward a counterproposal involving a Greek-Russian condominium on Athos. It proposed double citizenship for Athonite Russian monks and restricting other Orthodox states from taking part in the decision of the Athos question.[51] This proposal might have been the better way out for Russia as a patron of Slav interests in the Balkans. Its realization, however, was doubtful due to the resistance of Serbia and Bulgaria. Moreover, Greece would insist on changing the situation at the first opportunity.

With the beginning of the First World War, the question of the status of Athos did not arise again on a diplomatic level. Until the revolution of 1917, the Russian government did not recognize Athos as part of the territory belong to the Greek kingdom. We may definitely speak about the final uniting of Athos with Greece only in 1926, when the Greek government issued a law that all monks of the holy mountain should be Greek citizens. Thus, the long discussions on the international status of Athos ceased immediately after diplomatic pressure from Russia ended.

After the defeat of the Name Worshipers in 1913 and the beginning of the First World War in the following year, when many of the novices were called up for military service, a rapid decline of the Russian Athos began. From 1913 to 1917, the Russian population on Athos was reduced almost by half, from 4,100 to 2,460.[52] After 1917, when Russians lacked opportunities to visit Athos and the government no longer supported the monasteries, Russian monasticism on the holy mountain ceased until the end of the twentieth century.

The period between the end of the Russian-Ottoman War of 1877-78 and the beginning of the First World War was the "golden age" of Russian Athos. Despite opposition from the Ecumenical Patriarchate and the Greek monasteries (as well as of the Russian government), the aspirations of the Russian people for a presence on Athos were so strong that the Russian monastic population grew from year to year. In the difficult political situation at the turn of the century, the Russian government did not take active steps in the Balkans; its main policy was to keep the status quo. The fear of disrupting the balance of power and provoking a military conflict led to an extremely passive position on the part of the Russian Foreign Ministry, which preferred to withdraw on every question at issue. Sometimes even the rational proposals of the diplomats met no understanding in the Holy Synod; many matters that had to be solved immediately became entangled in red tape.

Because of the inconsistency of the policy toward the Russian monks on Athos, a strong political potential of Russia was not used to the fullest and did not bring the benefit it could have. One could say that Russian Athos acted not in coordination with the governmental policy but to some degree in spite of it. The enterprising, business-savvy Russian peasants, inspired by the liberty that they could not receive in their motherland created a unique phenomenon in southeastern Europe: a huge Russian community with strong economic and moral potential. One cannot doubt that this original "Russian island" in the eastern Mediterranean served as a great support to the Russian authority in the region. It is difficult to predict the fate of the Russians on Athos if the revolution of 1917 had not happened. Yet one thing is certain: Russian monasticism had a great influence on the political and spiritual life of the Balkans and of Eastern Christianity in general.

After 150 years of prevailing secular foreign policy, the Russian Empire at the end of the nineteenth century returned to the messianic ideology of the Third Rome in Near Eastern affairs. In this context, church policy became a fundamental component of Russian foreign policy. The Russian institutions in the Eastern Orthodox world—the Russian spiritual mission in Jerusalem and the Palestine society, as well as the Russian monasteries on Athos—were called to serve Russian interests in the Eastern Question and to strengthen Russian influence in the eastern Mediterranean.

After 1990, with the spiritual revival after the collapse of communism, Russian interest in Mount Athos has appeared again and is steadily growing. Many pilgrims from Russia visit the holy mountain every year, and many novices gather in the St. Panteleimon Metochion in Moscow. A number of Russians live in Greek monasteries as well. The spiritual authority of Athos among Orthodox believers in modern Russia is as high as it was in the nineteenth century. Striking evidence of it is the long lines of people waiting to bow and touch the relics brought from Athos to different Russian cities or visiting the exhibition of photos of Athos (held in Moscow in November 2011). The aspirations of the Russian people to the holy mountain today are spiritual or prompted by historical and cultural interest and do not seem to be enmeshed in the political rivalries characteristic of the Eastern Question of one hundred years ago.

Nevertheless, the present-day government policy of the Russian Federation supports these trends, so there is a wide field for dialogue between Russia, Greece, and the Athos monks. Numerous conferences on Athos (both scientific and public forums) in recent years have discussed different problems. A question of vital importance is the status of Athos in the modern secular world. The Greek Church together with the conservative segment of society, supported by Russian government structures, resist any attempts of Europe to open Athos to the public and to break its unique ancient regulations. Until now, the monks have managed to maintain this stronghold of Eastern spirituality in its more or less untouched Byzantine form, which makes it a calm gulf in the stormy, turbulent modern world.

NOTES

1. For arguments underscoring this strategic zone, see Sean McMeekin, *Russian Origins of the First World War* (Cambridge, MA: Harvard University Press, 2011); Ronald Bobroff, *Roads to Glory: Late Imperial Russia and the Turkish Straits* (London: I. B. Tauris, 2006); Barbara Jelavich, *The Ottoman Empire, the Great Powers, and the Straits Question, 1870–1887* (Bloomington: Indiana University Press, 1973); idem, *Russia's Balkan Entanglements, 1806–1914* (Cambridge: Cambridge University Press, 1991).

2. B. Braude, "Foundational Myths of the Millet System," in *Christians and Jews in the Ottoman Empire*, ed. B. Braude and Bernard Lewis, 2 vols. (New York: Holmes and Meier, 1982), 1:69–88; R. Clogg, "The Greek Millet in the Ottoman Empire," ibid., 1:185–208; K. H. Karpat, "*Millets* and Nationality: The Roots of the Incongruity of Nation and State in the Post-Ottoman Era," ibid., 1:141–70; D. Stamatopoulos, "The Splitting of the Orthodox Millet as a Secularizing Process: The Clerical-Lay Assembly of the Bulgarian Exarchate (İstanbul, 1871)," in *Griechische Kultur in Südesteuropa in der Neuzeit: Beiträge zum Symposium in Memoriam Gunnar Hering (Wien, 16–18 Dezember 2004)*, ed. M. A. Stassinopoulou and I. Zelepos, Byzantina et Neograeca Vindobonensia 26 (Vienna: Verlag der Österreichischen Akademie der Wissenschaften), 243–70.

3. V. F. Kurganov, "Istoricheskii ocherk greko-bolgarskoi raspri," *Pravoslavnyi sobesednik* 1 (1873): 187–260; V. Teplov, *Greko-bolgarskii tserkovnyi vopros po neizdannym istochnikam* (St. Petersburg: Tip. V. S. Balasheva, 1889); Kiril, patriarch Bylgarski, *Graf N. P. Ignatiev i bulgarskiiat tsurkoven vupros: Izsledvane i dokumenti* (Sofia: n.p., 1958); Z. Markova, *Bulgarskata Ekzarkhiia, 1870–1879* (Sofia: Izd-vo na Bulgarskata akademiia na naukite, 1989); V. Boneva, *Bulgarskoto tsurkovnonatsionalno dvizhenie, 1856–1870* (Veliko Turnovo: Za bukvite-O pismneh, 2010).

4. On the Russian position in the Greek-Bulgarian question, see L. A. Gerd, *Konstantinopol' i Peterburg: Tserkovnaia politika Rossii na pravoslavnom Vostoke (1878–1898)* (Moscow: Indrik, 2006), 225–308; idem, "Rossiia i greko-bolgarskii tserkovnyi vopros v 1901–1914 gg.," *Istoricheskie zapiski* 13 (2010): 225–73; E. Kofos, "Attempts at Mending the Greek-Bulgarian Schism (1875–1902)," *Balkan Studies* 18, no. 2 (1984): 347–75; I. Snegarov, "Ruski opiti za predotvrat'avane i vdigane na shizmata," *Macedonski Pregled* 5, no. 1; 5, no. 2 (1929): 1–44, 1–32.

5. These ideas were repeated many times in different documents. See, for example, the note of A. E. Vlangali from 15/28 December 1883, AVPRI, f. 180, op. 517/2, d. 3212, ll. 19–23.

6. A. N. Shebunin, *Rossiia na Blizhnem Vostoke* (Leningrad: Kubuch, 1926); I. S. Galkin, *Diplomatiia Evropeiskikh derzhav v sviazi s osvoboditel'nym dvizheniem narodov Evropeiskoi Turtsii 1905–1912* (Moscow: Izd-vo Moskovskogo universiteta, 1960); G. A. Georgiev et al., *Vostochnyi vopros vo vneshnei politike Rossii: Konets XVIII–nachalo XX veka* (Moscow: Nauka 1978); V. M. Khvostov, *Istoriia diplomatii*, vol. 2 (Moscow: Nauka 1963); I. V. Bestuzhev-Lada, *Bor'ba Rossii po voprosam vneshnei politiki: 1906–1910* (Moscow: Izd-vo Akademii nauk SSSR, 1961); K. B. Vinogradov, *Bosniiskii krizis 1908–1909* (Leningrad: Izd-vo Leningradskogo universiteta, 1964).

7. R. C. Hall, *The Balkan Wars 1912–1913: Prelude to the First World War* (London: Routledge, 2000), 22–24. Concerning Russia's policy during the Balkan Wars and its participation in the London Conferences of 1913, see I. A. Pisarev, "Balkany mezhdu mirom i voinoi (Londonskiie konferentsii 1912–1913 gg.)," *Novaia i noveishaia istoriia*, no. 4 (1984): 63–75; idem, "Balkanskii soiuz 1912–1913 gg. i Rossiia," *Sovetskoe slavianovedenie*, no. 3 (1985): 58–69; idem, "Rossiia i mezhdunarodnii krizis v period pervoi balkanskoi voiny (ok'tabr 1912–mai 1913 g.)," *Istoriia SSSR*, no. 4 (1986): 56–67.

8. The scholarship on Mount Athos is extensive. Useful guides include I. Doens, *Bibliographie de la Sainte Montagne de l'Athos* (Mount Athos: Agioreitiki Vivliothiki/Bibliothèque Athonite, 2001); D. Papachrysanthou, *Athonikos monachismos: Arches kai organosi* (Athens: Morphotiko Idryma Ethnikes Trapezes, 1992).

9. V. Grigorovich-Barsky, *Pervoe posescheniie svaitoi Afonskoi gory Vasiliia Grigorovicha-Barskogo, im samim opisannoe* (St. Petersburg: Pravoslavoe Palestinskoe Obshchestvo, 1885).

10. On the Russians on Athos, see A. A. Dmitrievskii, *Russkie na Afone: Ocherk zhizni i deiatel'nosti igumena russkogo Panteleimonova monastyr'a*

sviashchenno-arhimandrita Makariia (Sushkina) (St. Petersburg: Pravoslavoe Palestinskoe Obshchestvo, 1895); N. Fennell, *The Russians on Athos* (Oxford: Berg, 2001); Ierom. Ioakim (Sabel'nikov), *Velikaia strazha: Zhizn' i trudy blazhennoi pam'ati afonskikh startsev ieroshimonakha Ieronima i shiarkhimandrita Makariia; Kn. I. Ieroshimonakh Ieronim, starets-dukhovnik Russkogo na Afone Sviato-Panteleimonova monastyria* (Moscow: Izdatel'stvo Moskovskoi Patriarkhii, 2001); P. Troitskii, *Istoriia russkikh obitelei Afona v XIX–XX vekakh* (Moscow: Indrik, 2008); L. A. Gerd, *Russkii Afon 1878–1914: Ocherki tserkovno-politicheskoi istorii* (Moscow: Indrik, 2010); N. Fennell, P. Troitskii, and M. Talalai, *Il'inskii skit na Afone* (Moscow: Indrik, 2011).

11. Recounted in I. S. Iastrebov to A. I. Nelidov, 24 January 1891, RGIA, f. 797, op. 61.2 otd. 3 st., d. 146, ll. 8–12.

12. Ch. Kardaras, "I politiki drasi tou Patriarheiou Ioachim G' (proti patriarchia 1878-1884)" (PhD diss., University of Ioannina, 1993), 253–58.

13. T. Dokos to S. Dragoumis, 24 August 1887, Archeion Gennadion / Archeion St. Dragoumi, f. 32.1 (Athos-Mones Agiou Orous), 1–26. The report was edited following a copy in the Archive of the Greek Ministry of Foreign Affairs: I. A. Papaggelos, "Ekthesi tou proksenou G. Dokou peri tou Agiou Orous (1887)," *Hronika tis Halkidikis*, 40–41 (1985–86): 67–125.

14. Report from 5 August 1889, ibid.

15. AVPRI, f. 180, op. 517/2, d. 3212, l. 20.

16. On the Russian foundations in the Holy Land, see N. N. Lisovoi, ed., *Rossiia v Sviatoi zemle: Dokumenty i materialy*, 2 vols. (Moscow: Mezhdunarodnye otnoshenia, 2000); idem, *Russkoe duhovnoe i politicheskoe prisutstvie v Sviatoi Zemle i na Blizhnem Vostoke v XIX–nachale XX v.* (Moscow: Indrik, 2006); Nikodim Rotov, *Istoriia Russkoi Dukhovnoi missii v Ierusalime* (Serpukhov: Serpukhovskii Vysotskii Muzhskoi Monastyr, 1997).

17. Filaret Drozdov, metropolitan of Moscow and Kolomna (1782–1867), was the head of the ecclesiastical policy of Russia from the 1840s to the 1860s. All the diplomatic reports on church problems were sent to him. See the edition of his opinions on the matters of church policy in the Near East, *Sobranie mnenii i otzyvov Filareta mitropolita Moskovskogo i Kolomenskogo po delam pravoslavnoi tserkvi na Vostoke* (St. Petersburg: Sinodal'naia tipografiia, 1886).

18. Nelidov means the monastery of St. Simon Kananitis called "New Athos," founded in Abkhasia in 1875 by the Russian monks of St. Panteleimon Monastery on Old Athos.

19. A. I. Nelidov to N. P. Shishkin, 10 April 1890, AVPRI, f. 180, op. 517/2, d. 1193a, ll. 292–95.

20. K. Karpat, "The Transformation of the Ottoman State 1789–1908," *International Journal of Middle Eastern Studies* 3 (1972): 243–81; A. D. Novichev, *Istoriia Turtsii: Novoe vremia*, vol. 4, *1853–1875* (Leningrad: n.p., 1978); M. Todorova, *Angliia, Rusiia i Tanzimatyt* (Sofia: BAN, 1980); C. Findley, *Bureaucratic Reform in the Ottoman Empire: The Sublime Porte, 1789–1922* (Princeton, NJ: Princeton University Press, 1980); N. A. Dulina, *Tanzimat i Mustafa Reshid Pasha* (Moscow:

Nauka, 1984); F. Ahmad, *The Making of Modern Turkey* (London: Routledge, 1993); I. Ortaily, "Period Tanzimata i posleduiushchee administrativnoe ustroistvo," *Istoriia Osmanskogo gosudarstva, obshestva i tsivilizatsii*, vol. 1 (Moscow: Vostochnaia literatura RAN, 2006); I. F. Makarova, *Bolgary i Tanzimat* (Moscow: Knizhnyi dom Librokom, 2010).

21. *Pribavleniia k Tserkovnym Vedomostiam* (11 February 1917): 134; ibid. (18 February 1917): 161.

22. For example, in 1879 Ambassador A. B. Lobanov-Rostovskii declined to help the Georgian monks on the grounds that they, having become monks abroad, had lost their Russian citizenship. See AVPRI, f. 180, op. 517/2, d. 3672, ll. 11-12.

23. N. V. Kokhmanskii to I. A. Zinoviev, 1 November 1905, AVPRI, f. 180, op. 517/2, d. 3679, ll. 2-3.

24. N. V. Kokhmanskii to N. V. Charykov, 29 August 1909, l. 8; N. V. Kokhmanskii to N. V. Charykov, 29 August 1909, l. 9; a note by N. V. Kokhmanskii, Constantinople, 11 September 1909, ll. 6-7; N. V. Charykov to A. M. Petriaev, October 15 1909, l. 5, all in AVPRI, f. 180, op. 517/2, d. 3679.

25. A. Shopov to I. S. Geshov, 22 May 1900, CDA, f. 321k, op. 1, d. 1480, ll. 69-70.

26. Ibid., ll. 66-71.

27. A. Shopov to T. Ivanchov, 19, 26, and 27 April 1900, CDA, f. 321k, op. 1, d. 1480, ll. 4-5, 20-21, 26.

28. D. T. Bataković, *Dechansko pitanje* (Belgrade: Historical Institute-Prosveta, 1989), 9. The book is based on Serbian archives. See the reports of the Russian consuls on the Dechani affair, AVPRI, f. 146, op. 495, d. 4993-4998 (1902-16).

29. For the documents on this affair, see "Lavra prepodobnogo Kharitona Ispovednika (Ain-Farskoe delo) (1904-1914 gg.)," in Lisovoi, *Rossiia v Sviatoi Zemle*, 2:302-28.

30. Shahovskoi to the Russian Holy Synod, 1912, RGIA, f. 796, op. 195, VI otd. 1 st., d. 1116, l. 4.

31. *Kelliots* were the inhabitants of small monastic huts called *kellion* (cell, the third and smaller form of settlement behind the monasteries and the *sketes*). These foundations belonged to some of the large independent monasteries, and monks could only lease them. The Athos regulations limited inhabitants for the *kellia* to six, and they were considered hermits. Nevertheless, the Russian monks brought a much larger number there and built huge churches and edifices. The organization of the brotherhood made the *kelliots* a power comparable to St. Panteleimon Monastery. Their activities were a matter of constant controversies with the Greek owners of the *kellia*. See P. Troitskii, *Istoriia russkikh obitelei Afona v XIX-XX vekakh* (Moscow: Indrik, 2009), 111-88.

32. "O merakh dlia bor'by s zloupotrebleniami afonskikh kelliotov po sboru pozhertvovanik v Rossii," *Tserkovnye vedomosti*, 30 April 1911, no.18, pribal'eniia, razdel "Khronika."

33. A. A. Dmitrievskii, *Russkie afonskie monakhi-kellioty i ikh prositelnye o milostyni pis'ma, rassylaemye po Rossii: Rech, proiznesennaia pri otkrytii chtenii v Kievskom religiozno-prosvetitel'nom obshestve 9 oktiabria 1 905 g.* (Kiev: Kievskaia Dukhovnaia Akademiia, 1906).

34. G. Papamihail, *Apokalipseis peri tis Rosikis politikis en ti Orthodoxi Anatoli* (Alexandria: n.p., 1910); Meletios Metaxakis, mitr. Kritiou, *To Agion Oros kai i Rosiki politiki en Anatoli* (Athens: n.p., 1913).

35. *Patriarchikon sigillion peri kelliotikou zitimatos ekdothen epi tis patriarheias tou Panagiotatou Oikoumenikou Patriarheiou k. Ioachim G' tou apo Thessalonikis* (Constantinople: n.p., 1909).

36. N. Kokhmanskii to I. A. Zinoviev, 30 April 1906, AVPRI, f. 180, op. 517/2, d. 3680, ll. 1–6, 7, 8–9; 8 May 1907, RGIA, f. 797, op. 73, II otd. 3 st., d. 293, ll. 18–19; 21 May 1912, AVPRI, f. 180, op. 517/2, d. 3682, ll. 7–9.

37. AVPRI, f. 180, op. 517/2, d. 3686, ll. 1–4.

38. Ibid., ll. 5–9.

39. Ibid., ll. 20–27.

40. Ibid., l. 25.

41. AVPRI, f. 180, op. 517/2, d. 3689, ll. 1–21.

42. Ibid., d. 3686, ll. 29–36.

43. The stimulus for its spreading was the book *Na gorakh Kavkaza* by Hieromonk Ilarion. The leader of the movement became monk Antonii Bulatovich, a former officer. The Name Worshipers followed the Byzantine practice of the *hesychast* and in fact had no political inspirations. On this topic, see the excellent work by Ep. Ilarion (Alfeev), *Sviashchennaia taina Tserkvi: Vvedeniie v istoriiu i problematiku Imiaslavskikh sporov* (St. Petersburg: Izdatel'stvo Olega Abyshko, 2007); see also K. K. Papoulidis, *Oi Rossoi Onomatolatrai tou Agiou Orous* (Thessaloniki: IMXA, 1977); L. Graham and J. M. Kantor, *Naming Infinity: A True Story of Religious Mysticism and Mathematical Creativity* (Cambridge, MA: Harvard University Press, 2009), 7–18.

44. Reports of B. S. Serafimov to M. N. Giers, 24 September 1913; 1 October 1913; 7 October 1913, AVPRI, f. 180, op. 517/2, d. 3697.

45. See the Russian translation of this text in addition to the report of Serafimov, 21 October 1913, AVPRI, f. 180, op. 517/2, d. 3697, ll. 46–47.

46. Reports of Serafimov, 7 October 1913, AVPRI, f. 180, op. 517/2, d. 369, ll. 23–24, 34–35.

47. An extract from the protocol of the session of the Kinot on 28 October 1913. Quoted from the report of B. Serafimov, 2 November 1913, AVPRI, f. 180, op. 517/2, d. 3697, ll. 57–60.

48. Ibid., ll. 30–31.

49. Ibid., ll. 31–32.

50. H. K. Papastathis, "To kathestos tou Agiou Orous kai tis Ekklisias stin Makedonia meta tin synthiki tou Boukourestiou," in *Nomokanonikes meletes* (Athens: Protypes Thessalikes Ekdoseis, 2009), 61–63.

51. A secret telegram of M. N. Giers, 13 July 1914, AVPRI, f. 151, op. 482, d. 3877, l. 13. See O. E. Petrunina, "Afonskii vopros 1812-1917 gg. Po materialam russkikh diplomaticheskikh istochnikov," *Vestnik archivista*, no. 1 (2002): 74.

52. M. G. Talalai, "Russkoe monashestvo na afone 1913-1917 gg. Otchety A. A. Pavlovskogo v Rosiiskoe general'noe konsul'stvo v Salonikakh," in *Rossiia i Khristianskii Vostok*, II-III (Moscow: Indrik, 2004), 595-617.

Russian soldiers taking the oath at the Apostolic Church of Kars, 1915. (reprinted with permission from the State Archive of Audio Visual Documents of Georgia, A-298-91)

"Forty Years of Black Days"?
The Russian Administration of Kars, Ardahan, and Batum, 1878–1918

CANDAN BADEM

This chapter examines the basic tenets of the Russian "Military-Customary Administration" (*Voenno-narodnoe upravlenie*) and the Russian resettlement (colonization) policy in Kars, Ardahan, and Batum from the Russian annexation in 1878 until the Treaty of Brest-Litovsk in 1918.[1] While there is a sizable literature on the Russian administration in the Caucasus in general, very few studies in Russian, English, Armenian, or Turkish have been devoted to the Russian administration of this area.[2] Whereas contemporary Russian historians have almost forgotten about these territories, works by Turkish, Kurdish, Georgian, and Armenian historians are generally marked by nationalist interpretations, with few exceptions. Therefore, one of my goals is to dispel nationalist myths.

Another goal is to examine the out-migration of Muslims from the region following the Treaty of Constantinople (1879). In the three years following the Treaty of Constantinople between Russia and the Ottoman Empire, a treaty that generally affirmed the Treaties of San Stefano (1878) and Berlin (1878), more than 110,000 Muslims from Kars and Ardahan and more than 30,000 Muslims (with a few Armenians) from

Batum and Artvin abandoned their native lands and migrated to the Ottoman Empire. Turkish nationalist historiography until now has depicted the years under Russian rule (1878-1918) as "forty years of black days" (*kırk yıllık kara günler*) and has considered the Muslim exodus from 1879 to 1882 as forced by the Russian government.[3]

I argue that the Russian administration was not as "black" or bad as claimed by nationalist historians, and that the Russian administration did not force the local Muslim population to emigrate, although it encouraged out-migration by some indirect incentives. The out-migration of Muslims from these territories after the annexation was largely due to the unwillingness of the Muslim elites and the masses led by them to live as Russian subjects and to some Ottoman incentives to emigrate. These Muslim elites (notables, clergy, officials, and merchants dealing mainly with the state) feared loss of their privileged status under the new Russian administration. Some economic reasons also played a role for at least some of the emigrants. Second, I argue that nearly half of the Muslim emigrants from the region returned to Russia legally or illegally, a fact that is hardly mentioned in Turkish historiography. Further, I assert that the Russian policy in these territories was complex and inconsistent, and the Russian administration in the end was unsuccessful in colonizing the region with Russian peasants or even with Christians in general to a significant degree. Finally, although this chapter focuses on the relationship between Russian policy and the Muslim migration from the Caucasus, it is worth highlighting the role played by the many Russian-Ottoman wars and Eastern Question treaties in providing context for the Muslim migration and Russian decision making.

The Russian-Ottoman wars of the nineteenth century were fought in two main theaters of war: the Balkans and the Caucasus. Both empires always considered the Caucasian front as secondary. By 1877, Russia had already conquered the eastern Black Sea coast as far as Batum, as well as the once Ottoman districts of Akhaltsikhe and Akhalkalak. After the Russian-Ottoman War of 1877-78 and the Congress of Berlin, Russia further annexed the three Ottoman *sanjaks* of Kars, Ardahan (formerly Childir), and Batum. From these three *sanjaks* (*elviye-i selase* in Ottoman official parlance), the Russian government formed two oblasts: Kars (including Ardahan) and Batum. In 1883, the Batum oblast was dissolved and became part of the Kutaisi *guberniia*; however, the two districts (*okrugs*) of Artvin and Batum were still under the Military-Customary Administration. In 1903, the Batum oblast was restored.

The Military-Customary Administration was an administrative system developed by the Russian Empire in the nineteenth century, particularly during its wars in the northern Caucasus against the Muslim "mountaineer" peoples of the region. The system mixed Russian martial rule and local customs. In essence, it rested upon simple rules easily understood by the local populations instead of the complex corpus of Russian laws. This meant in practice a dual jurisdictional system in the region under consideration. In certain cases, local people could have recourse to local courts that delivered verdicts according to the sharia and customary laws. In other cases, locals were subjected to the same system of laws in operation throughout the entire Russian Empire. The Military-Customary Administration tried to conciliate the customs of the local population with Russian governmental institutions, and it allowed local people to exercise to a certain extent their customs in their internal affairs.[4]

The system was first put into practice in 1852, even before Imam Shamil's surrender in 1859. General Prince Aleksandr I. Bariatinskii (1815–79), the then chief of staff of the Army of the Caucasus and later the viceroy of the Caucasus (commander in chief of the Army of the Caucasus and governor-general of the Caucasus) from 1856 to 1862, had extensive experience in the Caucasus, and was familiar with local languages and Islamic practices. Hoping to learn from the administrative mistakes committed under General Ermolov at the beginning of the nineteenth century, Bariatinskii developed the Military-Customary Administration, which attempted to eliminate the problems of the former system of rule by incorporating native customs and procedures. In 1852, he set up a *mehkeme* (court) in Grozny, capital of Chechnya, to hear cases among Chechens. Presided over by a Russian officer, the court consisted of three members and a Muslim judge (*kadi* or *qadi*). The court's members took office after being elected by local people. The *kadi* decided all Islamic cases under his jurisdiction, where the president and members had only advisory votes. In other cases based on local customs (*adat*), the president and members were decisive, while the *kadi* had only an advisory vote.[5]

Besides justice, local population also took part in the administration of villages under the hybrid system developed under Russian rule. Village communities (*jamaat*) and tribal associations (*tohum*) retained their traditional structure of governance. Yet the final aim of Bariatinskii's innovation was to help people gradually grow accustomed to the tsarist regime and abide by its laws. Like Prince Mikhail S. Vorontsov (1782–1856), who had previously served as the viceroy of the Caucasus from 1844 to 1854, Bariatinskii also took care to incorporate Caucasian feudal landlords into the tsarist aristocracy. Based on experience, the tsarist regime considered local landlords its greatest allies in the conquered territories. In this respect, the Russian Empire did not significantly differ from other empires. Just as the Ottoman Empire appointed Kurdish beys as administrators of certain districts in Kurdistan, the Russian Empire entrusted local khans with the administration of some *uezds* in the Caucasus and Turkestan.[6] In fact, it is clear from the correspondence between Emperor Nicholas I and his generals (including the minister of war Aleksandr I. Chernyshev) that Russian colonialists had seriously examined the experiences of British and French imperialism in India and Algeria. Britain and France also examined Russia's experience in the Caucasus. After all, they were all inspired by the Ottoman system as well.[7]

The provisional regulation (*vremennoe polozhenie*) of 9 October 1878 endorsed by Grand Duke Mikhail Nikolaevich, the viceroy of the Caucasus and the commander in chief of the Caucasus army, briefly defined the boundaries and administrative divisions of the Kars oblast as well as the powers of the military governor. One of the two deputies of the military governor of Kars would preside over the Supreme Popular Court (*glavnyi narodnyi sud*), which was the provincial court of appeals, while the other one would be charged with military affairs. Local courts would see all cases except for those involving the local population's land affairs and crimes committed against the state. Rules pertaining to land ownership would be set forth later. A permanent gendarmerie unit (*militsiia*) consisting of four companies would be established in Kars to provide military-police services.[8] In short, the grand duke envisioned an administration that consolidated central authority in the hands of Russian military officials but left local affairs to native leaders. The Russian government tried to extend its experience from the Military-Customary Administration of the Caucasus into the two newly acquired oblasts of Kars and Batum. However, the Muslim population of the new region differed from the Caucasus Muslims in some ways.

A major distinction between the people of the northern Caucasus and those of the Kars and Batum oblasts was that the latter had been governed by the Ottoman Empire for centuries and so did not have such strong local *adat* (customary law) traditions as those of the former. Under the Ottoman system, İstanbul appointed a *kadi* to the district center (*kaza*), which meant the jurisdiction of a *kadi*. There were also the village councils of elders (*ihtiyar meclisi*) who settled petty matters. However, as reported by Lieutenant-General Viktor A. Frankini, the first Russian military governor of the Kars oblast from 1878 to 1881, local people hated those councils, which they thought had abused their authority. Now the Russian governor thought it would be unnecessary to set up such village councils. Furthermore, there were not enough literate persons to serve as secretaries.[9] Instead, each district (*okrug*) in the Batum and Kars oblasts would have its "popular court."[10]

A regulation dated February 1879 concerning the powers and responsibilities of the military governors of the Batum and Kars oblasts stipulated that these governors were responsible for maintaining order and safety in their respective provinces. They gradually were to prepare the population for civil citizenship (*grazhdanstvennost*), but the regulation cautioned against sharply disrupting their routine order and lifestyle unless a special need arose.[11] Governors were expected to integrate the material and moral interests of local influential people with Russia, inducing them to send their children to Russian schools. Governors had to obtain permission from the commander of the Army of the Caucasus to exile unwanted persons. Yet in cases of emergency, military governors were authorized to exile nuisance people and criminals to Tbilisi along with an explanatory report regarding the individuals and infractions in question. Military governors could also sentence subjects to fines as much as three hundred rubles and to imprisonment for up to three months. To arrest individuals from privileged classes, they first had to gain permission from the Caucasus administration in Tbilisi; however, they also had the power for immediate arrest in urgent cases so long as they informed the chief commander. Despite efforts to involve natives in the administration, the military governors thus retained enormous powers over the local populations in the districts under their control.

St Petersburg did support a policy of toleration concerning education and religious affairs. Military governors, for example, were not to interfere with the affairs of Muslim religious schools as long as those schools did not display fanaticism. In theory, the Russian secular schools administered by the Ministry of People's Enlightenment were open to Muslims as well. Few Muslims, however, sent their children to Russian schools. The Caucasus administration instructed military governors to support private enterprises but not to allow monopolies; to improve public works and transportation; to find new lands for Russian settlers without putting any limit on the rights of the local population; to preserve forests; to encourage volunteers for the mounted gendarme; to be attentive to the selection of gendarme officers; and to take necessary measures to increase provincial revenues.[12] Overall, Russian administrators provided better services for lesser taxes than was the case in the Ottoman Empire.

Migration and Colonization

The ethnic composition of the population in the two oblasts has been a battlefield for competing nationalisms, which makes any disinterested account of the colonization policies during the period under study highly important. Studying the demographic figures before and after the Russian annexation of the area as indicated in Russian and Ottoman sources will help sort through various competing nationalist claims to the region. Such analysis also illuminates underexplored aspects of the Eastern Question, particularly its impact on native populations. According to the Ottoman yearbook of the *vilayet* of Erzurum for the year 1877, the male population of the *sanjaks* of Kars and Çıldır (Ardahan) that went into the Kars oblast numbered 57,503 Muslims and 5,245 Christians, totaling 62,748 men.[13] From this figure, we can estimate that the total population including women and allowing for those who escaped census must have been more than 140,000 people. In the *sanjak* of Lazistan (Batum), the situation was similar, with an even smaller Christian population. Thus the majority of the population in these *sanjaks* was Muslim (Turks, Georgians, Kurds, and others), while Christians (mainly Armenians) constituted a small minority. Stepan Ermolaev, secretary of the statistics committee of the Kars oblast, also noted that at the time of its capture by Russians the entire population of Kars was Muslim with only a very small Christian population. Ermolaev wrote that according to Ottoman official local records, the male population amounted to 41,500 in 1878 excluding nomadic Kurdish tribes, and the Christians numbered 4,000, most of whom were Armenians.[14]

Conversely, the Soviet Armenian historian Artashes M. Poghosian has argued that on the eve of the Congress of Berlin in 1878, the number of Armenians in the *sanjaks* of Kars and Çıldır reached up to 280,000, referring to the journal *Ararat* in 1914.[15] However, Poghosian's source does not give any information on the population of these two *sanjaks*, but provides data only on other *vilayets* in Anatolia. Furthermore, Russian statistics do not support this number. Although the Armenian population in the Kars and Batum oblasts under Russian rule increased with Armenian immigrants and refugees, the total Armenian population (including the temporary population) in these oblasts did not exceed 115,000 in the former and 15,000 in the latter even on the eve of the First World War. Poghosian would be right if he gave that number for the war years beginning with 1915, when many Armenians from Anatolia indeed fled to Kars. However, Poghosian again makes a very surprising, implicitly nationalistic claim in his book, arguing this time without any reference, that before annexation by Russia, "the population of the Kars *sanjak* consisted of Armenians exclusively."[16]

Another nationalistic misrepresentation regarding the ethnic composition of the population comes from Tatiana F. Aristova, a Russian ethnographer and Kurdolog. Referring to an article by the Georgian ethnographer Dmitrii Z. Bakradze, Aristova argues that in the 1870s, Kurds dominated the ethnic composition of the Kars oblast.[17] However, Bakradze, to whom Aristova refers, writes that among the settlers in the Kars province, Kurds outnumbered any other ethnicity, followed by Karapapaks and Turkmens.[18] Using the term *vselentsy*, or "settlers," Bakradze does not mean the native population but rather a group of people settled in the region some time ago, most likely during the Ottoman period. Indeed, earlier, Bakradze describes the Kurds, Karapapaks, Turkmens, Caucasian highlanders, and others, as newcomers to the Kars province. Kurds thus did not constitute a majority or plurality in the whole population of the area, and Aristova therefore misunderstood either what she read or made a deliberate falsification.

While Armenian and Kurdish nationalism has thus tried to exaggerate the number of Armenians or Kurds within the population of the area, Turkish nationalism for its part in most cases has denied a substantial presence of Armenians in the area in the Middle Ages. Turkish nationalist historiography for its part has inaccurately claimed that Russia tried to colonize the area with Armenians after 1878. Similarly, for many years during the republican period in Turkey, Turkish nationalist historiography has also claimed that the Kurds in Turkey were just "mountain Turks." It would not be superfluous to note here that Fahrettin Kırzıoğlu, an influential historian on the history of Kars, was the inventor of this ridiculous mountain theory, according to which the name "Kurd" originated from sounds of "kart kurt" that were heard when people walked on the snow in mountains.

After the Congress of Berlin in 1878, when the three *sanjaks* were ultimately ceded to Russia, the Muslim population in these *sanjaks* began to immigrate to the Ottoman Empire. According to Article 21 of the

Treaty of San Stefano of 3 March 1878 and later Article 7 of the Treaty of Constantinople of 8 February 1879, the inhabitants of the Ottoman territories annexed by Russia were entitled to sell their property and immigrate to the Ottoman Empire within three years after the treaty was ratified. Similarly, Christians living in the Ottoman Empire could migrate to Russia.[19] After the three-year period, those who remained would automatically become Russian subjects.

It is some matter of debate whether Muslim emigration from the Russian Empire in the second half of the nineteenth century was a policy objective of the Russian government.[20] Evidence here suggests that the Russian government in general acted neutrally, neither forcing the Muslims in the two oblasts under consideration to immigrate to Turkey nor convincing them to stay. While Turkish nationalist historians have claimed that the Russian authorities forced the local Muslims to immigrate to Turkey in order to make room for Russian or Orthodox settlers, documents in the Ottoman, Russian, Georgian, and Armenian archives point to the religious motivation and voluntary nature of the Muslim exodus. The Ottoman authorities for their part, at least at the beginning of the three-year term, encouraged Muslim immigration into Anatolia by promising land, houses, and tax exemptions to the various delegations from the three *sanjaks*. The Muslim clergy (ulema or the mullahs, *muftis*, imams, *hodjas*) of these *sanjaks* actively propagated for immigration to Turkey. They thought that they would lose their influence under the Russian rule; therefore, they agitated for immigration to the Ottoman Empire together with their communities. In fact, they were able to collect money and goods for their "services" from their communities with the help of the Ottoman administration. Now the new Russian administration was not interested in defending the Muslim clergy's privileges. Therefore, the clergy opted for emigration together with as many people as possible. In their petitions to Ottoman authorities complaining of hardships in their new homes after their migration, the Muslim emigrants from the "three *sanjaks*" wrote that they did not want to live under Russian rule. For example, in a petition signed by thirty-three members of the ulema of Kars and Ardahan, dated July 1881, the petitioners stated that they left their homes due to their fateful invasion by Russia, but they did not mention any coercion by Russian authorities.[21]

Although the agitation of the Muslim clergy and the promises of the Ottoman authorities had an important effect, it is not possible to explain the whole process of migration by religious motives or by fanaticism, as other, economic reasons existed as well. By unfortunate coincidence, bad harvests marked the first two years under Russian rule in the two oblasts. Thus many peasants were unable to pay taxes. The economic situation of peasants was especially hard in those areas that had been affected most in the last war. Furthermore, the declaration of Batum as a free port (*porto franco*) was not in the interests of the neighboring population, which lost the opportunity to sell its products and to buy goods in Batum without paying taxes. Due to the severance of economic ties with İstanbul, some people had lost their opportunities and jobs. For example, single men in the Murgul valley used to go to İstanbul and other big cities for work. As General Komarov, military governor of the Batum oblast, argued, with the establishment of new borders, free passage of goods and men ceased and many people lost their means of subsistence.[22]

Prince Grigol D. Orbeliani, in his letter of November 1879 to the viceroy's deputy in charge of civil affairs, Adjutant General Prince Dmitrii I. Sviatopolk-Mirskii, complained of the Muslim exodus from Russia: "The Crimea became empty, more than 200 thousand Circassians left Kuban, Abkhazia is left without population. Now the inhabitants of Ajaria and Kars, even the Armenians, are running away from us, as if from the plague! Can all this be explained by fanaticism?"[23] Orbeliani, who had talked to local people in Batum, believed that although fanaticism had an impact, the incompetency and corruption of local administrators was a more important factor in the out-migration. He argued that corrupt local officials were alienating the people from Russian administration. He suggested that young, idealistic university graduates replace all administrators at the *uezd* (district) level in the region.

One year later, Lieutenant-General Dmitrii S. Staroselskii, head of the main administration of the viceroy, was sent to Batum to examine the reasons for the complaints of local people about the administration. He listened to local notables (the *bek*) and large merchants. In his report to the viceroy, Staroselskii wrote that he talked with ten *beks* separately, and these *beks* said that under Turkish rule they were in state service and received salaries, whereas only two or three *beks* had been accepted into Russian service. The rest were now deprived of their means of subsistence. Consequently, many *beks* tried to attract large groups to emigrate from Russia to Turkey with them, in order to be considered influential by Turkish authorities. Although the military governor of Batum had argued that he hoped to gain the respect and trust of the local population without paying attention to *beks* and other influential people, Staroselskii believed that this was a mistake; instead, the *beks* should be given some titles and salaries. "We have adopted such a system of action in the newly conquered places of the oblasts of Dagestan and Terek, and experience proved the rationality of this system," he added.[24] In the end, many *beks* in the two oblasts were entitled to large lands and to salaries in compensation for lost income they once had during Ottoman rule.

The Land Question

About nine-tenths of all fields, meadows, and pastures in the three *sanjaks*, now the oblasts of Kars and Batum, belonged to the treasury. According to the Ottoman Land Code of 1858, such permanently leased state lands (*arazi emiriye*) could not be alienated from their tenants (the peasants) as long as they paid their taxes. Ottoman law recognized full ownership only for houses with small gardens in villages and houses with land plots in cities. The rest was either state or *waqf* property. However, such categories of landed property were not compatible with the Russian laws of that time; the Russian administration thus faced a land problem that remained unsolved throughout Russian rule. When migration officially started in September 1878 in the Kars oblast, the sale of real estate owned by the residents of the province also became a problem.[25] General Frankini set up a commission called "*gorodskaia uprava*," to which real estate registers and transfer and sale procedures were handed over. Property rights were determined by Ottoman title deeds, in the absence of which one had to produce acceptable witnesses.

General Frankini, in a circular to the district and police administrations of the Kars oblast on 25 September 1878, stated that many residents appealed to migrate to Turkey and for permission to sell their movable and immovable properties before leaving. Other residents had asked whether landowners who wished to stay and to accept Russian nationality would be granted tenure over their lands as was the case under Ottoman rule. Frankini instructed the district governors that those would-be emigrants with title deeds should hand them over, while those without any title deed should sign written commitments attesting that they would not raise any claims for land ownership or tenure in the future. Frankini further stipulated: "Those wishing to stay here and accept Russian subjecthood shall not be deprived of their rights of land use provided that they document their rights. Those wishing to emigrate are not allowed to sell their lands, but those who want to depart immediately may sell all the harvest of this year (grass, fodder, barley, wheat, etc.) without having to pay the tithe." He required his agents to prepare and submit lists including first name, last name, family members (names and ages), and the amount of land at their disposal. Finally, Frankini granted "migration permits" only after he received these lists, the title deeds, and the aforementioned commitments to be handed over by the emigrants.[26] Authenticating the title deeds was difficult, however, and they were even unavailable in many places. The governors of Kars wrote to Tbilisi about the issue of title deeds several times, established commissions, proposed projects, but failed to receive a clear response from Tbilisi.[27]

On 9 February 1879, General Frankini wrote to Lieutenant General Alexander V. Komarov, head of the administration for Caucasus mountain tribes (*gorskoe upravlenie*) and a deputy of Grand Duke Mikhail Nikolaevich, that Article 21 of the Treaty of San Stefano was causing the Russian administration "much trouble," because of the right of emigration within three years.[28] Frankini argued that Russia had neither the right nor the means to resist emigration. Nor did Russia have any interest in doing so due to the stipulations of the treaty and the difficulty of controlling a practically open border. Furthermore, the Russian administration could not expect a population held by force to "fulfill its civic duties." Therefore, Frankini recommended that Russia not retain such a population. Still, the governor thought that emigrants should be paid appropriate sums close to the rent in return for their lands.

Governor Frankini wrote that the administration now needed to decide what to do about the emigrants' lands to ensure the "proper resettlement" of the oblast. He noted that a significant part of the Turkish population in the districts of Kağızman, Takht, and Oltu was prepared to emigrate if they felt any coercion from the authorities and worried that "Turks" (meaning Muslims) in other districts would join them. He also expressed concern over the problem of land speculation. If the administration allowed emigrants to sell their registered lands to any buyer, he argued, all free lands could soon be handed over to "speculators" in the face of the emigrants' desire to sell their immovable property as soon as possible. Subsequently, according to Frankini, the administration would be denied the opportunity to organize the province's settlement. Frankini suggested two measures to prevent this from happening. The first one was to announce that rural lands could be purchased only by permission of the administration. Such a measure would largely facilitate the settlement of the oblast but had limitations. He believed that (1) the government might be accused of arbitrariness; (2) it would be harder to have homogeneous village communities; and (3) the delay in title deed purchases would prolong the uncertainty surrounding prospective emigrants because of the treaty.

As an alternative to allowing would-be emigrants to sell the land on the free market, Frankini proposed that the Russian government buy the lands of all prospective emigrants by reimbursing the fees paid for the title deeds. The government would then colonize the oblast as it liked, and this would certainly prove to be very useful in the future, especially in case of a new war with Turkey. Frankini estimated that five hundred thousand rubles would be enough to buy the title deeds of the Muslims leaving the Kars oblast, given that the title deeds showed small amounts of rent for tax evasion purposes. The government could also give a loan to the new settlers for the land. Governor Frankini went on to say that if the loan project was ratified, immediate implementation would follow and detailed regulations would be drafted right away.[29]

While the Russian governor wrote that title deeds could be purchased cheaply, Fahrettin Erdoğan, the Young Turk Ittihadist agent who visited Batum and Kars many times from 1899 to 1914, interestingly claimed that Russians overpaid for the title deeds. Erdoğan wrote the following in his memoirs: "In and around Kars, Russians were following a cunning policy and exerting maximum efforts to drive the Turks living in Kars, Batum, and Ardahan away from their homelands by buying their real estate and lands at high prices."[30] Erdoğan also maintained that opposing the Russian policy of encouraging Turks to emigrate, Ismail Agha, his uncle from the Asboğa village in Sarıkamış, and some others propagandized against emigration. Their message penetrated the most remote villages and according to Erdoğan, thus "obviated emigration." Erdoğan also wrote that a treaty granted Muslims the right to emigrate within five years, which was, in fact, three years. Another claim by Erdoğan is that his uncle and others also made anti-emigration propaganda by saying that Kars, Batum, and Ardahan had been pledged to Russians for twenty years as indemnity, and these lands would again be given back to Turks at the expiry of the term. It is uncertain whether Erdoğan and his uncle believed these words they uttered, or they just told them for propaganda purposes. Whatever the case, their claims were false; no treaty provision existed stipulating that Kars would be returned to Turkey after twenty years or upon the payment of the indemnity. On one level, factual inaccuracies in Erdoğan's memoirs, and those like it, reflect contemporaneous construction of various nationalist narratives surrounding this region. On another, Erdoğan's memoirs suggest that contemporaries did indeed perceive an orchestrated attempt by the Russian government to force Muslim migration.

Colonization Policy and the Armenian Question

In another report to his superiors, General Frankini expressed his vision that the future population of the Kars province should be "entirely reliable and loyal" and should also be a mainstay against the "untrustworthy Muslim population in the Caucasus," detaching them from the surrounding Turkish provinces and centers of propaganda. The Muslim element should, he asserted, "make up only an insignificant part of the population, in the form of exceptions. The overwhelming element should be Russian, while it is possible to form the rest from Armenians and Greeks. I believe these last two elements should be counterbalanced. Around 4,000 Greek families are willing to immigrate to our lands from the provinces of Erzurum and Trabzon. They are a docile, obedient, and hardworking group of people engaged in farming and crafts with no political aspirations whatsoever. They would act as a counterweight against others. Our consulates in Erzurum and Trabzon should aid these Greeks."[31]

Here, in addition to casting aspersions on the Muslim population, Frankini also expressed discomfort with Armenians. He implied that Armenians had political aspirations, and he proposed using Greeks as counterweight against them. The governor believed that the oblast could in fact sustain twice as much as the population under Ottoman rule, which he estimated as eighteen thousand households, arguing that Ottoman censuses understated the population. For the colonization of the region, preference should be given first to Russians and then to Greeks, while the Armenian population should not be allowed to reach a significant percent of the population. For this reason, Frankini ordered the Armenian immigrants from Turkey to be distributed among Armenian villages, but they should not be allowed to create new villages.

According to Nikolai Shavrov (1826-99), a Russian nationalist retired general who published various books on Russian colonization in the Caucasus and numerous articles in the newspaper *Kavkaz* in Tbilisi, Mikhail Nikolaevich demanded that Russian peasants be settled (colonized) in the Kars oblast. However, General Mikhail T. Loris-Melikov, then minister of the interior and of Armenian descent, opposed the grand duke's demand.[32] Conqueror of Kars in 1877, minister of the interior from November 1880 to April 1881, Loris-Melikov was the author of the second Russian constitutional project and was known as a supporter of gradual liberal constitutional reforms. When Emperor Alexander II died of an injury from an assassination attempt on 13 March 1881, the more conservative segment of the ruling classes turned the new emperor against Loris-Melikov, and Loris-Melikov had to resign. Many historians consider his resignation from the post of minister of the interior as a turning point in nineteenth-century Russian political history.[33] Thus the new emperor, Alexander III, changed the political course toward conservatism, centralism, and Russian nationalism. He also saw Armenian nationalism as a threat to Russia. In 1882, he would order Count Dmitrii A. Tolstoi, the ultraconservative minister of the interior, to take serious measures against Armenian nationalism.

The opinions of General Frankini concerning regional settlement evolved during this change of regime and were apparently accepted by the Caucasus administration. Prince Sviatopolk-Mirskii wrote to Mikhail Nikolaevich in St. Petersburg that he had provided General Frankini with detailed instructions. In his report dated 16 February 1879, Sviatopolk-Mirskii outlined his plans for the region: Muslims in the Kars province should not be prevented from migrating to Turkey; and necessary precautions should be suggested to avoid foreign acquisition of the lands left behind by emigrants and to ensure complete government control over them. According to Sviatopolk-Mirskii, certain sums should be paid to emigrants in return for the lands they left behind. In turn, as many Russians as possible should be settled in the evacuated lands.

In the prince's opinion, this was such an important matter that the state should not hesitate to pay several million rubles. The Russian general argued that it had been a mistake to settle the lands around Akhaltsikhe and Gyumri with Armenians and Greeks from Turkey instead of Russian people in 1829, emphasizing that it would now be inexcusable to repeat that mistake in the settlement of the Kars province. He added that a few Russian villages in southern Caucasus had proved themselves very useful in many respects during the recent war.[34] In fact, Molokans and Dukhobors along the Ottoman border offered important services such as transport and provisions to the Russian army in return for compensation.[35] Although Armenians had also helped the Russian army in many ways during its war against Turkey, Sviatopolk-Mirskii still considered the settlement of Armenians a mistake, apparently because he thought that the Armenians intended to create an independent or autonomous Armenia.

Given that the Russian government had renounced an indemnity of 1.1 billion rubles in return for the Kars and Batum provinces, the amount of 500,000 rubles suggested by Frankini could not be considered excessive. Poghosian has written based on certain archival documents that Prince Sviatopolk-Mirskii had notified the governor of Kars through secret correspondence on 21 February 1879 of the government's decision to lend financial support to Russian peasants to settle in the Kars province.[36] Again, according to Poghosian, Sviatopolk-Mirskii had ordered that Russians were to be settled not only in vacant but also in inhabited villages. While Russian settlers in the Caucasus had been banned from emigrating in the past, they were now allowed to migrate into the Kars province.

Based on Sviatopolk-Mirskii's report and the grand duke's approval, Alexander II ordered an allocation of 500,000 rubles (the equivalent of 375,000 US dollars at that time) on 3 March 1879 for this purpose. Subsequently, Sviatopolk-Mirskii ordered General Frankini to move forward with active Russian settlement in the Caucasus. He also prohibited Russian officials from taking coercive measures to ensure Muslim migration. He wrote:

Colonization of the Kars oblast with Russian elements as largely as possible is, as demonstrated by the allocation of such a serious sum of money for this purpose, a significant state affair. But however important the aim is, the means to achieve this aim must conform to the glory and the just laws of our government. It would be unworthy of us to resort to artificial means to force the Muslims in the Kars province to emigrate. The attitude we need to adopt is simple and clear. We should fulfill the terms of the treaty in both letter and spirit and remain on legal and fair ground. The Muslim population has been granted a term of three years (starting from the ratification of the final treaty signed on 8 February of the current year) to decide between Russian and Turkish subjecthood. The term was granted precisely to ensure the proper conduct of migration without any commotion and destruction. It is also a moral imperative for us. The only thing we can and should do is to clearly explain to the Muslim population what their obligations as Russian subjects are and will be, not to impede those who wish to emigrate and on the contrary to make emigration easier for them. The most important precaution to be taken for this last issue is for the government to pay money [*voznagrazhdenie*, "reward"] to emigrants in return for their rights over the lands they will leave behind.[37]

Sviatopolk-Mirskii added that there were two principle ways to settle Russian immigrants in the Kars province, both of which had their advantages and disadvantages. The first involved waiting for the full body of

Muslims to emigrate and to register the amount and characteristics of the lands they left behind. At that point, a decision could be made about a deliberate redistribution of land among a large group of Russian settlers. Alternatively, Sviatopolk-Mirskii proposed a more gradual process of settling individual Russians as Muslims evacuated their lands. In the end, the government adopted the second option.

General Frankini reported to the viceroy of the Caucasus twice a month about emigrants from the oblast to Turkey. According to his reports, 32,494 individuals had emigrated by mid-August in 1879.[38] From 7 September 1878 until 13 June 1880, 4,383 households including 42,853 individuals applied for emigration to Turkey.[39] By 13 June 1880, the number of emigrants had reached 5,816 households consisting of 65,447 individuals.[40] The number of emigration permits (*bilets*) issued by the governor rose to 89,477 by the end of December 1881 and finally reached 111,202 (56,588 men and 54,614 women) by the end of February 1882, that is, when the three-year term stipulated by the Treaty of Constantinople expired.[41] In the Batum oblast, however, there was no such official count of emigrants. According to French and British consular reports, between 1879 and 1881, some 6,000 Georgian Muslim households (roughly 30,000–40,000 individuals) migrated to ports along the Black Sea coast in the Ottoman province of Trabzon. By February 1882, according to Ali Pasha of Çürüksu, a local notable appointed by the Ottoman government as an official for settling the migrants from the Batum region, the total number of Georgian Muslims who had immigrated to Ottoman Anatolia by sea was around 80,000; the number of migrants who had come overland was around 40,000.[42]

In his annual report for 1879, General Frankini also describes the various ethnic and religious elements of the local population of the Kars oblast in a section called "the settlement problem," which includes a telling analysis of the emigration of the Muslim population. He noted that the local people knew about the relations between Russia and the Ottoman Empire and the life-or-death struggle between the two empires through firsthand experience, not from books or hearsay information. These unfortunate people had shouldered all the burden of this struggle. According to Frankini, the suffering of the local people during the numerous Russian-Ottoman wars was extreme. In fact, the current generation alone had witnessed all three wars of the century. Listening to the artillery fire of General Paskevich at their mothers' bosom (the 1828–29 war), spending all their energy in a war with Russians in their youth (the

Crimean War of 1853–56), and finally, feeling the pain of surrendering to the Russian army for the third time at an old age, when they deserved to rest, this was a tragic generation. Thus, he said, "the present generation opened their eyes to the struggle of their homeland with Russia and [have] lived with it ever after." "Obviously," he continued, "in this case, a Turk would inevitably and naturally see his historical and national enemy in Russians. This is the origin of the local Turks' deep-seated distrust for us that no action could ever repair in any way."[43] General Frankini believed that the Turks' distrust was so "deep in their flesh and blood" and "had become such an inseparable part of their nature" that although they had "sound judgment and natural wisdom," they could not objectively evaluate the goodwill of Russian authorities toward them and saw a future under Russian rule with "a blind and foolish fear." Therefore, they chose to use their treaty-granted right to emigrate as soon as it became clear that the region would ultimately remain in Russian hands.

Governor Frankini's words in his annual report to describe the emigration of the people of Kars and Kağızman are highly interesting, surprising, and straightforward. An emphasis on religious "fanaticism" notwithstanding, Frankini writes with a sympathy that is uncharacteristic for any administrator of a conquered province:

The first ones to leave Kars were the Turks, who had been imbued with a religious-national spirit and who were the enemies not only of Russia but also of all Christendom: for all their lives, they had been fanatics-patriots who had read Arabic-Turkish literature and Islamic theology, and these formed a highly influential clerical class in Kars. They emigrated because of their fanaticism and patriotism; they deeply mourned the separation of their region from their homeland and its annexation by the hated Muscovites. Of course, they used all their rhetorical power and theological logic to rally the entire Turkish population of the province to their cause. They were followed by a whole group who had been dependent on the Turkish government for their means of existence: these were former Turkish officials and partly merchants. Then came the mass movement of those modeling the urban notables. It is hard to envisage a scene more heartbreaking than this long train of oxcarts covered by canvas, carrying silent and crestfallen women and children: before they left the lands they had tilled and improved by sweating blood since their young age, and set out for the gloomy uncertainty awaiting them and maybe even for misery and early death, the emigrants with women and children visited graveyards to bid farewell to the graves of their fathers, children, and companions of their labor life. In Kagyzman, where the people were engaged in horticulture, the emigrants not only painfully said good-bye to the cold graves of their beloved children but also hugged and kissed every tree in their gardens; trees that had been grown by centuries of labor and fed them with their fruits.[44]

Fahrettin Kırzıoğlu corroborated Frankini's account, writing that the Muslim population had been encouraged to emigrate by some *ulema*. The two quatrains below from an anonymous "epic of migration," as recorded by Kırzıoğlu, were recited in the courtyards of the large and small mosques in towns and villages. They constitute a good example of the rhetoric and theological logic described by Frankini:

Pay heed to the ulema's words
What do you wait for? Emigrate!
This is a duty for believers
What do you wait for? Emigrate!

On the rampage are these infidels
Burying you alive in graves
No literate man now remains
What do you wait for? Emigrate![45]

Frankini thought that the government had to take a neutral stance toward emigration to avoid undue suspicions. He reported that working to facilitate emigration would be morally improper, particularly given the "inevitable misery that migration to a country like Turkey would bring." On the other hand, trying to prevent emigration even through indirect means would also violate the treaty and the desires of the people. Therefore, he concluded that his government "fully acted in accordance with people's petitions and the terms of the treaty." However, we must not forget that despite Frankini's words, much depended on the local officials' attitudes.

The Question of Military Conscription

The question of military service in the tsarist army was an important factor in the Muslim emigrants' decision to relocate. In his annual report for 1879, General Frankini wrote that Muslim "agitators" going from village to village told the people, "Russians seek to recruit us as soldiers and force us to fight against our Muslim brothers. Then, they will ask our women to dress immodestly just like Russian women," an argument that was used in the Batum oblast as well and which probably many people believed.

As Russian officials discussed whether to encourage Muslims to migrate and made plans to purchase their lands, they also debated involving the Muslim population in the two oblasts in military service. In the Ottoman Empire, military recruitment of non-Muslims had been considered after the Crimean War, but somehow the idea was never put into practice. Now Russia was faced with a similar question: would it recruit the non-Christian population into its army? The tsarist government started working on introducing general military obligation in the Caucasus prior to the 1877–78 war, after which it began to recruit Christian men at the age of twenty in various regions in the Caucasus. The Caucasus administration also tried recruiting the Muslim population, but finally it gave up on the idea and levied taxes instead.

General Frankini submitted a report dated February 1879 to General Komarov, acting commander of the Army of the Caucasus. According to the report, Mikhail Nikolaevich had verbally informed General Frankini that recruitment of gendarmes (*militsiia*) should be considered a preliminary step to military recruitment soon to be implemented as a means to test the temper of the Muslim population. Thus, the governor ordered village communities to give one mounted gendarme for every ten households. Although the cavalrymen were called gendarme officers, their recruitment was opposed everywhere. Everywhere *militsiia* recruitment was regarded as drafting (*rekrutchina*); Muslims compared *militsiia* to Cossacks and Russian troops (*soldats*). Village communities and district governors petitioned the governor to cancel the obligation to provide mounted men. In response, the governor tried to convince the people that the mounted men to be recruited would serve as a gendarmerie, not as Cossacks. He argued that recruitment of mounted men was aimed at saving the people from the abuse of untrustworthy volunteers, and if the village communities rejected it, he would have to form the *militsia* from voluntary mercenaries, which would be inconvenient for both the government and the people. Such arguments proved persuasive, and Frankini successfully recruited *militsiia* men in many places.[46]

Still, the governor observed restlessness among the people against *militsiia* recruitment and the establishment of new courts. Locals met in mosques to discuss the policies of the Russian government, and Frankini noted that there was now a greater demand for temporary passes for travel to Erzurum for people interested in consulting the Turkish authorities there. Finally, he wrote that numerous delegations requested the cancellation of recruitment. They objected to the procedure of supplying men for cavalry, for they had been granted a term of three years by the treaty to decide on subjecthood; argued that central villages did not exist under Turkish rule; and stated that they had been pleased with the old courts. These delegations stated that they were ready to fulfill each and every obligation (carts, road building, tithes, etc.), but asked for exemption from providing gendarmes. The governor responded that he acknowledged the right granted to them by the treaty, but he himself never prevented anybody from migrating to Turkey, and they were supposed to act along with the government's instructions for their own benefit during their stay in the province, even if for a short term. Subsequently, delegations of Turks, Turkmens, and Kurds from the Takht district finally declared in an open manner that they were ready for immediate emigration under those circumstances. Takht was followed by Oltu district.

Thereupon, as the governor clarified in his report, he understood that explanations and meetings would get nowhere, and "repressive" measures had to be taken, such as sending the leaders of the agitation to exile. To do so, he first summoned identified agitators to Kars. He detained and threatened them for a few days and then released them after they promised that they would not confuse people anymore. Yet, he says, "I concluded that it would not be wise to impose coercive measures on a population that was ready to leave, and then the government's duty should be to thwart all hopes of the people for staying here without obeying our order."[47]

The governor reported that the agitation had started only a few months earlier when the surrender of Batum broke all the hopes of people for the final return of the Kars province to "Turkey." The turmoil was caused by the Muslims' common reluctance to live among Christians and under a Christian government; however, their reluctance was not sharpened after they learned about the government's new demands. Primary centers of the movement were Kağızman and Oltu. Concerned about what was going to become of their farms and seeing no remedy but the Turkish government's support supposedly based on certain privileges granted by intervening European states in Berlin, powerful landowners in these two areas went to visit Ismail Pasha in Erzurum, whose response to their demands was soon known all around the province.

According to Frankini, Ismail Pasha promised Muslim visitors from Kars that he would protest against the practice of recruiting gendarmes and other undertakings by the Russian government, a promise that he kept. Ismail Pasha also announced that Muslim residents of the Kars province would be provided with lands, animals, buildings, and other goods if they wished to migrate to Turkey. In fact, some lands in Erzurum, Erzincan, Bayburt, and along the Black Sea coast had already been reserved for immigrants for this purpose. The governor of Kars wrote:

> I suppose we should be happy about the Muslims' decision to emigrate in a state of panic caused by their concerns for an uncertain future and as they and Ismail Pasha acted in such an impulsive manner, for we would fall into a predicament if they had gone on rejecting our reforms and at the same time had not emigrated on the basis of the three-year term they have been granted. We would be at a loss, not knowing what to do with a mass of people who simply resist our rules with the power of inaction and inertia, finally having to force them to emigrate. Therefore, it is my belief that after the categorical declarations about an immediate emigration submitted to myself and the district governors, the government's duty is to support the people's inclinations and to wait until the spring, as it would be inappropriate to ask them to set off in winter, and in the meantime to deal with necessary formalities to secure an orderly migration process.[48]

As we learn from the governor's report, the reforms did not meet any resistance in the Shuragel district due to the composition of the population. In the Kağızman district, the *militsia* and the courts were established with some minor restrictions; however, petitions were submitted asking for emigration from certain Kurdish winter shelters (*kışlaks*) with some degree of pressure from the government. In Zarushad, council members were appointed by an order as the people refused to elect them. Not all central villages prepared the lists of the mounted militia. Everything was fine in the subdistricts of Çıldır and Horasan. The instructions were also implemented through meetings and explanations in the Ardahan district and Poskhov subdistrict. Yet part of the population in the Göle subdistrict submitted petitions for migration. Militiamen were selected from a smaller crop of volunteers where central villages refused to give any men for the mounted militia. In the Takht district, only Circassians (Kabardins, Ossetians, and Chechens) were convinced of the necessity to obey government instructions because apparently they wished to stay in the oblast. Local Turkmens were divided into two groups: one willing to stay, the other ready to leave immediately along with Turks and Kurds. Under these circumstances, the governor asked for a list of the families who wished to leave to verify that every family had decided for itself.

The census taken in 1886 to identify those to do military service once more caused some unrest within the Muslim population. Some Muslims who did not want to enter the military demanded permission to migrate to or take refuge in the Ottoman Empire. Hearing the news, the Ottoman government gave instructions to the Foreign Ministry to urge Russia to allow those seeking to emigrate from the Russian lands, even though the three-year term granted by the Treaty of Constantinople in February 1879 had expired.[49]

Finally, the Russian government abandoned the idea of recruiting Muslims as soldiers and gendarme officers at least for a while.[50] In 1889, the Russian administration levied a military tax on Muslim, Jewish, and Yezidi populations such as the one paid by non-Muslims in the Ottoman Empire for exemption from military service. The military tax for the entire Kars oblast was preset at 10,300 rubles, an amount shared among the non-Christian males in the cities and villages in proportion to the land taxes.[51] The Christian population was obliged to serve in the army, yet like Muslims albeit perhaps for different reasons, Dukhobors and many Molokans refused to enter military service. In 1891–92, only 59 men were recruited into the military from the Christian male population, of whom 32 were Armenians, 18 were Greeks, 8 were Russians, and 1 was an Estonian.[52] In 1901, of 314 young draftees, 177 were Armenians, 92 were Greeks, 43 were Orthodox Russians, and 2 were Estonians.[53] In other words, the efforts of the Russian military to recruit from the non-Orthodox population were less than auspicious.

After a period of Georgian and Armenian nationalist rule and the short-lived Turkish "Republic of South-West Caucasus" in 1919, Bolshevik and Kemalist forces eventually determined the Turkish-Soviet border in 1921, leaving Batum in Soviet Georgia and the rest of the two oblasts, as well as the Iğdır (Surmalu) district (*uezd*) of the Erivan *guberniia* in Turkey. Thus today's Turkish provinces of Artvin (southern part of the former Batum oblast), Ardahan, Kars, and Iğdır constitute the only territory gained by the Ottoman Empire at the end of the First World War, while it lost territory everywhere else. These provinces are also unique in the sense that their local Armenian populations did not experience the deportations and massacres of 1915 but later (at the end of the war in 1918) were involved in the mutual massacres and the war between Turkish forces and Dashnak Armenia. During the whole period of Russian rule, Kars occupied a special place in the Armenian nationalist movement as a training center for revolutionaries.[54]

The long history of Russian-Ottoman wars, combined with the Cold War polarity between the USSR and Turkey (as a member of NATO), served to unite traditional anti-Russian ideology with anti-Communism in Turkey. Soviet Georgian and Armenian claims to Kars and Ardahan in 1945, although abandoned shortly after being made, nevertheless further strengthened the anti-Russian and anti-Communist climate in Turkey. This led to a certain bias in Turkish historiography concerning Russian-Turkish relations, and many historians have viewed the history of Kars and Ardahan under Russian rule from this perspective. They characterized the forty-year period of Russian rule (1878–1918) through a negative light only, referring to it as the "forty years of black days," not unlike the characterization of Ottoman rule in the Balkans. During the Cold War years, Turkish historians had little contact with Russian sources, and even learning Russian was a suspicious activity from the Turkish state's point of view. Now the situation is changing. Many Turkish historians are learning Russian and are more likely to look at the Russian-Turkish relations in a more objectively detached way. Now we can try to evaluate the successes and failures of the Russian administration in Kars, Ardahan, and Batum.

First, it should be noted that not all tsarist ministers were enthusiastic about annexing the three *sanjaks*, except for the port of Batum. During the preparations for the Congress of Berlin in 1878, some prominent members of the Russian government, including the minister of war, Dmitrii A. Miliutin, suggested to Tsar Alexander II that Russia be satisfied with having the port of Batum only. They argued the advantages of leaving Kars and Ardahan to the Ottoman Empire, because the local people there were "at a very low level of culture," making them difficult to rule, and the territory was too mountainous. Because the region lacked roads and easily obtainable resources, tsarist officials considered it not worth maintaining at all. Miliutin and several other statesmen, such as the ambassador Nikolai Ignat'ev in İstanbul, also feared European accusations of Russian expansionism. Thus Miliutin believed that the area would be only a "burden" to Russia.[55] Indeed his words proved to be prophetic.

Nationalistic (pro-Turkish, pro-Armenian, etc.) and simplistic approaches portray Russian policies as uniform, coherent, relatively constant over time, and governed by a single dynamic, whereas they were in reality ambivalent, contradictory, changing over time, and dependent on many factors.⁵⁶ Also, an important factor was the bureaucracy. Whatever policy the Russian government pursued, it had to be implemented in part by local low-level government officials, who were in many cases either insignificant in numbers, or inefficient, corrupt, or politically unreliable from the official Russian perspective. Thus any policy, good or bad for Muslims or for non-Muslims, could be thwarted by these qualities of the local bureaucracy or by the lack of any properly functioning bureaucracy. A lack of qualified personnel with knowledge of the local languages constantly hampered the Russian administration in the Caucasus.⁵⁷

This was more acutely felt in Transcaucasia and even more so in the three *sanjaks* discussed here. For example, General Frankini, as the military governor of Kars, had many opportunities to confront problems associated with the lack of well-trained personnel. Touching on the problem of local staff in his annual report for 1879, he complained that Russia, a country with vast territories in Asia, lacked adequate staff to govern "Asian peoples." He also noted that whether they occupied civil or military posts, public officials of Russian origin did not know the history, geography, religion, customs, and language of the local people. In particular, he complained about the qualitative and quantitative insufficiency of low-level officials, whom he compared to capillary vessels in relation to the government's relations with the people. Therefore, he said, "most of the officials are locals and act on either what their tribe thinks or what they themselves think, paralyzing the government's influence."⁵⁸ In fact, General Frankini was perhaps the only qualified military governor in the oblasts of Batum and Kars for the entire forty-year period of Russian rule. On the other hand, Russian officials had reason to consider appointment to the two oblasts as a kind of punishment or exile due to the hardships of everyday life. As late as January 1913, an official wrote in the official newspaper of the Kars oblast that even an *uezd* center in inner Russia provided more facilities and a more comfortable life than in Kars.⁵⁹ Significant shortages included the perennial problem of housing. Low-level government officials had difficulty finding proper homes suited to the severe winter climate in the area. To make the situation worse, fuel prices were also very high.

The Russian administration was without doubt more modern and more efficient in comparison to the Ottoman administration. It built more roads and railways. It also opened more schools, although these schools did not attract Muslims. Moreover, the Russian government spent more than the revenues from the war indemnity and local taxes.

Here as in the Caucasus in general, the Russian government tried to integrate local elites into the Russian aristocracy. The Russian administration was more or less successful in integrating Muslim notables, although some of them went to the Ottoman side during the First World War.

It is remarkable that even Turkish nationalist politicians who lived in the region during Russian rule and who were afterward active in the Turkish republic wrote in their memoirs that the Russian government collected fewer taxes from the population, respected their religion and customs, and did other things to make its rule acceptable. However, these politicians also wrote in their memoirs that this was just a "policy of narcotization" (*uyuşturucu siyaset*) intended to blunt the Turks' national consciousness.[60] They also criticized the Russian government for not taking Muslims into the military, as this allegedly left them without military knowledge. What they did not want to remember is that the Muslims themselves did not want to enter military service in the Russian army. Turkish nationalist historians have also argued that the Russian government supported the Armenians in the region as a counterweight against the Muslims. However, this was not the case at least until the outbreak of the Great War in 1914.

The Russian administration did not force Muslims to emigrate; neither did it try to prevent them from emigrating. During the three years from 1879 to 1882, more than 140,000 people (about four-fifths of Muslims) in the two oblasts immigrated to Turkey. However, about half of these people returned to their homeplaces due to hardships in Anatolia, because the Ottoman government, economically bankrupt, could not fulfill its promises to the immigrants. Thus in 1914, on the eve of the war, slightly more than half the population in the Kars oblast and almost 90 percent of the population in the Batum oblast was still Muslim.

Unlike in Crimea and the northern Caucasus, the Russian administration utterly failed in colonizing the two oblasts with Russian peasants. By 1914, only about 5 percent of the permanent population (excluding troops and government officials) in the Kars oblast and less than 1 percent in the Batum oblast consisted of ethnic Russians, mainly the "sectarians," that is, Molokans and Dukhobors. Most of the Dukhobors had left Kars at the end of the 1890s due to their unwillingness to do military service. While the proportion of the Armenian population rose to 30 percent in the Kars oblast, it resulted not from intentional Russian policy, but rather from circumstances. Many Russian administrators like Prince Sviatopolk-Mirskii saw the settlement of Armenians from the Ottoman Empire in 1829 as a mistake that should not be repeated.

The refugee Armenians who fled the Ottoman Empire and illegally crossed the Russian border into the Caucasus during the Armenian massacres of the 1890s caused another perennial problem for the Russian administration, especially in the two oblasts as well as in the *guberniia* of Yerevan. These Armenians (about thirty thousand people, more than half of whom lived in the Kars and Batum oblasts) had come without any means of subsistence and had fallen into misery. Some of them eventually supported the Armenian revolutionary movement, which smuggled arms into the Ottoman Empire for the Armenian bands. Despite the Russian government's numerous representations to the Sublime Porte, Sultan Abdülhamid adamantly refused to permit the Armenian refugees back into the Ottoman Empire. Thus the Russian government was obliged to offer those refugees Russian citizenship in 1902. While most of the Armenian refugees became Russian subjects, some of them did not, and some of them returned to Turkey after the 1908 constitutional revolution in Turkey. There were also Ottoman Kurdish bands violating the Russian border to pillage and plunder.

The outbreak of the First World War and the ensuing violence led to further deterioration of interethnic and interconfessional relations in the oblasts of Batum and Kars. The vacuum of power left after the dissolution of the Russian army in the wake of the Russian Revolutions of 1917 led to further massacres of both Muslims and non-Muslims in the two oblasts. By 1921, the two regions except for the city of Batum became the territory of the new Turkish republic. The dissolution of economic ties with the Caucasus and the rest of the Russian Empire led to seclusion and backwardness in this area. One of the most volatile sites for population movements in the history of the Eastern Question, the area became the periphery of the Turkish republic instead of the Russian Empire. The fact that the region was still in dispute between the USSR and Turkey in 1945 shows the long-lasting legacy of the violence and migrations associated with the Russian-Ottoman wars and the Eastern Question.

NOTES

Research for this study has been supported by Tunceli University under Project no. MFTUB011-02.

1. It is difficult to translate the Russian term *Voenno-narodnoe upravlenie* into English or any other language. Alternative translations are as follows: military-civil, military-communal, military-native, or military-popular administration. In this chapter all translations from Russian and Turkish sources are mine.

2. Soviet-Armenian historian Artashes M. Poghosian's *Karsskaia oblast' v sostave Rossii* (Yerevan: Hayastan, 1983) is the only monograph on the Kars oblast' in Russian. For a recent work from an Armenian perspective, see Richard G. Hovannisian, ed., *Armenian Kars and Ani* (Costa Mesa, CA: Mazda, 2011). In Armenian, see Ararat Hagopyan, *Karsi Marz 1878-1917* (Yerevan: Chartaraket, 2000). In Turkish, see my own *Çarlık Rusyası Yönetiminde Kars Vilayeti* (İstanbul: Birzamanlar, 2010). Aleksandr B. Shirokorad, *Uteriannye zemli rossii: Ot Petra I do grazhdanskoi voiny* (Moscow: Veche, 2006), includes a chapter on this region from a Russian nationalist perspective.

3. The historian Fahrettin Kırzıoğlu (1917-2005), a native of Kars, was the main protagonist of this approach. His books *Kars Tarihi* (İstanbul: Işıl Matbaası, 1953) and *Edebiyatımızda Kars* (İstanbul: Işıl Matbaası, 1958) as well as his numerous articles have been quoted by many other historians who have simply repeated his claims.

4. Semen Esadze, *Istoricheskaia zapiska ob upravlenii Kavkazom*, 2 vols. (Tbilisi: Guttenberg, 1907), 2:257-58. See also Timothy K. Blauvelt, "Military-Civil Administration and Islam in the North Caucasus, 1858-83," *Kritika: Explorations in Russian and Eurasian History* 11, no. 2 (Spring 2010): 221-55.

5. Esadze, *Istoricheskaia zapiska*, 1:165-98. See also Alla S. Kondrasheva, "Sistema voenno-narodnogo upravleniia kak forma politicheskogo kompromissa rossiiskoi administratsii i severo-kavkazskikh gortsev (2-ia polovina XIX veka)," *Vestnik SevKavGTU Seriia "Pravo"* 1, no. 6 (2004).

6. In the Ottoman Empire, this province, with its center in Diyarbekir, was officially called "Kurdistan" between 1847 and 1867. The Turkish words *bey* and *bek* have the same meaning; the former is the official version, and the latter is a local variant.

7. For a comparative study of Russia's "military-communal administration" in the northern Caucasus and the French system in Algeria in the nineteenth century, see Vladimir O. Bobrovnikov, "Voenno-narodnoe upravlenie na Severnom Kavkaze (Dagestan): Musulmanskaia periferiia v rossiiskom imperskom prostranstve, XIX-XX vv," in *Prostranstvo vlasti: Istoricheskii opyt Rossii i vyzovy sovremennosti*, ed. B. V. Ananich and S. I. Barzilov (Moscow: Moskovskii obschestvenny nauchny fond, 2001), 372-90; and idem, *Musulmane Severnogo Kavkaza: Obychai, pravo, nasilie* (Moscow: Vostochnaia Literatura, RAN, 2002), 171-75.

8. *Proekt vremennogo polozheniia ob upravlenii Karsski oblasti*, 27 September (9 October) 1878, HAA, f. 274, op. 1, d. 1.

9. Governor Frankini to the Viceroy of the Caucasus, 27 February 1879, HAA, f. 1262, op. 2, d. 1, ll. 9–11.

10. STsSA, f. 1087, op. 3, d. 215, l. 5.

11. The concept of *grazhdanstvennost*, popularized by the historian Karamzin and the poet Pushkin, denoted European culture and civilization. See Jörg Baberowski, "Tsivilizatorskaia missiia i natsionalizm v Zakavkaz'e: 1828–1914 gg.," in *Novaia imperskaia istoriia postsovetskogo prostranstva*, ed. I. Gerasimov (Kazan: Tsentr Issledovaniy Natsionalizma i Imperii, 2004), 314.

12. "Proekt instruktsii o pravakh i obiazannostiakh voennykh gubernatorov Karsskoi i Batumskoi oblastei po narodnomu upravleniiu, po gorodskoi chasti i po ustroistvu kraia," HAA, f. 274, op. 1, d. 3.

13. *Sâlname-i Vilâyet-i Erzurum sene 1293* (Erzurum: Erzurum Vilayet Matbaası, 1876–77), 144.

14. *Pamyatnaia knizhka i adres kalendar Karsskoi oblasti za 1904 god* (Kars: Oblastnaia tipografiia, 1904), opisatelny otdel, 4.

15. Poghosian, *Karsskaia oblast*, 71.

16. Ibid., 72.

17. Tatiana Fedorovna Aristova, *Material'naia kultura kurdov. XIX–pervoi poloviny XX v.* (Moscow: Nauka, 1990), 56.

18. Dmitrii Bakradze, "Pri zaniatii nami oblasti, iz vselentsev, v chislitel-nom otnoshenii, osobenno preobladali kurdy, zatem karapapakhi i, nakonets, turkmeny," and "Istorichesko-etnograficheskii ocherk Karsskoi oblasti," *Izvestiia Kavkazskago Otdela Imperatorskago Russkago Geograficheskago Obshchestva* 7 (Tbilisi, 1883): 6.

19. For the Ottoman-French texts of the Treaty of Constantinople, see BOA, İ. MMS. 60/2855-1. For the Russian text, see E. A. Adamov, ed., *Sbornik dogovorov Rossii s drugimi gosudarstvami 1856–1917 gg.* (Moscow: Politicheskaia Literatura, 1952), 159–75. James Meyer has inaccurately written that Article 7 of this treaty stipulated a span of "six months" for emigration. See Meyer, "Immigration, Return, and the Politics of Citizenship: Russian Muslims in the Ottoman Empire, 1860–1914," *International Journal of Middle East Studies* 39 (February 2007): 25.

20. Meyer, "Immigration, Return, and the Politics of Citizenship," 16.

21. "Hasb'el-kader Rusya tarafından vatan-ı mukaddeslerimizin istilasıyla beraber ... ," BOA, İ. DH. 834/67140 lef 1, quoted in Badem, *Çarlık Rusyası Yönetiminde Kars Vilayeti*, 112.

22. Shamshe V. Megrelidze, *Ajaris Tsarsulidan (Muhajiroba 1878–1882 tslebshi)* (Tbilisi: Metsniereba, 1964), 83–84. See also idem, *Zakavkaz'e v russko-turetskoi voine 1877–1878 gg.* (Tbilisi: Metsniereba, 1972), 260.

23. Prince Grigol D. Orbeliani to Adjutant General Prince Dmitrii I. Sviatopolk-Mirskii, 9 November 1879, quoted in Megrelidze, *Ajaris Tsarsulidan*, 79. The original letter is in Russian.

24. Ibid., 82.

25. *Godovoi otchet voennogo gubernatora Karsskoi oblasti o sostoianii vverennoi emu oblasti za 1879 god* (Kars: June 1880), 60. This source is subsequently cited as *Otchet 1879*.

26. General Frankini to district and police administrations of the Kars oblast, 25 September 1878, Kopiia s tsirkiularnago predpisaniia Voen. Gub. Karsskoi oblasti okruzhnym i politseiskim upravleniiam ot 13 sent. 1878 g. N. 5703, HAA, f. 1262, op. 1, d. 7(II), ll. 5-6.

27. Komissiia dlia okonchaniia soslovno-pozemelnago voprosa v chastiakh Kavkazskago kraia voenno-narodnago upravleniia 11 marta 1903 g. N. 807, v sovet Glavnonachalstvuiushchago grazhdanskoi chastiu na Kavkaze, 23 March 1903, STsSA, f. 231, op. 1, d. 309.

28. The name of this administration was changed to Caucasus Military-Customary Administration (Kavkazskoe voenno-narodnoe upravlenie) toward the end of 1879.

29. General Frankini to General Komarov, Zapiska o pereselenii musulmanskago naseleniia, 28 January 1879, N. 394, HAA, f. 1262, op. 1, d. 7(II), ll. 16-25.

30. Fahrettin Erdoğan, *Türk Ellerinde Hatıralarım* (İstanbul: Yeni Matbaa, 1954), 18.

31. General Frankini to General Komarov, Kars, 6 (18) February 1879, no. 1053, HAA, f. 1262, op. 1, d. 7(II), ll. 65-75.

32. Svetlana Lur'e, "Rossiiskaia i britanskaia imperii na srednem vostoke v XIX-Nachale XX veka: Ideologiia i praktika" (*kandidat* thesis in history, Moscow Institute of Oriental Studies of the Russian Academy of Sciences, 1996). Lur'e believes that a significant number of Armenians were settled in the Kars province, and Armenians assumed the function of colonization, but she has not provided any evidence to support her argument.

33. See, for example, B. S. Itenberg and V. A. Tvardovskaia, eds., *Graf M. T. Loris-Melikov i ego sovremenniki* (Moscow: Tsentrpoligraf, 2004).

34. "Doklad General Adyutanta Kn. Sviatopolk-Mirskago ot 4 fevralya 1879 g., no. 39," HAA, f. 1262, op. 1, d. 7(II), ll. 76-79. See also Bakradze's report, 5 March 1879, STsSA, f. 229, op. 1, d. 12, l. 14.

35. Nicholas Breyfogle, *Heretics and Colonizers* (Ithaca, NY: Cornell University Press, 2005), 140; and Megrelidze, *Zakavkaz'e v Russko-Turetskoi voine*, 101.

36. Poghosian, *Karsskaia oblast*, 124.

37. Bakradze's report, 5 March 1879, STsSA, f. 229, op. 1, d. 12, l. 14.

38. General Frankini to the Viceroy, 17 August 1879, HAA, f. 1262, op. 1, d. 7(II), l. 117.

39. General Frankini to the Viceroy, 23 June 1880, HAA, f. 1262, op. 1, d. 7, l. 27.

40. *Otchet 1879*, Prilozhenie N. 15: 176-77. The report was signed on 27 June 1880.

41. Bakradze, Report of the Land Commission of Kars, 17 March 1882, STsSA, f. 229, op. 1, d. 12, l. 16, also see f. 545, op. 1, d. 3008, ll. 16-43.

42. Oktay Özel, "Migration and Power Politics: The Settlement of Georgian Immigrants in Turkey (1878-1908)," *Middle Eastern Studies* 4 (July 2010): 478.

43. *Otchet 1879*, 50.

44. Ibid., 51.

45. For the full original text of the epic in Turkish, see Kırzıoğlu, *Edebiyatımızda Kars* (İstanbul: Işıl Matbaası, 1958), 53-54.

46. The Governor of Kars to the Commander of the Caucasian Army, Kars, 28 January (9 February) 1879, no. 388, HAA, f. 1262, op. 1, d. 7(II), ll. 29-40.

47. Ibid.

48. Ibid.

49. The Grand Vizier to the Foreign Minister, 28 Temmuz 1302 [9 August 1886], BOA, A. MKT. MHM. 491/23 lef 4.

50. Having visited Kars in 1893, H. F. B. Lynch wrote that he had heard from the local Muslim population that military service would be made compulsory in ten years by a decree issued in 1890, but he had not investigated the validity of the news. Lynch also noted that Muslim people wished to emigrate due to the decree. See Lynch, *Armenia. Travels and Studies*, 2 vols. (London: Longmans, Green, 1901), 1:75.

51. *Kavkazskii Kalendar na 1894 god* (Tbilisi: Tipografii Gruzinsk. Izdatelsk. Tovarıshchestva i M. Martirosiantsa, 1893), V otdel, 139.

52. Ibid., 140.

53. *Obzor Karsskoi oblasti za 1901 god* (Kars: Tipografiia Kantselyarii Voennago Gubernatora Karsskoi Oblasti, 1901), 20.

54. See Rubina Peroomian, "Kars in the Armenian Liberation Movement," in Hovannisian, *Armenian Kars and Ani*, 245-69.

55. Shamshe V. Megrelidze, *Voprosy Zakavkazya v istorii russko-turetskoi voiny 1877-1878 gg*. (Tbilisi: Metsniereba, 1969), 87.

56. Peter Holquist, "The Politics and Practice of the Russian Occupation of Armenia, 1915-February 1917," in *A Question of Genocide: Armenians and Turks at the End of the Ottoman Empire*, ed. R. G. Suny, F. M. Goçek, and N. M. Naimark (New York: Oxford University Press, 2011), 151-52.

57. Blauvelt, "Military-Civil Administration and Islam," 228.

58. *Otchet 1879*, 104.

59. A. Bezrukov, "Kvartirny vopros v Karse," *Kars* 2, no. 8 (20 January 1913): 3, quoted in Badem, *Çarlık Rusyası Yönetiminde Kars Vilayeti*, 241-42.

60. Yasin Haşimoğlu, *Oltu Şura Hükümeti'nin Ermeni Mücadelesi* (Erzurum: Salkımsöğüt Yayınları, 2005), 39; and Erdoğan, *Türk Ellerinde Hatıralarım*, 27-29.

The Idea of an Eastern Federation
An Alternative to the Destruction of the Ottoman Empire

JOHN A. MAZIS

It is clear today, with the benefit of hindsight, that the idea of an Eastern federation, the volunteer union based on equality of the various peoples of the Balkans and Anatolia, was doomed from the start. The late nineteenth and early twentieth centuries, when this idea emerged, were characterized by rising nationalism and attempts, or rather hopes, of breaking down great empires and creating nation states. While this sentiment was widespread in central and Eastern Europe, it was more pronounced in the Balkans, where wars (Greek-Turkish in 1897 and the two Balkan Wars in 1912-13), uprisings (the Ilinden revolt), and guerrilla warfare (Macedonia, 1903-8) kept the peninsula in a constant state of war.[1] If the idea of cooperation among the peoples of the Balkans in general sounds impossible, the peaceful coexistence as equal partners of Turks and Greeks under the same polity sounds even more far-fetched. The two peoples found themselves in the occupier/subject role for over four centuries, and since the successful Greek revolt and the

Ion Dragoumis, circa 1914. (from the personal collection of John Mazis)

creation of the modern Greek state their relations have been antagonistic at best, hostile at worst, but seldom, if ever, "normal." That sentiment was particularly present among the Greeks, who, after all, had been the (mostly) unwilling subjects of the Ottoman Empire and the ones who found themselves after their independence living in a small and vulnerable state, wanting to expand at the expense of the Ottoman Empire but at the same time feeling threatened by it.[2]

The fact that the people of the Balkans and the Turks seldom agreed on anything should not be viewed as an insurmountable obstacle to their cooperation. Such cooperation did occur from time to time due to outside pressures or threats.[3] Nothing illustrates better the need for regional cooperation, but also the depth of enmity among those involved, than the way the various states treated each other's people in times of war or how they treated each other using war as an excuse.[4] The genocides at the hands of the Ottoman state and those of the early Republic of Turkey, of Armenians, Greeks, and Assyrians highlight both the need for a multiethnic Eastern federation based on equality of its members, but also one of the main reasons that the Eastern Idea remained just an idea and never came to fruition.[5]

The imperfect treaties that brought the First World War to its close had as their result, among many others, the redrawing of the maps of Europe and the Middle East as well as the destruction of the German, Austrian-Hungarian, Russian, and Ottoman Empires.[6] While ending four empires created many hardships and future problems for the people involved, arguably the disappearance of the Ottoman Empire left a more lasting legacy. With the collapse of Ottoman rule, the political makeup of the Middle East and the eastern Mediterranean basin changed forever, and the diplomatic implications from that change are evident to this day. To be sure, the destruction of the Ottoman Empire was considered long overdue; the so-called Eastern Question was formulated as early as 1844, if not before, when the Russian tsar Nicholas I labeled the Ottoman Empire "the sick man of Europe."[7] By the turn of the twentieth century, the most pressing concerns were not if but rather when the empire would dissolve, and which country would benefit the most from that demise. The various European powers, which foresaw if not actively sought the dissolution of the Ottoman Empire, attempted to answer the Eastern Question to their advantage. Various non-Muslim (former) subjects of the sultan, now citizens of small Balkan states, were also looking forward to the end of the Ottoman state; some were even working to hasten the end of the empire. The Greek irredentist ideology of the Μεγάλη Ιδέα (Megali Idea, Great Idea) represents just one example, albeit the best known, of the aspirations of the Balkan peoples at the expense of the Ottoman State.[8]

As one would expect, Ottoman statesmen and intellectuals sought ways to avoid the destruction of their empire. Starting with the changes of Sultan Mahmud II (1808–39), continuing with the so-called Tanzimat (Reform) era of the mid- to late nineteenth century, and culminating with the Young Turk revolt of 1908, a number of Ottoman statesmen attempted (with uneven results) to modernize the government.[9] Many Young Turks sought even to institute a democratic, multiethnic state. As a result, the Eastern Question has been presented as a dilemma whose solution was in the hands of either the Ottoman Turkish elite or the European powers that could preserve or destroy the Ottoman Empire at will.[10] As Christine M. Philliou has noted: "The framework of the Eastern Question . . . does not allow for complexity and implications of changes within Ottoman politics, but tends instead to reinforce a polar opposition between reform and conservatism within Ottoman politics and to place most of the dynamism and potential to enact change in the hands of the great powers."[11] Philliou points to the traditional way of approaching the Eastern Question. According to that model, the only active players, and thus the only sources of a possible solution, were either the Turkish elite or the European powers. Under that rubric, the Ottoman subjects who were not part of the ruling elite (both Muslims and Christians) as well as the people of the newly independent Balkan states were passive observers of actions and policies that were to determine their fate. As this discussion will show, the traditional view needs reassessing.[12] A number of individuals who were part of neither the Ottoman governing elite nor the Western political and diplomatic establishments were seeking an alternative which would potentially result in benefits to the people of the area. Thus, while reforming the empire was the solution embraced by the Muslim Ottoman elite and European interests, some of the Sultan's Christian subjects championed other alternatives that could have helped modernize and strengthen the country. This third way has been forgotten in the traditional binary-centered presentation of the Eastern Question. While this third alternative failed to materialize, it should nevertheless be studied as part of examining the subaltern reaction to great-power policies.

Among those who advocated a radical, and rather imaginative, reform of the Ottoman Empire, Ion Dragoumis is the most unexpected.

Dragoumis (1878–1920) is a major figure in the intellectual, cultural, and political history of modern Greece. As a diplomat, politician, political theorist, and writer, he had a sixteen-year meteoric career in the Greek Foreign Service culminating with his appointment as Greek ambassador to Russia.[13] Elected to Parliament in 1915, Dragoumis became a foe of Greek prime minister Eleftherios Venizelos and his pro-Entente policies.[14] A founding member of the "Council of the Sixteen Members of the United Opposition," Dragoumis and his party were preparing to challenge Venizelos in the November 1920 elections. However, a few months before the elections, on 13 August 1920, an attempt on Venizelos's life set in motion a series of countermeasures (arrest of opposition leaders, attacks on individuals and offices) by his followers culminating in the assassination of Dragoumis by Venizelist paramilitary troops.[15]

During the late nineteenth and early twentieth century, a number of Ottoman subjects (many but not all of them Greeks) expressed interest in the idea of transforming the state. During the Congress of Berlin (1878) the Ottoman representative, Karatheodori Pasha, and the sultan's private banker, George Zarifis (both ethnic Greeks) were working on a project aimed at the creation of a Greek-Turkish state.[16] The timing and the identity of the people involved are crucial in understanding the impetus behind alternative plans of reforming the empire. Beginning in the 1870s, Greek irredentist aspirations were on a collision course with similar movements among other Balkan nationalists, particularly the Bulgarians. Both the Greeks and the Bulgarians viewed the Ottoman province of Macedonia as an area populated by a large number of their co-nationals and thus ripe for annexation at a future date. Since there were competing claims about the ethnic composition of the province, nationalists from both countries wanted to make sure that their co-nationals would be the dominant element in Macedonia by the time the Ottoman Empire dissolved. To achieve their competing ends, Greeks and Bulgarians organized educational and religious institutions in Macedonia, but they also came to rely on armed bands to protect their interests and harm those of their antagonist.

During this time of attempts to fend off both the Ottoman Empire and competing Balkan claims by Bulgaria, some Greek patriots reached the conclusion that the outright realization of the Megali Idea was impossible and an alternative might be in order. Both Karatheodori and Zarifis were accustomed to working in the Ottoman state as high-level bureaucrats and financiers. Despite their Greek heritage, both men enjoyed great influence and preferential treatment. To privileged Greeks such as these men, a Greek-Turkish state was an attractive proposition; as ethnic Greeks they wanted to achieve some of Greece's irredentist goals, while as privileged members of the Ottoman elite they did not want the demise of the Ottoman Empire. Their intentions notwithstanding, Karatheodori and Zarifis did not attempt to present concrete plans for the success of their ideas.

Another idea for a "Near Eastern Federation" came from the Greek socialist P. Argyriades, a member of the International League for Peace and Liberty and president of its subgroup League for Balkan Confederation. Speaking in Paris in 1894, Argyriades proposed a federation consisting of the following Balkan countries and territories: Greece with the island of Crete, Bulgaria, Romania, Serbia, Bosnia-Herzegovina (at the time administered by Austria-Hungary), Montenegro, and the Ottoman provinces of Macedonia, Albania, and Thrace. Argyriades wanted to add to the new state some of the non-European parts of the Ottoman Empire such as the Asia Minor littoral, Armenia, and Constantinople as a free city and the confederation's capital.[17]

According to this plan, the constituent states would have internal autonomy but coordinate matters of mutual interest, defense, and foreign policy. While the earlier plan proposed by Karatheodori and Zarifis was advocated by members of the Ottoman establishment, Argyriades, a socialist working outside mainstream politics, was inspired not so much by considerations of nationalism and self-preservation as by dreams of brotherhood among peoples and restructuring of the economy and society.

Somewhere between these two vague ideas stood the Federative Union of the Peoples of the East, a supranational organization created in 1909 and headed by an ethnic Greek Ottoman citizen and doctor, Constantine Roccas. The Federative Union of the Peoples of the East was supported by the influential nationalist Greek newspaper of Constantinople Λαός (The People). Part of its program (similar to the Karatheodori-Zarifis proposal) advocated "the division of Turkey into independent federal states . . . an alliance of the federal citizens . . . in order to defend the Empire from the frequent foreign attacks and to prevent it from partition."[18] Roccas's program also envisioned that the new state, whose official language would be French, would be comprised of the following peoples: Albanians, Armenians, Bulgarians, Greeks, Jews, Kurds, Kutsowallachs, Lebanese, Montenegrins, Serbs, Syrians, Turks, and Wallachs. Also, the Kingdoms of Greece, Serbia, Bulgaria,

Romania, Montenegro, and Hungary were invited to join the federation, which was to be based on "justice, equality, and history."[19] At the same time, the program of the Federative Union supported some of Argyriades's socialist ideas, for it also renounced despotism and class divisions.

While the Greeks took a leading role in devising possible alternatives to the Ottoman state, they were not the only ethnic group thinking along these lines. Roccas's organization was not exclusively Greek in composition and included members from a variety of Balkan nationalities. In October 1912, days before the Balkan Wars started, the International Socialist Bureau published the *Manifesto of the Socialists of Turkey and the Balkans, 1912*. This document condemned the coming war as a capitalist tool seeking to destroy the Ottoman Empire for the benefit of the great powers and not the Ottoman people, nor the people of the Balkans in general. The *Manifesto* called for the people of the Balkans and the Near East to unite "in the most democratic form of government, without racial or religious discrimination." The authors proclaimed that only radical reform would revive and safeguard the Ottoman state and "render possible the democratic federation of the Balkans."[20]

The people involved in formulating these ideas and plans had clearly identifiable motives for wanting the creation of a Greek-Turkish state. Greeks living in the Ottoman Empire, especially those with privileges, would benefit from a Greek-Turkish state in which they would be on equal footing with their Turkish neighbors. Socialists, like Argyriades, with their tradition of downplaying nationalism, were also willing to champion a Balkan/Anatolian federated state. The possibility, however, of a Greek living in the Greek Kingdom and steeped in the Megali Idea wanting the same sounds improbable. Yet Ion Dragoumis, a nationalist icon in Greece to this day, championed a Greek-Turkish federation. Dragoumis will be forever remembered, above everything else, as a patriot who became the soul and the brain of the successful Greek attempt to counter Bulgarian influence in Ottoman Macedonia. His three years (1902–5) as secretary to the Monastir (Macedonia) consulate represent his most dynamic work on behalf of Hellenism and the fulfillment of the Megali Idea.[21]

Dragoumis arrived in Monastir at a time when Bulgarian irredentist actions in Ottoman Macedonia seemed to be bearing fruit. Several Bulgarian educational and religious institutions were thriving, and Bulgarian armed bands were acting with impunity. At the same time, a cautious

Greek state was directing its consular officers in the area to refrain from openly promoting Greek nationalist goals. Whatever instructions Dragoumis was given by his superiors became, in his view, secondary to the real work that needed to be done. He used the freedom of movement and the prestige of his diplomatic position to create a Greek nationalist network in the middle of Ottoman Macedonia. In a letter to his father, dated 18 December 1903, Dragoumis articulated his master plan for action in Macedonia.[22] He wanted to create a network of Greek patriots who, in coordination with and financed by the Greek government, would provide the Macedonian countryside with Greek teachers and priests. He also wanted to encourage rich Greeks to buy land from Bulgarians and to invest in commercial and industrial enterprises with an eye to making the Greek element in the area stable and attractive to those who might be wavering in their allegiance.

During the three years that Dragoumis spent in Macedonia, he devoted all his energies to achieving these goals. In general, the scope of Dragoumis's work in Macedonia has not been properly understood. Most often, if not exclusively, his role is described as being that of a logistical organizer for the guerrilla bands, a coordinator of action with local notables, a purveyor of nationalist propaganda, and a conduit by which the Greek government could pass money and supplies to various places in Macedonia. These functions were indeed a major part of Dragoumis's work, and the dedication and energy he brought to these tasks cannot be overestimated. But there was another element of his work largely absent from most accounts. In the last days of 1902, Dragoumis and some local Greeks of Monastir created an organization called Macedonian Defense (Μακεδονική). This was a conspiratorial organization (indeed, one would call it a terrorist organization today) dedicated to creating a close-knit network of Greeks who would be willing to defend Greek interests in their area. Such defense was often in the form of propaganda and education but intimidation and murder of those who supported the Bulgarian cause were also common.[23]

Dragoumis's role in awakening the local Greeks was so central that he was nicknamed "the alarm clock."[24] As a result of his well-known activities in Ottoman Macedonia, Dragoumis's patriotism, irredentist credentials, and his adherence to the Megali Idea were beyond reproach. Nevertheless, it was Dragoumis who looked at the political and diplomatic landscape of his time, changed course, and became the champion of what came to be known as the Ανατολική Ιδέα or Ανατολική Ομοσπονδία (Eastern Idea or Eastern Federation).[25]

The Eastern Idea was an attempt to strengthen the Ottoman state by changing its nature from that of an empire with a particular ethnic/religious group as the dominant one (Turks/Muslims) to a federation in which a number of ethnic/religious groups (Greeks, Turks, and Armenians, Christians and Muslims) would coexist on an equal basis. Thus, while part of the elite in the Greek context, Dragoumis clearly belongs to the greater subaltern of the Balkan/Ottoman world whose ideas about the fate of their countries and future has been neglected in favor of the more traditional approach to solutions to the Eastern Question.

Dragoumis articulated his ideas about the Eastern Federation in books, newspaper and journal articles, letters, and in his private journals from 1908 until 1920. Although he was never particularly precise about the details of the proposed state, he left enough material for us to recreate a fairly clear image. Dragoumis's substitution of the Megali Idea with the Eastern Idea was a process fueled by political conditions of the Balkans and the Near East, the diplomatic landscape of Europe, and the author's personal beliefs about such concepts as state, nation, and culture. Ironically, Dragoumis's greatest contribution to the Megali Idea, his service in Ottoman Macedonia, might have convinced him to seek an alternative way to achieve his ends. The Ottoman province of Macedonia, which is divided today between Bulgaria, Greece, and the Former Yugoslav Republic of Macedonia, was populated by a mix of people including, among others, Turks, Greeks, Bulgarians, Serbs, Albanians, Jews, Vlachs, and Pomaks, with none of these peoples constituting a clear majority in the province as a whole.[26] Claiming territory according to a clearly defined ethnic majority population was an issue of the utmost contention, as each side developed cartographic arguments to best support its claims. The possibility then of absorbing into a Greater Greece only the areas easily identified as populated by a clear Greek majority was rather remote. The alternative, to incorporate these areas into Greece proper without the consent of their non-Greek inhabitants, was clearly a recipe for creating a new set of problems. Additionally, while the collapse of the Ottoman state was in theory good for Greek national aspirations, the reality was rather different.

Dragoumis had no confidence in the Greek state and its ability to gain from the decaying Ottomans. One major problem was Bulgaria, whose vibrant nationalism represented a real threat to the future of Hellenism. As Greece and Bulgaria fought for supremacy in Macedonia, it became clear that they were involved in a zero-sum game.[27] Since both sides claimed the same territory and people as their own, any gain by one was a net loss for the other. Bulgarian successes were celebrated as major nationalist accomplishments in Sofia and as catastrophic events in Athens (and vice versa). If the threat posed to Hellenism by Bulgaria was not enough, the dissolution of the Ottoman Empire would also attract the attention of the great powers, which could not miss an opportunity to augment their empires at the expense of the fledgling Balkan states. Adding to Dragoumis's anxiety, Bulgaria's patron, imperial Russia, had its own long-standing claims on the Ottoman Empire.[28] These claims (notably Constantinople) included areas that Dragoumis considered indispensable parts of the Hellenic world.[29]

Comparing the danger posed to Greece's irredentist aspirations by Bulgaria and the great powers, Dragoumis believed that the differences between Greece and the Ottoman Empire, however serious, could be bridged. Since the Greek state was clearly not in a position to impose its views on others, an alternative approach was needed. Dragoumis reached the conclusion that the interests of Hellenism were best served not by the destruction of the Ottoman Empire but rather by its survival. In short, Dragoumis went against the ideology that dominated modern Greece almost from the moment of its inception and proposed cooperation and coexistence of the Greeks with the Turks in a federated Greek-Ottoman state. Given the fact that Bulgarian nationalism and great-power politics posed equal threats to Hellenism and the Ottoman Empire, Dragoumis could foresee a situation in which an exhausted Turkey might be easy to manipulate and even eager to accommodate Greek nationalist demands. Thus, Dragoumis proposed cooperation, not confrontation, with the Ottoman Empire.[30]

While Dragoumis's Eastern Idea was in great part based on pragmatic considerations, such as the diplomatic dynamics of the time, he was also motivated by his beliefs about the role of Greece vis-à-vis both East and West. His thoughts on the subject are an integral part of his Eastern Idea and shed light on his way of thinking about the subject.[31] Greece, like Russia and the German Empire, noted Dragoumis, is located somewhere on the border between East and West. On the one hand, the West had been beneficial to Greece inasmuch as it helped the Greeks to better understand themselves and their ancient past. On the other, the West viewed modern Greek culture as inferior, or at best a bad copy, of its modern Western counterpart.[32] While Greece was in a position of weakness vis-à-vis the West, Dragoumis believed that Greek culture could deal with the East from a position of strength. The reason that the Greeks could prevail in the East, according to Dragoumis, was to be found in the social development of the people living in the Ottoman Empire.³³ In an interesting twist, Dragoumis applied the same negative views that the West had about Greece to the people and cultures located to the east of Greece. In an attitude that would be labeled today as Orientalist, Dragoumis viewed the Muslim people of the Ottoman Empire as culturally inferior to the West (in that scheme Greece is located closer to the West both geographically and culturally). According to Dragoumis, most, if not all, of the subject people of the empire, such as the Arabs and the Albanians, had not yet developed a distinct national identity.³⁴ The Turkish element of the empire, which was politically dominant, could not impose its culture on its Christian minorities, which were culturally more advanced.³⁵

Dragoumis believed that the Greeks should concentrate their political, economic, and cultural activities in the East, culturally incorporate other ethnic groups, such as the Albanians, and strengthen the Greek element in the Turkish Empire.³⁶ In time a Greek-Turkish understanding would elevate the Greeks to the position of corulers.³⁷ At first glance, Dragoumis's notions of a multiethnic state do not appear new. Indeed, a closer look at the ideals of the early Greek revolutionary Rigas Velestinles as well as the leader of the 1821 revolution, Alexandros Ypsilantis, reveal that both had in mind the creation of a multiethnic state.³⁸ By the early twentieth century, many Greeks perceived fulfillment of the Megali Idea as being the re-creation of either the Byzantine Empire or more outlandishly the empire of Alexander the Great. In opposition to these plans and the Megali Idea, some Greek politicians believed that the country should limit itself to the borders of the time. Dragoumis disagreed with both views; he believed that diplomatically and numerically the Greeks were too weak to create a new Greek empire. Since both Alexander's and the Byzantine empires were not purely Greek but rather multiethnic, re-creating them under a Greek polity would incite nationalist aspirations by the subject people and create many new problems, rather than solving the old ones.³⁹

Dragoumis rejected the idea of Greece as a nation-state as well. Some of his contemporaries, claimed Dragoumis, were mistaken to equate the nation with the state. In his view, the whole notion of the nation-state was a Western one that was transplanted in Greece without any alterations to account for local realities; he was suspicious of such one-size-fits-all solutions. Hellenism was much broader and not synonymous with the Greek state. Those Greeks who were unhappy with the territorial and political status quo had, according to Dragoumis, three options at their disposal. Two of them were impractical. He rejected, first, the attempt to re-create old paradigms of ancient Greece and Byzantium, and second, he believed that the modern paradigms of socialism and anarchism had yet to be tested. Dragoumis was convinced, therefore, that the third approach, his idea of an Eastern Federation, while also untested, represented the best possible outcome.[40]

Although ideology and diplomatic considerations were at the heart of Dragoumis's attempts to answer national questions, two political developments of the time were also important in the formulation of his Eastern Idea theory. During the late nineteenth and early twentieth century, when Dragoumis was formulating his theories, another model for Greek irredentism had emerged. The island of Crete moved from being part of the Ottoman Empire (up to 1896) to becoming a semi-independent entity (1897–1912) to finally uniting with Greece. In the Cretan story, Dragoumis saw a possible model.[41] Instead of the Greek state gradually conquering parts of its historical lands, an easier solution might be the simultaneous existence of a number of small Greek states that eventually, when the time was ripe, could unite.[42] Another political development that influenced Dragoumis's thinking was the revolt of the Young Turks. Western-educated and reform-minded, the Young Turks, mainly military officers, wanted to change the course of the empire by reversing its steady decline.[43] A main component of their program was equality of the various ethnic groups within the empire. The Young Turk regime, which ostensibly represented the dawn of Western-style political reforms, encouraged those ethnic minorities within the empire who wanted a democratic, multiethnic state based on modern European models.[44] Initially Dragoumis accepted the sincerity of the public statements of the Young Turks and expected them to accommodate the minorities of the Ottoman Empire and come to an understanding with Turkey's neighbors.[45] Following the Young Turk revolt, an anonymous Greek diplomat was quoted as saying: "The Great Idea in its political sense, it's impracticable for the present and will indefinitely remain so. Why then should we Greeks . . . quarrel with the Turks? Why should we object to living under a Turkish sovereign in Turkey as we live under a Danish sovereign in Greece? All that we ask from the Young Turks is not to interfere with our national language and customs."[46] A. J. Panayotopoulos deduces (I believe accurately) that the unnamed Greek diplomat was Ion Dragoumis.[47]

Clearly, after 1908 Dragoumis had come to believe that the Young Turk government working with the Greek element in the empire would create a Greek-Turkish partnership.[48] While Dragoumis hoped that the Young Turk government would bring about meaningful changes in the realm of political rights and democratization, he was also careful to explore other options. Thus, while calling for Greek-Turkish cooperation on the basis of equality and preservation of the Ottoman state, Dragoumis also advised Ottoman Greeks to take advantage of the new parliamentary system introduced by the Young Turks. Dragoumis argued for the creation of powerful Greek local and regional communities and other social, cultural, and political organizations within the empire, which would help ensure progress and safeguard Greek interests from intrusions "either legal or illegal by the Turkish state."[49] If the new state proposed by the Young Turks flourished, then the Greeks would be positioned favorably to become political equals. In the event that the Young Turk experiment failed and the empire collapsed, then the Greeks would be positioned to win the lion's share of the territorial spoils.[50]

While the idea of an Eastern Federation was but one of the issues occupying Dragoumis's time and thoughts, it was important enough to his vision for the future for him to attempt some initial planning for the state's possible borders and political system. Although he abstained from devising detailed plans of action and organization, he did provide some general idea of his vision, based interestingly enough on the Austro-Hungarian Empire.[51] On a trip to Austria-Hungary in October 1910, Dragoumis was impressed by the three different languages often encountered in public spaces such as on street signs and in railroad stations. He noted that Austria allowed the subject peoples the freedom to manage their religious, cultural, and educational affairs.[52] He also commented on the fact that the various peoples enjoyed equal political rights with the Austrians in the empire as a whole, while at the same time they enjoyed local autonomy and even, in the case of the Hungarians, controlled their own parliament. If the Eastern Federation was to emulate Austria-Hungary, the Greeks would play the role of the Hungarians. That is, the Greeks would be the junior partner in the state but with wide administrative, political, and cultural freedoms. The Hungarians and the Austrians were governing their respective halves of the Austro-Hungarian Empire but in questions of federal foreign policy and defense the Hungarians, even thought they were the junior partner, had veto powers. At the same time, the Hungarians were given a free hand in administering their ancestral territories and exercised control over the non-Hungarian people who resided there. Additionally, the

Hungarians took a free hand in controlling parts of the empire populated by non-Magyars (such as the Slovak lands), allowing them in essence to have an empire within the empire.[53]

Dragoumis envisioned a polity in which the Turks and the Greeks would be corulers, but at the same time the Greeks would be allowed broad powers, especially when it came to relationships with other Christian minorities. Envisioning the Greeks of the Greek-Turkish Empire as the Hungarians of Austria-Hungary might also explain certain of Dragoumis's equivocations regarding his commitment to a so-called Eastern Federation. Just as the Hungarians (although partners in the Austro-Hungarian Empire) were often perceived as less than wholeheartedly invested in the preservation of the Habsburg dominion, so Dragoumis's commitment to the preservation of the Greek-Turkish state would be provisional. Dragoumis's aim with the proposal of an Eastern Federation was not necessarily to preserve the territorial integrity of the Ottoman Empire prior to the First World War but rather to gain more political power for the Greek and Christian minority.

In the period 1914–19, Dragoumis was too busy with other issues to give much thought to his Eastern Federation idea. As Greek ambassador to St. Petersburg, he was involved in the high-level deliberations regarding Greece's position in World War I. Dragoumis was of the opinion that Greece should stay neutral and proposed a coalition government as the best way to govern the country under those difficult circumstances, but the proposal was rejected by the main political parties.[54] In 1915 Dragoumis was elected to parliament as a foe of the Greek prime minister Venizelos and his policy of entering the war on the side of the Triple Entente. Soon Dragoumis (through newspaper articles and parliamentary speeches) became a thorn in the side not only of the government but also of the Entente, whose troops controlled parts of northern Greece.[55] In June 1917, Dragoumis and a number of other opposition leaders were exiled to Corsica for the duration of the war. For about two years, Dragoumis's letters were censored, and his access to the news was limited; as a result he was in no position to comment on contemporary events. In April 1919, Dragoumis was allowed to leave Corsica for Greece. Unfortunately for him, instead of being allowed to return to Athens and resume his life, he was sent to the island of Skopelos for a term of internal exile that lasted until November of that year.

Today Skopelos is a major tourist destination with thousands of foreign visitors and regular connections with the mainland. In 1919 the island was a backwater without electricity or running water; a perfect place to isolate someone from the public eye. The long spell of inactivity and his return to internal exile affected Dragoumis's health. Reportedly he experienced some problems with his "nerves" and was treated by the local doctor.[56] Between exiles, isolation, and health problems, Dragoumis had very little time to contemplate the Eastern Federation. The only public communication dealing with the future of the Balkans and Anatolia that Dragoumis had during that time came in 1919 while he was in Skopelos. In a letter to friends, Dragoumis noted with satisfaction the fact that the proposed settlement with the Ottoman Empire (which became known as the Treaty of Sèvres in 1920) would leave mostly Greeks and Turks in Asia Minor. This development made the possibility of an Eastern Federation easier to accomplish, for it took from the Ottoman Empire those elements that Dragoumis considered backward (mostly Muslim Arabs and Kurds) while forcing the two main nationalities in the area, the Turks and the Greeks, to come to grips with the new realities of the post–World War I era.[57]

Dragoumis envisioned the creation of a new Greek-Turkish state to exist alongside but independent from Greece proper with autonomous local government for the various ethnic groups, full political freedoms, and two official languages. This state's capital would be Bursa or Ikonium or another inland city. He argued that Constantinople, Thrace, and the Dardanelles should constitute another independent state committed to neutrality and free navigation through the straights due to its strategic importance. Thus the Eastern Federation was to be composed of three states, one Greek and two Greek-Turkish, but ethnic minorities would be allowed to exist within each of the three states and their rights, presumably, safeguarded. Eventually autonomous areas would be allowed within the various states. Dragoumis did not provide details about the exact governing structure of the Eastern Federation. He did not explain such important issues as what kind of constitution would govern the state or what kind of government would run the day-to-day affairs of the country. However, examining some of his writings does permit certain hypotheses. Since Dragoumis modeled his Eastern Federation on Austria-Hungary, it is safe to assume that the Eastern Federation would resemble that state. Because Austria-Hungary was governed by a parliamentary, or quasi-parliamentary system, one can also assume that Dragoumis had a similar arrangement in mind. He had no problem with the monarch of the Eastern Federation being a constitutional one more or less like the king of Greece or the Austrian emperor.[58] Allowing the Ottoman sultan to fulfill such a limited role as ceremonial head of state was acceptable to Dragoumis.

If this federation had come to pass, what would have happened to the Danish royal family, which occupied the Greek throne? Was the king of Greece to be subordinate to the sultan? (The king of Bavaria and his relationship with the German emperor come to mind). Or was there another arrangement in the making? Dragoumis left no answers to those questions. Time and again in his writings about the Greek state, Dragoumis complains of the tyranny of the central government and describes an ideal condition with powers accorded the prefectures and the municipalities. While at times he wanted a military officer in charge of the prefectures, he allowed for an elected municipal government as well as an elected prefecture council. Since he was suspicious of the powers of central governments, Dragoumis would most likely have wanted the role of the central government of the Eastern Federation to be limited as well.[59] The new state would be based on two pillars: autonomous communities and cooperative associations.[60] In general, the state that Dragoumis envisioned would be a loose confederation with significant powers devolving from the central government to the constituent units.[61] Thus, the power of the federal government would be limited while state, municipal, and local elected bodies would run their affairs. Although the Eastern Federation would be a democratic state, the voters would have an indirect role in electing their representatives.[62] This notion derived from Dragoumis's belief that parliaments had a role to play in governing the state, but that role was mostly consultative rather than legislative or supervisory vis-à-vis the executive branch. Dragoumis did not oppose parliaments per se, but he mistrusted parliamentarians as being parochial in outlook and beholden to their local electorate to the detriment of the greater common good.[63] Since the main groups that would constitute the Eastern Federation were to be Muslims and Christians, and both religions had traditionally played important roles in political decision making, some mention of church-state relations (especially since the sultan was traditionally both a temporal and a religious leader) seems in order. Here again Dragoumis demurs from direct comment, but his voluminous auxiliary writings allow for some informed conclusions.

Dragoumis was a secularist who, although he recognized a public role for organized religion, envisioned the political authority of the state in firm control over church affairs.[64] In short, Dragoumis envisioned an Eastern Federation as a secular state with a Muslim monarch as its figurehead. The people of the federation would be free to worship in any faith, but their religious institutions and leaders would be firmly under the control of the political leadership.

Dragoumis hoped that his Eastern Idea of a Greek-Turkish state would have fulfilled a number of goals as far as the Greeks were concerned. More specifically, the plan would have advanced the irredentist needs of the Greek state, albeit without outright annexation of land, while protecting the interests of the 1,500,000–2,000,000 Greeks living in the Ottoman Empire. As it appeared on paper, the new state would have been strong enough to counter the attempts by the Slavs (Russians, and Bulgarians) to annex territories that Dragoumis considered Greek. While the interests of Hellenism remained paramount in Dragoumis's plans, his proposed state (strong, prosperous, modern, and democratic) would have also bestowed benefits on all its citizens.[65] The people of the Eastern Federation, regardless of their ethnic background or religion, would be free to pursue their interests and become the beneficiaries of a social, political, and economic renaissance.

Although Dragoumis and like-minded thinkers thought of the Eastern Federation as a solution to the ethnic problems of the Balkans and the Near East, their plan would have had wider implications. The Eastern Federation was a departure from the conventional political wisdom of its time. Indeed, part of its allure and interest today stems from its originality. In early twentieth-century Europe, two paradigms of viable states reigned supreme. One was that of the nation-state as represented by countries such as France or Italy, where the overwhelming majority of the people were identified as having a shared language, culture, and religion. The other alternative consisted of a multiethnic empire such as Russia or Austria-Hungary. In both empires, the population was diverse with different linguistic and cultural characteristics. In the case of Russia, the dominant group attempted with little success to retain power by pushing the minorities to integrate linguistically, culturally, and even religiously.[66] In the case of Austria-Hungary, the dominant group gave up part of its power and created a partnership with one of its minority groups (Austrians with Hungarians). The Eastern Federation was an attempt to forge a new course: the creation of a federal state on a voluntary basis. In the Eastern Federation, there would be no dominant group but rather a voluntary association of people who would agree to a union in order to safeguard their interests from infringement by more powerful states. The Eastern Federation represented a new paradigm, for its time, of a modern state.[67] Such a hybrid, it was hoped, combined the best elements of the dynamic nation-state with that of a powerful empire, an ingenious solution to a complex problem. The Eastern Federation also represented the potential for the creation of a new great power, which would change the balance of power in Europe and serve as a model for the Near East, and beyond. Located in a strategic part of the world, the Eastern Federation was destined to play a dynamic international role.

For the past two centuries, as the Ottoman Empire was weakened year after year, the strategic confluence of eastern Mediterranean, the Black Sea, and the Middle East was at the mercy of other more powerful states, which allowed its existence only because they could not agree among themselves on the spoils. While the Ottoman Empire was allowed to exist, it was ruthlessly exploited economically—by the great powers as well as by its own elites—to the detriment of its people regardless of their religion or ethnic origin. One of the most visible signs of foreign exploitation of the Ottoman Empire were the so-called capitulations, a system that gave Western merchants preferential treatment and thus a competitive edge to the detriment of Ottoman subjects and the empire's economy. The capitulations were also used to keep a large number of people, foreigners but also locals working for foreign firms, immune from the jurisdiction of Ottoman law and its authorities.[68]

Indeed, both the corrupt domestic elites and the great powers exploited national and religious differences in order to promote their interests. The dream for an Eastern Federation entailed a super state in which Christians and Muslims (perennial competitors for supremacy in the area) could coexist and cooperate, rid the country of the old, corrupt elites, and end foreign economic and military domination. The Eastern Federation would have also been a new way of addressing the problem of coexistence among different peoples in the same state. For the past one hundred years, the declining Ottoman Empire had been in more or less constant war with its Christian subjects. The result of those wars, regardless of who won, was violence, destruction, and dislocation of the population. In the end, the Ottoman Empire and its Muslim citizens were weakened, while the Christian peoples, even after achieving independence, found their new, small states vulnerable to outside pressure. The Eastern Federation held the promise of the peaceful coexistence of Muslims and Christians, as well as a way to counter threats from outside.

Finally, Dragoumis hoped that this new Greek-Turkish state would have all the potential of the Ottoman Empire with all the vigor of the

Greek element, which would allow it to resist outside pressures, mainly from the West.[69] Considering the history of the Near East since the Great War, the importance of a strong Eastern Federation becomes evident. One wonders how successful outside powers would have been in controlling either physically or economically parts of this sensitive area of the world with its strategic location and oil reserves. The existence of a strong Eastern Federation would have changed the diplomatic dynamics of the area, and Europe in general, with unforeseen impact on such developments as the Second World War and even the Cold War.

Unfortunately for Dragoumis, his dreams for a union of the Greek and the Turkish people in an Eastern Federation failed to materialize, and its potential and promise remained unfulfilled. One reason, maybe the main one, was the area's long history. There had been too much animosity between the Turks and their subject peoples. For most Greeks, Armenians, and other minorities, the Turks represented not a future partner but an enemy and oppressor. Following a number of wars between Turkey and its former subject peoples, culminating in the Balkan Wars of 1912-13, most Turks were also unwilling to cooperate. Their former subjects had been able not only to create independent states but also to humiliate a formerly glorious empire. As Turkish refugees fled the Balkans and resettled in Turkey proper, their tales of suffering at the hands of their Christian enemies hardened the political stance of those who contemplated, however remotely, cooperation. To be sure, even before the Balkan Wars the coexistence of Greeks and Turks in Asia Minor was far from idyllic.[70] After the Young Turk revolt, while the Greeks and the Turks of the Asia Minor littoral, presumably more sophisticated and open to new ideas due to their commercial ties to the West, embraced the promised changes of democratization and secularism, their brethren in the hinterland were unsure about, if not outright hostile to, those ideas.[71]

The Young Turks also share a great part of the responsibility for the failure of any kind of Muslim-Christian rapprochement. Their initial message—full of high-minded ideals of democracy and respect for minority rights—resonated with the empire's subject people, who rushed to support the new regime. Soon after taking control of the state, however, the Young Turks not only reverted to the Ottoman state's policies of discrimination against minorities but also became the catalyst for the strengthening, if not the emergence, of Turkish nationalism. As Ion Dragoumis noted in his journal in July 1914, the Young Turks attempted to create a modern multiethnic state based on equality under the law, but they failed and instead "created Turkish nationalism, reinforced the nationalism of Greeks, Bulgarians, Armenians, and awakened the nationalism of the Kurds, Albanians, Circassians, and Arabs."[72] The tragic history of the Armenian genocide illustrates why the idea of an Eastern Federation was premature or even impossible.[73] It clearly demonstrates how deep and impossible to heal was the animosity between the peoples of the Near East. While most of the killing occurred during, and as a result of, the First World War, part of its planning and even some pogroms had occurred before the war itself. The main motivating factor was not state security, as one might claim for the 1915 genocide, but rather an attempt by the Turkish state to ensure that the subject people would be unable to translate their economic strength into political power, what the historian Sia Anagnostopoulou labels "nationalizing economy and space."[74] While the case of the Armenian genocide is the most notorious, the Greeks were also targeted for elimination through political, economic, and military measures.[75] To achieve these ends, the Young Turks used organized terror, forced relocation, and even widespread killings of Asia Minor Greeks by military and paramilitary units under the supervision of the Turkish government even before World War I started.[76] The expulsions of minorities and the Armenian genocide were but the closing chapter in the history of an empire and the opening one in the history of a strictly homogeneous nation-state. A modern and democratic multiethnic state, of the type the Eastern Federation could have become, would have able to prevent such tragedies.

Another reason that might account for the failure of a Greek-Turkish state is the fact that such ideas remained limited to discussions among certain members of the elite. For reasons that are unclear, there were no efforts to communicate such plans to a wider audience. As a result, the various ideas for supranational cooperation failed to achieve popular support. Any talk of wider Eastern cooperation of peoples remained just talk and failed to gain any real traction in popular political discourse. A major shortcoming of Ion Dragoumis's plans for an Eastern Federation was his failure to grasp the changing diplomatic landscape of the world. Did he really believe, despite his experience in foreign affairs, that the great powers would allow the genesis of such a powerful federation, which was going to compete with them and hinder their geopolitical and economic plans? Further, the spirit of the times was moving in a direction that differed from Dragoumis's way of thinking. The end of the First World War became the apogee of the nation-state. United States president Woodrow Wilson became a hero in Europe because of his ideas of democratization and self-determination. As a result, the treaties that ended the war attempted (albeit at times half-heartedly or/ and unsuccessfully) to redraw the map of Europe based on the principle of national self-determination.[77] In such a climate, the idea of creating multiethnic empires was anachronistic; at the time the trend was to split great empires into many small nation-states, rather than allowing the creation of new powers. While the great powers allowed, indeed encouraged, the creation of Czechoslovakia and Yugoslavia, these states were not strong enough to become either empires or a serious challenge to the powers of the day. Additionally, Czechoslovakia's peaceful split and, more tragically, Yugoslavia's violent ending are not hopeful signs for what might have happened to the Eastern Federation.

The EU is a contemporary entity that might be a better example of what the Eastern Federation could have been. The fact that it took the major trauma of the Second World War to push the Europeans closer indicates that the 1920s were too early for such developments. Also, the European states that came together in the 1950s to create the nucleus of today's EU were at a more advanced stage economically, socially, and politically than the areas that would have been partners in the Eastern Federation. France, West Germany, Italy, Belgium, the Netherlands, and Luxemburg were industrialized states with a long tradition of democratic governance (Germany less so) that served as a guide for the structure and procedures of EU. In contrast, the Balkans and Anatolia were still agrarian-based societies with very little, if any, experience with democratic governments and modern societies. In any case, before we rush to proclaim the EU a success, we should keep in mind that the recent economic downturn has put strains on the partnership, and one can only speculate if the EU will survive in the future in its current form. Additionally, the economic crisis has revealed that the EU is not as cohesive as previously thought (or hoped), and far from being a partnership of equals, it is an entity dominated by unified Germany. At the same time, it is also in the context of the EU that Turkish-Greek coexistence under the same federation-like entity is, however remotely, possible. If at some point in the future Turkey joins the EU, then it will join other member states such as Greece, Bulgaria, Romania, and Cyprus, as well as countries of the former Yugoslavia, which are or will be members by that time. If this scenario materializes, then a modified version of the Eastern Federation might yet come to exist.

The fact that we are left to speculate about a future (and remote) possibility of realizing a version of the Eastern Idea indicates that the "original" idea of an Eastern Federation, however promising, was either unrealistic or at best belonged to the nineteenth-century way of thinking while the nation-state was the new paradigm of the early twentieth. Indeed, a major victim of that policy of nation-state creation was Dragoumis's ideal model of modern empire based on the principles of democracy and respect for ethnic minority rights; the Treaties of Trianon and Saint-Germain brought about the dissolution of the Austro-Hungarian Empire and replaced it with a number of nation-states.

NOTES

An earlier version of this work was presented at the conference "Mediterranean and its Seas," September 2008, Minneapolis, Minnesota.

1. While the bibliography of the history of the Balkans is extensive, a sample of works, from Barbara Jelavich, *History of the Balkans*, 2 vols. (New York: Cambridge University Press, 1983), to Thanos Veremis, *Valkania apo ton 19o os ton 200 aiona* [The Balkans from the 19th to the 21st century] (Athens: Patakis, 2004), indicates the experience of almost constant warfare among the Balkan peoples at the time under examination.

2. While works by historians of Greek history are more prone to emphasize Greek-Turkish problems, those of Ottoman scholars give them less attention, usually because the former write studies more specific to Greece, while the latter examine the Ottoman Empire in its totality. See Richard Clogg, *A Concise History of Greece*, 2nd ed. (Cambridge: Cambridge University Press, 2002); Thomas Gallant, *Modern Greece* (New York: Oxford University Press, 2001); Karen Barkey, *Empire of Difference: The Ottomans in Comparative Perspective* (New York: Cambridge University Press, 2008); and Şükrü M. Hanioğlu, *A Brief History of the Late Ottoman Empire* (Princeton, NJ: Princeton University Press, 2008).

3. The best known case of such cooperation is the agreement between Greece and Turkey in the late 1920s. See Evanthis Hatzivassiliou, *O Eleftherios Venizelos, e Ellinotourkike Prosegise kai to Provlema tis Asfalias sta Valkania 1928–1931* [Eleftherios Venizelos, the Greek-Turkish rapprochement and the problem of security in the Balkans 1928–1931] (Thessaloniki: IMXA, 1999).

4. See *Report of the International Commission to Inquire into the Causes and Conduct of the Balkan Wars* (Washington, DC: Carnegie Endowment for International Peace, 1914).

5. For recent works on the various genocides by the Ottoman Empire and the Republic of Turkey, see Taner Akçam, *From Empire to Republic: Turkish Nationalism and the Armenian Genocide* (London: Zed Books, 2004); idem, *The Young Turks' Crime against Humanity* (Princeton, NJ: Princeton University Press, 2012); and George N. Shirinian, ed., *The Asia Minor Catastrophe and the Ottoman Greek*

Genocide: Essays in Asia Minor, Pontos, and Eastern Thrace, 1912–1923 (Bloomington, IL: Asia Minor and Pontos Hellenic Research Center, 2012).

6. The treaties in question are those of Versailles (28 June 1919) with Germany, Saint-Germain (10 September 1919) with Austria, Trianon (4 June 1920) with Hungary, and Sèvres (10 August 1920) with the Ottoman Empire. The case of Imperial Russia is different because that state "morphed" into the USSR due to domestic developments. Nevertheless, the Treaty of Brest-Litovsk (3 March 1918) between Russia and Germany, however short lived, can be taken as the "official" end of the Russian Empire. For more on the treaties in question, see Margaret Macmillan, *Paris 1919: Six Months That Changed the World* (New York: Random House, 2002); David Fromkin, *A Peace to End All Peace* (New York: Avon Books, 1989); and Nikolaos Petsales-Diomedes, *Greece at the Paris Peace Conference (1919)* (Thessaloniki: IMXA, 1978).

7. While the term "sick man of Europe" is the most common one, according to W. Bruce Lincoln, *Nicholas I, Emperor and Autocrat of All the Russias* (Bloomington: Indiana University Press, 1978), 222–23, Tsar Nicholas I said, "Turkey is a dying man."

8. The term itself is a bit misleading. While Great Idea is the direct English translation of the Greek term Μεγάλη Ιδέα, Μεγάλη can mean "great," but it can also mean "important" or "profound," which is more descriptive of the spirit of this ideology. Proponents of the ideology (the majority of the Greek leadership as well as the people) advocated either the outright destruction of the Ottoman Empire and the re-creation of a Byzantine/Greek one, or the acquisition of as much land from the Ottoman state as possible. From the 1840s to the 1920s, the Megali Idea was at the center of Greek politics and foreign affairs. For a detailed treatment, see Adamatia Pollis's "The Megali Idea: A Study of Greek Nationalism" (PhD diss., Johns Hopkins University, 1958); see also Michael Llewellyn Smith, *Ionian Vision: Greece in Asia Minor, 1919–1922* (New York: St. Martin's Press, 1973), 2–3; Jerry Augustinos, "The Dynamics of Modern Greek Nationalism: The 'Great Idea' and the Macedonian Problem," *East European Quarterly* 6, no. 4 (1972): 444–53.

9. On the attempted reforms and the difficulties encountered, see Roderic Davison, *Reform in the Ottoman Empire, 1856–1876* (Princeton, NJ: Princeton University Press, 1963); Hanioğlu, *Brief History of the Late Ottoman Empire*, 72–149; and Stanford Shaw and Ezel Kural Shaw, *History of the Ottoman Empire and Modern Turkey*, 2 vols. (New York: Cambridge University Press, 1977), 2:155–71.

10. The so-called Greek Project, associated mainly with Catherine the Great and Alexander I, is a prime example of the attempts by outsiders to impose their will on the people of the Balkans and the Ottoman Empire. Whatever one might attribute to such plans, it is clear that they were conjured to benefit Russia first, if not exclusively. See Janet Hartley, *Alexander I* (New York: Longman, 1994), 100–101.

11. Christine M. Philliou, *Biography of an Empire: Governing Ottomans in an Age of Revolution* (Berkeley: University of California Press, 2011), 224n7.

12. Some historians do portray the peoples of the Balkans as having some agency, but this is usually understood as some form of revolt aimed at weakening or outright destroying the Ottoman Empire, rather than reforming and reviving it. See A. J. Grant and Harold Temperley, *Europe in the Nineteenth and Twentieth Centuries (1789-1932)* (London: Longmans, Green, 1932), 257.

13. Ion Dragoumis Archives, pt. A, file 29, Gennadius Library, American School of Classical Studies, Athens (henceforth cited as Dragoumis Archives). All translations from Greek to English are mine. See also Gerasimos Augoustinos, *Consciousness and History: Critics of Greek Society, 1897-1914* (Boulder, CO: East European Monographs, 1977).

14. Given Venizelos's importance in modern Greek history, one would expect several available works about him, but that is not the case. Besides Doros Alastos's hagiographical *Venizelos: Patriot, Statesman, Revolutionary* (Gulf Breeze, FL: Academic International Press, 1978), there is also Thanos Veremis and E. Nikolopoulos, *O Eleftherios Venizelos kai e Epoche Tou* [Eleftherios Venizelos and his era] (Athens: Greek Letters, 2005); and Paschalis Kitromilides, ed., *Eleftherios Venizelos: The Trials of Statesmanship* (Edinburgh: Edinburgh University Press, 2006). Macmillan, *Paris 1919*, provides a vivid portrayal, especially the chapter titled "The Greatest Greek Statesman since Pericles," 347-65.

15. Pavlos Drandakis, ed., *Megali Elliniki Engiklopedia* [Great Greek encyclopedia], 24 vols. (Athens: Phoenix Ekdoseis, n.d), 9:530. One would think that a culture that emphasizes its long history (like that of modern Greece) would have a tradition of historical biography. This is not the case, however; thus biographical information on Dragoumis exists mainly as encyclopedia entries.

16. See Evangelos Kofos, *Greece and the Eastern Crisis, 1875-1878* (Thessaloniki: IMXA, 1976), 20.

17. A. J. Panayotopoulos, "The Great Idea and the Vision of Eastern Federation: Apropos of the Views of I. Dragoumis and A. Souliotis—Nicolaidis," *Balkan Studies* 21 (1980): 332-33; and L. S. Stavrianos, *Balkan Federation* (Hamden, CT: Archon Books, 1964), 150-51. Although a number of historians have dealt with the Eastern Question, most of them follow the traditional route of viewing the problem from the perspective of the great powers and the Ottoman governing elite. In contrast, only the works of Panayotopoulos and Stavrianos have addressed the plans for a third way via a Balkan federation.

18. Panayotopoulos, "Great Idea," 348.

19. Ibid., 348-49. One could see a federation based on justice and equality, but "history" is problematic. Clearly, the people who would participate in the federation had some common history, but historically they viewed themselves as distinct groups. Since there is no explanation of what the framers had in mind by "history," any speculation now would be of little use.

20. Panayotopoulos, "Great Idea," 356-57.

21. Dragoumis Archives, pt. A, file 30. There is no evidence that Dragoumis knew of the plans presented here. While he must have known Karatheodori and Zarifis by reputation, he most likely had never heard of Argyriades, his organization, or his ideas.

22. Ion Dragoumis, *Ta Tetradia tou Ilinden* [Notebooks from the Ilinden uprising], ed. George Petsivas (Athens: Petsivas, 2000), 401-3.

23. See K. A. Vakalopoulos, *Ion Dragoumis-Pavlos Gyparis: Koryfees Morfes tou Makedonikou Agona (1902-1908)* [Ion Dragoumis-Paul Gyparis: Leading individuals of the struggle for Macedonia (1902-1908)] (Thessaloniki: Barbounakes, 1987), 37-44.

24. See anonymous, *Epitafia Styli ston Iona Dragoumi* [Epitaph monument for Ion Dragoumis] (Athens: Ekdoseis Efthynes, 1978), 67.

25. *Istoria tou Ellinikou Ethnous* [History of the Greek nation], 16 vols. (Athens: Ekdotiki Athenon, 1978), 15:485. Dragoumis's Eastern Idea was developed as early as 1908 with the help of his good friend Athanasios Souliotis-Nicolaidis. See Philip Dragoumis, *Imerologio: Valkanikoi Polemoi 1912-1913* [Private journal: Balkan Wars 1912-1913], ed. Ioannis K. Mazarakis-Ainian (Athens: Dodoni, 1988), 331; and *Imerologio: Dichasmos 1916-1919* [Private journal: The National Split 1916-1919], ed. Mark Dragoumis and Christina Varda (Athens: Dodoni, 1995), 65.

26. For a fairly balanced treatment of the Macedonian question (although sympathetic to the Greeks), see Douglas Dakin, *The Greek Struggle in Macedonia, 1897-1913* (Thessaloniki: IMXA, 1966).

27. Ion Dragoumis, *To Monopati* [The footpath] (Athens: Dodoni, 1925), 49.

28. There is a tradition of Russia being thought of as Bulgaria's patron, while Bulgaria has been viewed as Russia's tool. In reality, Russian-Bulgarian relations were never as harmonious as presented. See Barbara Jelavich, *Russia's Balkan Entanglements, 1806-1914* (New York: Cambridge University Press, 1991), 178-96.

29. Ion Dragoumis, "Prokyrixe stous sklavomenous kai tous asklavotous Ellines" ([Manifesto to the free and unredeemed Greeks], Dragoumis Archives, pt. A, file 37, 2.

30. See D. P. Tagopoulos, ed., *Deka Arthra tou Ionos Dragoumi ston Nouma* [Ten articles by Ion Dragoumis in *Noumas*] (Athens: Ekdosis Typou, 1920).

31. Ion Dragoumis, "Oxi pros tin Dysin, pros tin Anatolin einai o dromos" [The road leads to the east, not to the west], *Atlantis*, 3 September 1927, 2-5. See Dragoumis Archives, pt. A, file 37.

32. For a modern scholarly treatment of the issue, see Maria Todorova, *Imagining the Balkans* (New York: Oxford University Press, 1997).

33. The idea that the Greek element could, under the right conditions, prevail in a new Turkish democratic empire was not Dragoumis's (or his fellow Greeks') alone. In a letter to Dragoumis dated 4 February 1920, a British acquaintance of his, William Ramsay, notes that the anticipated Greek control

of Asia Minor would result in the Greek element ruling its western part and also having a great degree of influence in the center of the peninsula. For the letter, see the Gennadius Library, Allilografia Ionos Dragoumi, letter 0648.

34. See Ion Dragoumis, "Ypomnima ston Ekumenikon Patriarchin Ioakem III, 1907" [Note to the ecumenical patriarch Joachim III, 1907], Dragoumis Archives, pt. B, file 16-18, 2.

35. See Dragoumis Archives, pt. B, file 16-18; and Ion Dragoumis, "I Thesi tes Tourkias" [Conditions in Turkey], *Noumas* 460 (11 December 1911).

36. Ion Dragoumis, "O Ellinismos mou kai oi Ellenes" [My sense of Hellenism and the Greeks], in *Apanta Ionos Dragoumi* [The collected works of Ion Dragoumis] (Athens: Nea Thesis, 1991), 81, 108.

37. Ion Dragoumis, "Osoi Zontanoi" [Those who are alive], in *Apanta Ionos Dragoumi* [The collected works of Ion Dragoumis]) (Athens: Nea Thesis, 1991), 119, 127, 140. Dragoumis was not alone in his belief in the superiority of Greek culture in the Ottoman Empire. Even some other, non-Greek members of the first Young Turk parliament (1908-9) recognized that Greek national identity was more advanced than that of other ethnic groups in the empire. See Emre Sencer, "Balkan Nationalisms in the Ottoman Parliament, 1909," *East European Quarterly* 38, no. 1 (2004): 56-59.

38. Panayotopoulos, "Great Idea," 359.

39. Ibid., 336, 342.

40. See Ion Dragoumis, *Fylla Imerologiou, 6, 1918-1920* [Pages from the private journal, v. 6, 1918-1920], ed. Theodoros Soteropoulos (Athens: Hermes, 1987), 116.

41. Ion Dragoumis, *Politikoi Programatikoi Stochasmoi* [Political thoughts] (Athens: Byron, 1972), 16. See also his "Osoi Zontanoi," 148.

42. In a letter to Charises Vamvakas, 26 July 1913, Dragoumis proposes an independent State of Thrace with Adrianople as its capital. In this way certain objections by the great powers could be overcome, and the possible future threat to the area by Bulgaria could be averted. See Gennadius Library, Allilografia Ionos Dragoumi, letter 0276.

43. See Barkey *Empire of Difference*, 292-94; John Patrick Kinross, *The Ottoman Centuries* (New York: Morrow Quill, 1977), 575-76; and Shaw and Shaw, *History of the Ottoman Empire and Modern Turkey*, 2:255-71.

44. Sencer, "Balkan Nationalisms," 53.

45. Dragoumis was not the only Greek to accept the sincerity of the Young Turk program. A number of Greek newspapers in Constantinople, representing the views of a large segment of the over two hundred thousand Greeks in the city, welcomed the possibility of a new beginning. See Panayotopoulos "Great Idea," 348-49; and G. F. Abbott, *Turkey in Transition* (London: Edward Arnold, 1909), 84-85.

46. Abbott, *Turkey in Transition*, 85-86.

47. A. J. Panayotopoulos, "Early Relations between the Greeks and the Young Turks," *Balkan Studies* 21 (1980): 91. Eventually Dragoumis and others realized that the Young Turk manifesto on citizen equality regardless of religious and ethnic background was just a slogan, and not government policy. See Panayotopoulos, "Great Idea," 352; and Abbott, *Turkey in Transition*, 106-7.

48. Smith, *Ionian Vision*, 30.

49. Tagopoulos, *Deka Arthra*, 85.

50. Th. Papakostantinou, *Ion Dragoumis kai Politike Pezografia* [Ion Dragoumis and political prose] (Athens: Zaharopoulos, 1957), κγ'.

51. In his journal (January 1911) Dragoumis wrote: "I would accept my nation to exist in the way Hungary exists in Austria." Dragoumis noted how privileged the Hungarian part of the Austro-Hungarian Empire was and wanted a similar Greco-Turkish polity. See Ion Dragoumis, *Fylla Imerologiou, IV, 1908-1912* [Pages from the private journal, vol. 4, 1908-1912], ed. Thanos Veremis and John Koliopoulos (Athens: Hermes, 1985), 158.

52. See Ion Dragoumis, *Fylla Imerologiou, IV, 1908-1912*, 140.

53. For a sophisticated but readable explanation of the creation and workings of the dual monarchy of Austria-Hungary, see A. J. P. Taylor, *The Habsburg Monarchy, 1809-1918* (Chicago: University of Chicago Press, 1976), 130-40. In describing the compromise that allowed the creation of the new polity, Taylor shows how the Hungarians were able to gain almost complete independence from Vienna in domestic matters while keeping the right to veto, or at least shape, imperial policies. The author notes how in the years 1900 to 1914 (the time that Dragoumis visited the empire), a number of national minorities within the empire had achieved a large measure of cultural autonomy. At the same time, the agreements that accorded a degree of autonomy to different nationalities in the empire did not solve all the ethnic problems. Dragoumis's views were based on a short visit without any in-depth study of the Austro-Hungarian Empire, its political system, and its ethnic challenges. One wonders if the various national minorities in the Austro-Hungarian Empire thought of themselves as privileged as Dragoumis believed them to be. Indeed, Taylor, *Habsburg Monarchy*, 196-213 and 224-27, notes that for all the deals and compromises, by 1914 the Austro-Hungarian Empire faced major ethnic problems that could not be solved by peaceful political means.

54. George Leontaritis, *Greece and the First World War: From Neutrality to Intervention, 1917-1918* (Boulder, CO: East European Monographs, 1990), 140, 108; and Petros Horologas "E politike Drase tou Dragoumi" [Dragoumis's political actions], in *Nea Estia "Teuchos Afieromeno ston Iona Dragoumi"* [Special issue dedicated to Ion Dragoumis] 29, no. 342 (1941): 256.

55. Dragoumis Archives, pt. A, file 12-14 (now renamed "International Relations I 1915-1916" and "II Foreign Intervention").

56. See Philip Dragoumis, *Imerologio*, 432.

57. Dragoumis Archives, pt. B, file 16-18, letter dated 1 July 1919, 3-5.
58. See Ion Dragoumis, "Osoi Zontanoi," 164.
59. Ibid., 154-55, 167-68; and Ion Dragoumis, *Samothraki to Nisi* [The island of Samothrace] (Athens: Dodoni, 1926), 42; idem, *Politikoi Programatikoi Stochasmoi*, 22, 24; and idem, "O Ellinismos mou kai oi Ellenes," 122.
60. See Ion Dragoumis, *Fylla Imerologiou*, 6, 1918-1920, 14 August 1919, 116.
61. While Dragoumis named his state "Ομοσπονδία" (federation), it is clear that he had a much looser union in mind; thus the term "Συνομοσπονδία" or "confederation," would be more appropriate.
62. Ion Dragoumis, *Koinotis, Ethnos kai Kratos* [Community, nation and state], ed. Philip Dragoumis. (Thessaloniki: Heteria Makedonikon Spoudon, 1967), 78; and idem, "O Ellinismos mou kai oi Ellenes," 31.
63. Dragoumis, "O Ellinismos mou kai oi Ellenes," 135-36.
64. Ibid., 85-86.
65. Dragoumis did not hypothesize about the interests of the Greeks of the Ottoman Empire. Presumably a confederation would have offered religious and ethnic minorities some protection from infringement of their rights by the majority.
66. For details on imperial Russia's policy of Russification, see Theodore R. Weeks, *Nation and State in Late Imperial Russia* (DeKalb: Northern Illinois University Press, 1996).
67. The post-World War I creations of Czechoslovakia and the Kingdom of Serbs, Croats, and Slovenes are examples of states created on the basis of voluntary cooperation of the constituent ethnic groups. The difference between those two states and the proposed Eastern Federation is that whereas the ethnic groups in the former cases were quite close culturally, in the latter case the state would be truly multicultural.
68. Shaw and Shaw, *History of the Ottoman Empire and Modern Turkey*, 2:97-98; and Mark Mazower, *Salonica City of Ghosts: Christians, Muslims and Jews, 1430-1950* (New York: Vintage Books, 2004), 165-66.
69. Constantine Svolopoulos, *E Ellinike Exoterike Politike apo tis Arches tou 20ou Eona os to Deutero Pagosmio Ploemo* [Greek foreign policy from the beginning of the 20th century to the Second World War] (Thessaloniki: Sakkoula, 1983), 47.
70. Sia Anagnostopoulou, *Mikra Asia, 19os ai.-1919: Hoi Hellenorthodoxes Koinotetes* [Asia Minor, 19th c.-1919: The Greek Orthodox communities] (Athens: Greek Letters, 1998), 12-13.
71. Ibid., 459-60.
72. Ion Dragoumis, *Fylla Imerologiou, V, 1913-1917* [Pages from the private journal, v. 5, 1913-1917], ed. Theodoros Soteropoulos (Athens: Hermes, 1986), 76.
73. The topic of the Armenian Genocide is not open to interpretation. The overwhelming majority of scholars accept that what occurred in 1915 was a

state-sponsored genocide of the Ottoman Empire's Armenian minority. See International Association of Genocide Scholars, 20 July 2012, www.atour.com/~aahgn/news/20080311a.html (accessed 14 October 2013). Denying that what occurred was genocide, as in the case of Shaw and Shaw, *History of the Ottoman Empire and Modern Turkey*, 2:315-16, or blaming the exigencies of war, as in the recent case of Sean McMeekin, *The Russian Origins of the First World War* (Cambridge, MA: Harvard University Press, 2011), 242, are considered acts of scholarly misconduct. http://www.voelkermord.at/docs/Scholars_Denying_IAGS.pdf (accessed 14 October 2013).

74. Anagnostopoulou, *Mikra Asia*, 529; Akçam, *From Empire to Republic*, 144-49; and Donald Bloxham, *The Great Game of Genocide* (New York: Oxford University Press, 2005).

75. Akçam, *From Empire to Republic*, 144.

76. See reports of the Greek consulate in Smyrna to the Greek Ministry of Foreign Affairs in Anagnostopoulou, *Mikra Asia*, 597-604; and Taner Akçam, *A Shameful Act: The Armenian Genocide and the Question of Turkish Responsibility*, trans. Paul Bessemer (New York: Metropolitan Books, 2006), 97, 106-8.

77. For the trials and tribulations of state formation in the post-World War I Balkans, see Charles and Barbara Jelavich, *The Establishment of the Balkan National States, 1804-1920* (Seattle: University of Washington Press, 1977), 298; and Leften Stavrianos, *The Balkans since 1453* (New York: New York University Press, 2000).

Sergei Sazonov. (from Eugene de Schelking, *Recollections of a Russian Diplomat: The Suicide of Monarchies* [New York: Macmillan, 1918])

Squabbling over the Spoils
Late Imperial Russia's Rivalry with France in the Near East

RONALD P. BOBROFF

The Franco-Russian Alliance, from its beginnings in 1891 through its demise with the Russian Revolution in 1917, is best remembered for the way France and Russia cooperated primarily to resist what was perceived as a growing threat from Germany. Indeed, this alliance formed one side of a diarchy of alliances that engendered the tensions facilitating the beginning of the First World War in 1914. However, while the two partners stood together against Germany, their cooperation regarding the Ottoman Empire was strained, as Paris and St. Petersburg had quite different interests in the Ottoman Empire and its ultimate fate. That these differences over the Eastern Question nearly wrecked the Dual Alliance, even in the midst of war, shows how vital Near Eastern issues were to France, to Russia, and to Europe as a whole.

Before the First World War, France sought to handle the Sublime Porte carefully in order to preserve the Ottoman Empire for as long as possible to protect its own financial interests and influence in the Near East. Indeed, France had often maintained a working relationship with the Ottomans as far back as the sixteenth century. Russia, in contrast, usually a rival of the Ottomans, had little monetary investment, so could afford to pursue a blunter approach. Russia's security concerns, however, were great as the Ottoman navy began to modernize. Russia felt obligated to respond with the construction of its own capital ships on the Black Sea, leading to a naval race of sorts between the two countries. With the outbreak of war in 1914, the disparate financial engagement largely gave way to disagreements about the Ottoman Empire's ultimate partition, which exposed the misalignment of France and Russia's geostrategic goals. This discord over the Ottoman Empire during the last decade of Romanov rule illuminates the precarious nature of the Franco-Russian Alliance. Disagreement over administration and partition of Ottoman lands strained the alliance to the limit during the First World War.

Scholars have studied the Franco-Russian relationship both as a subject in its own right and via studies of the events of the time. Most monographs that examine the alliance concentrate on its origins.[1] Shorter works have looked more broadly at the alliance, yet authors have predominantly focused on the financial relationship between the two states.[2] Furthermore, each of the crises on the road to war in 1914 has received attention by historians, but no one has analyzed the French and Russian positions over the whole series of crises—particularly those crises that related to the Ottoman Empire—in order to draw out lessons about the alliance dynamic. Indeed, the Franco-Russian disagreement over the Ottoman Empire and its inheritance shows us how the Eastern Question could magnify as well as transcend the issues that usually defined relationships within Europe.

Though rather overshadowed by the military history of the war, valuable studies of the diplomacy of the First World War exist in a variety of languages based on archives from nearly all the belligerent parties. These studies have run the gamut from the diplomacy of the war as a whole to the resolution of specific concerns.[3] Works on the allied decision in March 1915 to award the Turkish Straits—the Bosporus and the Dardanelles—to the Russians upon the defeat of the Central Powers have tended to concentrate on Great Britain's willingness to accept Russia's gain. Britain had long opposed Russian expansion into the region, so scholars have sought to understand such an about-face in attitude.[4] Historians, however, have little scrutinized France's stubborn resistance to awarding this most valuable prize to its ally. Similarly, much has been written about the legendary Sykes-Picot talks, credited with beginning the imperialist division of the Near East and laying the groundwork for the modern Middle East. Less attention, however, has been devoted to Russia's role in these talks or its objectives.[5] A recent trend in the scholarship of Russia and the Eastern Question has been to examine Russian-Ottoman relations directly. Michael Reynolds and Sean McMeekin have both used the archives of Russia and Turkey to offer new interpretations of the struggle between the two aging empires.[6] Neither, however, draws France sufficiently into the picture, with McMeekin even mistakenly suggesting that the Eastern Question was not "terribly urgent" for France, leaving a significant part of the dynamic unappreciated.[7] This essay seeks to uncover the pattern of Franco-Russian disagreement over the Ottoman Empire on the eve of and during World War I.

The Eastern Question provides the critical (if neglected) context for this relationship. This dispute over the pace and management of perceived Ottoman decline dominated no small amount of international relations in the long nineteenth century. Indeed, given the importance of the Eastern Question to relations among European states in this period and the influence of European rivalries on the Near East, any study of the Russian-Ottoman borderlands ought to consider the diplomatic arena. International history offers valuable insights into the nature of relations among states and into the connections between international relations and nonpolitical developments in cultures and societies as well. As Zara Steiner reminds us, international history constitutes far more than what one foreign minister said to another.[8] Given the inherently transnational nature of a *borderland*, a field that relies on multinational studies achieved through work in the archives of many states offers important insights into the problem, lost in the vales and dunes of any single land.[9] This chapter aims to do just that with archival sources from Russia, France, Great Britain, and the United States. The international-history approach to the borderlands shows how intractable questions about their fate could be, even in the face of the life-or-death struggle playing out in western and eastern Europe.

The Eastern Question played an especially significant role in the foreign policy of Russia, which engaged in at least six wars with the Ottoman Empire during this time and slowly but inexorably pushed the mutual border further south on both sides of the Black Sea. The Eastern Question also featured in the relations of France and Russia, given the former's long connection with the Sublime Porte. For example, among the reasons for the Crimean War (1853-56) was a Franco-Russian dispute over stewardship of the holy places within Ottoman Palestine.[10]

The war did not unseat newly installed French influence over the holy places, much to the frustration of St. Petersburg, long accustomed to the role of protector of Orthodox Christians in Ottoman domains. French interest in the Near East was thus confirmed and enhanced, while Franco-Russian relations were left strained by the humiliating loss that the Russians suffered on their own territory.

The Franco-Russian Alliance, formed in the early 1890s, thus represented a new landmark in the diplomatic landscape. For the first time in decades, Russia and France found common ground in their mutual concerns about the rise of Germany following the forced retirement of German chancellor Otto von Bismarck. Bismarck had worked to keep France isolated while preserving peace between Russia and Austria-Hungary by binding St. Petersburg first into tripartite agreements with Berlin and Vienna and then into the bilateral Reinsurance Treaty.[11] In 1890, however, Kaiser Wilhelm II decided to let lapse the Reinsurance Treaty between Russia and Germany. Wilhelm was sure that autocratic Russia and republican France could never put aside their ideological differences to breach Paris's isolation. With financial links already growing after Bismarck closed the Berlin bond markets to Russian needs, the end of the agreement between Berlin and St. Petersburg encouraged Russia to turn to Paris as a strategic partner, lest Russia find itself isolated as well by the increasingly powerful German Empire. A political agreement in 1891 was followed by a military alliance, ratified by 1894, which pledged the two powers to mutual aid in case of an attack by Germany or by another rival with Germany's support. Given the French rivalry with Great Britain in Africa and the Russian challenge to Britain in Asia, the alliance took on an anti-British tinge as well for approximately a decade. Tension with Great Britain, however, subsided as first Paris and then St. Petersburg decided to solve their colonial conflicts with London via ententes in 1904 and 1907.[12] Growing concern over German intentions acted to concentrate the attention of the Entente powers on affairs in Europe.

The first decade of Franco-Russian cooperation was not free from difficulties, of course. For example, Paris's low level of support for St. Petersburg during the Russian-Japanese War of 1904–5 deeply disappointed the Russians. Nevertheless, France ultimately offered Russia loans that allowed it to survive both the severe losses it suffered during the war in Asia and the revolution beginning in January 1905, which unsettled both city and countryside.

In the wake of tsarist losses during the Russian-Japanese War, the Revolution of 1905 and the ensuing governmental reform, the new Russian premier, Pyotr A. Stolypin, rose to power as Russia's first Western-style prime minister. He provided some coordination among the Russian ministers who typically competed for influence on the tsar, and dominated the foreign policy of Russia over the years 1907 to 1911.[13] Stolypin sought to avoid any diplomatic adventure that might threaten war, given how weak Russia had become and how slowly reconstruction and rearmament were progressing. Talented and well-connected but egotistical to a fault, foreign minister Aleksandr P. Izvolskii followed this line at first. In 1908, however, Russia's Balkan rival, the Austro-Hungarian Empire, began building a railway through Ottoman dominions in the Balkans to connect Austrian possessions with the Aegean port of Salonika and appeared ready to push their influence further into the heart of the Balkan Peninsula by finally annexing the Ottoman provinces of Bosnia and Herzegovina, administered by Vienna since 1878. As these moves violated decades-old understandings, Izvolskii thought that an opportunity had arisen to advance Russian interests at the straits though an agreement with Vienna.[14] Izvolskii and the Austrian foreign minister, Alois Lexa von Aehrenthal, met quietly in September 1908 at the latter's estate, and as far as Izvolskii later claimed to understand, the two had agreed that Russia would accept Austrian annexation of Bosnia-Herzegovina in return for Austrian support for an alteration of the regime at the straits in Russia's favor. However, before Izvolskii could gain the acceptance of the other great powers for such a change at the straits, Austria declared the annexation in October 1908, leaving Izvolskii exposed. When Russia tried to resist Vienna's move, Berlin threatened St. Petersburg with an ultimatum, forcing Russia to back down and further lose prestige and influence in the region.

The Bosnian crisis spelled the end of Izvolskii's ministry. Once the crisis had passed, Stolypin arranged for Izvolskii's removal from his ministerial post. Izvolskii's dismissal could not happen immediately in order to save face, so his departure awaited the opening of an appropriate ambassadorial post. Simultaneously, Stolypin installed as assistant foreign minister someone he could trust more fully, and who would rise to foreign minister once Izvolskii was gone. That person was Sergei D. Sazonov, Stolypin's brother-in-law, with far fewer connections and without an independent base in St. Petersburg, thus subject to Stolypin's influence. Both as assistant and, starting in November 1910, as full minister, Sazonov toed the line that the prime minister set out: an avoidance of foreign tension in order to preserve the peace that Russia needed to continue its rebuilding. Indeed, an examination of Sazonov's tenure through the outbreak of the world war, even after Stolypin's assassination in September 1911, reveals that he assiduously sought to prevent discussion of the Turkish Straits whenever a crisis around the Ottoman Empire emerged. Russia was at the time too weak to ensure that an alteration in the straits regime would occur along lines that Russia desired, so Sazonov sought to prevent any change until Russia was strong again.[15]

Yet while not at this point seeking a change at the straits, Russia did attempt to influence the Ottoman Empire on a couple of occasions between 1912 and 1914, as diplomatic tensions increased across Europe. In trying to defend its interests, Russia sought the cooperation of France, because Russian pressure alone rarely succeeded in persuading the Porte to change policy. France, with its significant investment in the Ottoman economy, possessed levers of influence that Russia did not have, and St. Petersburg hoped its ally would assist in pressuring the Porte to change its ways. Paris, however, was rarely willing to do so.

The Balkan Wars of 1912–13 exposed the first rift within the Franco-Russian Alliance over Ottoman affairs. During the First Balkan War, Montenegro, Serbia, Bulgaria, and Greece attacked Ottoman forces, seeking to push the Ottoman Empire out of the Balkan Peninsula.[16] In this conflict, the Bulgarian army met unanticipated success against Ottoman forces. Their victory was becoming so complete by late October 1912 and again in March 1913 that the Russian government grew very concerned that the Bulgarians might seize Constantinople. This possibility the Russians could not allow, as interested as they were in preventing any state but the Ottoman Empire or their own from controlling the Turkish Straits and in allowing no other leader but the tsar the honor of bringing Constantinople back under Christian rule. St. Petersburg thus sought any enticement it could find to hold back the Bulgarians. One tack the Russians took in the spring of 1913 to persuade Sofia to keep its forces out of the Ottoman capital was to gain the great powers' acceptance of an Ottoman indemnity for Bulgaria. In mid-March 1913, Bulgarian envoys had requested support from St. Petersburg for a revision of the Bulgarian-Ottoman border along with an indemnity, a typical levy forced on a losing power.[17] Foreign Minister Sazonov hoped that once the powers promised such compensation to Sofia, Bulgaria would accept an armistice and relinquish the intention of attacking Constantinople. Although the revised borderline through Thrace had received easy approval, France in particular reacted hostilely to the indemnity.

Already afraid that these new changes to the arrangements of the Ambassadorial Conference of the great powers in London would lead Vienna to put forward demands serving its own interests, Paris felt that such an addition to the Ottoman Empire's financial burden directly affected France's own interests in the Ottoman Empire.[18] France carried 45 percent of the Ottoman debt and had huge capital investments there, so the French particularly feared the Ottoman Empire going bankrupt under an added burden.[19] The French furthermore posited that other powers, especially Germany, would surely resist if an indemnity were imposed on the Ottomans. French diplomats argued that the Germans would make use of this pressure to present itself as a better friend of the Sublime Porte.[20] As much as Sazonov insisted on meeting the Bulgarians on this issue, the French would only agree to allow the commission in Paris in charge of the Ottoman debt to examine the issue after the war.

In late March 1913, Russia pondered the merits of a unilateral dispatch of a flotilla to the Bosporus, ready to deploy to Constantinople if Ottoman power in the capital should collapse. While the British government implicitly opened the door to whatever action the Russians thought necessary, the French were panicked by the thought of such a Russian coup.[21] The French were suspicious of what Russia might do once it was in actual possession of the Ottoman capital and how that might affect the French position there. The French ambassador to London, Paul Cambon, strongly opposed allowing Russia to act in a way that would leave it in control of Constantinople. In March he spoke of an international force to occupy Constantinople to avoid a unilateral Russian occupation, and then he derided H. H. Asquith, the British prime minister, and Andrew Bonar Law, the opposition leader, who opposed the ambassador's suggestions, as "being led astray by their classical memories" when they resisted protecting the Ottomans in a way that was reminiscent of Disraeli's policies.[22] At the beginning of April, Cambon told the British foreign secretary, Sir Edward Grey, that "Russia could not be left to go to Constantinople alone."[23] Indeed, the French may not have hidden their concerns about Russian designs on Constantinople from St. Petersburg. As early as November 1912, Sazonov complained to Izvolskii, then the Russian ambassador to Paris, of his suspicions that the French were trying to encourage the Bulgarians to take the city.[24]

In the Second Balkan War, the Russians again turned to the French for help, but now in opposition to the Ottomans, who had joined Bulgaria's erstwhile allies in a redivision of the spoils of the war. It appeared during the summer of 1913 that the Ottomans might be able to reconquer lands predominantly populated by Christians, a turn of events that above all the Russians were unwilling to countenance. While it is unclear who suggested it, Sazonov fastened onto the idea of a great-power financial boycott of the Ottoman Empire that would force it to cooperate with the powers. France was the only power to oppose this strategy.

Paris and St. Petersburg became the poles of a debate over such a boycott.[25] The French insisted that Ottoman debt was a European concern, and Paris could not act without cooperation from the other powers with investments and interests in the empire. Cambon observed in late July 1913 that "the European financial world would not permit the governments to drive Turkey to bankruptcy."[26] The French pointed to fears that if they acted unilaterally, other nations, especially Germany, might fill the gap left by the French. Paris first tried to suggest that contracts were private, so the French government could not interfere.[27] The French then claimed that even if they were to seek approval of the council in charge of the Régie des Tabacs, the Germans and the Austrians on the council would never go along with such a step.[28]

Sazonov countered these strokes as they arrived. His own advisors had examined the possibility of others profiting at France's expense and denied that either minor powers or the United States would take advantage of the French withdrawal. The Germans themselves indicated that Berlin was prepared to join a boycott.[29] As to the lack of cooperation by the Germanic powers on the council, both the Austrian and the German ambassadors in St. Petersburg told Sazonov that France dominated the committee, and Vienna and Berlin would be willing to act on the council in a manner compatible with Sazonov's suggestions.[30] This Franco-Russian spar over the boycott reveals that France, via its many excuses and claims, was the real obstacle to Russian attempts to influence the Ottomans. Moreover, the dispute shows that the Central Powers had some success at using this issue to drive a wedge between the two allies.[31] Ultimately, the French dragged their heels long enough to undermine Russian attempts at employing such a means against Constantinople.

Another example of Franco-Russian disagreement relates to the growing naval race between Russia and the Ottoman Empire on the

Black Sea.[32] After the Young Turk coup in Constantinople in 1908, the Ottoman government applied itself more seriously to the task of improving its armed forces. For the navy, this meant the acquisition of modern warships, including the new dreadnought-class battleships, introduced by the British in 1906 as a quantum advance in firepower, armor, and speed. Everything else afloat was obsolete in comparison, or so it seemed at the time. The Ottomans did not try to build such boats themselves but instead sought them abroad, either by ordering their own built from scratch or by purchasing those already under construction for other states. Such boats could then be sailed by the Ottomans into the Black Sea. Both the Russian navy and the Russian Foreign Ministry feared such a development, because the Russians could only build compensating dreadnoughts in their Black Sea shipyards.[33] The relevant international agreements still prohibited other states from sailing warships through the Turkish Straits, thus preventing St. Petersburg from adopting the same purchasing strategy as Constantinople. While the Russians tried to compensate by improving their Black Sea shipyards and plowing money into new construction, such a method promised no results before the Ottomans could put their own boats in the Black Sea. Therefore, the Russians also tried to deny the Ottomans the boats that they sought. On the one hand, they sought cooperation from the British in slowing the completion of the ships under construction in Britain. London officially demurred but was able to slow the completion of two dreadnoughts nearly finished so that at the start of the war they were still in the shipyards and sequestered by the Royal Navy.[34] Less successfully, Sazonov complained about continuing French loans to the Ottomans. He claimed that this money was facilitating the new Ottoman acquisitions. The French denied that these transactions were having an effect, shortsightedly noting that the Ottoman Empire had to use their first tranche to pay off their debt from the Balkan Wars, while the second tranche would depend on the maintenance of the peace.[35] The French were also convinced that if they held their funds back, the Germans would step in to fill the Ottomans' needs, thereby gaining even more influence over the Porte.[36] Sazonov had never succeeded in obtaining French financial support for his external policies toward the Ottoman Empire, and this case was no exception.

Once the First World War had begun and the Ottoman Empire had entered the conflict at the end of October 1914, the focus of Russian policy moved from pressure to partition. With war under way, the Stolypinesque caution could be put definitively aside. It had long been the religious dream of the Russians to put the cross back on top of the Hagia Sophia in Constantinople, but the secular goal of control over the Turkish Straits that would ensure the economic and military security of Russia had grown in importance through the long nineteenth century. For those in Russia who cared about war aims, no prize was more attractive. For Foreign Minister Sazonov, seizure of this territory was to happen "now or never."[37] By March 1915, with the Anglo-French operation at the Dardanelles (and ultimately Gallipoli) under way, Sazonov put forth Russian claims. The Russians sought both Constantinople and nearly the whole of the straits for themselves. Petrograd (as St. Petersburg was now known) expected the British to resist, still believing that London was committed to keeping the Russians out of the eastern Mediterranean Sea in the tradition of the great foreign secretaries Palmerston and Salisbury. The talk in the foreign ministry was that they would need French help to persuade Great Britain to change its policy.[38] More than a decade earlier, however, the British had already decided that they no longer needed the straits closed to maintain the security of the Suez Canal and other British interests in the region. They therefore quickly informed Petrograd of their assent to the Russian claim, requiring only that Russia cooperate with the as yet undetermined British claims in the rest of the Ottoman Empire and assuming that the war was seen through to victory.[39]

Instead, the real trouble came from the French. Paris was very concerned about the impact of an extension of Russian power on its economic interests in the Ottoman capital and hinterland. Paris also feared that Russian control of the straits would allow the projection of Russian naval power into the eastern Mediterranean, a region in which the French too had special interests. Privy to the details of Russian naval planning before the war, the French knew that the Russians possessed plans for a blue-water navy. Such a fleet, able to shelter in Russian Black Sea ports or Constantinople, could fundamentally alter the balance of power in the region. So concerned was Paris about this possible shift that Raymond Poincaré, the French president, wrote an unusual, direct letter to the French ambassador in which he said,

> The possession of Constantinople and its vicinity would not only give Russia a sort of privilege in the inheritance of the Ottoman Empire. It would introduce her, via the Mediterranean, into the concert of Western nations, and this would give her, via the open sea, the chance to become a great naval power. Everything would thus be changed in the European equilibrium. Such an enlargement and such added strength would only be acceptable to us if we would ourselves

receive the same benefits of war. Everything is thus inevitably linked. We can agree to the Russian desires only in proportion to the satisfactions that we ourselves receive.[40]

In short, Poincaré argued that Russian control of the Turkish Straits would completely upset the European balance of power, which the French expected to dominate after the defeat of Germany. The French thus used various stratagems to avoid the dispatch of an acceptance of the Russian demands. This temporizing frustrated Petrograd, and Sazonov pressed Paris to come in line with the British.[41] During one argument with Maurice Paléologue, the French ambassador to the tsar, over the neutralization of the straits, an exasperated Sazonov threatened Paléologue that if the Russian demands were not accepted, he would immediately tender his resignation to Nicholas II. The implied threat was that the next minister might not have the commitment to the unified war effort that Sazonov possessed and thus could be more receptive to a separate-peace proposal by the Central Powers.[42] Almost two weeks later, Sazonov told the British ambassador, Sir George Buchanan, that the line of Paléologue's negotiation "had made a very bad impression and a comparison was being drawn between the manner in which the French and British Govts. [sic] treated various questions connected with Constantinople and the Straits, much to the disadvantage of the former."[43] By the end of the first week of April, fearing that further delay might cause Sazonov to make good his threat, the French approved the Russian measure.[44] With Paris's acquiescence, Russia at last stood on the verge of realizing its epochal aspiration: Russian possession of Constantinople and the straits with European support. The dream would become reality once the Entente powers had won the war. However, victory was not yet in their grasp, as the fighting and the diplomatic wrangling continued.

These promises given by the British and the French were predicated on Russia accepting Allied desires elsewhere in the Ottoman Empire. London, especially, began to sort out exactly what it desired in the lands south of Anatolia. Here British and French interests more directly clashed. In the southwest, the British sought to provide the greatest possible buffer for the defense of the Suez Canal, while the French sought to claim control over a "Syria" that Paris defined as reaching all the way through Palestine to the edge of the Sinai Peninsula. In the east, there was disagreement over who would get northern Mesopotamian areas, such as Mosul.[45] The resolution of the latter concerns was in the end left to Sir Mark Sykes and François Georges-Picot, English and French diplomats with experience in the Middle East. Before these historic exchanges took place, however, the Franco-Russian argument over Palestine presented another rancorous debate over the post-Ottoman future.

From the first discussions with the Russians in the fall of 1914 through the tense negotiations over the Russian demands in March 1915, Paris sought to steal a march on London, by trying to convince Petrograd to side with France on its objectives. In mid-November 1914, in the context of preliminary discussions about war aims soon after the Ottoman Empire had entered the war, Paléologue used the occasion to describe to the tsar French interests in general by referring to France's long interest in Syria and Palestine. The ambassador asked Nicholas II if he would oppose France taking the measures it believed necessary to protect its "patrimony" in the region. He received a laconic "certainly not" in reply.[46] Théophile Delcassé, the French foreign minister, echoed his ambassador in January 1915, when he too referred to French interests in those two regions, though he conceded that no one European power could control Palestine alone.[47]

Paléologue returned to the theme during the March 1915 negotiations over the straits with the Russian Foreign Ministry and the tsar. On his way to see Nicholas, Paléologue told the assistant foreign minister that he believed Syria included Palestine, but the official refused to accept the claim.[48] The ambassador said the same to the tsar, insisting that Syria's border stretched to the Egyptian frontier, thus including Palestine, in which relevant nineteenth-century statutes would protect the holy places. He also put forward specific lines of territory to include Cilicia in the north. Afterward, Paléologue met with Sazonov to seek Russia's acceptance of French possession of Cilicia and a Syria that included Palestine. While the tsar remained noncommittal, Sazonov refused to allow any thought of another Christian power having full control over the holy sites, even making a veiled threat by referring to past conflicts, telling the ambassador: "You know how Russian opinion is sensitive to religious questions. Remember that the Crimean War had its origin in the argument over the holy places."[49] Sazonov was so disturbed that he wrote his own ambassador in Paris to learn whether the French government really felt the way Paléologue implied.[50] Izvolskii replied that Delcassé thought that France might seek some specific parts of Palestine but that as Sazonov suggested, serious discussion was still required regarding the holy places.[51]

Indeed, concerned as the British and the French were about the possibility of a Russian separate peace with Germany, Sazonov's reference to the Crimean War must have been especially alarming. If the French were trying to present a fait accompli to the British, they utterly failed given this Russian resistance and the fact that the Russians informed the British of Paléologue's proposition. The Russians themselves suggested internationalization of the holy places to the British, the solution eventually adopted by the Sykes-Picot Agreement.[52] Even in these early negotiations about the postwar disposition of Ottoman territories, the differences between Russia and France were clear. That Sazonov should escalate to threats so quickly indicates how seriously the Russian government took these questions, now that the whole of the Ottoman corpse appeared ready for dismemberment. France furthermore appears to have tried to separate Russia from Great Britain during the March negotiations over the straits, perhaps in an effort to strengthen its play for Palestine. Early in March 1915, Delcassé led Izvolskii to believe that the key to resolving the straits question lay in London and that while Delcassé would do all he could to meet Russia's wishes, the British Cabinet stood opposed.[53] In further conversation, Delcassé, trying to convince Izvolskii that the straits would need to remain unfortified, noted that Russia's establishment on the Asiatic coast of the straits "depend[ed] on the resolution of yet another question, the question of the partition of the Asian possessions of Turkey."[54] Delcassé perhaps hoped that were Petrograd to believe that the French were being more cooperative than the British, the tsar might accept the French desires in Palestine. The Russians, under little illusion about the real obstacle—the French—remained unsympathetic to Paris's views. The Russian position was helpful to the British, who themselves were thinking about the postwar Middle East. The British appear to have expected Anglo-French rivalry to reemerge after the war and so thought about limiting French territorial gains in the Middle East and at the same time protecting their strategic position in the eastern Mediterranean.[55] Early British discussions in fact considered seizing the whole coast from Egypt to Alexandretta, just south of modern Turkey, but the politicians understood that this was politically impossible. Keeping Palestine out of French hands, however, came to assume increasing strategic significance, and the Russian attitude made that easier.

Interestingly, in late March 1916, as the negotiations in Petrograd over changes to the Sykes-Picot Agreement initialed in London were concluding, Paléologue again sought Sazonov's acceptance of a French

Palestine, with the proviso that the holy sites would have an international regime. Under those circumstances, Sazonov was willing to support the change if France could get British approval. This however was a nonstarter, as Sazonov likely expected, and internationalization remained the plan. The archives have still not clarified if this was an independent attempt on Paléologue's part or something suggested by Paris, but either way it could only have further raised suspicions about the French.[56]

As for the arrangement of territory in the eastern Ottoman Empire, the Russians had a position to stake out here too, but these talks progressed with some, if less, conflict. In approximately six weeks in late 1915, British and French diplomats, led by Sir Mark Sykes, who had been Lord Kitchener's man on the committee that had done preliminary work on British interests in the region, and the English-speaking François Georges-Picot, briefly consul-general in Beirut, hammered out the agreement that was to carry their names.[57] According to the agreement initialed on 3 January 1916, France and Great Britain both gained areas that they would directly control (for France this was a crescent from northern Galilee through Lebanon and the Syrian coast, through Cilicia to the Persian border; for Britain this was central and southern Mesopotamia and the northern coast of Arabia with the port of Haifa to serve as a railhead and naval station).[58] The two countries then were to have zones of influence over northern parts of the forecast Arab state, the legendary zones A and B. Central Palestine, containing the holy sites, was to be under international administration.

Once they had accomplished this draft partition, the two men brought the document to Russia for approval. The changes that the Russians made give us a better sense of Petrograd's concerns at the time. The primary change that Sazonov effected was to exchange territory with France. While France sought a band of territory that would run all the way to the Persian border, leaving all of Armenia to the Russians, Petrograd insisted on taking that French territory along the Persian border and in northern Kurdistan in exchange for western Armenia. On seeing the draft for the first time, Sazonov manifested extreme surprise, saying that he had "never foreseen the establishment of France on the frontiers of Persia."[59] In April and May 1916, France and Great Britain accepted the Russian changes, and the agreement as a whole was ratified in October 1916. Clearly, Russian security was paramount in Petrograd's decisions. On top of the insistence on full possession of the straits with the ability to fortify them, Russia kept France farther from the borders of the Russian Empire as well as mostly from Persia, in the northern part of which Russia was increasingly influential.

Subordinated to taking control of the straits region and preventing France from approaching Russian-dominated borderlands was the fate of the Armenians.[60] While Sazonov's initial reaction to seeing the draft document included concern about the treatment of the Armenians, and the tsar said something similar a couple of days later, this may have been just a ploy to buy time for the Russians to deliberate over the proposal.[61] In March 1915, Nicholas II had told Paléologue that he wondered if it would not be possible to guarantee autonomy for the Armenians under the nominal sovereignty of the Ottomans, and almost exactly a year later, the tsar told the ambassador that he had never dreamed of conquering Armenia, save for strategic areas such as Erzerum and Trebizond.[62] In a meeting on the subject with the relevant ministers, Sazonov explained that such a division was warranted based on the topography and religious differences among the Armenians in the region.[63] Reynolds argues, furthermore, that Sykes also supported such a redistribution of the Armenian lands by suggesting that this arrangement would put the center of gravity of Armenian nationalism in the French areas and that the territory Russia would take had in fact been largely stripped of its Armenian population by Ottoman actions and disease.[64] In the end, the Russians preferred splitting Armenia between themselves and the French in order to take as much of the French zone along the Persian border as possible, keeping a major European power farther from Russia itself.

This essay reveals the high level of tension that existed within the Franco-Russian Alliance, both in peacetime and in war. The Eastern Question was central to those tensions, obscured until now by foci on the other allies and topics of greater concern to them. Nevertheless, divergent interests in the Ottoman Empire presented here were not enough to destroy the alliance, even as the Germans offered cooperation in Sazonov's desired financial boycott of the Ottoman Empire in 1913 and during the world war dangled a promise of Constantinople before Russia to lure it away. The tsar and his foreign minister remained faithful to their ally and do not appear ever to have given serious thought to a separate peace. While frustration was common for St. Petersburg before the war, one wonders whether the Russians were not just tremendously successful in successive games of chicken with the French and the British during the war, and had the British foreign secretary or French foreign minister been more stubborn whether Sazonov might have made concessions. Regarding the straits, at least, that is doubtful, given Sazonov's belief that this was Russia's one real chance to seize them. In the other areas, it is less clear that Russian diplomats did not simply outlast allied negotiators. Russia made the most of its strong negotiating position to protect its interests during the war, which, bigger failings aside, reflects well on Russia's wartime diplomacy. Russia's success during the war, in contrast with its regular frustration in its dealings with France before the war, speaks to its better bargaining position once the French were dependent on the Russian war effort for their national survival. Though tension grew over the last years before the outbreak of war in 1914, the stakes were not yet high enough for Paris to sacrifice central interests. After 1914, with Germany in occupation of an important swathe of French territory, the situation had changed.

Overall, these cases also make clear what the French and Russian governments felt to be core strategic interests. For France, its financial and economic position in the Ottoman Empire was crucial. Government, enterprises, and individuals were well invested in the eastern empire, and Paris sought to ensure the security of this important income and influence. Implicitly before the war, then explicitly from 1914 onward, France also was interested in the fate of the physical Ottoman territories, not just for their financial value but also for their utility in extending French influence as it expected to reassume the role of predominant European power. The Russians, too, were interested in imperial expansion, with attention always centered on the Turkish Straits. Gaining this exit to the open seas seemed to promise economic security as well as military advantage. Furthermore, Russia desired neither to have France too close to the Caucasian borderlands nor to allow it substantive access to Persia, where Russia was trying to develop its influence, and this influence trumped its purported concern for its fellow Christians, the Armenians. This suggests that had the alliance succeeded in its primary objective of resisting and defeating the Germans, it would not have lasted long into the postwar period, as the divergent interests of the two empires drew Paris and Petrograd into a rivalry that only wartime necessity kept at bay. Thus regardless of the Bolshevik revolution, the struggle over the fate of Ottoman domains was destined to continue well into the twentieth century.

NOTES

Research for this paper was funded in part by a grant from the International Research and Exchanges Board (IREX), with funds provided by the National

Endowment for the Humanities and the US Department of State. Funding for research was also provided by the following divisions of Duke University: the Graduate School, the History Department, the Center for Slavic, Eurasian, and East European Studies, and the Center for International Studies; and of Wake Forest University: the Griffin Fund of the History Department and the Archie Fund for Arts and Humanities. The author also thanks the editors of the volume, Mara Kozelsky and Lucien J. Frary, as well as participants in a session on this volume at the 2012 meeting of the ASEEES, for their helpful suggestions.

Dates in this paper follow the Gregorian calendar, not the Julian calendar still in use in Russia at the time.

1. See most notably, George F. Kennan, *The Fateful Alliance* (New York: Pantheon, 1984); I. S. Rybachenok, *Soiuz s Frantsiei vo vneshnei politike Rossii v kontse XIX v.* (Moscow: Institut istorii SSSR AN SSSR, 1993); Anne Hogenhuis-Seliverstoff, *Une Alliance Franco-Russe* (Brussels: Bruylant, 1997); William L. Langer, *The Franco-Russian Alliance, 1890-1894* (Cambridge, MA: Harvard University Press, 1929); and Boris Nolde, *L'alliance franco-russe: Les origines du systeme diplomatique d'avant-guerre* (Paris: Droz, 1936). But see also Georges Michon, *L'alliance franco-russe, 1891-1917* (Paris: Delpeuch, 1927) for a longer view.

2. See, for example, Dietrich Geyer, *Russian Imperialism* (New Haven, CT: Yale University Press, 1987); John P. Sontag, "Tsarist Debts and Tsarist Foreign Policy," *Slavic Review* 27 (1968): 529-41; and D. W. Spring, "Russia and the Franco-Russian Alliance, 1905-14," *Slavonic and East European Review* 66 (1988): 562-92.

3. On the war in general, see, for example, David Stevenson, *The First World War and International Politics* (Oxford: Oxford University Press, 1988); V. A. Emets, *Ocherki vneshnei politiki Rossii v period pervoi mirovoi voiny: Vzaimootnosheniia Rossii s soiuznikami po voprosam vedeniia voiny* (Moscow: Nauka, 1977); Z. A. B. Zeman, *A Diplomatic History of the First World War* (London: Weidenfeld and Nicolson, 1971); W. W. Gottlieb, *Studies in Secret Diplomacy during the First World War* (London: George Allen and Unwin, 1957).

4. Geoffrey Miller, *Straits: British Policy towards the Ottoman Empire and the Origins of the Dardanelles Campaign* (Hull: University of Hull Press, 1997); Zara S. Steiner and Keith Neilson, *Britain and the Origins of the First World War*, 2nd ed. (New York: Palgrave Macmillan, 2003).

5. See, for example, F. W. Brecher, "French Policy toward the Levant 1914-18," *Middle Eastern Studies* 29, no. 4 (October 1993): 641-63; Stevenson, *First World War and International Politics*,130; Emets, *Ocherki*, 148; A. V. Ignat'ev, ed., *Istoriia vneshnei politiki Rossii: Konets XIX-nachalo XX veka* (Moscow: Mezhdunarodnye otnosheniia, 1997), 523-24; and Edward Peter Fitzgerald, "France's Middle Eastern Ambitions, the Sykes-Picot Negotiations, and the Oil Fields of Mosul, 1915-1918," *Journal of Modern History* 66, no. 4 (1994): 697-725. Exceptions are Dmitri L. Shevelev, "K istorii zakliucheniia soglasheniia o razdele aziatskikh territorii osmanskoi imperii 1916 g.," *Vostok* 5 (2001): 39-43; Michael

A. Reynolds, *Shattering Empires: The Clash and Collapse of the Ottoman and Russian Empires, 1908-1918* (Cambridge: Cambridge University Press, 2011), 140-41; and especially Sean McMeekin, *The Russian Origins of the First World War* (Cambridge, MA: Harvard University Press, 2011), 194-213.

6. Reynolds, *Shattering Empires*; and McMeekin, *Russian Origins*.
7. McMeekin, *Russian Origins*, 11.
8. Zara Steiner, "On Writing International History: Chaps, Maps and Much More," *International Affairs* 73, no. 3 (July 1997): 531-46, esp. 533.
9. Ibid., 545.
10. David M. Goldfrank, *The Origins of the Crimean War* (London: Longman, 1994).
11. Jonathan Steinberg, *Bismarck: A Life* (Oxford: Oxford University Press, 2011), 328-29.
12. In 1904, the British and the French reached a set of agreements that resolved some of the most intractable colonial disputes that had plagued the two empires during the nineteenth century. Britain's influence over Egypt and France's over Morocco were recognized. Siam was understood to be a buffer between the two empires in Southeast Asia. Canadian differences were resolved as well. The Russians were less interested in an understanding until their defeat at the hands of Japan in 1905. After this, with the encouragement of the French, the British and the Russians agreed to divide Persia into two zones of influence separated by a neutral zone, and special British interests in Afghanistan and Tibet were recognized. On the conclusion of the ententes, see Christopher Andrew, *Théophile Delcassé and the Making of the Entente Cordiale: A Reappraisal of French Foreign Policy, 1898-1905* (London: Macmillan, 1968); Steiner and Neilson, *Britain and the Origins*, 30-32, 84-92; I. V. Bestuzhev, *Bor'ba v Rossii po voprosam vneshnei politiki 1906-1910* (Moscow: Izd-vo AN SSSR, 1961), 127-50; Samuel R. Williamson Jr., *The Politics of Grand Strategy: Britain and France Prepare for War, 1904-1914* (London: Ashfield, 1990), 1-29; M. B. Hayne, *The French Foreign Office and the Origins of the First World War, 1898-1914* (Oxford: Clarendon Press, 1993), chaps. 2-8; and George Monger, *The End of Isolation: British Foreign Policy, 1900-1907* (London: Thomas Nelson, 1963).
13. David MacLaren McDonald, *United Government and Foreign Policy in Russia, 1900-1914* (Cambridge, MA: Harvard University Press, 1992), 103-26. See also Abraham Ascher, *P. A. Stolypin: The Search for Stability in Late Imperial Russia* (Stanford, CA: Stanford University Press, 2001); and Fiona Tomaszewski, *A Great Russia: Russia and the Triple Entente, 1905-1914* (Westport, CT: Praeger, 2002).
14. D. C. B. Lieven, *Russia and the Origins of the First World War* (London: Macmillan, 1983), 37. On the Bosnian crisis, see Lieven, *Russia*, 33-37; David Stevenson, *Armaments and the Coming of War, Europe 1904-1914* (Oxford: Clarendon Press, 1996), 112-22; Samuel R. Williamson Jr., *Austria-Hungary and the Origins of the First World War* (New York: St. Martin's, 1991), 69-72; Luigi

Albertini, *The Origins of the War of 1914*, trans. Isabella M. Massey, 3 vols. (London: Oxford, 1952-57), 2:190-300.

15. See Ronald P. Bobroff, *Roads to Glory: Late Imperial Russia and the Turkish Straits* (London: I. B. Tauris, 2006), 19.

16. On Russian policy toward the straits during the Balkan Wars more generally, see Bobroff, "The Balkan Wars: Choosing between the Balkan States and the Straits," chap. 3 in *Roads to Glory*. See also Ernst C. Helmreich, *The Diplomacy of the Balkan Wars, 1912-1913* (Cambridge, MA: Harvard University Press, 1938); Edward C. Thaden, *Russia and the Balkan Alliance of 1912* (University Park: Pennsylvania State University Press, 1965); Stevenson, *Armaments*; Richard C. Hall, *The Balkan Wars, 1912-1913* (London: Routledge, 2000); and McMeekin, *Russian Origins*, 21-27.

17. Sazonov to Benckendorff, 22 March 1913, tel. 680, in *Der diplomatische Schriftwechsel Iswolskis, 1911-1914, aus dem Geheimakten der russischen Staatarchiv*, ed. Friedrich Stieve (Berlin: Deutsche Verlagsgesellschaft für Politik und Geschichte, 1926) (hereafter cited as *DSI*), 3, no. 783.

18. Izvolskii to Sazonov, 31 March 1913, tel. 139, *Un Livre Noir: Diplomatie d'avant guerre d'après les documents des archives russes, novembre 1910-juillet, 1914*, ed. René Marchand, 3 vols. (Paris: Librarie du Travail, 1922-34) (hereafter cited as *LN*), 2:59.

19. Note de Directeur des Affaires politiques (Paléologue), 7 April 1913, France, Ministrère des Affaires Etrangères, *Documents diplomatiques français (1871-1914)* 2e et 3e série (Paris: Impr. Nationale, 1929-54) (hereafter cited as *DDF*), 3.6, no. 222.

20. Ibid.

21. On the British side, see Grey to Bertie, 3 April 1913, ltr. 235, *British Documents on the Origins of the War 1898-1914*, ed. G. P. Gooch and Harold Temperley, 11 vols. (London: H. M. Stationary Office, 1926-38) [hereafter cited as *BD*], 9.2, no. 800; Benckendorff to Sazonov, 3 April 1913, tel. 298, RGIA, f. 1276, op. 9, d. 600, l. 6; and Benckendorff to Sazonov, 3 April 1913, tel. 301, RGIA, f. 1276, op. 9, d. 600, l. 7.

22. Cambon to Pichon, 6 April 1913, dep. 197, *DDF*, 3.6, no. 216.

23. Grey to Bertie, 1 April 1913, ltr. 232, *BD*, 9.2, no. 783.

24. Sazonov to Izvolskii, 8 November 1913, tel. 2502, AVPRI, f. 151, op. 482, d. 130, l. 110.

25. Bobroff, *Roads to Glory*, 68-70.

26. P. Cambon to Pichon, 21 July 1913, tels. 204, 205, *DDF*, 3.7, no. 433. See also P. Cambon to Pichon, 18 July 1913, tels. 199, 200, *DDF*, 3.7, no. 412.

27. P. Cambon to Pichon, 24 July 1913, dep. 436, *DDF*, 3.7, no. 465.

28. Izvolskii to Sazonov, 12 August 1913, tel. 396, *Materialy po istorii franko-russkikh otnoshenii za 1910-1914 gg.* (Moscow: Izd. Narodnogo komissariata po inostrannym delam, 1922), 398-99; and *LN*, 2:120. See also Pichon to Delcassé, 12 August 1913, tel. 860 and 860 bis, *DDF*, 3.8, no. 13; and the departmental

source for Pichon's note in Note du Département, 11 August 1913, *DDF*, 3.8, no. 1.

29. Sazonov to Izvolskii, 20 August 1913, tel. 2338, *LN*, 2:136-37 and incorrectly numbered as tel. 2238 in *Materialy po istorii*, 410-11. Bronevskii to Sazonov, 11 August 1913, tel. 201, AVPRI, f. 151, op. 482, d. 3715, l. 107. More than a willingness to put pressure on the Ottomans, with whom the Germans were trying to gain favor, this enthusiasm to cooperate with St. Petersburg is more likely another case of Berlin attempting to use the differences within the Franco-Russian Alliance by siding with Russia against France, in the hopes of drawing Russia out.

30. Sazonov to Izvolskii, 21 August 1913, ltr. 777, in *Materialy po istorii*, 411; and *LN*, 2:137-38. In contrast, Germany showed less willingness to follow such a course when speaking with other powers. See Goschen to Grey, 20 August 1913, disp. 301, *BD*, 9.2, no. 1248; and Helmreich, *Diplomacy of the Balkan Wars*, 401, who does not consult the Russian document, so misses the double game that the Central Powers appear to play here, and which Sazonov detects, as he notes in this letter to Izvolskii.

31. Bertie to Grey, 26 July 1913, tel. 101, *BD*, 9.2, no. 1180 and minutes; Sazonov to Izvolskii, 1 August 1913, tel. 2194, in *Materialy po istorii*, 396, and *LN*, 2:116.

32. See K. F. Shatsillo, *Russkii imperializm i razvitie flota nakanune pervoi mirovoi voiny (1906-1914)* (Moscow: Nauka, 1968); McMeekin, *Russian Origins*, 33-40.

33. McMeekin misses both Navy Minister I. K. Grigorovich's late conversion to concern over the Turkish buildup and the French financial role in the Ottoman purchases of capital ships. McMeekin, *Russian Origins*, 34-37; and Bobroff, *Roads*, 76-95.

34. Benckendorff to Sazonov, 12 June 1914, tel. 149, in *Entente Diplomacy and the World: Matrix of the History of Europe, 1909-1914*, ed. G. A. Schreiner (London: Knickerbocker, 1921), no. 853; Miller, *Straits*, 200-201.

35. Doumergue to Paléologue, 23 April 1914, tels. 193, 194, *DDF*, 3.10, no. 147.

36. Boppe to Doumergue, 25 January 1914, tels. 56, 57, *DDF*, 3.9, no. 152.

37. G. N. Mikhailovskii, *Zapiski: Iz istorii rossiiskogo vneshnepoliticheskogo vedomstva, 1914-1920 gg.*, 2 vols. (Moscow: Mezhdunarodnye otnosheniia, 1993), 1:87. McMeekin, *Russian Origins*, 98-111, glosses over the fact that the Russians did not make demands on the Ottoman Empire, and Sazonov tried to keep the Ottoman Empire *out* of the war until the Ottomans actually entered the war in October 1914. See also, Bobroff, *Roads*, 96-115. On Ottoman entry, see Reynolds, *Shattering Empires*, 108-14. While McMeekin suggests that a desire for capturing the straits defines virtually every decision any Russian leader made in 1914, including in the July crisis and the months before Ottoman entry, Reynolds, *Shattering Empires*, 115, with more subtlety, correctly notes that the

Russians "who preferred to keep the Ottomans out of the war did so because they believed that it was more important to concentrate on defeating Germany, not because they lacked ambitions in the Ottoman lands."

38. Mikhailovskii, *Zapiski*, 1:85-88, and Paléologue to Delcassé, 4 March 1915, tel. 367, Archives de Ministère des Affaires Etrangères (hereafter cited as MAE) Pa-ap 211 Delcassé, v. 25, p. 94.

39. Steiner and Neilson, *Britain and the Origins*, 87; Marian Kent, "Constantinople and Asiatic Turkey, 1905-1914," in *British Foreign Policy under Sir Edward Grey*, ed. F. H. Hinsley (Cambridge: Cambridge University Press, 1977), 156; Miller, *Straits*, 11; and Monger, *End of Isolation*, 116-17. McMeekin, *Russian Origins*, 120-31, misses this earlier conversion of the British and spends much more time discussing London's part in this than in examining the strong French resistance.

40. Poincaré to Paléologue, 9 March 1915, ltr., *DDF*, 1915 t. 1 (Brussels: P. I. E.-Peter Lang, 2002), no. 320.

41. Sazonov to Izvolskii, 23 March 1915, tel. 1315, in *Konstantinopol i prolivy: Po sekretnym dokumentam b. Ministerstva inostrannykh del*, ed. E. A. Adamova, 2 vols. (Moscow: Izdanie Litizdata NKID, 1925-26), vol. 1, no. 88; and Sazonov to Izvolskii, 3 April 1915, tel. 1518, in *Konstantinopol i prolivy*, vol. 1, no. 95.

42. Diary of Foreign Ministry, 5 March 1915, in *Mezhdunarodnye otnosheniia v epokhu imperializma: Dokumenty iz arkhivov tsarskogo i Vremennogo pravitel'stv, 1878-1917 gg.* (Moscow: Gos. Sots-Econ. Izd, 1931), 7.1, no. 312; Paléologue to Delcassé, 5 March 1915, tel. 374, Hoover Institution Archives (hereafter cited as HI), Basily MSS.; Buchanan to Grey, 5 March 1915, tel. 257, TNA FO 371/2481/26072.

43. Buchanan to Grey, 3/17/15, tel. 314, TNA FO 371/2449/30806.

44. Bertie to Grey, 10 March 1915, tel. 87, TNA FO 371/2449/25014/28338; Bertie to Grey, 11 March 1915, tel., TNA FO 371/2449/25014/28458; and "Verbal'naia nota frantsuzskogo posol'stva v Petrograde ministru inostrannykh del," 10 April 1915, *Konstantinopol' i prolivy*, vol. 1, no. 99. See also William A. Renzi, "Great Britain, Russia, and the Straits, 1914-1915," *Journal of Modern History* 42, no. 1 (1970): 1-20.

45. See Fitzgerald, "France's Middle Eastern Ambitions."

46. Paléologue to Delcassé, 11/22/14, tels. 957-58 and 959-62, *DDF*, 1914 (Paris: Imprimerie Nationale, 1999), nos. 561, 562.

47. Izvolskii to Sazonov, 10 January 1915, tel. 740, in *Razdel aziatskoi Turtsii*, ed. E. A. Adamov (Moscow: Izd. Litizdata NKID, 1924) (hereafter cited as *RAT*), no. 3. McMeekin, *Russian Origins*, 203-4, suggests that the issue of Palestine arises in 1916 only as a "British red herring" and that Sazonov paid lip service to the concern in order to leverage Russia's own demands. He misses the longer story and Russia's real concern laid out here.

48. Neratov to Sazonov, 15 March 1915, tel. 1156, *RAT*, no. 28.

49. Paléologue to Delcassé, 17 March 1915, tels. 426–428, *DDF*, 1915, t.1, no. 358. See also Buchanan to Grey, 17 March 1915, tel. 314, TNA FO 371/2449/30806.

50. Sazonov to Izvolskii, 16 March 1915, tel. 119, AVPRI, f. 138, op. 467, d. 469/488, l. 87.

51. Izvolskii to Sazonov, 17 March 1915, tel. 140, *RAT*, no. 31.

52. Buchanan to Grey, 18 March 1915, tel. 320, TNA FO 371/2449/31923.

53. Izvolskii to Sazonov, 4 March 1915, tel. 113, in *Mezhdunarodnye otnosheniia*, 7.1, no. 305.

54. Izvolskii to Sazonov, 4 March 1915, tel. 115, in *Mezhdunarodnye otnosheniia*, 7.1, no. 307.

55. Benckendorff on 7 March 1915 wrote Sazonov that Foreign Secretary Grey feared a discussion about the partition of Asiatic Turkey given French and Italian interests, while Delcassé was pushing the topic forward. Benckendorff felt sure that there was disagreement between the British and the French on the future of Ottoman Asia and the Mediterranean Sea. Benckendorff to Sazonov, 7 March 1915, tel. 159, in *Mezhdunarodnye otnosheniia*, 7.1, p. 402n1.

56. See Paléologue to Briand, 26 March 1916, tel. 254, MAE, pa-ap 133 Paléologue, v. 3, p. 30; Paléologue to Sazonov, 26 March 1916, letter, *RAT*, no. 91; Sazonov to Paléologue, 28 March 1916, ltr. 247, *RAT*, no. 92.

57. On Georges-Picot, see Brecher, "French Policy toward the Levant"; on Sykes, see Efraim Karsh and Inari Karsh, *Empires of the Sand: The Struggle for Mastery in the Middle East, 1789–1923* (Cambridge, MA: Harvard University Press, 1999), 202; and Elie Kedourie, "Sir Mark Sykes and Palestine 1915–16," *Middle Eastern Studies* 6, no. 3 (1970): 340–41.

58. Karsh and Karsh, *Empires of the Sand*, 225.

59. Paléologue to Briand, 11 March 1916, tel. 203, MAE, pa-ap 43, Cambon, Jules, v. 79, p. 26.

60. On the Russian relationship to Armenia during the war, see especially Peter Holquist, "The Politics and Practice of the Russian Occupation of Armenia, 1915–February 1917," in *A Question of Genocide: Armenians and Turks at the End of the Ottoman Empire*, ed. Ronald Grigor Suny, Fatma Müge Göçek, and Norman M. Naimark (Oxford: Oxford University Press, 2011), 151–74; but also Reynolds, *Shattering Empires*, 140–66; and McMeekin, *Russian Origins*, 141–74.

61. Paléologue to Briand, 11 March 1916, tel. 204, MAE, pa-ap 133, Paléologue, v. 1, pp. 19–20; Paléologue to Briand, 13 March 1916, tel. 210, HI, Basily, box 9.

62. Paléologue to Briand, 13 March 1916, HI, Basily, box 9.

63. Osoboe soveshchanie, 17 March 1916, Protocol, *RAT*, no. 96. Attending were the chairman of the Council of Ministers, Stürmer; navy minister Grigorovich; Sazonov, for the army minister, Beliaev; and for the viceroy of the Caucasus, Nikol'skii. See also Sazonov to Izvolskii and Benckendorff, 17 March 1916, tel. 1098, AVPRI, f. 133, op. 470, d. 77, l. 53.

64. Reynolds, *Shattering Empires*, 141.

The Eastern Question in Turkish Republican Textbooks
Settling Old Scores with the European and the Ottoman "Other"

NAZAN ÇIÇEK

On a cold January day in 1923 in Eskişehir, a small Anatolian town near Ankara, Mustafa Kemal (Atatürk) gave a lengthy speech to the officials and notables who had gathered at the governor's office to hear him. During the address, which touched upon many pressing matters, Mustafa Kemal discussed the Lausanne Conference (1922–23), which was still in progress. He complained that despite several long and tiring sessions, there was still no good news to celebrate. He vehemently protested that "enemies" held the Ankara government responsible for a series of matters concerning many centuries of history that had nothing to do with the people of today's Turkey. "If our enemies were fair, humane, and conscientious, the problem would be solved in two days" he argued, "but we know that they are not."[1] A few days later, this time in the movie house of İzmit, a small town east of İstanbul, he repeated that the Lausanne Conference did not look promising. "Nevertheless," he added, "this is only natural, because this conference has not been trying

The Turkish Historical Society visits the Museum of Old Eastern Historical Artifacts, 15 September 1934. Those pictured, including Afet İnan, who was also Mustafa Kemal's adopted daughter, and Yusuf Akçura, were the architects of the Turkish History Thesis. (reprinted with permission from the Turkish Historical Society, file HEE-D 57-N 23-Ön Yüz)

to sort out and settle accounts that merely emerged yesterday. It has been dealing with problems that first appeared hundreds of years ago and became extremely acute recently. It is never an easy task to resolve such abstruse, profound, intricate, and corrupt matters."[2] By "enemies" and "intricate and corrupt matters," Mustafa Kemal meant Europeans and the Eastern Question, although he did not employ the term as such.

As the phrase the "Eastern Question" itself suggests, the Western world defined the East, represented by the Ottoman Empire, as a problem, and "problematized" it discursively.[3] For the Western world, the Eastern Question was, in simplest terms, the answer sought to the question of "what to do with the Turk?"[4] Could he be reformed, civilized, or even if possible Christianized? Or would it be better to leave him alone to meet his fate in his "barbaric," "backward," and "Islamic" state? Should the Ottoman Empire be supported in order to slow its possible dissolution and delay its final collapse? These questions appeared as by-products of more complicated questions of far-reaching effect that had been keeping European political decision makers busy for some time: Who (or what) would fill the vacuum in the region after the seemingly imminent collapse of the Ottoman Empire? Who would become the hegemonic power governing the eastern Mediterranean? How would the parameters of the Concert of Europe and the balance of power established after the Congress of Vienna in 1815 change, and at whose expense?

In a framework constructed by these questions, maintaining the independence and territorial integrity of the Ottoman Empire, tottering but intact, became increasingly more important for Great Britain, which could ill afford to lose commercial control of the eastern Mediterranean and the Indian dominions to Russia. Moreover, the Ottoman Empire, with its *provisionist economic policy* inherited from Byzantium, was becoming a center of attraction for Britain, "the world's workshop, the world's shipbuilder, [and] the world's banker" in the nineteenth century.[5] Britain saw in the Ottoman Empire a largely untouched market for customs-free mass-produced factory goods and finance capital. Nevertheless, British jealousy with respect to the eastern Mediterranean and the Ottoman Empire also applied to Russia, which had its own plans for the region.

Simply put, the interests of the British and Russian Empires in the Ottoman Empire and Near East were openly antagonistic, at least until the last quarter of the nineteenth century. In this context, at the beginning of the century Britain set out to fortify the Ottoman Empire against Russian attacks. For the British Foreign Office, the empire of the tsars, motivated by the ideal of "building a universal Russian Kingdom," posed a draconian threat to British interests in the Near East.[6] Thus, "Palmerstonism," which would later become the traditional policy of Britain vis-à-vis the Eastern Question, aimed to protect and maintain the territorial integrity and political independence of the Ottoman Empire. Both Conservatives and Liberals vigorously supported Palmerstonian policy until the last quarter of the nineteenth century. Britain proved its commitment by siding with the Ottomans against Russia in the Crimean War (1853–56). While it managed to avoid engaging its army in other potentially endless wars between Russia and the Ottoman Empire, Britain employed all other means possible, including coercion, intimidation, threats, and psychological violence at the negotiating table.

The British media at the time hailed Palmerstonian policy as the "project of saving the Turk." The policy encompassed issues ranging from opening the Ottoman economy to free trade and European money markets, to the conscription of non-Muslims into the Ottoman army, from threatening the rebellious governor of Egypt, Mehmed Ali Paşa, into submission, to opposing the Slavic-Orthodox union of the Danubian principalities. Concrete action included fighting in the Crimean War and "convincing" Greece to withhold her support during the Cretan uprising of the 1860s. As one historian of the "Eastern Question" has argued, "In the quadrille of the balance of power, England had the special role, she led the dance."[7]

In the meantime, Palmerstonian policy sought to introduce some degree of liberalization and reform into the Ottoman political and administrative system in order to generate cohesion within a fragmented Ottoman society, as well as to turn the Ottoman state into a "modern state" with infrastructural power.[8] In implementing its aims, Great Britain developed a form of cooperation that at times seemed more like coercion and pressure than friendly collaboration with the Ottoman ruling elites. As Foreign Secretary Lord Palmerston put it: "A community is not like a man or a tree or a building whose parts are not renovated but remain the same, and are worn out and decay by age and use. All that is requisite to keep an Empire vigorous for an indefinite period of time is that its institutions and laws should adapt themselves to the changes which take place in the habits of the people and in the relative position of the community as compared with other countries."[9]

The allies of the Ottoman Empire therefore undertook a mission of reforming "the Turk," who was otherwise incapable of his own preservation, and set out to teach him how to be "modern" and "civilized." Their embassies vigilantly oversaw the implementation of a series of reform edicts that the sultan promulgated to ensure that they did not remain dead letters. British consuls and agents actively interfered in the affairs of the Porte whenever they believed that "fanatical" Muslim conservatism had reared its ugly head and hindered the modernization project. The so-called reforms that the Ottoman ruling elites had been expected to implement clearly reflected the "cultural mission of the Western world which was heavily tainted by a romanticized crusader perspective, professing as its object the liberation of [the] Christian population under the yoke."[10] Palmerstonian policy, in this sense, was self-contradictory, for it aimed to preserve the territorial integrity and political independence of the Ottoman Empire as a free-trade region, while it also desired to free Christians from Muslim rule.[11]

As the century progressed, Palmerstonism gradually lost its allure. In the last quarter of the nineteenth century, it became evident in the eyes of the British that the "sick man" was long past rehabilitation. Concurrent with Ottoman financial bankruptcy, the Christian revolt in

Bosnia and Herzegovina in 1875, followed by the Bulgarian uprising in 1876, played a considerable role in rebuilding the image of the Turk in Europe as "the great anti-human specimen of humanity."[12] Accordingly, the Disraeli cabinet refrained from openly backing the Ottoman Empire during the Russian-Ottoman War of 1877–78, which would end in absolute defeat for the latter. Yet the terms of the Treaty of San Stefano, concluded between Russia and the Ottoman Empire on 3 March 1878, prompted Britain once more to intervene in favor of its old ally since the treaty had brought about an unacceptable increase in Russia's influence in the eastern Mediterranean, which in a way invalidated almost a century-long British attempt to retain the balance of power in Europe. The modifications in the Treaty of San Stefano, which took the form of the Treaty of Berlin (1878), coupled with the Cyprus Convention and the Euphrates Valley Railway project, signified a conspicuous shift in Britain's traditional Near Eastern policy. Britain no longer attempted to support Turkish rule in the Balkans and concentrated instead on the straits as well as the Asian dominions of the sultan as a bulwark against Russian encroachments. The complete dissolution of Ottoman rule in the Balkans (1912–13) and the worst nightmare of every Ottoman political leader, namely, a Russian-British alliance in the First World War, sealed the end of the Ottoman Empire and the Eastern Question by creating fertile ground for the long-delayed dismemberment plans.

The preceding description of the so-called Eastern Question demonstrates, briefly, how the West with its arrogant solipsism of colonial knowledge understood and portrayed the position of the Ottoman Empire in a European-dominated world system during the nineteenth and early twentieth centuries. The Eastern Question as a product of alteritist discourse that established the East as antithetical to the West was a politically constructed phenomenon that increasingly determined the Ottoman Empire's position vis-à-vis the European powers. It also worked as a site of discursive struggle that produced a Eurocentric, hegemonic discourse that was dichotomist, reductionist, imperialistically driven, and by and large Orientalist in Saidian terms. In this sense, the Eastern Question was the Ottoman Empire's Western Question, yet even Ottoman policy makers themselves adopted and internalized the concept, as demonstrated by the many documents produced by Ottoman statesmen of the time, a situation that attests to the term's hegemonic quality.[13]

This chapter explores narrations of the Eastern Question as they appeared in a series of Turkish primary, secondary, and high school history textbooks printed between 1940 and 2007. Republican social science and history textbooks since 1923 have covered the topic of the Eastern Question (although not necessarily under this heading) as part of Turkish historiography. Unlike the Ottoman ruling elite, whose perception of their own empire was widely affected by its tainted reflection in the mirror of the Eastern Question, the republican founding elite was determined to create a new image of Turks and Turkish history, purged of the unpleasant associations with the Eastern Question. This did not necessarily mean that the events that had constituted the phenomenon called the Eastern Question were forgotten or ignored. However, the term was conspicuously absent in early republican-era textbooks, implying that the Eastern Question, with its powerful discursive connotations, was no longer accepted as a defining vehicle for Turkish self-perception. On some occasions when writers used the term, they employed it as an unmistakably foreign concept coined and circulated by the Western world as part of its imperialistically driven alteritist attitude toward the Ottoman Empire and/or Turks. The significance of the term as a potent vehicle marking the "othering," dichotomist, and Orientalist features of the Western construction of the Turks increasingly made itself felt in the Kemalist framework as the "official imagining of identity."[14] The founding narratives it produced were gradually subject to alterations in accordance with the new dynamics, challenges, and changes in Turkey's identity-formation politics and its relationship with the idea of the West.

Drawing on the assumption that history textbooks are political texts through which national and historical consciousness, as well as the perceptions of the "other" and the "self," are both constructed and reflected, this chapter examines Turkish textbooks in order to understand the meaning and place of the Eastern Question in the cognitive map of several generations of republican elites. These elites, with their cultural and "symbolic capital," have undertaken the task of rewriting the history of the Turks as a nation-building and nation-state consolidation strategy.[15]

Since the Eastern Question was the Turks' Western Question, its narrative in republican textbooks can be read as the long story of the Turks' interaction with Europe, which had been and still is marked by many inner conflicts, contrasts, and tensions, whereby an antagonistic discourse toward the West coexists alongside oblique (and sometimes overt) praise and admiration. It can also be read as the story of the Turkish Republic's problematic relationship with its Ottoman past and legacy, which is intrinsically linked to the way that the Eastern Question played out in the nineteenth century. Considering the ways in which Ottoman memory is associated with Turkish identity in power relations and in power holders' particular worldview and analyzing the shifts in the portrayal of this extremely traumatic part of the Ottoman past provide an understanding of the changing trends in modern identity formation. This chapter contributes to such an understanding through an in-depth examination of twenty-nine Turkish history textbooks.

After a brief discussion of the vital role attributed to textbooks as "authoritative texts that not only represent politics in their contents, but also set up the terms of citizenship in the nation," this chapter delves into the treatment of the Eastern Question in the history textbooks taught in Turkish schools between 1940 and 1980.[16] After detecting an almost complete avoidance of the term in those textbooks and ascertaining the possible reasons behind this void, the chapter examines history textbooks published between 1980 and 2007. The reintroduction of the term "Eastern Question" into the textbooks after the military intervention of 1980 is extremely significant, in that it provides valuable insights into the changing parameters of Turkey's sense of national security, self-perception, and identification with Europe. The emergence of the Eastern Question as an *omnipresent* term toward the twenty-first century marks yet another shift in Turkey's relationships with both its Ottoman past and Europe. The reappearance of the term in textbooks demonstrates a new historical continuum between Islamic civilizations, the Ottoman Empire, and today's Turkey based on supposedly "deep-seated" and "constant hostility" displayed by the Western world towards its Muslim "other."

Competing for Memory and Identity: Turkish History Textbooks

For the members of the political-bureaucratic elite that founded the Turkish Republic on the heritage of the Ottoman Empire, the project of creating a nation-state also entailed "imagining" and "inventing" a new history fit for national needs. As Ernest Gellner suggests, "nations as a natural, God-given way of classifying men, as an inherent political destiny, are a myth; nationalism, which sometimes takes pre-existing cultures and turns them into nations, sometimes invents them, and often obliterates pre-existing cultures: that is reality."[17] In the process of creating nations as "imagined communities," the nation-states, alongside many other social-engineering measures, also invent a new history for the nation.[18] E. J. Hobsbawm argues that "naturally states would use the increasingly powerful machinery for communicating with their inhabitants, above all the primary schools, to spread the image and heritage of the 'nation' and to inculcate attachment to it and to attach all to country and flag often 'inventing traditions' or even nations for this purpose."[19] Thus official rewriting of history and its dissemination through compulsory state-controlled primary education becomes an ineluctable enterprise of nation-states in imagining and constructing the nation and national belonging. The Turkish republican case in this sense epitomizes the imagining and inventing of a nation with a brand-new history that would take the form of the *Turkish History Thesis* in the 1930s. This meticulously composed narrative bore all the signs of official history rewriting. It sought to prove "scientifically" that the Turks as a nation had existed since time immemorial. Unlike the stereotyped images generated by the Orientalist literature, the new narrative portrayed the Turks as the inventors and representatives of the highest civilization on the planet.

With the foundation of the Republic in 1923, history teaching in schools was hailed as an essential component in the construction of the new Turkish identity, state, and nation.[20] As Akçuraoğlu Yusuf summarized in the First History Congress (1932), the priority of the new Turkish historiography was to "narrate the past according to national interests, rather than merely copying the histories written from the perspectives of other nations."[21] Republican elites argued that "knowing the profound Turkish history" was "a sacred gem feeding the Turk's skills and might, and his unbeatable strength in the face of any currents that would harm national existence."[22] Moreover, the new Turkish national history aimed to eradicate the "inferiority complex" engendered by the traumatic experience of the Eastern Question, as well as challenge the centuries-long European anti-Turkish discourse in Gladstonian terms. "The Republican conversion narrative," which professed an ontological fracture between the Ottoman Empire and the Turkish Republic, attempted to reconstruct the memory of society along "national" lines.[23] The new narrative found its expression in crystallized form in history textbooks, which the Ministry of Education has strictly controlled from the beginning of the Republic.[24]

As social memory studies suggest, memory is an essential factor in identity formation. Therefore, nation-states appear keen on "achieving the dominance of national memory over other memories and thus excluding and eliminating other contestants for control over other types of identity for primary allegiance."[25] As Mark Beissinger notes, "nationalism is not simply about imagined communities; it is much more fundamentally a struggle over defining communities, and particularly a struggle for control over the imagination about community."[26] While the nation-building elites struggle to replace other forms of identity with the national one and to reshape the cultural and collective memory, historiography becomes a powerful tool in overpowering and silencing rival voices and narratives that represent different memories than the "nationally constructed" one.

By identifying and analyzing the portrayal of the Eastern Question in republican history textbooks, this chapter attempts to understand how Turkish policy makers used the theme of the Eastern Question as an integral element of the republican founding narrative, as they fought their way into constructing a national identity and a new social memory for the Turkish people. Comparing the coverage of the Eastern Question in a number of textbooks published in a relatively long period also helps us comprehend the ongoing negotiation process between national memory and identity in the Turkish context.

The Eastern Question as a Fading Memory in Early Republican-Era Textbooks

Of the seventeen history textbooks published between 1940 and 1980 examined here, only a few openly use the phrase "Eastern Question," although they all extensively narrate and discuss the eventful years of the Ottoman Empire's long nineteenth century.[27] While the term "Eastern Question" is completely absent from many textbooks, some textbooks mention the term only in passing. For example, in the 1941 study by Sadri Ertem and Kazım Nami Duru, the section on the "Period of External Intervention" describes the "Eastern Question" as the "discord between Mahmud II and Mehmet Ali Paşa [that] became a great concern for the European states. Around that time, the term Eastern Question was coined and gained popularity. It was used to refer to all issues regarding the Near East. In fact, the Eastern Question was completely about the Ottoman Empire's position vis-à-vis the European states. The Ottoman Empire had been in decline since the eighteenth century. [Europeans] had planned to parcel it out one day just like Poland. This was an issue of grave importance. This is the essence of what is called the Eastern Question."[28]

Another textbook, published by Mustafa Cezar in 1951, states that "in this century [the nineteenth] England's democracy improved unprecedentedly. Her industry and trade made great progress. She enormously enlarged her commercial fleet and her naval force. Her colonial territory also became very large. England paid utmost attention to the issue called the Eastern Question, which consisted in the dismemberment of the Ottoman Empire, and she struggled to prevent Russia from tearing off large pieces from the Ottoman territory. Around this time, England became a worldwide influential power."[29]

Bedriye Atsız and Hilmi Oran, in 1953, describe the setting as follows: "Thus Russia [thanks to the Treaty of Unkiar Skelessi, 1833], found a way to meddle with the Ottoman Empire's internal matters and increased her influence over the Empire. She also secured her position in the Black Sea and acquired the most influential role on the stage of the Eastern Question."[30]

As one scholar opines, in the early years of the Republic "it would have been anathema to suggest that the Ottoman Empire might have a positive legacy to pass on to the new nation. The door to the past was to be not merely firmly closed but slammed shut and locked tight to prevent any seeping of influence or temptation to nostalgia."[31] The founding elites of the Turkish Republic were determined to disown the memory of the Ottoman Empire in their quest to create a new nation. They looked upon the Ottoman past with disdain and desperately sought formulations that would distance the "glorious" history of the Turkish nation from the "shameful acts" of the Ottoman dynasty. This dynasty, according to Mustafa Kemal, "had acquired the power to rule over the Turkish nation for more than six centuries by violence" and were a bunch of "madmen," "dissolute spendthrifts," and "pure evildoers."[32]

In the early 1920s, historians vehemently argued over the place of the Ottoman Empire in the history writing of the Republic. Some writers even went so far as to suggest eliminating the Ottoman Empire from Turkish history altogether. Muhittin Birgen, for example, called for a total rejection of the Ottoman past and ventured that "the solution to the problem of Ottoman and Turkish history [could not] be procured by sticking the word Turk onto the tail of the word Ottoman."[33] The majority of scholars, however, were in favor of integrating Ottoman history into Turkish history in a peculiarly selective and pragmatic way. Accordingly, the well-known attempts to design a narrative of "dis-continuity," which took the form of notorious Turkish History Thesis, ensued.[34]

The Turkish History Thesis is the quintessence of creative memory making. The thesis found the ancestors of the Turks on the steppes of Central Asia, whose civilization manifested itself in the Orkhon

Inscriptions. It invented the legend of the great exodus of the Turkish clans westward and related them to the earliest inhabitants of Anatolia, who built the ancient civilizations of Asia Minor, such as the Hittites and the Sumerians. This last aspect of the formula allowed the Turkish Republic to assert that Anatolia belonged to the Turks long before the ancestors of the contemporary Greeks and Armenians became its inhabitants, thereby refuting the territorial claims of those nations over this "prehistorically" Turkish land. Like another grandiose theory, called the *Sun Language Theory*, read at the Third Turkish Language Conference in August 1936, which claimed that Turkish was the first language of primitive man from which all other languages were derived, the Turkish History Thesis asserted that the ancestors of the contemporary Turks were the first and real owners of the territory on which the Republic was built. Thus the Turks, as conveyers of the world's first language, were not a barbarous and inferior "race." In fact, the Turks were the very progenitors of civilization.

The first outcome of the Turkish History Thesis was the book titled *Türk Tarihinin Ana Hatları* (The main forms of Turkish history), which devoted only fifty pages to the Ottoman Empire out of its total six hundred pages. The Turkish qualities of the Ottoman Empire as a state were highly questionable, and its relationship with the Turkish Republic was a puzzle consisting of many ambiguous, self-contradictory, and blurry references.[35] For example,

the political elite tried both to distance themselves from their imperial legacy (which included glorification of this history) and hold onto particular periods of this same history. In other words, the attitude was not a complete dismissal of the Ottoman past. Rather, there was an attempt at picking and choosing specific elements and periods of this past: moreover, whatever was deemed good in this history was talked about as the deeds of the Turkish elements, whereas everything bad was attributed to the sultans and to external actors. Thus, for example, the earlier periods of the empire were discussed with admiration. It was the later periods that were defined as corrupt and full of religious conservatism and susceptibility to external influences—factors that they argued eventually led to the demise of the empire.[36]

As for Europe, Kemalists had mixed feelings. In "Nutuk" (the long speech delivered by Mustafa Kemal from 15 to 20 October 1927 at the Second Congress of Cumhuriyet Halk Partisi [Republican People's Party]) two competing perspectives on Europe emerge. "The first perspective resents Europe, the second admires it. . . . [Mustafa Kemal]

Atatürk distrusts European nations. The great powers of Europe argue for human rights, peace and civilized methods, but they see no harm in occupying a country that does not belong to them, and in dividing, colonizing and annihilating it."[37] Yet it was no mystery that the Turkey of his dreams was constructed along Western lines, a country where people would be rehabituated in the Bourdieuan sense through a Western mentality and lifestyle.

The preface of *Türk Tarihinin Ana Hatları* states, "The main motivation for the creation of such book, apart from writing a long-overdue proper national history for the Turkish nation, was to correct the prevailing false beliefs and ideas about Turks that predominate in academia across the world."[38] The book indeed appeared in a constant "dialogical conversation" in the Bakhtinian sense with the Western world.[39] Employing Western science to challenge and counter the Western world's biased ideas and attitudes toward Turks speaks volumes about the Kemalists' approach to the West. The new regime's insistence on deriving its ideological discursive instruments from so-called scientific truth, as well as its belief in the authoritative status of Western scholars as the ultimate representatives of the temple of science, was clearly discernible in the foundational texts of Turkish nation building. The architects of the Turkish History Thesis and the Sun Language Theory characteristically sought the approval of Western social scientists—in fact mostly Orientalists—and considered it a yardstick for the credibility of their ideology. As Etienne Copeaux points out, although Western Orientalist scholars, who had almost exclusively created the academic literature on the history of Turks, partly caused this attitude, the unchallenged position of the West as the monopolistic producer of scientific knowledge must have been the real reason behind it.[40]

According to Cemil Aydın, "the modern historical memory of international relations in the past two hundred years, inscribed into the foundational texts of Turkish nationalism, includes the betrayal of the Ottoman-Turkish desire to become an equal member of the European state system by the European powers. . . . But the Republican elite adopted a radical Westernist modernization project at home, an indication that the universal West was already divorced in their minds from the imperialist West. Gradually, a pro-Western Occidentalism was constructed in Turkish intellectual life mainly for the justification of the radical cultural revolution that the Republican regime began to implement."[41]

This "pro-Western Occidentalism" did not necessarily preclude the textbook authors of the early republican era from disseminating some negative stereotypical images of Europe in the context of nineteenth-century international relations. In other words, undertaking a project of wholesale Westernization at home did not readily generate a white-washing campaign, so to speak, that ignored Western imperialism and its devastating effects on the Ottoman Empire.[42] The difficulties that the Republic was experiencing with "establishing the European paradigm as a part of Turkey's over all magnum opus or Utopia," namely the modernization vis-à-vis "the Sèvres apology, a notion that holds the outer world, especially the West, as responsible for Turkey's problems ranging from economic instability to domestic unrest" were discernible in this attitude.[43]

Early republican-era textbooks keep talking about the "arrogant," "conceited," "insolent," "equivocal," "untrustworthy," and "opportunist" characteristics of the Western powers, yet always as outdated things. Besides, the Ottoman sultans and officials with their "feckless," "short-sighted," "spineless," and "selfish" policies were partly responsible for the disaster that befell the Ottoman Empire. Altogether, the Ottoman state belonged to the domain of Western imperialism. The young Turkish Republic, "free from the shackles of the imperialism after Lausanne," a notion proudly repeated in all textbooks, belonged to the domain of Western universalism. The immediate memory of Europe as the "toothless monster" of the days of the Turkish War of Independence (1919–23) was balanced with the image of a Western world that Turkey, a staunch believer in the merits of Western civilization, wished to emulate and join. Although the West continued to operate as an external "other" in the construction of Turkishness, "efforts to frame Turkish identity as distinct among a global community of nations coexisted with attempts to associate Turkey indisputably with the West."[44] As Çağlar Keyder aptly suggests, "in contrast to the anti-colonial sentiment which fuelled the majority of third-world national movements, Turkish nationalism did not exhibit an anti-Western nativism. [Turkish reformers and their epigones] saw their society as backward, but not essentially different. They were all Nehrus, and there was no Gandhi among them."[45] Thus, the seventeen history textbooks published between 1940 and 1980 (except for the three examples mentioned earlier) refrain from mentioning the term "Eastern Question."

All this, however, was to change by the 1980s, when the policy makers of the Republic opted to resurrect the Western ghosts of late Ottoman times in order to remind Turkish children that if not safeguarded vigorously, their country's independence was in danger. The "toothless monster," albeit in different attire, was back. As the discourse of Western "betrayal" represented by the "Sèvres apology" was recalled and reestablished, the term "Eastern Question" reclaimed its place in the textbooks.

During the 1990s, although it kept a relatively low profile, the Eastern Question nevertheless preserved its place as a separate topic in textbooks. In the twenty-first century, with Turkey's national pride bruised in the process of seeking EU candidacy, and a new political party with Islamist background (Adalet ve Kalkınma Partisi [AKP] [Justice and Development Party]) in power since 2002, the term "Eastern Question" has been revisited by the textbooks and interpreted in a way to redefine Turkey's stance vis-à-vis Europe and the Ottoman past. Once more, the term has proved its symbolic power.

The Rediscovery of the Term "Eastern Question" from the 1980s Onward

Unlike the early republican-era textbooks that treated the Eastern Question as a painful yet seemingly ineluctable sequence in Ottoman history, the textbooks of the 1980s reflected the militarist, conservative, and securitist zeitgeist of Turkish politics after the coup d'état of September 1980. The new narrative cautioned Turkish youth that the Eastern Question was not as dead as it had seemed.[46]

In the 1980s, "Turkey was attempting to reaffirm national integrity and utilize traditional Kemalism as a unifying force. During the period of extreme political polarization and increasing religious fundamentalism, Atatürk nationalism was employed to enhance solidarity."[47] Yet, as Copeaux asserts, after 1980 a narrative polyphony is present in the textbooks, where two different approaches to Turkish history coexist: Kemalism and the Turkish-Islamic Synthesis.[48] The Turkish-Islamic Synthesis, which emphasized Islam and Turkish culture as interdependent and mutually constructive entities, inevitably ushered in a desire to restore the grandeur of the Ottoman Empire and integrate it into Turkish history in a more pronounced way.[49] Given that "the past, for Kemalists, [was] another country," the Turkish-Islamic Synthesis was a détente between Turkey and the Ottoman Empire.[50] Since the 1950s, the inclination of republican policy makers to reestablish Turkey's ruptured relations with the Ottoman past enabled the authors of textbooks to gradually enlarge the space devoted to the Ottomans at the expense of world history (specifically ancient) and to tone down the harsh criticism directed at the empire. In the meantime, "the Turkish History Thesis was not totally abandoned but restricted as background knowledge."[51] Thus with the Turkish-Islamic Synthesis as the new paradigm of official Turkish national identity, placing not Atatürk himself but his attachment to the West in a secondary position to the Turkish-Islamic identity, history textbooks in the 1980s eagerly rediscovered the term "Eastern Question."[52]

The defensive mentality of the 1980s textbooks, while invoking the traumatic memories of the Treaty of Sèvres era, ironically benefited from the conditions laid by the pro-Ottoman Turkish-Islamic Synthesis, which facilitated the identification process with the Ottomans. The term "Eastern Question" came to represent the allegedly systematic hostility faced by Turks since the foundation of the empire. Moreover, the contemporary international threats perceived by the Turkish state were supposedly specters of the same Eastern Question. Although Europe was never openly named, there was little doubt as to the identity of "some other quarters and great powers" that aided and abetted the anti-Turkish plots and politics in the region. According to a popular high school history textbook first published in 1981 (later editions followed):

It is a great pity that since the establishment of the Ottoman state, the number of enemies that have eyes for our beloved fatherland has never dwindled. When the Ottoman state started to decline, an extremely obnoxious scheme was launched and carried out until the end of the Independence War. This involved *all the efforts that sought the partition of our land and annihilation of our national existence* [emphasis in original]. The Eastern Question, which lasted hundreds of years, was assumed to end with the final collapse of the Ottoman State at the end of the First World War.... Yet since then, those who wish to dismember Turkey have not diminished. Yes, perhaps some of our former foes seem to have turned into our friends. Nevertheless, the number of powers that are unhappy with a united and prosperous Turkey has increased. One of our neighbors wishes to seize the whole Aegean Sea and suffocate Turkey. Two of our neighbors hanker after our eastern and southeastern regions hoping to capture and turn them into their own protectorates. Another neighbor has never changed its aspirations regarding the straits, and it will never cease to want them. The existence of Turkey as the symbol of peace and unity in the Middle East prompts the jealousy of its neighbors. They wrongly assume that Turkey as a power growing ever stronger will pose a threat to themselves. There are also some other quarters that manipulate the balance of power in the Middle East to their own advantage, and some great powers foster and back this shady business as they see fit for their own interests. These unscrupulous desires and policies that aim to send Turkey back to the days of the Treaty of Sèvres find supporters in many circles and keep Turkey under a constant threat both from within and without.[53]

As this passage clearly shows, the term "Eastern Question," which was not very popular with the textbook authors of the earlier decades, reappears in the narrative. The phrase gained the status of a topic that deserved exclusive attention. Its remarkable return marks an indisputable shift both in the perception of Europe and in Turkish policy makers' attempts to form national memory.

From the 1980s onward, the image of Europe has undergone an unmistakable change in Turkish textbooks. The antagonistic quality of past and present relationships between Turkey and Europe derives increasingly from and is constituted through its otherness. As a scholar drawing on his work on Turkish history textbooks published in the 1990s and the twenty-first century suggests, "Europe is relocated from a distant 'other' to an 'other' that is hostile and aggressive towards the Ottoman State—and by implication, the Turkish nation."[54] This "new" notion of Europe promoted by the power holders of the time leaves its undeniable imprint not only on the accounts of the Eastern Question but also on the prominence and explanatory force of the phrase in textbooks. As the textbook authors choose to "remember" the role of the Eastern Question in the tragic and traumatic collapse of the Ottoman Empire and reincorporate it into national memory, Europe slowly and irreversibly turns into the epitome of "hypocrisy," "Machiavellianism," "greed," and "injustice." Unlike the textbooks of earlier decades, however, this image is not confined to distant times but is vibrant today. The Ottoman Empire as Europe's prey in the context of the Eastern Question attracts more sympathy and acquires a new status. Previously attributed qualities such as "incompetence," "pusillanimity," and "devilry" are replaced by more neutral or moderate traits. A newly emerging discourse of victimization, when read together with other accounts on the Ottomans in the nineteenth century, tends to picture the empire as a helpless sufferer at the hands of the Western imperialists.

Rediscovery of the term "Eastern Question," in other words, goes hand in hand with a new rapprochement with the Ottoman legacy. This process, however, is by no means one way. Changing perceptions of Europe and the Ottoman past are intertwined and mutually constitutive. As the Kemalist founding narrative and rhetoric gradually lose ground, and their original assumptions and dictates are reinterpreted according to the needs of the time, contextualization of republican history with regard to the Ottoman past changes, which in turn reconstructs the image of Europe. On the other hand, changing perceptions of Europe contribute to the dwindling credibility of the national memory fashioned by the Kemalist founding narrative in the first decades of the Republic.

In the textbooks of the 1990s, the Eastern Question reinforces its place and remains a separate topic described in seemingly value-free terms that nevertheless accentuate Europe's share in the destiny of the Ottoman Empire. The problem of setting a chronological framework for the Eastern Question is also a topic addressed in a popular textbook:

> There has been no consensus on the exact time that the Eastern Question first emerged. Some trace it as far back as the Crusades. In this book, the Eastern Question will be defined as an issue engendered by the power politics among the European states in the nineteenth century. Most of the European states believed that the Ottoman state was not capable of maintaining its existence on its own. Its untimely collapse could give rise to large-scale conflicts among the European powers. Therefore, some European states opted to protect the Ottoman state. In the simplest sense, the term "Eastern Question" was used to refer to the policies of maintaining the integrity and independence of the Ottoman state in the first half of the nineteenth century. In the second half of the century, it meant the partition of the Ottoman territory in Europe. In the twentieth century, it referred to the dismemberment of all Ottoman territories. Each and every crisis in the internal or foreign affairs of the Ottoman state were placed under the rubric of the Eastern Question by Europeans.[55]

Another example that starkly defines the Eastern Question as a long-term European imperial project aimed at Ottoman dismemberment states that the phrase:

> was first used at the Vienna Congress of 1815. European States convened this conference in order to sort out the problems caused by the French emperor Bonaparte. At the congress, the Russian tsar Alexander asked the other participants to become involved in the Greek cause and used the term *Eastern Question* [emphasis in original]. However, the Austrian prime minister Metternich, who had made great efforts to convene the conference and who was against nationalist movements, vehemently opposed the tsar's view. England, anxious about a possible Russian advance in the East, also objected. Thus, the congress did not deal with the Greek issue. The term "Eastern Question," however, became a political term and was frequently used afterward. In the first half of the nineteenth century, it was used to explain the policies aiming at the maintenance of the territorial integrity of the Ottoman state. In the second half of the century, it meant the division of *Turks'* territory in Europe [emphasis in original]. In the twentieth century, it meant the dismemberment of all territory that the Ottoman

State still possessed. Europeans attempted to explain the Ottoman state's every crisis by using the term "Eastern Question." Politicians perceived it as a term related to the prevailing situation and the future of the Ottoman Empire. European historians used it in order to narrate and expound the past relationships between Turks and Europe. Thus, the Eastern Question turned into a concept and term of the discipline of history. Regarding the beginning of the Eastern Question, the opinion of the historians was largely accepted. They in fact offered different views on this matter. European historians asserted that the Eastern Question was rooted in the emergence of Islam. Some argued that the beginning of the Eastern Question coincided with the conquest of İstanbul. In reality, the Eastern Question first appeared in the second half of the eighteenth century, was named so at the Vienna Congress of 1815, continued throughout the nineteenth and the first two decades of the twentieth century, and finally culminated in the disintegration of the Ottoman state. The Eastern Question from beginning to end was a question of European imperialism. The Eastern Question in the sense that was understood by Europeans was in fact a Western Question for Turks.[56]

Writing on the Turkish debate over the nature and legacy of the Ottoman past, one scholar suggests that it is, "at one level, an enactment of the tension between European and post-colonial narratives." However, because the Ottomans were never actually colonized, "the Turkish debate can be read not so much as an attempt to assert post-colonial particularity in the face of European universalism, but rather a bid to resurrect Ottoman universalism in the face of Kemalist particularism."[57] As many scholars argue today, the official imagining of the Turkish national history by the republican founding elites, namely, the glorification of a mythic past without any significant reference to Islam (and by implication the Ottoman Empire) and overtly Western in nature, did not appeal to the majority of the population.[58] "Religious leaders and intellectuals who felt that Islam should have some place in the new order were in conflict with the nationalist ethos of the early Republican era. To those who felt that Islam should play a part in the new national identity, the answer was unequivocally negative. Islam had overshadowed the true greatness of the Turks, ultimately causing the decline and fall of the Ottoman Empire, and thus was not to play a part in the new national identity."[59]

Since then, intellectuals and politicians with Islamist backgrounds have been persistently asking for a corrective intervention into the national memory as constructed by the early republican Kemalist narrative. This intervention inevitably involves a rehabilitation of Turkey's relationship with its Ottoman past and the creation of an alternative narrative that places stronger emphasis on the religious, imperialist, and Orientalist aspirations of the Western world vis-à-vis the Ottoman Empire. With the Justice and Development Party in power since 2002, the re-Islamization of the Turkish public sphere since 1990s along with the emergence of neo-Ottomanism[60] movement is well in progress.[61] The desire for a more nuanced history that accentuates and underlines the "systematic wrongdoings of Christian Europe" toward "Muslim Ottomans and Turks" has been discernible in the narrations of the Eastern Question in the textbooks. For example:

The Eastern Question: It was first used as a political term by the Western diplomats at the Vienna Congress of 1815. Its beginning goes back to very old times. This term refers to all kinds of relationships that took place between the Christian Western world and the Turkish-Islamic world starting from 1071 [the Battle of Manzikert] and ending in 1923. The first part of the Eastern Question covers the period in which Turks began to advance toward the West, and Europe attempted yet failed to stop them through Crusades. Although they proved abortive, the Crusades nevertheless brought about a mentality mainly built on religious thinking. That mentality was called the *Crusader's mentality* in the Islamic world [emphasis in original]. The goal of the Eastern Question at that time was to drive Turks from Balkans and Anatolia, which Europeans considered Christian territory. Europeans came near their goals when the Ottomans were defeated at Vienna in 1683 and signed the Treaty of Karlowitz in 1699. The second phase of the Eastern Question covers the period between 1699 and 1923. The goal of Europeans during this time was ostensibly to protect the Christian minorities living under Ottoman rule, but actually to tear off Ottoman territories and destroy the Ottoman state. In the second half of the nineteenth century, they combined colonialism with their Crusader's mentality, but skillfully concealed their real intentions and acted under the false pretense of protecting the rights of Christian subjects of the Ottoman state. In following decades, Europeans attributed several different meanings to the term Eastern Question. They were aware that Russia with her increasing power was pursuing the policy of acquiring access to warm seas that posed a threat to their own interests. Therefore, during the first half of the nineteenth century European states promoted the policy of maintaining the territorial integrity of the Ottoman state that was in harmony with their interests in the region. They preferred a weak Ottoman state to a powerful state that could jeopardize their interests. In the second half of the century, the Eastern Question came to refer to Europe's plans to evict the Ottoman state from Europe as well as to recapture İstanbul with a view to resurrecting the Byzantine Empire. Throughout the centuries in which the Eastern Question unfolded, Europeans always adopted a hostile and two-faced attitude toward Turks.[62]

By examining twenty-nine Turkish history textbooks published between 1940 and 2007, this chapter sheds light on the role and the place of the Eastern Question as both a historical term and a phenomenon within the "symbol system that makes up official [Turkish] national identity."[63] The chapter began by exploring the republican founding elite's nation-building strategy to actively control the domain of national identity and carry out a project of identity formation by constructing a new history for the Turkish nation. Although the state was the sole actor in devising the official national identity, it nevertheless was open to myriad influences from social and international forces. In time, these forces evidently shaped the trajectory of the official line and the process of national memory construction, and hence brought about discernible shifts in the official historiography. This fluid nature of Turkish identity formation found its expression in history textbooks. The changing narrations of the Eastern Question in the textbooks as an undeniably powerful term that not only linked the history of the Ottoman Empire to the Turkish Republic but also portrayed the Western world in a particular way reflected the ongoing struggle among the several actors as to what should be included in official Turkish identity. In this sense, the Eastern Question came to serve as a litmus test for detecting and perceiving the way the Turkish state positioned itself vis-à-vis the Ottoman Empire and the Western world.

In its early decades, the young Turkish Republic could be compared to a rebellious child who gained independence from strict parents through a painful and systematic struggle that terminated in family disaster, so to speak. Like an individual with a childhood trauma who rejects parental influence after the relationship with them is irreversibly damaged, the Turkish Republic distanced itself from its Ottoman predecessors and attempted to settle the score with them by "inventing" a brand-new Turkish "family" history that vacillated between almost completely ignoring the Ottomans and eagerly revealing their "betrayals." Although the past mattered enormously, the children of the Republic were expected to focus on the present and the future and "remember" the overall magnificence of their nation since ancient times, rather than become entangled with the recent past mostly associated with Eastern Question disasters. The tension caused by the difficulty of reconciling two different images of the Western world, one being the "toothless monster" that had threatened the very existence of the Turks, and the other as the highest form of civilization, which the Turkish nation state wished to emulate, did not help either. The term "Eastern Question" had to go, and so it did, as the history textbooks from the period between 1940 and 1980 testify. Although the 1970s saw a reinstatement of the Ottoman legacy into the official Turkish national identity in the form of the Turkish-Islamic Synthesis, the term "Eastern Question" nevertheless had to wait until after the coup of 1980 to make its remarkable comeback. Proving once again its symbolic value and singularity in the cognitive map of Turkish policy makers in the context of identity formation, the term "Eastern Question" in history textbooks became the locus of reinterpretation of the self and the "other." As the increasingly stronger emphasis placed on the culturally and religiously charged aspects of the Eastern Question in history textbooks in the 1990s and the twenty-first century demonstrates, the term continues to mirror the changing dynamics in the Turkish state's intricate relationships with the Western world.

As Turkey's thirty-year-long efforts and aspirations to become a member of the EU seem to wane unprecedentedly in the second decade of the new millennium, and as Europe gradually loses its status as the sole point of reference for Turkish policy makers, the impact on the narration of the Eastern Question in the history textbooks in coming years is yet to be seen. Turkish history textbooks, after all, have never ceased to transmit what the state wishes the Turkish nation to know about its history, although the definition, the content, and the components of that history have been in constant deconstruction and reconstruction since the foundation of the Republic.

NOTES

1. Mustafa Kemal, "Eskişehir Mutasarrıflık Dairesinde Konuşma, 15.01.1339 [1923]," in Mustafa Kemal, *Eskişehir-İzmit Konuşmaları* (İstanbul: Kaynak Yayınları, 1993), 57.

2. Mustafa Kemal, "İzmit Sinema Binasında Konuşma, 19. 01.1339 [1923]," in Kemal, *Eskişehir-İzmit Konuşmaları*, 183.

3. I use the term "problematization" in the Foucauldian sense, that is, "the set of discursive or nondiscursive practices that makes something enter into the play of the true and false, and constitutes it as an object for thought (whether under the form of moral reflection, scientific knowledge or political analysis, etc.)." See Michel Foucault, "The Concern for Truth," in *Foucault Live (Interviews 1966-1984)*, ed. Silvère Lotringer (New York: Semiotext(e), 1989), 456-57. Of course, Edward Said's Orientalism theses that draw from Foucault's concept of

"problematization" should be kept in mind. See Edward W. Said, *Orientalism* (New York: Vintage, 1978).

4. An anonymous work titled *What Is to Be Done with Turkey? Or Turkey, Its Present and Future* (Henry Colburn: London, 1950) gives insights into the way the Eastern Question was conceptualized and perceived in the Western world.

5. Asa Briggs, *Victorian People: Reassessment of Persons and Themes, 1851–1867* (London: Penguin Books, 1955), 10.

6. Hans Kohn, *The Mind of Modern Russia: Historical and Political Thought of Russia's Great Age* (New Brunswick, NJ: Rutgers University Press, 1955), 17.

7. İnari Rautsi, *The Eastern Question Revisited: Case Studies in Ottoman Balance of Power* (Helsinki: Helsinki University Printing House, 1993), 12.

8. The concepts of "infrastructural power" and "modern state" should be understood as used in Michael Mann's "The Autonomous Power of the State, Its Origins, Mechanisms and Results," *Archives Européennes de Sociologie* 25 (1984): 185–213. Mann defines the modern state as "the state with infrastructural power" and terms the infrastructural power as "the capacity of the state actually to penetrate civil society, and to implement logistically political decisions throughout the realm."

9. Palmerston to Beauvale (Private Communication), 25 August 1839, quoted in F. S. Rodkey, "Lord Palmerston and the Rejuvenation of Turkey 1830–41, Part II," *Journal of Modern History* 2, no. 2 (1930): 202.

10. Çağlar Keyder, *State and Class in Turkey: A Study in Capitalist Development* (London: Verso, 1987), 21–22, 34.

11. M. H. Yavuz, "The Transformation of 'Empire' through Wars and Reforms: Integration vs. Oppression," in *War and Diplomacy: The Russo-Turkish War of 1877–1878 and the Treaty of Berlin*, ed. M. Hakan Yavuz and Peter Sluglett (Salt Lake City: University of Utah Press, 2011), 21.

12. W. E. Gladstone, *Bulgarian Horrors and the Question of the East* (London: John Murray Gladstone, 1876), 13.

13. David M. Goldfrank also offers a discussion of the Eastern Question as a Western Question in *The Origins of the Crimean War* (New York: Longman, 1994).

14. Bedia Tanyel Taysı, "For the People in Spite of the People? Official Turkish Identity from 1960" (PhD diss., Washington State University, 2004), 53–54.

15. I use the term "symbolic capital" in a Bourdieuan sense that "refers to the degree of accumulated prestige, celebrity, consecration of honour and is founded in a dialectic of knowledge and recognition." See Pierre Bourdieu, *The Field of Cultural Production: Essays on Art and Literature* (New York: Columbia University Press, 1993), 7.

16. Sam Kaplan, "'Religious Nationalism': A Textbook Case from Turkey," *Comparative Studies of South Asia, Africa and the Middle East* 25, no. 3 (2005): 669.

17. Ernest Gellner, *Nations and Nationalism* (Oxford: Blackwell, 1983), 48–49.

18. Benedict Anderson, *Imagined Communities* (London: Verso, 1983), 5-6.

19. E. J. Hobsbawm, *Nations and Nationalism since 1780* (Cambridge: Cambridge University Press, 1990), 91.

20. Apart from history teaching, school life was structured in a way to inculcate attachment to the nation and create bonding among the citizens of the Republic. Elementary school pupils wearing black uniforms started each school day by repeating an oath in which they promised to be industrious and truthful as an ideal Turkish child should be, and swearing that they would love those younger than themselves, respect their elders, and happily sacrifice their lives for their nation and fatherland if necessary. Secondary and high school pupils also wore uniforms. Monuments and busts of Mustafa Kemal Atatürk were erected in schoolyards. On every Monday and Friday in front of Atatürk busts, flag ceremonies were held, and the national anthem was sung collectively. Atatürk's "Address to the Turkish Youth," one of the cult texts of Kemalism that exhorts youth to be ready for duty in times of danger in hyperbolic language, was reproduced in almost all course material and was regularly repeated by students. Several national festivals were invented, and pupils wore special costumes for the occasion and performed in pageants to celebrate them. See Nazan Çiçek, "The Role of Mass Education in Nation-Building in the Ottoman Empire and the Turkish Republic, 1870-1930," in *Mass Education and the Limits of State Building, c. 1870-1930*, ed. Laurence Brockliss and Nicola Sheldon (New York: Palgrave Macmillan, 2012), 234-41. For a selection of biographies and autobiographies that reflect the indoctrination campaign of the early republican regime in schools, see Bekir Onur, *Türkiye'de Çocukluğun Tarihi* (Ankara: İmge Yayınları, 2005), 376-83. As a work of oral history that dwells on the perceptions of children circa the foundation of the Republic, several accounts of school life can be found in Mine Göğüş Tan et al., *Cumhuriyette Çocuktular* (İstanbul: Boğaziçi Üniversitesi Yayınları, 2007).

21. Ebru Boyar, *Ottomans, Turks and the Balkans: Empire Lost, Relations Altered* (London: I. B. Tauris, 2007), 19.

22. Yeşim Bayar, "The Dynamic Nature of Educational Policies and Turkish Nation Building: Where Does Religion Fit In?," *Comparative Studies of South Asia, Africa and the Middle East* 29, no. 3 (2009): 367.

23. Murat Ergin, "Chromatic Turkishness: Race, Modernity and Western Scholars in the Construction of Turkish National Identity" (PhD diss., University of Minnesota, 2005), 9, 173.

24. In Turkey, curriculum and textbook content have been always controlled at the national level. As explained in an Organisation for Economic Co-operation and Development (OECD) report, "the curriculum, subject matter, syllabi, textbooks and teacher's guides are subject to national regulations prescribed in minute detail from Ankara. The rule in educational management in Turkey is that 'Ankara knows best'" (OECD Reviews of National Policies for Education: Turkey 1989, OECD Publishing, 19 April 1989, 20). All textbooks have to be

examined and approved by the Committee of Instruction and Pedagogy at the Ministry of National Education. Although today many publishers produce textbooks, the contemporary textbook selection and approval procedure does not differ from that of 1930s. See F. J. Childress, "The Republican Lessons: Education and Making of Modern Turkey" (PhD diss., University of Utah, 2001), 130.

25. Jonathan Boyarin, ed., *Remapping Memory: The Politics of TimeSpace* (Minneapolis: University of Minneapolis Press, 1994), 126, quoted in Jeffrey K. Olick and Joyce Robbins Joyce, "Social Memory Studies: From 'Collective Memory' to the Historical Sociology of Mnemonic Practices," *Annual Review of Sociology* 24 (1998): 105-40, 117.

26. Mark Beissinger, "Nationalisms That Bark and Nationalisms That Bite: Ernest Gellner and the Substantiation of Nations," in *The State of the Nation: Ernest Gellner and the Theory of Nationalism*, ed. John A Hall (Cambridge: Cambridge University Press, 1998), 175.

27. This study is built on an in-depth examination of twenty-nine Turkish history textbooks published between 1940 and 2007. Seventeen of those textbooks were taught in all Turkish private and public schools between the 1940 and 1980, while twelve of them were used between 1980 and 2007. These textbooks were chosen for this study because they are the history textbooks that could be obtained by the writer in the Turkish National Library in Ankara. Since the Turkish Republic was founded in 1923, undoubtedly other history textbooks were published and used before 1940. The history textbooks titled *Türk Tarihinin Ana Hatları* (The main forms of Turkish history), taught in high schools between 1931 and 1939, were the revised and abridged versions of the texts that made up the Turkish History Thesis. Those textbooks were somewhat controversial, and in 1935, Mustafa Kemal Atatürk commissioned some historians to devise a new program for history writing. From 1939 onward, new history textbooks that were not the abridged version of *Türk Tarihini Ana Hatları* but were written for the exclusive use in the schools were published and used. This study chooses the year 1940 as the starting point because the republican regime reached its point of consolidation around that time. The republican official ideology constructed (and constructed by) the Turkish History Thesis embedded in national education crystallized toward the end of the 1930s. The time frame of this study ends in 2007, because in the following years the same textbooks published in the middle of the first decade of the new millennium went into new editions. Because this study analyses a series of textbooks produced for the consumption of primary, secondary, and high school students, the targeted audience of the textbooks examined here include the whole body of students attending those schools. As mentioned, textbook content has always been controlled at the national level in Turkey. No textbook uninspected and unauthorized by the Ministry of National Education finds its way into the classroom. This has assured uniformity and almost complete homogenization in the curriculum of all schools across the country. In some cases, the textbooks do not even

bear the names of the authors, demonstrating that the Ministry of National Education has paid attention to content, rather than authorship, in choosing textbooks. As the examination of seventeen textbooks published between 1940 and 1980 demonstrates, although different authors wrote them, the content of the textbooks remained identical. This also applies to the twelve textbooks used between 1980 and 2007. The Ministry of Education picked the textbooks whose content complied with the particular understanding of Ottoman-Turkish history that was championed by the power holders of the time. The fourteen textbooks that I examined (yet do not refer to in this study because they avoid the term "the Eastern Question") are the following: (1) Enver Behnan Şapolyo, *Kemal Atatürk ve Milli Mücadele Tarihi* (no grade) (Ankara: Berkalp Kitabevi, 1944); (2) *Tarih V* (fifth grade) (İstanbul: Maarif Matbaası, 1945); (3) Arif Müfid Mansel, Cavid Baysun, and Enver Ziya Karal, *Yeni ve Yakın Çağlar Tarihi Lise Üçüncü Sınıf* (eleventh grade) (Ankara: MEB Yayınları, 1947); (4) Faruk Kurtuluş and Osman Kurtuluş, *Tarih V* (fifth grade) (İstanbul: Nebioğlu Kitap, 1950); (5) Enver Koray, *Tarih III Liseler İçin Yeni ve Yakın Çağlar* (eleventh grade) (İstanbul: İnkılap Kitabevi, 1951); (6) Ali Ekrem İnal and Nurettin Ormancı, *Tarih Orta III* (eighth grade) (İstanbul: Atlas Yayınevi, 1953); (7) Zuhuri Danışman, *Tarih V* (fifth grade) (İstanbul: Samim Sadık Özaygen Neşriyat, 1955); (8) Hilmi Oran, *İlkokullar için Tarih V* (fifth grade) (İstanbul: İnkılap Kitabevi, 1955); (9) Emin Oktay, *Tarih Orta III* (eighth grade) (İstanbul: Atlas Yayınevi, 1956); (10) Halit Aksan and Büruz Sarmat, *Tarih İlkokul V* (fifth grade) (İstanbul: İnkılap Kitabevi, 1956); (11) Enver Ziya Karal, *Yeni ve Yakın Çağlar Tarihi* (eleventh grade) (İstanbul: Maarif Basımevi, 1957); (12) Enver Behnan Şapolyo, *Yeni Lise Kitapları Yeni ve Yakın Çağlar ve Türkiye Tarihi Lise III* (eleventh grade) (İstanbul: İnkılap Kitabevi, 1960); (13) Ali Ekrem İnal and Rakım Çalapala, *Tarih V* (fifth grade) (İstanbul: Atlas Yayınevi, 1962); (14) Yılmaz Öztuna, *Tarih Lise III* (eleventh grade) (İstanbul: Milli Eğitim Bakanlığı, 1976).

28. Sadri Ertem and Kazım Nami Duru, *Ortaokul İçin Tarih III* (eighth grade) (Ankara: Maarif Matbaası, 1941), 119.

29. Cezar Mustafa, *Ortaokullar İçin Tarih III* (eighth grade) (İstanbul: Okul Kitapları Türk, 1951), 133.

30. Bedriye Atsız and Hilmi Oran, *Yeni Lise Kitapları, Tarih III* (eleventh grade) (İstanbul: Yeni ve Yakın Çağlar, İnkılap Kitabevi, 1953), 162.

31. Amy Singer, "The Ottoman Legacy for Contemporary Turkish Culture, Institutions, and Values," *Comparative Studies of South Asia, Africa and the Middle East* 31, no. 3 (2011): 553–56.

32. Aysel Morin, "Crafting a Nation: The Mythic Construction of the New Turkish National Identity in Atatürk's Nutuk" (PhD diss., University of Nebraska, 2004), 170.

33. Boyar, *Ottomans, Turks and the Balkans*, 18.

34. Büşra Ersanlı, "The Ottoman Empire in the Historiography of the Kemalist Era: A Theory of Fatal Decline," in *The Ottomans and the Balkans: A*

Discussion of Historiography, ed. Fikret Adanır and Suraiya Faroqhi (Leiden: Brill, 2002), 121.

35. Büşra Ersanlı Behar, *İktidar ve Tarih Türkiye'de Resmi Tarih Tezinin Oluşumu (1929-1937)*, 2nd ed. (İstanbul: Afa, 1996); Etienne Copeaux, *Tarih Ders Kitaplarında (1931-1993) Türk Tarih Tezinden Türk-İslam Sentezine* [De L'Adriatique à La Mer de Chine], trans. Ali Berktay (İstanbul: Tarih Vakfı Yurt Yayınları, 1998).

36. Bayar, "Dynamic Nature of Educational Policies," 368.

37. Morin, "Crafting the Nation," 246-47.

38. Türk Tarihi Heyeti Azaları, *Türk Tarihinin Ana Hatları* (İstanbul: Devlet Matbaası, 1930), 1.

39. Mikhail Bakhtin, *The Dialogic Imagination: Four Essays* (Austin: University of Texas Press, 1980), 281.

40. Copeaux, *Tarih Ders Kitaplarında*, 51-53.

41. Cemil Aydın, "Between Occidentalism and the Global Left: Islamist Critiques of the West in Turkey," *Comparative Studies of South Asia, Africa and the Middle East* 26, no. 3 (2006): 451.

42. For an analysis of "the epistemological difference between the West and the process of Westernization" in the Turkish collective conscious, and the national aporia of Westernization against and/or in spite of the West, see Emre Kayhan, "Between Apology and Utopia: A Study on the Sources of Turkish Conduct" (PhD diss., Fletcher School of Law and Diplomacy, 2009), 103.

43. Ibid., 169-71.

44. Ergin, "Chromatic Turkishness," 11.

45. Çağlar Keyder, "A History and Geography of Turkish Nationalism," in *Citizenship and the Nation-State in Greece and Turkey*, ed. Faruk Birtek and Thalia Dragonas (London and NewYork: Routledge, 2005), 12.

46. Twelve textbooks published between 1980 and 2007 have been examined for this study. In addition to the four textbooks quoted later in the chpater, the eight unquoted textbooks are the following: (1) Rakım Çalapala, *Sosyal Bilgiler V* (fifth grade) (İstanbul: İnkılap Kitabevi, 1988); (2) *İlkokullar İçin Sosyal Bilgiler V* (fifth grade) (İstanbul: Milli Eğitim Basımevi, 1993); (3) Erdoğan Şahin Tahir, *Osmanlı Tarihi Lise I* (ninth grade) (Ankara: Koza Eğitim Yayıncılık, 1993); (4) Kara Kemal, *Milli Tarih Orta II* (seventh grade) (İstanbul: Serhat Yayınları, 1994); (5) *Tarih Lise II* (tenth grade) (İstanbul: Milsan Basım A.Ş, 2003); (6) Erdoğan Şahin Tahir and Ali Kaya, *Osmanlı Tarihi II* (tenth grade) (Ankara: Koza Eğitim ve Yayıncılık, 1993); (7) Ahmet Güneş and Süleyman Özbek, *Tarih Lise II* (tenth grade) (İstanbul: Tutibay Yayınları: 2006); (8) Ahmet Başaran, Ali Sert, Lütfi İlgün, and Liseler İçin Osmanlı Tarihi (ninth-tenth-eleventh grade) (Ankara: Devlet Kitapları MEB, 2007); Ahmet Güneş and Süleyman Özbek, *Tarih Lise II* (tenth grade) (İstanbul: Tutibay Yayınları, 2006).

47. Avonna Deanne Swartz, "Textbooks and National Ideology: A Content Analysis of the Secondary Turkish History Textbooks Used in the Republic of Turkey since 1929" (PhD diss., University of Texas, 1997), 78.

48. Copeaux, *Tarih Ders Kitaplarında*, 62.

49. Turkish-Islamic Synthesis as a political ideal and discourse began to germinate in the 1970s. The ideologues of the right-wing organization Aydınlar Ocağı (The Hearth of the Enlightened) were mainly responsible for its formulation. As Zürcher correctly points out, "according to this theory, Turkish culture was built on two pillars: a 2500-year-old Turkish element and a 1000-year-old Islamic element." See Erik J. Zürcher, *Turkey: A Modern History* (London: I. B. Tauris, 1998), 303. As Taysı suggests, between 1970 and 1980, "the general nature of the ideology of those in power had more of a Turkist and Islamist tinge to it, thus the state tolerated, and in some cases fostered Islamic and Turkist expressions of identity." See Taysı, "For the People in Spite of the People?," 97. It was only after 1980s, however, that the Turkish-Islamic Synthesis came to encompass and represent the main parameters of official Turkish national identity. Kemalist secularism was reassessed in order to reach a resolution between the Islamic Ottoman past and the secular Turkish present. For further reading on the Turkish-Islamic Synthesis, see Gökhan Çetinsaya, "Rethinking Nationalism and Islam: Some Preliminary Notes on the Roots of 'Turkish-Islamic Synthesis' in Modern Turkish Political Thought," *Muslim World* 89 (1999): 350–86; Bozkurt Güvenç, Gencay Şaylan, İlhan Tekeli, and Şerafettin Turan, *Türk-İslam Sentezi* [Turkish-Islamic Synthesis] (İstanbul: Sarmal, 1991); İlhan Tekeli, "Türk-İslam Sentezi Üzerine" [On Turkish-Islamic Synthesis], *Bilim ve Sanat* 77 (1987): 5–8; Paul J. Magnarella, "State Politics: Desecularization, State Corporatism, and Elite Behavior in Turkey," in *Human Materialism: A Model of Sociocultural Systems and a Strategy for Analysis* (Gainesville: University Press of Florida, 1993), 87–113.

50. Nora Fisher Onar, "Echoes of a Universalism Lost: Rival Representations of the Ottomans in Today's Turkey," *Middle Eastern Studies* 45, no. 2 (2009): 233.

51. H. Kaya, M. Öztürk, D. Kahyaoğlu, and A. Çetiner, "The Structure of the Turkish Education System," in *Clio in the Balkans: The Politics of History Education*, ed. C. Koulouri (Thessaloniki: CDRSE, 2002), 507.

52. Taysı, "For the People in Spite of the People?," 125.

53. Mükerrem K. Su and Ahmet Mumcu, *Liseler İçin T.C İnkılap Tarihi ve Atatürkçülük*, 9th ed. (İstanbul: MEB Basımevi, 1989), 306–7.

54. Nihat Gürel Kahveci, "Teaching 'Europe' in Turkey: An Analysis of Secondary History Textbooks 1956–2005" (PhD diss., University of Illinois at Urbana-Champaign, 2007), 53.

55. *Tarih, Lise II* (tenth grade) (İstanbul: MEB TTK Basımevi, 1993), 55.

56. Veli Şirin, *Tarih II, Liseler İçin* (tenth grade) (İstanbul: Gendaş, 1995), 92–93.

57. Onar, "Echoes of a Universalism Lost," 229.

58. Çağlar Keyder, "'Whither the Project of Modernity?' Turkey in the 1990s," in *Rethinking Modernity and National Identity in Turkey*, ed. Sibel Bozdoğan and Reşat Kasaba (Seattle: University of Washington Press, 1997), 42–43.

59. Taysı, "For the People in Spite of the People?," 11.

60. Many members of the currently incumbent Adalet ve Kalkınma Partisi (Justice and Development Party) are neo-Ottomanists pitting Ottoman pluralism against universalist republicanism. The neo-Ottoman narrative emphasizes moderate Islamic conservatism over the strict secularist principles of Kemalism. It also suggests as much, if not more, political, economic, and cultural engagement with Islamic countries as with Europe. See Erikli Cihan, "Through the Turkish Looking Glass: Turkey's Divergent Narratives, National Identity and Foreign Policy" (master's thesis, Georgetown University, 2010), 30.

61. Drawing on the analysis of Türkmen, we can assert that history textbooks in the twenty-first century are not the only ones in the curriculum that reflect a new emphasis on Islam, which by definition points to a more embracing attitude toward the Islamic Ottoman past. As Türkmen asserts, "the way Atatürk is presented in textbooks changes from 1995 to 2007-8. The 2007-8 textbooks show a new concern for Atatürk's religiosity and his knowledge about Islam. Anecdotes proving his deep Qoranic knowledge are inserted into chapters and supported with photographs of him in prayer in the unit 'Religion and Secularism. . . .' Such a concern is not seen in the 1995 textbooks." See Buket Türkmen, "A Transformed Kemalist Islam or a New Islamic Civic Morality? A Study of 'Religious Culture and Morality' Textbooks in the Turkish High School Curricula," *Comparative Studies of South Asia, Africa and the Middle East* 29, no. 3 (2009): 381-97, here 394.

62. Vicdan Cazgır, Servet Yavuz, and Niyazi Ceyhun, *Tarih Lise II* (tenth grade), 2nd ed. (Ankara: Devlet Kitapları, 2007), 58-59.

63. Taysı, "For the People in Spite of the People?," 47.

Epilogue
Legacies of the Eastern Question

LUCIEN J. FRARY and MARA KOZELSKY

Macedonia Square, the central meeting place in Skopje, Republic of Macedonia, is part of an ambitious "antiquization" project financed by the government that reflects the bustling capital as a historical crossroads. Synthesizing more than two millennia of history, the square's centerpiece features an enormous white marble fountain with a twenty-two-meter-high bronze Alexander the Great on a rearing Bucephalus. Gotse Delchev and Dame Gruev, revolutionary leaders and founders of nineteenth-century independence movements in Bulgaria and Macedonia, flank statues of the Byzantine emperor Justinian I (whose birthplace is twelve miles outside Skopje), and Tsar Samuel, the leader of the medieval Bulgarian Empire. Newly imagined twentieth-century heroes, such as the lexicographer Dimitrija Chupovski and the Yugoslav politician Metodija Andonov-Chento, complete this pantheon of nationalistic kitsch, incorporating the native champions of several Balkan states. Anachronistic public monuments like these illuminate the confusing nature of borders and identities in the Balkans. The "Skopje 2014" project, which includes plans for about twenty buildings and forty monuments, underscores the fraught politics of historical memory and

Statue of Alexander the Great on horseback in Macedonia Square, Skopje, Macedonia. (photo by Raso MK / Wikimedia Commons)

the attempt of Macedonians to grapple with a state created, in part, by the Eastern Question.

When the Ottoman Empire collapsed in the wake of the First World War, the Eastern Question by all appearances expired. Many contemporary observers regarded the Treaties of Sèvres (1920) and Lausanne (1923) as the denouement to the struggle for the Ottoman inheritance. British politician and historian J. A. R. Marriott concluded the fourth edition of his landmark study, published in 1940, with the transference of the Turkish capital from İstanbul to Ankara and the creation of the modern Turkish Republic. According to Marriott, "the birth of a new Nation in the bracing atmosphere of Anatolia" closed one aspect of the Eastern Question. He vaguely conceded, however, that other factors still awaited solutions.[1] More decisively, M. S. Anderson ended his 1966 survey with a discussion of the peace treaties of the postwar years: "With the Lausanne settlement the Eastern Question was no more."[2] Anderson argued that the disappearance of empires limited the rivalries of the great powers and fostered the well-being of nation-states. Still, Anderson also hinted at the troubles embedded in unsatisfied territorial claims. In such a manner, the two standard works of the Eastern Question alluded to issues unresolved by the postwar settlement.[3]

Beginning in the nineteenth century, the Eastern Question evolved from European presumptions to manage a perceived Ottoman decline into an elaborate international contest involving millions of people and dozens of states. The pattern of competition and rivalry, however, did not suddenly halt with the partition of the Ottoman Empire according to the Treaty of Sèvres. Instead, the contrived solution of the Eastern Question, the creation of the mandate states of the Middle East, unleashed a new generation of problems that have dominated the twentieth century. Thus, American historian L. Carl Brown has suggested that the Eastern Question "still exists," albeit "in muted form."[4] More generally, it could be said that the Eastern Question has shaped many of "the structural issues and conflicts of modern Eastern European and Middle Eastern politics."[5]

This book understands the Eastern Question as belonging to a particular historical era with specific historical actors. The concept emerged in the vocabulary of European politics in the 1820s as publicists and politicians retrospectively applied the Eastern Question to past events, in some cases dating its origins as far back as the Persian invasion of Greece. For a century, contemporaries applied the concept to describe the tensions unleashed by the Russian-Ottoman confrontation of the late eighteenth century through the end of the First World War. As chapters in this book demonstrate, European concerns about the Eastern Question had real and often devastating consequences for peoples of the Ottoman Empire and inhabitants of its western and northern borderlands. Historical phenomena of such significance do not simply exit the stage of history without leaving a lasting legacy. In these final pages, we propose that contemporary national identities, territorial boundaries, conflicts, and cultures from the Balkans to the Caucasus have deep roots in Eastern Question policies, wars, and migrations.

As historians, we do not intend this brief foray into affairs of the present as an exhaustive research essay. Such is the domain of political scientists and journalists. Rather, we are taking the opportunity to reflect in a general way on the legacy of the Eastern Question. Here we aim to highlight the literature that has already begun to contemplate the Eastern Question's heritage in the twentieth and twenty-first centuries and to encourage scholars to further explore how this past international dilemma has shaped the present. Although the Eastern Question may no longer survive as formulated by nineteenth-century diplomats, illuminating its legacy provides a key to understanding the political culture that still exists in the Balkans, the Black Sea region, the Caucasus, and the Middle East. As illustrated by the Macedonian monuments, the Eastern Question still frames how indigenous actors create collective identities and relationships to the world around them. On a more dangerous level, many current conflicts in the borderland regions between the former Russian and Ottoman Empires continue to exhibit the political pattern of Eastern Question disputes. Recognizing the unintended consequences of foreign intervention, whether for peace enforcement, humanitarian reasons, or economic self-interest, has much to teach us about the unforeseen challenges of international relations and interstate rivalry in a persistently volatile and fragmented region of the world. The ouster of Crimean President Yanukovych and Russia's foray into Crimea in February 2014 attests to the relevance of the Eastern Question when contemplating the history of the present.

Unsurprisingly, centuries of the Eastern Question have left their toll. Although the activity of native populations mediated external intrusion, great-power politics swept up local actors who regularly bore the burden of ensuing wars. Treaties designed by Western powers, even when integrating desires of select indigenous intellectuals and nationalists, typically failed to correspond to native realities. By the early twentieth century, the relative ethnic and religious harmony fostered by centuries of Ottoman rule had disintegrated. A mixture of foreign and domestic forces had imposed a new framework based on national sovereignty and ethnic homogeneity. As a result, neighbors turned on neighbors in continuous localized violence sparked by new geographic divisions and economic dislocations. Christian state powers in the Balkan Peninsula and northern Black Sea basin pushed Muslims southward and further east. The Ottomans, meanwhile, removed Armenians from their midst.[6]

The European powers responded to the localized violence (which they, in part, provoked) with cartographic experiments and humanitarian interventions. Decisions made in smoke-filled European conference halls in the nineteenth century generated much of the twenty-first century's political map of southeastern Europe. Similarly, the imaginary geography of politics and identity that has settled over the space between the Balkans through the Middle East is mostly the result of foreign thinking.[7] The new Europe and Middle East created by the peace treaties ending the First World War failed to resolve the problems of ethnic violence that they ostensibly sought to address. Instead, friction immediately ensued between Muslims and Christians, Serbs and Croats, Bulgarians and Greeks, Jews and Palestinians, Kuwaitis and Iraqis, and so on. In the Caucasus, similarly, hostility among Armenians and Azerbaijanis, Georgians and Russians detonated with the end of tsarist rule, as myths of "ancient hatreds" were born.

The violence of the First World War persisted after 1918 for many of the new states created by the European powers, as uprisings and border wars continued in the space of the former Ottoman Empire. In some cases, such as in the interwar Kingdom of Yugoslavia, unresolved tensions erupted during the Second World War and beyond.[8] Experiments of self-rule in the Caucasus ended through the application of brute force.[9] Subsequently, the Soviet Union continued the process of expelling Muslims from the northern Black Sea shore. European penetration continued to guide the developments of the new mandate states as the struggle for the Ottoman succession continued into the Cold War.[10]

Naturally, not all the region's contemporary conflicts are due to the policies generated by the Eastern Question. Yet nearly all of them have some origin in the predominant problem of nineteenth-century international relations. An illustrative example is the infamous exchange between Churchill and Stalin in 1944 known as "the percentages agreement," which presumed the right of the great powers to divide Eastern Europe into spheres of influence. Both wartime leaders, well versed in modern European history, relied on the clear precedent generated by centuries of Eastern Question interventions in Eastern Europe to carve up the region into zones of dominion. In a similar instance, when discussing the question of the Turkish Straits during the wartime conference at Potsdam in July 1945, Soviet foreign minister Vyacheslav Molotov relied on the Eastern Question treaties of 1805 (the Russian-Ottoman Defensive Alliance) and 1833 (Unkiar Skelessi) to press for Soviet bases on Turkish territory.[11]

During the Cold War, the imposition of a strong, unifying nationalist principle in the Soviet Union, Yugoslavia, and the Republic of Turkey, appeared to suppress the sectarian and ethnic violence generated in the crucible of the Eastern Question. The Yugoslavian wars of the 1990s, the Nagorno-Karabakh conflict, and the resurgence of Kurdish nationalism soon shattered this impression. The revival of ethnic and sectarian clashes revealed that authoritarian national policies had not solved the old conflicts embedded in Eastern Question affairs but had merely put them into a deep freeze. Similarly, present-day conflicts over symbols, heroes, and homelands in the Balkans, the Black Sea region, and the Caucasus directly stem from great-power rivalries in the territory of the former Ottoman Empire. An ongoing issue involves commonplace assumptions about the meaning of "East" and "West" constructed by Eastern Question political discourse and how these categories can cloud our appreciation of reality.[12]

Perhaps more than any of the borderland regions of the former Ottoman Empire, Turkey battles the legacy of the Eastern Question today. Whether coming to terms with long-standing fears of dismemberment or debates over Turkey's entry into the EU, echoes of the Eastern Question endure. Memory of the Eastern Question permeates Turkish conceptions of its own statehood and its foreign policy. In some cases, as Nazan Çiçek points out in this volume, this memory has created a lingering resentment of Western interference. In other cases, as Ohran Kemal Cengiz, a columnist for the Turkish newspaper *Zaman*, has argued, the legacy manifests itself in a "security state neurosis." In the aftermath of centuries of European debates about partitioning the Ottoman Empire, Turkey's founders and subsequent ruling parties have had "a deep fear of losing the homeland as a whole."[13]

Meanwhile, the lexicon of nineteenth-century international relations (and the scholarly and journalistic literature that lent it legitimacy) promoted the deep-seated notion of Turkey as a non-European power. "Othering" discourse that undergirded the Eastern Question still exists in European politics and the continuing debate over Turkey's candidacy for the EU. Is Turkey part of Europe, or not? Such questions and their answers have assumed a consistently essentialist tone, with much of the opposition revolving around the nature of Turkish culture and whether Muslims can be considered European. The Cyprus dispute, meanwhile, has magnified the problem profoundly. Discourse around Turkey's entry into the EU, in other words, has much in common with the Western portrayal of the Ottoman Empire during the nineteenth century and the legacy of European intervention in Ottoman affairs.[14]

As Turkish interest in joining the EU wanes, Mustafa Kemal Atatürk's vision of a highly modernized, secular, and homogenous ethnic nation-state has given way to a nationalist model based on a more distant past. In place of Kemalism, Turkish politicians and nationalists have turned to the Ottoman Empire for inspiration. The result has been called "neo-Ottomanism," and more popularly, "Ottomania."[15] Many books, theatrical works, and television shows set in the Ottoman era have reached Turkish audiences in recent decades. Turkish fashion incorporates Ottoman style, and restaurants feature Ottoman dishes. Many Turkish women have returned to the veil. Neo-Ottoman policy makers celebrate the Islamic and multiethnic history of Turkey's past and envision an important economic and cultural role in the former Ottoman space. The Turkish government has increased trade with neighboring countries.[16] The recently established Black Sea Economic Cooperation (BSEC) and the Southeastern European Cooperation Process (SEECP) provide a framework for this new orientation.[17] Turkish missionaries, many of whom follow the teachings of Muslim cleric Fetullah Gülen, spread their practice of Islam to the peoples of Crimea, the Caucasus, and Central Asia. Gülen supporters distinguish Anatolian Islam from Arabian Islam. They characterize the former as influenced by Sufi mysticism and the teachings of Said Nursi, a Muslim theologian who emphasized pairing the tradition of Ottoman classical learning with modern advances in science. Rooted in education initiatives, the movement's expansionist impulse follows the contours of the former Ottoman Empire and the Muslim regions of the former Soviet Union.[18]

Historical memory invigorates Turkish interest in areas of the former Ottoman realm, although pragmatic ties with the populations of Crimea and the Caucasus inform Turkish political and economic behavior. Descendants of the refugees who fled Russia and the Balkans during the numerous Russian-Ottoman wars and Eastern Question conflicts, for example, constitute active minority groups in Turkey. Some, such as the large diaspora communities of Circassians and Crimean Tatars, who immigrated to Turkey in multiple large waves throughout the nineteenth century, advocate for Turkish support in the affairs of their homelands.[19]

Beyond Turkey, the legacy of the Eastern Question can be seen in the borderland regions between the former Russian and Ottoman Empires. In Bulgaria, for example, Bulgarian Muslims, or Pomaks, thrive despite centuries-long sporadic ethnocultural antagonism with their non-Muslim neighbors. Although the most recent state-directed onslaught against Bulgarian-speaking Muslims and Bulgarian Turks under Todor Zhivkov resulted in the tragic exodus of thousands of individuals, over half a million Bulgarian Muslims and Bulgarian Turks still reside within Bulgaria. Concentrated in the Eastern Rhodopes and northeastern Ludogorie region, many Bulgarian Muslims have mobilized behind the banner of the Movement for Rights and Freedoms (Dvizhenie za prava i svobodi), a centrist political party that has become increasingly visible in recent years. Their presence adds complexity and texture to an intriguing region and constitutes one of the many sensitive locales shaped by the Eastern Question.

For those of us benefitting from hindsight, it seems obvious that the twentieth-century experiments in socialism in the Balkans resolved few of the underlying causes of conflict. One of the more important debates today consists of the disputed territory of Kosova, the most recent state created through great-power intervention. In fact, for those looking for a link between past and present, Kosova testifies to the failure of international mediation to overpower the region's inhabitants. Kosovars today still associate with the clan, family, and regional ties that the forces of a NATO- or EU-guided "independent" state could not harness.[20] The stubborn parochialism alive in Kosova is similar to that encountered by nineteenth-century diplomats when they tried to mold the region along "Western" patterns. Kosova also stands as a testimony to the longevity of Eastern Question alignments in the post-Ottoman world. Ninety-eight UN states recognize its independence, while Russia and Serbia continue to dispute its existence.

The status of Macedonia as an independent state and the question of Macedonian identity, alluded to at the beginning of this epilogue, similarly illuminate the contested nature of politics and identity in the historical area of the Eastern Question. Although the Republic of Macedonia has been a member of the UN since 1993, Greece continues to challenge the usage of the name "Macedonia," because of the historical and territorial ambiguity of the term and the millions of Greeks who identify themselves as Macedonian. Thus, the provisional reference of the Former Yugoslav Republic of Macedonia (FYROM) remains the official moniker. Macedonian politicians struggle to create a "Macedonian identity" in a state composed of many different ethnic and religious groups, including Turks, Serbs, Bosnians, Aromanians, Roma, and a quarter of the population that self-identifies as Albanian.

Like Turkey and the Balkan Peninsula, the Caucasus also bears the imprint of the Eastern Question. Arguably, of all the areas under discussion, the legacy here is currently the most volatile and the least understood. Problems in the Caucasus range widely to include ethnic and sectarian disputes, regionalization, and stalled transitions to democracy. Wars fought over Abkhazia, Chechnya, and Karabakh in the 1990s and the first decade of the new millennium failed to resolve latent tensions, leading many experts to describe the region as one of "frozen conflicts."[21] Displaced peoples from these regions fan out into surrounding states and struggle for survival. Moreover, in what appears to be a modern reenactment of the Eastern Question, Russia, the EU, and Turkey vie for influence in the region. In the past, great powers were interested in the Caucasus for its ports, geostrategic location at the intersection of the Russian and Ottoman Empires and Eurasian trade routes, and, in the case of Britain, access to Persia.[22] Today competition takes a similar pattern of foreign interference but revolves around oil reserves in the Caspian Sea and marks the entry of the United States as a key player. The problem here is not the purchasing of oil but the characterization of the region as intrinsic to national security interests, a platform that increasingly justifies interference.[23]

In an effort to maintain its traditional sphere of influence in the southern Caucasus as well as its monopoly over energy supplies to Europe, Russia maneuvers to block or control Caspian oil trade with the West.[24] Although hesitant to antagonize Russia by granting membership to the states of the southern Caucasus, NATO began reaching out to the region after the Soviet Union collapsed. Currently no Caucasian states belong to NATO, but they all participate in the NATO program Partnership for Peace. Turkey, meanwhile, with fewer resources than Russia or the West, nevertheless actively engages the

Caucasus through BSEC, SEECP, and BlackSeafor, a naval-based "peacekeeping" force.

At the moment, the southern Caucasus is split fairly evenly between spheres of influence, with Armenia seeking support from Russia, Azerbaijan from Turkey, and Georgia from the EU and NATO institutions.[25] Twenty-first-century great-power politics in this region of the world, among other things, has assisted the rearmament of states of the Caucasus. Petrodollars from Russia, the United States, and Turkey have sped up this process.[26] The Russian-Georgian War of 2008 illustrates the dangerous consequences of external competition in this region. Russia's intervention on behalf of South Ossetia and Abkhazia has guaranteed neither independence nor stability. It did, however, cost millions of dollars, resulted in thousands of refugees, and caused tremendous damage to the Georgian economy. Estimates of human casualties range from a few to a few thousand. Analysts such as Vicken Cheterian ascribe these conflicts either to the rise of nationalism or to the "historic upheaval caused by the Soviet collapse."[27] We suggest, however, that many of the conflicts in the Caucasus also stem from a pattern of geopolitics that date to the Eastern Question; internal ethnic tensions and external competition for the Caucasus among the great powers have roots in the conflicts of the nineteenth century.

Present-day Ukraine, like the Balkans and the Caucasus, bears the mark of the Eastern Question. Political scientists often note Ukraine's identity conflict between ethnic Ukrainians and those who are either ethnically Russian or culturally identify with Russia.[28] However, the Ukrainian-Russian divide is only part of the story, more reflective of its recent past in the Soviet Union. Before Russia absorbed Ukraine in the late seventeenth century, much of the region fell under Ottoman sway. After Russia pushed down to the Black Sea in the eighteenth century, what is now southern Ukraine existed as a frontier zone between the Russian and the Ottoman Empires.

The many border changes, migrations, and population exchanges associated with Eastern Question conflicts in the eighteenth, nineteenth, and twentieth centuries have left Ukraine with a diverse population of Crimean Tatars, Hungarians, Moldovans, Bulgarians, Armenians, Poles, and others. Crimean Tatars, whose fate has been closely tied to the Eastern Question, rank among the largest and most influential ethnic groups. They are locked in a battle with Russians for influence in the peninsula, while memory of the Crimean War continues to haunt Russian and Tatar relations. Tatars today view the Crimean War as an expression of Russian colonialism, bigotry, and a forerunner to Stalinist deportations. Ultranationalistic Cossacks have reprised their Crimean War-era paramilitary roles with anti-Islamic activities, an ugly phenomenon also transpiring in the Caucasus.[29] Following Russia's re-annexation of the peninsula in 2014, painful memories of the recent and distant past have left many Tatars uncertain of their future. Some have once again begun to leave their homelands.

The future of mainland Ukraine also hangs in a terrible uncertainty. Torn between NATO and the EU to the west and Russia to the east, Ukrainian citizens struggle to assert their sovereignty amid heavily fortified great powers. Diplomatic patterns reminiscent of the Eastern Question operating in Ukraine today include: external provocation of nationalist sentiment; clandestine intervention; regional nationalists appealing to big states for assistance; big states presuming to manage the affairs of small nations; and Western suspicion of Russian motivation. To be sure, many of Ukraine's present problems flow from seventy years of Soviet policy and the challenges of the post-Soviet transition.[30] Still, it is hard not to see the imprint of nineteenth-century diplomatic behaviors.

Any discussion of the lasting influence of the Eastern Question must make reference to the Middle East. Whereas diplomats influenced by Wilsonian ideals of national sovereignty may have seen the creation of the mandate states from the partitioned Ottoman Empire as a rupture with the past, scholars who have studied the region in the decades since have also emphasized continuities.[31] In this view, the British and French mandate states directly stemmed from diplomatic projects to partition the Ottoman Empire during the nineteenth century. Western diplomats' presumption to generate a new political geography in the Treaties of Sèvres and Lausanne followed traditional patterns of European interventionism in Ottoman affairs. As in the Treaty of Berlin following the Russian-Ottoman War of 1877–78, new boundaries often did not reflect the desires of all indigenous populations. Thus, the problem of Kurdish statehood, the Israeli-Palestinian conflict, and sectarian strife in the former mandate states can be directly and indirectly attributed to the Eastern Question.[32] Recently, Huseyin Yilmaz has even suggested that the term "Middle East" is virtually synonymous with the Eastern Question, without the "question attached."[33]

In the twenty-first century, the toll of the Eastern Question is everywhere evident in states from the Balkans to the Caucasus. It can be seen in awkwardly crafted borders and an altered demography, as well as the nationalist movements that draw inspiration from a fraught past. Further, the present presumption of the great powers to regulate affairs in this region follows worn patterns and threatens to create new problems. At worst, the Eastern Question reveals itself in inconclusive wars over territory and peoples. Understanding the Eastern Question in its past and present complexity grows ever more important, as the re-emerging states at its center establish themselves.

NOTES

1. J. A. R. Marriott, *The Eastern Question*, 4th ed. (Oxford: Oxford University Press, 1940), 577.

2. M. S. Anderson, *The Eastern Question, 1774–1923: A Study in International Relations* (London: Macmillan, 1966), 388.

3. The entries on the "Eastern Question" in the three editions of the *Bolshaia Sovetskaia Entsiklopediia* (1929, 1951, 1971) likewise end demonstratively with the First World War and the October Revolution, when "the term departed from usage" (2nd ed.) and "exited the arena of world politics" (3rd ed.).

4. L. Carl Brown, *International Politics and the Middle East: Old Rules, Dangerous Game* (Princeton, NJ: Princeton University Press, 1984), 7; idem, *Diplomacy in the Middle East: The International Relations of Regional and Outside Powers* (London: I. B. Tauris, 2004), xv.

5. Mujeeb R. Khan, "The Ottoman Eastern Question and the Problematic Origins of Ethnic Cleansing, Genocide, and Humanitarian Interventionism in Europe and the Middle East," in *War and Diplomacy: The Russo-Turkish War of 1877–1878 and the Treaty of Berlin*, ed. Peter L. Sluglett and M. Hakan Yavuz (Salt Lake City: Utah University Press, 2011), 99.

6. For a collection of pathbreaking essays on this topic, see Ronald Grigor Suny, Fatma Müge Göçek, and Norman M. Naimark, *A Question of Genocide: Armenians and Turks at the End of the Ottoman Empire* (Oxford: Oxford University Press, 2013).

7. For reassessments of the creation of borders in the Balkans and the Arabian Peninsula, see Isa Blumi, *Foundations of Modernity: Human Agency and the Imperial State* (New York: Routledge, 2012); idem, *Reinstating the Ottomans: Alternative Balkan Communities, 1800–1912* (New York: Palgrave Macmillan, 2011); Eugene Rogan, *Frontiers of the State in the Late Ottoman Empire: Transjordan, 1850–1921* (Cambridge: Cambridge University Press, 1999); Frederick Anscombe, *The Ottoman Gulf: The Creation of Kuwait, Saudi Arabia, and Qatar* (New York: Columbia University Press, 1997).

8. Joseph Rothschild, *East-Central Europe between the Two World Wars* (Seattle: University of Washington Press, 1977), remains unsurpassed. See also Hugh Seton-Watson, *Eastern Europe between the Wars, 1918–1941* (Cambridge:

Cambridge University Press, 1944); and Balázs Trencsényi *The Politics of "National Character": A Study in Interwar East European Thought* (New York: Routledge, 2012).

9. Richard Pipes, *The Formation of the Soviet Union: Communism and Nationalism, 1917-1923*, 2nd ed. (Cambridge, MA: Harvard University Press, 1964); Ronald Suny, *The Revenge of the Past: Nationalism, Revolution, and the Collapse of the Soviet Union* (Stanford, CA: Stanford University Press, 1993); Firuz Kazemzadeh, *The Struggle for Transcaucasia (1917-1921)* (New York: Columbia University Press, 1951); R. G. Hovannisian, *The Republic of Armenia*, 4 vols. (Berkeley: University of California Press, 1971-96); Ronald Suny, *The Making of the Georgian Nation*, 2nd ed. (Bloomington: Indiana University Press, 1994); idem, *Looking toward Ararat: Armenia in Modern History* (Bloomington: Indiana University Press, 1993).

10. Brown, *International Politics and the Middle East*, 93-196; A. L. Macfie, *The Eastern Question, 1774-1923* (London: Longman, 1996), 78-80.

11. J. C. Hurewitz, "Russia and the Turkish Straits: A Reevaluation of the Origins of the Problem," *World Politics* 14, no. 4 (July 1962): 605-32; idem, *The Middle East and North Africa in World Politics: A Documentary Record*, 2 vols. (New Haven, CT: Yale University Press, 1975), 1:162-67, 252-53.

12. See the essays in Andrew Hammond, *The Balkans and the West: Constructing the European Other, 1945-2003* (Aldershot, Hampshire: Ashgate, 2004).

13. Ohran Kemal Cengiz, "Can We Totally Get Rid of 'Security State' Neurosis?," 6 August 2010, http://www.todayszaman.com/columnist-218272-can-we-totally-get-rid-of-security-state-neurosis.html; for an extended analysis of the Sèvres syndrome, see Fatma Müge Göçek, *The Transformation of Turkey: Redefining State and Society from the Ottoman Empire to the Modern Era* (London: I. B. Tauris, 2011), 98-184.

14. Beyza Ç. Tekin, *Representations and Othering in Discourse: The Construction of Turkey in an EU Context* (Amsterdam: John Benjamins, 2010).

15. Omer Taspinar, "Turkey's Middle East Policies: Between Neo-Ottomanism and Kemalism," *Carnegie Papers* 10 (2008), http://carnegieendowment.org/files/cmec10_taspinar_final.pdf; Alexander Murinson, *Turkey's Entente with Israel and Azerbaijan: State Identity and Security in the Middle East and Caucasus* (New York: Routledge, 2009), 82, 119, 121.

16. Göçek, *Transformation of Turkey*, 2-9.

17. Charlotte Mathilde Louise Hille, *State Building and Conflict Resolution in the Caucasus* (Amsterdam: Brill, 2010), 3. See also Oleksandr Pavliuk and Ivanna Klympush-Tsintsadze, eds., *The Black Sea Region: Cooperation and Security Building* (Armonk, NY: M. E. Sharpe, 2003).

18. M. Hakan Yavuz and John L. Esposito, eds., *Turkish Islam and the Secular State: The Gülen Movement* (Syracuse: Syracuse University Press, 2003); Bekim Agai, " Fetullah Gülen and His Movement's Islamic Ethic of Education," *Critique: Critical Middle Eastern Studies*, 11, no. 1 (2002): 27-47; Pınar Akçalı and Cennet

Engin-Demirb, "Turkey's Educational Policies in Central Asia and Caucasia: Perceptions of Policy Makers and Experts," *International Journal of Educational Development* 32, no. 1 (January 2012): 11–21.

19. Hille, *State Building and Conflict Resolution*, 4.
20. Blumi, *Reinstating the Ottomans*, 189.
21. See, for example, Svante E. Cornell, *Small Nations and Great Powers: A Study of Ethnopolitical Conflict in the Caucasus* (London: Curzon Press, 2001), 2; and Stephen Blank, "Russia and the Black Sea's Frozen Conflicts in Strategic Perspective," *Mediterranean Quarterly* 19, no. 3 (Summer 2008): 23–54.
22. Charles King, "Imagining Circassia: David Urquhart and the Making of North Caucasus Nationalism," *Russian Review* 66, no. 2 (2007): 238–55. The Eastern Question and the Great Game frequently overlapped, and the Caucasus was often the intersection.
23. For a recent summary of outside interests in affairs of the Caucasus, see Stefan Georgescu, Marilena Munteanu, Tabriz Garayev, and Stanca Costel, "Positions of the States Involved in Energy Projects in the South Caucasus," *Analele Universitatii Maritime Constanta* 13, no. 18 (2012): 89–296. The authors also point to China and Iran as actors of rising importance in the Caucasus.
24. Cheterian, *War and Peace in the Caucasus*, 356–67.
25. Hille, *State Building and Conflict Resolution*, 316–18. For BlackSeafor, see the official website of the Republic of Turkey's Ministry of Foreign Affairs, "BlackSeafor," http://www.mfa.gov.tr/blackseafor.en.mfa.
26. Vicken Cheterian, *War and Peace in the Caucasus: Ethnic Conflict and the New Geopolitics* (New York: Columbia University Press, 2008), 365–71.
27. Ibid., 5.
28. Stephen Shulman notes that these categories do not necessarily follow strict ethnic, cultural, linguistic, or even geographic alignment and distinguishes between those Ukrainian citizens who identify with an "ethnic Ukrainian identity" versus those of an "East Slavic identity." Those of the "ethnic Ukrainian identity," according to political analysts, tend to show greater interest in open markets and democracy, specifically participation in the EU, while those who identify with an "East Slavic identity" tend to favor heavy state involvement in the economy, authoritarian political structures, and economic union with Russia. See Stephen Shulman, "National Identity and Public Support for Political and Economic Reform in Ukraine," *Slavic Review* 64, no. 1 (Spring 2005): 59–87; and Mykola Riabchuk, "Ukraine's 'Muddling Through': National Identity and Postcommunist Transition," *Communist and Post-Communist Studies* 45 (2012): 439–46.
29. Ibraim Abdullaev, "Otgoloski kolonial'noi Voinyi," *Golos Kryma*, 17 October 2003, 7. See also idem, "Postup' Kresnostsev v Krymu," *Golos Kryma*, 24 November 2000, 4; and Gul'nara Abdullaeva, "Krymskie Tatary v Krymskoi Voine 1853–1856," *Advet*, 15 February 2005, 3; "Muslim Imam in Crimea Accuses Cossacks of Using Children in Provocation," *Religious Information Service of*

Ukraine, 13 February 2013, http://risu.org.ua/en/index/all_news/community/protests/51274/; and Ellen Barry, "The Cossacks Are Back: May the Hills Tremble," *New York Times*, March 16, 2013, http://tinyurl.com/mf2ljer.

30. For a good introduction to post-Soviet Ukrainian politics, see Taras Kuzio, *Contemporary Ukraine: Dynamics of Post-Soviet Transformation* (New York: M. E. Sharpe, 1998); Paul D'Anieri, *Understanding Ukrainian Politics: Power, Politics, and Institutional Design* (New York: M. E. Sharpe, 2007).

31. For a discussion of diplomats' perception of the novelty of their task, see Toby Dodge, *Inventing Iraq: The Failure of Nation Building and a History Denied* (New York: Columbia University Press, 2003).

32. D. K. Fieldhouse, *Western Imperialism in the Middle East, 1914–58* (Oxford: Oxford University Press, 2006); Timothy J. Paris, *Britain, the Hashemites and Arab Rule, 1920–1925: The Sherifian Solution* (London: Routledge, 2003). See also Edward Knox, *The Making of a New Eastern Question: British Palestine Policy and the Origins of Israel, 1917–1925* (Washington, DC: Catholic University Press, 1981); and W. Roger Louis, "The United Kingdom and the Beginning of the Mandates System, 1919–1922," *International Organization* 23, no. 1 (1969): 73–96.

33. Huseyin Yilmaz, "The Eastern Question and the Ottoman Empire: The Genesis of the Near East and the Middle East in the Nineteenth Century," in *Is There a Middle East? The Evolution of a Geopolitical Concept*, ed. Michael E. Bonine, Abbas Amanat, and Michael Ezekiel Gapser (Stanford, CA: Stanford University Press, 2012), 32.

Contributors

CANDAN BADEM (PhD, Sabancı University, İstanbul, 2007) is an assistant professor in the Department of History, Tunceli University, Tunceli, Turkey. He is the author of *The Ottoman Crimean War* (Brill, 2010) and *Çarlık Rusyası Yönetiminde Kars Vilayeti* (Birzamanlar, 2010). Currently, he is continuing research on the Russian administration of the Kars and Batum provinces and on World War I in this area.

RONALD P. BOBROFF (PhD, Duke University, 2000) is an associate professor in the Division of History, Politics, and International Studies at Oglethorpe University. His concentrations are in European international and Russian histories. He also holds an MSc from the London School of Economics through the Department of International History. He is the author of *Roads to Glory: Late Imperial Russia and the Turkish Straits* (I. B. Tauris, 2006). He has also taught at Wake Forest University, where he is currently interim chair of the History Department, and Duke University.

NAZAN ÇIÇEK (PhD, School of Oriental and African Studies, University of London, 2006) is the author of *The Young Ottomans: Turkish Critics of the Eastern Question in the Late Nineteenth Century* (I. B. Tauris, 2010). She currently teaches at Ankara University in the Faculty of Political Sciences. She has published articles on the political and intellectual history of the Ottoman Empire and the Turkish Republic in several journals including *Middle Eastern Studies* and *Études Balkaniques*.

JACK FAIREY (PhD, University of Toronto, 2004) is an assistant professor of history at the National University of Singapore. His research deals primarily with the Orthodox Christian peoples of the Near East and the history of the nineteenth-century Mediterranean. He was the Ted and Elaine Athanassiades Post-Doctoral Research Fellow at the Program in Hellenic Studies at Princeton in 2005-6 and previously taught Mediterranean and Ottoman history at Queens

University and York University in Ontario, Canada. He is currently completing a monograph on the international crisis over religious privileges and protectorates in the Ottoman Empire that gave rise to the Crimean War.

LUCIEN J. FRARY (PhD, University of Minnesota, 2003) is an associate professor of history at Rider University. His main areas of interest are Mediterranean, Slavic, and Eastern Orthodox studies. He is the author of articles and reviews in scholarly journals such as *Russian History, Mediterranean Historical Review, Kritika,* and *Modern Greek Studies Yearbook*. He is currently completing a monograph about Russia and the making of modern Greece.

MARA KOZELSKY is an associate professor of history at the University of South Alabama. Her areas of interest include religious and political history, history of Russia and Ukraine, and the Crimean War. Her study *Christianizing Crimea: Shaping Sacred Space in the Russian Empire and Beyond* was published in 2010 (Northern Illinois University Press), and she is completing a book about war and recovery in Crimea.

LORA GERD is the author of forty-five articles and three books on Byzantine and post-Byzantine canon law, the history of Byzantine studies, church history, and relations between Russia and the Greek world in the nineteenth and early twentieth centuries. She is a professor at St. Petersburg State University and chief researcher at the Russian Academy of Sciences (Institute of History). Her current research examines church history from the nineteenth century through 1917.

JOHN A. MAZIS is a professor of European history at Hamline University in St. Paul, Minnesota. He is the author of *The Greeks of Odessa: Diaspora Leadership in Late Imperial Russia* (East European Monographs, 2004) as well as several articles on Russian and modern Greek history. His current research interests focus on Greek intellectual and political history at the turn of the twentieth century.

THEOPHILUS C. PROUSIS is Distinguished Professor of History (2006) at the University of North Florida in Jacksonville. He specializes in European, Russian, and Near Eastern history and has published extensively on a variety of topics, including imperial Russia's contacts with Eastern Orthodox communities in the Ottoman Empire, British encounters with the Ottoman Levant, and European designs in the Eastern Question. His publications rely on Russian and British archives, and he is currently working on a multivolume compilation of British embassy documents from Constantinople in the early 1820s.

VICTOR TAKI (PhD, Central European University, Budapest) is currently affiliated with the Center of Ukrainian and Belorussian Studies at the Faculty of

History of Moscow State University. His doctoral dissertation, "Russia on the Danube: Imperial Expansion and Political Reform in Moldavia and Wallachia, 1812-1834," examined discursive and institutional aspects of relations between the Russian Empire and the elites of the two Romanian principalities at the dawn of the modern epoch. He has held positions at Carleton University (Ottawa), the University of Alberta (Edmonton), and Dalhousie University (Halifax). From 2011 to 2013 he was a postdoctoral fellow and lecturer at the University of Alberta working on a book project devoted to the Russian encounters with the Ottoman Empire in the eighteenth and nineteenth centuries. His most recent publications are "Orientalism at the Margins: The Ottoman Empire under Russian Eyes" (*Kritika*, 2011) and a coauthored monograph, *Bessarabiia v sostave rossiiskoi imperii, 1812-1917* (Novoe Literaturnoe Obozrenie, 2012).

Index

Page references in italics indicate illustrations.

Abdulaeva, Gul'nara, 182
Abdülhamid II, Sultan, 32–33n73, 246
Abdülmecid I, Sultan, 120, 134, 142, 148, 155
Abkhazia, 229, 339–40
Adlerberg, Nikolai, 167, 170–74
Adrianople, Treaty of (1829), 43–44, 48
Aehrenthal, Alois Lexa von, 285
Ahmed Kasım Efendi, 139–40
Aivazovsky, Ivan: *View of Constantinople by Evening Light*, *132*
Akçura, Yusuf, 304
Akkerman, Convention of (1826), 43–44
Akty sobrannye Kavkazskoiu arkheograficheskoiu kommissiei, 12
Alabin, Petr Vladimirovich, 54–55
Alberoni, Cardinal, 3, 7
Aleksei Mikhailovich, Tsar, 38–39
Alexander I, Tsar, 50, 76–77, 107, 174, 203
Alexander II, Tsar, 176, 178, 234–35, 243
Alexander III, Tsar, 234
Alexander the Great, 261, 331, 332
Alexandra Fedorovna, Empress, 137
Ali Paşa, 16, 236
Amalfitani, 201
Anagnostopoulou, Sia, 270
Anderson, M. S.: *The Eastern Question: 1774–1923: A Study in International Relations*, 4–5, 7, 14–15, 333
Andonov-Chento, Metodija, 331

Anna Ioannovna, Empress, 40
Anthimos IV, Patriarch, 147
Anthimos VI, Patriarch, 150
Anthimos VII, Patriarch, 198
Ardahan, 221–22, 226, 228, 232, 241–43
Argiri, Jean, 116
Argyriades, Pavlos, 256–57
Aristova, Tatiana F., 227
Armenian Apostolic (Gregorian) Church, 142–43, 153
Armenians, 335; genocide (1915), 12–13, 270; massacres of (1895 and 1909), 13; nationalist movement among, 242–43; revolutionary movement among, 246; Russian acquisition of lands of, 143; Sykes-Picot Agreement on, 295. *See also under* Kars-Batum
Arsenije III, Patriarch, 38
Asquith, Herbert Henry, 287
Ataliotissa, Artietu, 113
Athos. *See* Mount Athos
Athos Regulations (Kanonismos), 203
Atsız, Bedriye, 312
Austria-Hungary: attitude toward Thessaloniki region, 209; collapse of, 253, 272; as a model for an Eastern Federation, 263–67
Aydın, Cemil, 314
Ayion Potirion (Holy Grail) of Vlatades, 135, 136–41, 153–54

Baconschi, Teodor, 59
Badem, Candan, 20, 183; *The Ottoman Crimean War*, 16
Bakradze, Dmitrii Z., 227
Balkan Alliance, 198
Balkan nationalism, 195-96
Balkan Wars (1912-13), 4, 198, 207, 209, 269, 286-88
Bariatinskii, Aleksandr I., Prince, 223-24
Băsescu, Traian, 60
Bass, Gary, 18
Batum. *See* Kars-Batum
Bazili, Konstantin, 112
Beissinger, Mark, 310-11
Beliaev, Alexei K., 208
Belkovkii, Stanislav Aleksandrovich, 60
Benazet, Théodore, 8-9
Berlin Congress (1878), 195, 222, 227, 255
Berlin Treaty (1878), 203, 221, 307, 341
Bessarabia, 42, 58-59, 182
Bibescu, Gheorghe, 44
Birgen, Muhittin, 312
Bismarck, Otto von, 195, 284
Bitis, Alexander, 17
Black Sea Economic Cooperation (BSEC), 337, 339-40
BlackSeafor, 339-40
Blanc, Louis, 46
Blumi, Isa, 16
Blunt, Charles, 136, 138-40, 147-50, 156
Bobroff, Ronald, 17, 20-21
Bogdanovich, Khatib Aleksandr Usmanov, 179
borderlands, transnational nature of, 283
Bosnian crisis (1908-9), 198, 285
boyars, 40-44, 54-56
Brătianu, Ion C., 58
Brest-Litovsk, Treaty of (1918), 221
Brotherhood of Russian Kelliots, 206
Brower, Daniel, 153
Brown, L. Carl, 333
Bryce, James, Viscount, 12-13
BSEC (Black Sea Economic Cooperation), 337, 339-40
Buchanan, Sir George, 291
Bucharest, Treaty of (1812), 76
Bucharest, Treaty of (1913), 209

Bulgaria: Balkan claims by, 255, 257-60; in the Balkan Wars, 209, 286; creation of, 195; Muslims in, 338; nationalism of, 259-60; Ottoman indemnity for, 286-87; Turks in, 338; uprising in, 306-7
Bulgarian conspiracies (1840s), 45
Bulgarian Exarchate, 196-97
Bulgarian Horrors and the Question of the East (Gladstone), 11
Bulgarian massacres (1875), 13
Bulgarian nationalist movement, 197
Bulgarian schism (1872), 196-97, 209, 211
Burning of the Government Buildings at Kertch, 166
Byzantium, 40, 136, 142, 193, 196, 199, 262, 305

Cambon, Paul, 287-88
Canning, Stratford de Redcliffe, 136, 140, 144-45, 156
Cantacuzino, Mihai, 41
Cantacuzino, Șerban, Prince, 38
Cantemir, Constantine, Prince, 38
Cantemir, Dimitrie, 39-40
Caspian oil trade, 339
Castlereagh, Robert Stewart, 78. *See also* Strangford files
Catherine II, of Russia, 8, 40-41, 174
Catherine the Great, 50
Caucasus, generally, 224-25, 339-41
Ceaușescu, Nicolae, 59
Cengiz, Ohran Kemal, 336
Ceza, Mustafa, 311-12
Chabert, Francis, 90, 92
Charge of the Light Brigade, 168. *See also* Crimean War
Charles XII of Sweden, King, 39
Chechnya, 223, 339
Cheterian, Vicken, 340
Chicherin, B. N., 10
Chios Massacre (1822), 9, 79, 86-88, 107-9
Chorgun, 174
Choublier, Max: *La question d'Orient avant la Traité de Berlin*, 11-12
Christian captives during the Greek Revolution, 101-21; apostatized, 115;

enslavement conditions/process, 110; European response to, 109-10; families' searches for, 103; humanitarian intervention for, 103, 106; number of, 108, 112; Ottoman enslavement of captives and Russian ransoming of, 102, 110-21; Ottoman responses to the revolution's outbreak, 104-10; overview of, 20, 101-3
Chupovski, Dimitrija, 331
Churchill, Winston, 36, 336
Çiçek, Nazan, 15, 19, 336; *Young Ottomans*, 16
Çıldır. *See* Kars-Batum
Circassian migration, 183
Clarendon, George Villiers, 133-34, 156
Cold War, 243, 336
Commerce, Treaty of (1783), 76
Congress of Focşani (1772), 41
Constantine, King, 210-11
Constantine V, Patriarch, 198
Constantinople, 132; fears of Russian occupation of, 287, 295; Ottoman conquest of (1453), 9, 193; Russian ecclesiastical politics in, 197-98; strategic importance to Russia, 193
Constantinople, Treaty of (1879), 221-22, 227-28, 236
Copeaux, Etienne, 314, 316
Cor, Mathurin-Joseph, 149
Cossacks, 169-70, 180, 341
Council of the Sixteen Members of the United Opposition, 255
Crete, 262
Crews, Robert, 153
Crimean War (1853-56), 4, 165-83; Allied invasion of Crimea, 168, 170; Battle of Balaklava, 168; British support of the Ottomans in, 305; causes of, 283; "the chaos," 168-70; Cossacks' role in, 169-70, 180; devastation in Crimea, 173; Eastern Question studies sparked by, 9-10; martial law imposed, 171; overview of, 165-68; present-day Tatars' view of, 340-41; racialist settlement following, 174-75; religion's role in, 17, 131-35; Russian occupation of Moldavia and Wallachia as triggering, 47; Russian responsibility for, 134-35; Russian-Tatar tensions during, 169-70; siege of Sevastopol, 168-69, 179-80; start of, 168; starvation/poverty caused by, 173; Tatar conditions/losses during, 171-76, 180-82; and Tatar nationalism, 168, 170; Tatars blamed for Russian losses, 171, 174, 180. *See also* Tatar exodus following the Crimean War

Custine, Marquis de, 9
Cyprus Convention, 307
Cyprus dispute, 21, 337
Czartoryski, Adam, 45, 51-52
Czechoslovakia, 271

Daly, John, 17
Damalas, N., 200
Damianos, Patriarch, 205
Danilevskii, Nikolai Iakovleich, 36, 60; *Rossiia i Evropa*, 10, 55-56
Dantz, Jacques, 114, 116
Danubian principalities, 35-61; and current Russian-Romanian relations, 57-61; and the Greek myth in Russian culture, 50-51, 57; Moldavian/Wallachian map, 34; Moldavia/Wallachia nationalism, 18-19, 37, 48, 53-54, 59; Moldova's reunification with Romania, 59-60; Ottoman capitulations to Moldavian/Wallachian, 37, 41-44, 46-48, 58 (*see also* Kuchuk Kainardji, Treaty of); overview of, 18-19, 35-37; Russian perceptions of Romanians, 48-57; Russia protection of, 37-48, 49-50; Russian-Moldavian treaties, 39-43; Strangford on, 88-89; Western influence in, 53-54; and the young Romanians, 45-47
Dardanelly, Bosfor i Chernoe more v XVIII veke (Ulianitskii), 10
Dashkov papers, 74-75
Dechani monastery, 204-5
Delacroix, Eugène: *La Grèce sur les ruines de Missolonghi*, 109; *Massacre at Chios* (*Les Scènes des Massacres de Scio*), 79, 109

Dela Turtsii i Egipta v 1832 i 1833 godakh (N. N. Murav'ev), 10
Delcassé, Théophile, 292–93
Delchev, Gotse, 331
Demidoff, Anatole, 54
Destunis, Spyridon, 107
devshirme (type of enslavement), 111
Dionysios IV, Patriarch, 38
Dionysios V, Patriarch, 198
Disraeli cabinet, 307
Dmitrievskii, Alexei, 206–7
Dnevnik pisatelia (Dostoevsky), 11
Dobrogea, 58
Dokos, G., 200–201
Dosifei, Metropolitan, 37–38, 41
Dostoevsky, Fyodor: *Dnevnik pisatelia*, 11
Doumanis, Nicholas, 16
Dragoumis, Ion, 19, 252, 254–55, 257–70, 272
Dragoumis, Stephanos, 200
Drăgunescu, P., 40
dreadnought-class battleships, 289
Driault, Edouard: *La question d'Orient*, 12
Druzhinina, E. I., 166
Dugin, Alexander Gelievich, 60
Dupin, Charles, 8–9
Duru, Kazım Nami, 311
Dzhaniiskii, Abdulla Murza, 176

Eastern Crisis (1821–22). *See* Strangford files
Eastern Crisis (1875–78), 4, 11
Eastern Federation concept, 251–72; Argyriades proposal, 256–57; Dragoumis proposal, 19, 254–55, 257–70, 272; emergence of, 251; and the end of the Ottoman Empire, 253–54; and the EU, 271; failure of, 251, 270–72; and the Federative Union of the Peoples of the East (Roccas proposal), 256–57; Karatheodori-Zarifis proposal, 255–56; and the *Manifesto of the Socialists of Turkey and the Balkans, 1912*, 257; vs. the Megali Idea (the Great Idea), 19, 253–55, 257–59, 261; as a new paradigm, 267–68; obstacles to cooperation, 251, 253; overview of, 19, 251, 253; and redrawing of maps after the First World War, 253, 271, 335
Eastern Question, 3–21; definitions of, 4–6; emergence/evolution in European/Russian thought, 7–13, 253, 319–21, 333–34; as European response to Ottoman decline, 3–4, 6, 304; humanitarian intervention in, 18, 103, 106, 335; importance to relations among European states, 283; international relations shaped by, 6–7, 17; Islam's role in, 16–17; legacy of, 21, 333–42; major episodes of, 4; Marriott on, 4–5, 13–15, 333; new definitions of, 13–18; new directions for scholarship on, 18–21; overview of, 3–7; religion's role in, 19 (*see also* Mount Athos; Ottoman Christian religious affairs); Russian involvement in, 16–17, 19; scholarship/journalistic literature on, 4–5, 7–13; traditional approach to, 254. *See also* Turkish republican textbooks on the Eastern Question
The Eastern Question: 1774–1923: A Study in International Relations (Anderson), 4–5, 7, 14–15, 333
The Eastern Question: An Historical Study of European Diplomacy (Marriott), 4–5, 13–15, 333
Echmiadzin cathedral, 143–44
Edhem, Ibrahim, 115
Emrence, Cem, 16
Entente, 58–59, 255, 264, 284
Erdoğan, Fahrettin, 232–33
Ermolaev, Stepan, 226
Ertem, Sadri, 311
Etaireia uprising (1821), 50–51, 77
EU (European Union), 271
Euphrates Valley Railway project, 307
Eurasian Union, 341
Europa, Rusia și România (D. A. Sturdza), 35–36, 47, 57, 61n1
Evmorfopoulos, Zanni, 113
Evpatoria, Allied occupation of, 170, 176

Fadeev, Rostislav Andreevich, 36, 56
Fairey, Jack, 17, 19

Index

Federative Union of the Peoples of the East, 256–57
Feodor Alexeevich, Tsar, 37–38
Figes, Orlando, 17
First World War (1914–18), 4; and British view of the Eastern Question, 12–13; redrawing of maps following, 253, 271, 335; studies of the diplomacy of, 282; tensions leading to, 281; violence following, 335. *See also* Franco-Russian Alliance
Fisher, Alan W., 167, 183
Fonton, Felix Petrovich, 48–49, 51, 58
Former Yugoslav Republic of Macedonia (FYROM), 339. *See also* Macedonia
Franco-Russian Alliance, 281–96; anti-British aspect of, 284; during the Balkan Wars, 286–88; demise of, 281; and discord over Palestine, 292–94; and discord over the Ottoman Empire, 281–83, 286, 289, 292–93, 295; establishment of, 284; and fears of Russian occupation of Constantinople, 287, 295; and French opposition to Ottoman indemnity for Bulgaria, 287; overview of, 20–21, 281, 295–96; and proposed boycott of the Ottoman Empire, 288, 295; and the Russian-Japanese War, 284; and Russian naval power, 289–91; scholarship on, 282; and the Sykes-Picot Agreement, 294–95; and the Turkish Straits, 285–86, 289–96
Frankini, Viktor A., 225, 230–41, 244
Frary, Lucien, 20
French Revolution, 50
Fuad Paşa, Mehmet, 150

Gedeon, 38
Gellner, Ernest, 309
Gennady, 205
genocides, 183
Georges-Picot, François, 291–92, 294
Gerd, Lora, 16, 19
Germanos, Archbishop, 104–5
Germany, 253, 284
Ghica, Alexandru, 44

Ghica, Ion, 46–47
Gianib Efendi, 85, 120
Giers, Mikhail N., 212
Ginkulov, Iakov Danilovich: *Nachertanie pravil moldovlakhiiskoi grammatiki*, 53
Gladstone, William Ewart, 11
Goldfrank, David, 17
Gooch, Brison, 134
Gorchakov, Alexander Mikhailovich, 58
Gorchakov, Mikhail Dmitrievich, Prince, 167, 171–72
Gordon, Thomas, 108
Gorgoli, Ivan Savvich, 137, 141
Gorski, Philip, 131
Great Britain: during the Eastern Crisis, 78 (*see also* Strangford files); French vs. British interests in the Ottoman Empire, 291–92; interest in the Turkish Straits, 290, 293; interests in/protection of the Ottoman Empire, 305–7
Great Idea. *See* Megali Idea
La Grèce sur les ruines de Missolonghi (Delacroix), 109
Greece: in the Balkan Wars, 286; independence for, 120; on Macedonia, 339; as a nation-state, 261; in relation to the East and the West, 260–61; role in the First World War, 264
Greek-Ottoman relations and the Megali Idea, 19, 40, 197–98, 253–55, 257–59, 261
Greek Revolution (1821–30), 4; Eastern Crisis triggered by, 75–76 (*see also* Strangford files); humanitarian intervention in, 103, 106; sectarian/ethnic violence during, 9, 102–7 (*see also* Christian captives during the Greek Revolution); as a source for the Eastern Question, 8–9; start of, 104; Sublime Porte's response to, 102; Ypsilantis's role in, 104. *See also* Chios Massacre
Greek-Turkish state. *See* Eastern Federation concept
Gregory, Patriarch, 205
Gregory Palamas, Saint, 210
Grigorios V, Patriarch, 76, 105–6
Grigorios VI Fourtouniadis, Patriarch, 146–47, 151, 155

Gruev, Dame, 331
Gülen, Fetullah, 337

Habsburg Empire. *See* Austria-Hungary
Halet Efendi, 80–81
Hatt-ı Şerif of Gülhane, 148–49
hesychasts, 210
Hieronym, Archimandrite, 194, 199
Hilandar monastery, 204–5
Hobsbawm, Eric, 310
Holy Alliance, 50, 89
Holy Apostle Andrew, 199
Holy Grail. *See* Ayion Potirion of Vlatades
Holy Prophet Ilias, 199
Holy Synod (Russia), 110, 196–97, 203, 206–7, 213
Hroch, Miroslav, 45
Hubsch, Konstantin, Baron, 114–16

Iastrebov, Ivan S., 200
identity and memory, 310
Ignat'ev, Nikolai, 195, 243
Ilarionov, N. A., 204
İnan, Afet, 304
Institut d'Égypte, 8
International Socialist Bureau, 257
Ioannikios II, Archbishop, 147
Ionian Islands, 78, 146
Isaiah, Archimandrite, 38
Islam: place in Turkish republican textbooks, 320–21; role in the Eastern Question, 16–17; slavery sanctioned by, 111, 118; spread of, 337
Ismail Agha, 232
Ismail Paşa, 240–41
Israeli-Palestinian conflict, 341
Iuzefovich, T., 10
Ivan V, Tsar, 38
Izvolskii, Aleksandr P., 285, 287, 292–93

Jalussi, Stamatis and Nikorisi, 113
Jelavich, Charles and Barbara, 16
Jesus prayer, 210
Joachim III, Patriarch, 197–200
Joachim IV, Patriarch, 198
John Chrysostom, Saint, 142

Justice and Development Party (Turkey), 321
Justinian I, Emperor, 331

Kabuzan, V. M., 166
Kalamata, 104
Kalavryta, 104
Kalmyks, 101
Kane, Eileen, 153
Kapodistrias, Ioannis, 118, 120
Kara Ali, 108
Karabakh, 339
Karamanoğlu, Yakub Paşa, 139
Karatheodori Pasha, 255–56
Karpat, Kemal, 15–16, 167, 177–78
Kars-Batum, 221–46; and the Armenian nationalist movement, 242–43; Batum declared a free port, 229; Batum oblast dissolved/restored, 222; bureaucratic administration of, 244; vs. the Caucasus, 224–25; court system for, 224–25; ethnic composition of the population in, 226–27; governors' responsibilities/authority in, 225–26; *kadi* in, 224–25; land in, 230–34, 236; local elites' integration into Russian aristocracy, 245; military conscription in, 238–42, 245; and the Military-Customary Administration, 221, 223–24; military tax in, 242; Muslim migration from, 183, 221–22, 226–31, 235–38, 245; Muslim religious schools in, 225; overview of, 20, 221–26, 243–46; population of, 226; provisional regulation for, 224; Russian annexation of, 221–22, 243; and the Russian-Ottoman wars, 222, 236–37, 246; Russian Revolution's impact on, 246; Russian secular schools in, 225; Russian settlement and the Armenians, 222, 232–37, 245–46; Russian soldiers taking oath at the Apostolic Church, 220; and the Treaty of Brest-Litovsk, 221
Kazakhs, 101
Kerr, Niven, 147

Keyder, Çağlar, 315
Khomiakov, Aleksei Stepanovich, 51, 52
Kiselev, Pavel Dmitrievich, 51
Kırzıoğlu, Fahrettin, 227, 238
Kogălniceanu, Mihai, 45, 58
Kokhmanskii, Nikolai V., 203-4
Komarov, General Alexander V., 229, 231, 239
Kosova, 338
Kovalevskii, Egor Petrovich, 53
Kozelsky, Mara, 17, 20
Kuchuk Kainardji, Treaty of (1774), 8, 18, 41-42, 76, 106, 152
Kurd, origin of term, 227
Kurdish nationalism/statehood, 336, 341
Kurdistan, 224

labor, racialized notions of, 174
Laiotă Basarab, 41
Lampsei, Ivan, 180-81
Lausanne, Treaty of (1923), 18, 333, 341
Lausanne Conference (1922-23), 303-4
Lavra of Dechani, 204-5
Lavra of St. Chariton, 205
Law, Andrew Bonar, 287
Lazistan. *See* Kars-Batum
League of Nations, 13
Lebanon, 205-6
Ledru-Rollin, Alexandre-August, 46
Lenin, V. I., 13
Leont'ev, Konstantin Nikolaevich, 55-56
Liprandi, Ivan Petrovich, 54
Lisovoi, Nikolai, 16
Logothetis, Lykourgos, 108
London Conference (1912-13), 207, 209
London Treaty (1913), 209
Loris-Melikov, Mikhail Tarlevich, 233-34
Loukou, Nikolas and Frangouli, 115
Lupu, Vasilie, 38
Lutsk, Treaty of (1711), 39

Macedonia, 4, 195, 255, 257-59, 331, 333, 338-39
Macedonian Defense, 258
Macedonia Square (Skopje, Macedonia), 331, 332

Mahmud II, Sultan, 148, 154
Makarii Sushkin, Abbot, 199, 202
Malinovskii, Vasilii Feodorovich, 51
Mandelshtam, Andrei N., 208-9
Manifesto of the Socialists of Turkey and the Balkans, 1912, 257
Marriott, J. A. R.: *The Eastern Question: An Historical Study of European Diplomacy*, 4-5, 13-15, 333
Martens, F. F., 11
Marx, Karl, 9, 13
Massacre at Chios (*Les Scènes des Massacres de Scio*; Delacroix), 79, 109
Mazis, John A., 19
Mazzini, Giuseppe, 46
McMeekin, Sean, 17, 283
Megali Idea (the Great Idea), 19, 40, 197-98, 253-55, 257-59, 261
Mehmed Ali Paşa, 4, 8-9, 16, 306
Mel'nikova, L. V., 17
memory and identity, 310
Menshikov, Aleksandr Sergeyevich, Prince, 155-56, 168-71
Metaksakis, Meletios, 207, 210-11
Meyer, William, 119
Middle East, Eastern Question's impact on, 341
migrations, 166-67, 183. *See also* Kars-Batum, Muslim migration from; Tatar exodus following the Crimean War
Mikhail Feodorovich, Tsar, 39
Mikhailii, Mavra, 174
Military Intendancy, 179
Miliutin, Dmitrii Alekseevich, 243
Minchaki, Matvei (Minciaky), 113-17
Ministry of Education (Turkey), 310
Ministry of People's Enlightenment, 225
Ministry of State Domains (St. Petersburg), 174-75, 181
Mircea the Old, 41
Missolonghi, 104, 116
Moldavia. *See under* Danubian principalities
Moldavian Church, 37-38
Molotov, Vyacheslav, 336
Molotov-Ribbentrop Pact (1939), 59
Montenegro, 211, 256-57, 286

Morfanou, 201
Mount Athos, 193–214; citizenship of monks on, 203–4, 212; diplomatic patronage for non-Greek monks on, 195; Greek annexation of, 207; Greek delegation to, 200–201; Greek monasteries on, 194, 199–200; Hilandar monastery, 204–5; international status of, 208–12; *kelliots* of, 205–7; Kinot of, 210–11; Name Worshipers movement on, 209–10, 212; Ottoman conquest of (1423–24), 199; overview of, 19, 194–95; Russian-Greek authority proposed for, 211–12; and Russian-Greek tensions, 194, 207–8; Russian monasteries' and *sketes*' prosperity, 199–200, 206; Russian pilgrims/monks on, 200–204, 208, 212–14; spiritual significance for Orthodox Christians, 195, 198–99, 205, 213–14; strategic location of, 194–95, 198–99, 211; union with Greece (1926), 212
Mourousi, Constantine, 78
Movement for Rights and Freedoms (Dvizhenie za prava i svobodi), 338
Münnich, Burkhard Christoph von, 40
Murav'ev, Andrei Nikolaevich, 136
Murav'ev, N. N.: *Dela Turtsii i Egipta v 1832 i 1833 godakh*, 10; *Russkie na Bosfore v 1833 godu*, 10
Murav'ev-Goluchwski agreement (1897), 198
Museum of Old Eastern Historical Artifacts, 304
Mustafa Kemal (Atatürk), 303–4, 312, 337; "Nutuk," 313–14
Mustoksidi, Angelos, 119, 137–41, 154

Nabucco, 60
Nachertanie pravil moldovlakhiiskoi grammatiki (Ginkulov), 53
Nafplion, 117–18
Nagorno-Karabakh conflict, 336
Naimark, Norman, 183
Name Worshipers movement, 209–10, 212
Napoleonic era, 50
Napoleonic Wars, 8, 173

NATO, 339–40
Navoni, M., 86
Nelidov, Alexander I., 202
neo-Ottomanism, 337
Nesselrode, Karl Vasil'evich, 43, 106–7, 117, 132–35, 154–56
Nicholas I, Tsar, 42–43, 46, 132–34, 143, 151, 155–56, 174, 176, 253
Nicholas II, Tsar, 292, 295
Nikolaevich, Mikhail, Grand Duke, 224, 233–34, 239
Nogais, 101
Nursi, Said, 337
Nuzla estate, 211

Obrenović, Miloš, 45
Odessa, refugees in, 112, 167
oil reserves in the Caspian Sea, 339
Oran, Hilmi, 312
Orbeliani, Grigol D., Prince, 229
Organic Statutes (1827–28), 44, 46
Orientalism (Said), 15
Orkhon Inscriptions, 312–13
Ottoman Christian religious affairs, 131–57; Ayion Potirion (Holy Grail) of Vlatades, 135–41, 153–54; British interest in secularizing Ottoman society, 153; and Catholic claims at holy places, 155–56; Orthodox clergymen's appointment/removal, 135, 145–51; overview of, 19, 131–36; politicization/internationalization of, 135–36, 151–54, 156–57; prayer books and liturgical commemorations, 135, 141–45, 155–56; role in the Crimean War, 131–35; Russian mistrust of the British and French regarding, 154–55
The Ottoman Crimean War (Badem), 16
Ottoman Empire: boycott of, 288, 295; capitulations by, 268 (*see also under* Danubian principalities); collapse of, 2, 13, 253, 307, 333; in the First World War, 289; foreign exploitation of, 268; immigration to, 167; *millet* system in, 195–96; modernization/secularization of, 202–3, 306 (*see also* Tanzimat); perceived decline of, 3–4, 7 (*see also*

Eastern Question); refugees from, 17–18; Russian consuls in, 102–3, 112, 196; as the "sick man of Europe," 80, 253; slavery under, 20, 101, 110–12, 120 (*see also* Christian captives during the Greek Revolution); withdrawal from southeastern Europe, 195. *See also* Sublime Porte
Ottomania, 337
Ottoman Land Code (1858), 230

Pahlen, F. P., 117
Paisios, 38–39
Paléologue, Maurice, 291–95
Palestine: French and Russian interests in, 292–94; Israeli-Palestinian conflict, 341; politicization/internationalization of, 152, 294; Russian monasteries in, 205–6
Palmer, William, 144–45
Palmerston, Henry John Temple, 134, 144, 306
Palmerstonism, 305–6
Panayotopoulos, A. J., 262
Panesh, A. D., 17
Panin, Viktor N., 118
Pan-Slavism: Bulgarians' place in, 52–53; and current Russian-Romanian relations, 57–58; growth of, 51–52; and Romanian distinctiveness/independence, 56–57; Romanian elites' attitude toward, 55–56; and the Slavic origin of Romanians, 52–53
Panteleimon, Abbot, 205
Paparrigopoulos, Ioannis, 119
Parembli, Michael and Coco, 113
Paris, Treaty of (1856), 165, 168, 176–78, 181–83
Partnership for Peace, 339
Paskevich, General Ivan Fedorovich, 236–37
Patras, 104–5
Pavlidis, P., 200
Peloponnese, 104
percentages agreement (1944), 336
Pestel, Vladimir Ivanovich, 169, 170–71
Peter the Great, 38–40, 49–50
Petriaev, A. M., 208

Petrovitch, George, 51
Phanariote Greeks, 40, 43, 51, 53–54
Philhellenism, 50–51, 107, 109
Philiki Etaireia (Society of Friends), 77–78. *See also* Etaireia uprising
Philliou, Christine M., 254
Pinson, Mark, 167
Pitzipios, Iakovos, 144
Poghosian, Artashes M., 226–27, 235
Pogodin, Mikhail Mikhailovich, 52, 55
Poincaré, Raymond, 290–91
Ponsonby, John, 144, 147
Potsdam Conference (1945), 336
Prousis, Theophilus, 16, 20
Pruth Campaign (1711), 39–40, 49–50
Puryear, Vernon, 14
Putin, Vladimir, 60, 341

La question d'Orient (Driault), 12
La question d'Orient au XVIIIe siècle (Sorel), 12
La question d'Orient avant la Traité de Berlin (Choublier), 11–12
La questione d'Oriente innanzi l'Europa (Ubicini), 9
Quran on slavery, 118

Rakov, V. S., 170
Rauf Paşa, Mehmed Emin, Grand Vizier, 150
Reinsurance Treaty, 284
relics: Ayion Potirion (Holy Grail) of Vlatades, 135–41, 153–54; at Echmiadzin, 143; as gifts, 137–38
religious turn, 131
Republic of South-West Caucasus, 242
Reşid, Mehmed, 119
Reşid Paşa, Mustafa, 148–49
Reynolds, Michael, 17, 283, 295
Ribop'er, Alexander I. (Ribeaupierre), 117–18
Rizos-Neroulos, Iakovos, 118
Roccas, Constantine, 256–57
Rodogno, Davide, 18
Romania, 35–36; Bessarabia's unification with, 59; disputes with Ukraine, 61; in the EU and NATO, 59–61; Moldova's

Romania (*continued*)
reunification with, 59-60; participation in World War I, 58-59; participation in World War II, 59; populism in, 59; relations with Turkey, 59-60. *See also* Danubian principalities; Pan-Slavism
Romanian language, 53
Rossiia i Evropa (Danilevskii), 10, 55-56
Rumelia, 195
Russia: Bulgarians supported by, 196-97; on the Caspian oil trade, 339; collapse of, 253; Eastern Question research after the Crimean War, 10; on Kosova, 338; Military-Customary Administration (*see under* Kars-Batum); naval power of, 21, 289-91; Ottoman Christians protected by, 19; populism in, 59; racialist settlement policies of, 175; relations with Austria, 285; relations with France (*see* Franco-Russian Alliance); relations with Germany, 284; relations with the West, 59-60; Serbs supported by, 204; spiritual enterprise in the Ottoman Empire, 193-97; as successor of Byzantium, 193, 196
Russian Foreign Ministry: Athos policy of, 202, 207; Balkan/Near Eastern policy of, 10, 195-98, 213 (*see also* Mount Athos)
Russian-Georgian War (2008), 340
Russian-Japanese War (1904-5), 284-85
Russian Old Believers, 174
Russian-Ottoman Defensive Alliance (1805), 336
Russian-Ottoman War (1677-81), 39
Russian-Ottoman War (1735-39), 40
Russian-Ottoman War (1768-74), 40, 50
Russian-Ottoman War (1828-29), 53
Russian-Ottoman War (1877-78), 8, 11, 183, 222, 307; causes of, 16. *See also* Kars-Batum
Russian-Persian War (1826-28), 4
Russian Revolution (1905), 285
Russian Revolution (1917), 246

Russian-Romanian relations. *See* Danubian principalities
Russkaia politika v vostochnom voprose (Zhigarev), 11
Russkie na Bosfore v 1833 godu (N. N. Murav'ev), 10

Saab, Ann Pottinger, 153
Said, Edward: *Orientalism*, 15
Samiote Greeks, 79, 87-88, 108. *See also* Chios Massacre
Samuel, Tsar, 331
Sandrini, Antoine F., 105
San Stefano, Treaty of (1878), 195, 221, 227-28, 231, 307
Sazonov, Sergei D., 280, 285-96
SEECP (Southeastern European Cooperation Process), 337, 339-40
Selim III, 42
Serafimov, Boris S., 194, 208, 210-12
Serbia, 56, 142, 204-5, 211-12, 286, 338
Serbian uprising (1804-13), 51
Sergeevich, Konstantin and Ivan, 52
Seton-Watson, Robert William, 14
Sèvres, Treaty of (1920), 265, 315-17, 333, 341
Shamil, Russian defeat of (Caucasus, 1859), 4, 9-10, 183, 223
Shavrov, Nikolai, 233
Sheremet, Vitalii, 17
Shopov, Atanas, 204
Shuvalov, P. A., 58
Silvia, Aspasia, 113
Skete of St. Andrew, 194, 210-11
Skopelos, 264-65
Skopje 2014 project, 331, 333
Sluglett, Peter: *War and Diplomacy*, 16
Smyrna Massacre (1821), 107, 109
Smyrna slave market, 108
Sobieski, Jan, 38
Solov'ev, Sergei Mikhailovich: "Vostochnyi vopros," 11
Sorel, Albert: *La question d'Orient au XVIIIe siècle*, 12
Southeastern European Cooperation Process (SEECP), 337, 339-40

Index

South Ossetia, 340
Soutso, Michael, 77
Soviet Union, 243, 335-36, 339, 341
Spiridov, A. M., 52
Stalin, Joseph, 175, 183, 336, 340-41
Staroselskii, Dmitrii S., 229
Stavrou, Theofanis, 16
Ștefan, Gheorghe, 38-39
Steiner, Zara, 283
St. Ilias Shuaya monastery, 205-6
St. John Chrysostom monastic cell, 204-5
St. John the Theologian monastery, 203
Stolypin, Pyotr A., 285-86
St. Panteleimon Metochion, 213
St. Panteleimon monastery, 199, 210
St. Petersburg Protocol, 114
Strangford, Percy Clinton Sidney Smythe, 73, 74, 78-80
Strangford files, 73-94; on abuses of foreign-flagged vessels, 85-86; on bribing Halet Efendi, 81-82; on Chios, 86-88; on commerce, 91-92; on conference with Ottomon ministers, 82-84; on the Danubian principalities, 88-89; on direct Russian-Ottoman negotiations, 84-85; Eastern Crisis context of, 73-78; on Greek-Ottoman naval clashes, 92-93; on Greek-Ottoman sectarian violence, 78-80; overview of, 20, 74-75, 81; on the Porte's right to search British ships, 89-91; on Russian demands regarding Black Sea navigation, 93-94; specificity/urgency of, 80
—DOCUMENTS BY DATE: 10 Jan. 1822 (no. 3), 81-82; 25 Feb. 1822 (no. 27), 82-84; 25 Feb. 1822 (no. 29), 84-85; 10 Apr. 1822 (no. 47), 85-86; 25 Apr. 1822 (no. 55), 86-88; 10 May 1822 (no. 70), 88-89; 10 Jun. 1822 (no. 85), 89-91; 25 Jun. 1822 (no. 97), 91-92; 26 Jun. 1822 (no. 101), 92-93; 3 Sept. 1822 (no. 145), 93-94
Stroganov, Andrei Nikolaevich, 167, 171, 173-76, 178, 181
Stroganov, Grigorii Aleksandrovich, 76-80, 89, 106

Sturdza, Dimitrie Alexandru, 45, 58; *Europa, Rusia și România*, 35-36, 47, 57, 61n1
Sturdza, Michael, 44
Sublime Porte, 8-9, 16, 43; allegations of offenses against the Orthodox Church, 133-35 (*see also* Ottoman Christian religious affairs); on the Armenian Church's relations with Russia, 143-44; authority shared with local leaders, 16; British ambassadors to, 73 (*see also* Strangford files); centralizing reforms by, 76; response to the Greek Revolution, 102; Russian ambassadors to, 106, 117; treaties with Russia, 76-77 (*see also* Kuchuk Kainardji, Treaty of); tsarist influence at, 9
Suez Canal, 290-91
Sufi mysticism, 337
Suleiman Pașa, 46
Sun Language Theory, 313, 314
Sviatopolk-Mirskii, Dmitrii I., Prince, 229, 234-36, 245-46
Sykes, Sir Mark, 291-92, 294
Sykes-Picot Agreement (1916), 3, 282-83, 293-96
Symeon the New Theologian, 210
Syria, 205, 292

Taki, Victor, 18-19
Tanzimat (Restructuring/Reforms), 120, 196, 202-3, 254
Tash-Basty (now Bol'shoe Sadovoe), 172
Tatar exodus following the Crimean War, 165-83; alarm over/investigation of, 179-81; Crimea's resettlement following, 182; first wave of migration, 170, 176; forced relocation as a cause of, 167-68, 171-72, 175-76, 180, 183; and holy war rhetoric, 168; Ottoman encouragement of, 177-78; overview of, 20, 167; population loss's impact on Crimea, 167, 178-79, 182; preventing further migration, 181-82; religious reasons for, 177-78, 181; Russian encouragement of, 167, 176, 178, 181; scope of the migration, 165-66, 178,

Tatar exodus (*continued*)
    182; second wave of migration, 177; Treaty of Paris's role in, 168, 176-77, 181; vs. other migrations/genocides, 183
Tatars: deportations under Stalin, 183; present-day view of the Crimean War, 340-41; slave trade of, 101, 111-12. *See also under* Crimean War
Tauride Statistical Committee, 182
Tbilisi, 225
Temperley, Harold, 14
ten-years' crisis (1831-41), 4
textbooks, Turkish. *See* Turkish republican textbooks on the Eastern Question
Thouvenel, Édouard, 152
Titov, Vladimir Pavlovich, 151
Tolstoi, Dmitrii Andreevich, 234
Totleben, Eduard, 180-81
Toynbee, Arnold J., 12-13
Transcaucasia, 244
Transnistria, 59-60
Trikoupis, Charilaos, 197
Tripolitza Massacre (1821), 104
Turkey: anti-Communism in, 243; during the Cold War, 336; coup d'état in (1980), 316, 323; cultural missions of, 341; EU admission sought by, 21, 271, 316, 336-37; foreign trade by, 337; founding of, 120, 310, 333; industrial plans of, 341; in NATO, 243; refugee minorities in, 338; relations with Russia, 36, 76-77; relations with the USSR, 243, 336
Turkish Historical Society, 304
Turkish History Thesis, 304, 310, 312-14, 317
Turkish-Islamic Synthesis, 316-17, 323
Turkish republican textbooks on the Eastern Question, 307-23; Eastern Question as a fading memory in, 311-16; "Eastern Question" term rediscovered (1980s), 309, 315-23; Europe's image in, 313-15, 317-19, 322-23; history books, 309-11, 323; Islam's place in, 320-21; and nation building, 309-11, 314, 322; overview of, 19, 307-9, 322-23; Sun Language Theory, 313, 314; Turkish History Thesis, 304, 310, 312-14, 317; and Turkish identity, 308-10, 322; and the Turkish-Islamic Synthesis, 316-17, 323; *Türk Tarihinin Ana Hatları*, 313-14; and Westernization, 314-15
Turkish Straits, 145, 193, 282, 285-86, 289-96, 336
Turkmenchai, Treaty of (1828), 143
Türk Tarihinin Ana Hatları (The main forms of Turkish history), 313-14

Ubicini, A.: *La questione d'Oriente innanzi l'Europa*, 9
Ukraine, 61, 340-41
Ulianitskii, V. A.: *Dardanelly, Bosfor i Chernoe more v XVIII veke*, 10
United States, oil interests of, 339
Unkiar Skelessi, Treaty of (1833), 336
Urquhart, David, 9
Uspenskii, Feodor I., 206
USSR. *See* Soviet Union

Valsamaky, Konstantin, 114, 116
Vasil'chikov, Viktor Ilarianovich, Prince, 179-81
Vatopedi monastery, 210
Velestinles, Rigas, 261
Venelin, Iurii Ivanovich, 52-53
Veniamin, Archimandrite, 138-40
Veniamin Karypoglou, Bishop, 137-38
Venizelos, Eleftherios, 211-12, 255, 264
View of Constantinople by Evening Light (Aivazovsky), 132
Vlangali, A. E., 201
Vlassopoulos, Ioannis, 104-5, 116
Vorontsov, Mikhail Semenovich, Prince, 112-16, 171, 224
"Vostochnyi vopros" (Solov'ev), 11

Wallachia. *See under* Danubian principalities
Wallachian Revolution (1848), 45-46, 48
Walsh, Robert, 105-6, 109

War and Diplomacy (Yavuz and Sluglett), 16
war captives, 101–2. *See also* Christian captives during the Greek Revolution
Werth, Paul, 143, 153
Wilhelm II, Kaiser, 284
Williams, Bryan Glyn, 167
Wilson, Woodrow, 270–71
World War I. *See* First World War

Yanukovych, Viktor, 334
Yavuz, M. Hakan: *War and Diplomacy*, 16
Yermanos IV, Patriarch, 147, 150
Yilmaz, Huseyin, 341
Young Ottomans (Çiçek), 16

Young Turks, 4, 254, 262–63, 269–70, 289
Ypsilantis, Alexander, 50, 52, 77, 104, 261. *See also* Etaireia uprising
Yugoslavia, 271, 335–36
Yushchenko, Viktor, 341
Yusuf Paşa, 105

Zakadi, Gavril, 139
Zakharov, Zakharia, 114, 116–17
Zarifis, George, 255–56
Zhigarev, Sergei: *Russkaia politika v vostochnom voprose*, 11
Zhivkov, Todor, 338
Zinoviev, Ivan A., 206

www.ingramcontent.com/pod-product-compliance
Lightning Source LLC
Chambersburg PA
CBHW060939230426
43665CB00015B/1997